A+ CERTIFICATION

INTERACTIVE WORKBOOK

EMMETT DULANEY
ROBERT BOGUE

PH PTR

Prentice Hall PTR
Upper Saddle River, NJ 07458
www.phptr.com/phptrinteractive

ISBN 0-13-084847-6

90000

9 780130 848475

Editorial/production supervision: *Mary Sudul*
Acquisitions editor: *Jill Pisoni*
Development editor: *Ralph Moore*
Technical Contributor: *Corinne Gregory*
Marketing manager: *Lisa Konzelman*
Manufacturing manager: *Maura Goldstaub*
Editorial assistant: *Linda Ramagnano*
Cover design director: *Jerry Votta*
Cover designer: *Anthony Gemmellaro*
Art director: *Gail Cocker-Bogusz*
Series design: *Meryl Poweski*
Page layout: *FASTpages*
Web site project manager: *Craig Little*

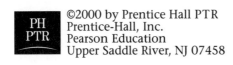

Prentice Hall books are widely used by corporations and government agencies for training, marketing, and resale.

The publisher offers discounts on this book when ordered in bulk quantities. For more information, contact: Corporate Sales Department, Phone: 800-382-3419; Fax: 201-236-7141; E-mail: corpsales@prenhall.com; or write: Prentice Hall PTR, Corp. Sales Dept., One Lake Street, Upper Saddle River, NJ 07458.

ISBN 0-13-084847-6

Prentice-Hall International (UK) Limited, *London*
Prentice-Hall of Australia Pty. Limited, *Sydney*
Prentice-Hall Canada Inc., *Toronto*
Prentice-Hall Hispanoamericana, S.A., *Mexico*
Prentice-Hall of India Private Limited, *New Delhi*
Prentice-Hall of Japan, Inc., *Tokyo*
Simon & Schuster Asia Pte. Ltd., *Singapore*
Editora Prentice-Hall do Brasil, Ltda., *Rio de Janeiro*

CONTENTS

C H A P T E R 7 Customer Satisfaction   **297**

C H A P T E R 8 Operating System Functions, Operation, and File Management **311**

C H A P T E R 9 Memory Management   **363**

FROM THE EDITOR

Prentice Hall's Interactive Workbooks are designed to get you up and running fast, with just the information you need, when you need it.

We are certain that you will find our unique approach to learning simple and straightforward. Every chapter of every Interactive Workbook begins with a list of clearly defined Learning Objectives. A series of labs make up the heart of each chapter. Each lab is designed to teach you specific skills in the form of exercises. You perform these exercises at your computer and answer pointed questions about what you observe. Your answers will lead to further discussion and exploration. Each lab then ends with multiple-choice Self-Review Questions, to reinforce what you've learned. Finally, we have included Test Your Thinking projects at the end of each chapter. These projects challenge you to synthesize all of the skills you've acquired in the chapter.

Our goal is to make learning engaging, and to make you a more productive learner.

And you are not alone. Each book is integrated with its own "Companion Website." The website is a place where you can find more detailed information about the concepts discussed in the Workbook, additional Self-Review Questions to further refine your understanding of the material, and perhaps most importantly, where you can find a community of other Interactive Workbook users working to acquire the same set of skills that you are.

All of the Companion Websites for our Interactive Workbooks can be found at `http://www.phptr.com/phptrinteractive/`.

Jill Pisoni
Editor
Prentice Hall PTR Interactive

ACKNOWLEDGMENTS

ROBERT BOGUE

I would like to acknowledge the effort that is involved in any book project by saying thank you to Jill Pisoni for her understanding when the schedules just didn't come together like they should, to Ralph Moore for shepherding me through Prentice Hall's writing process, and Emmett Dulaney for getting me involved in the project. I would most of all, however, like to thank Ben & Kathy Gibson for their dedication to educating people every day in every situation. It's an example that I continue to try to live up to.

INTRODUCTION

Welcome to the *A+ Certification Interactive Workbook*. You're about to embark on a unique learning experience, one that we hope will not only help you to pass the A+ Certification exam, but will also give you a complete understanding of the subject matter and make you a successful technician. Much like learning to repair an automobile, it's one thing to read about procedures in a book and answer questions about what you read. But it's another thing entirely to lift up the hood and dig right in, and you won't get to the other end of this book without doing that. In fact, in the very first chapter, you will completely disassemble your PC and reassemble it again!

WHO THIS BOOK IS FOR

Frankly, this book is for anybody who wishes to pass the A+ Certification exam, *no experience necessary*. Even more importantly, this book is for anybody who wishes to become a good computer technician.

If you are already an experienced technician who needs to become certified, you are free to pick and choose the Exercises that you need to freshen up your skills, take the Self-Review quizzes for practice, and be on your way. This book should also serve you well in the field as a comprehensive reference.

If you are relatively new to this business but would like to gain some experience and become certified, this book will help you get there. It will also help you not just to memorize information (which is all too easily forgotten), but also to roll up your sleeves and learn by doing. And when you become active in your learning process, you retain far more than you would by simply memorizing abstract information.

You should note that the exam assumes only six months of on-the-job experience. This is an important point for all audience members. If you are a seasoned technician, don't assume that the test is beneath you or will be a breeze to pass. Do you know how many feet in front of a Stop sign you are supposed to stop like you did when you first passed your driving test? There are bound to be some fundamental details like this that you have forgotten, so the best way to make sure that you are pre-pared is to study and practice. And that applies to everybody! That's where this book can help!

HOW THIS BOOK IS ORGANIZED

The Interactive Workbook series offers an extraordinary opportunity to explore your computer system and learn through a journey of discovery. In this book, you are presented with a series of interactive Labs that are intended to map to each of the CompTIA objectives. Each Lab begins with Learning Objectives that show you what Exercises (or tasks) are covered in that Lab. This is followed by an overview of the concepts that will be further explored through the Exercises, which are the heart of each Lab.

Each Exercise consists of a series of steps that you will follow to perform a specific task, along with questions that are designed to help you discover the important things on your own. The answers to these questions are given at the end of the Exercises, along with more in-depth discussion of the concepts explored.

At the end of each Lab is a series of multiple-choice Self-Review Questions, which are designed much like the questions you will see on the A+ exam. If you feel certain that you already understand a certain Objective, you are free to skip that Exercise, but are still encouraged to take the Self-Review quiz at the end of the Lab, just to make sure. The answers to these questions appear in Appendix A. There are also additional Self-Review Questions at this book's companion Web site, found at http://www.phptr.com/phptrinteractive/. But more on that in a moment ....

Finally, at the end of each chapter you will find a Test Your Thinking section, which consists of a series of projects designed to solidify all of the skills you have learned in the chapter. If you have successfully completed all of the Labs in the chapter, you should be able to tackle these projects with few problems. There are not always 'answers' to these projects, but where appropriate, you will find guidance and/or solutions at the companion Web site.

There are actually two exams. You will note from this book's table of contents that it is split into two separate parts: The first part is "The Core Exam," and the second part is "The DOS/WIN Exam." The Core Exam is mostly concerned with how well you understand hardware issues, including installing new hardware, cleaning, troubleshooting, repairing, and so forth. It also covers safety and customer-service issues. The DOS/WIN Exam is primarily concerned with software issues related to Microsoft operating systems. You must pass both of these exams within 90 days of each other in order to become certified. It is recommended that you plan to take both at the same time.

As mentioned, each chapter maps directly to the CompTIA domains for the exam, and each Lab covers the core concepts of each domain. However, you will notice that while there are 13 domains in the CompTIA blueprint, there are only 12 primary chapters in this book. This is because the topic of Domain 4.0, Motherboard/Processors/Memory, is already covered interactively in Chapter 1, "Installation, Configuration, and Upgrading." Therefore, Domain 4.0 has been moved to the back of the book as Appendix B to avoid unnecessary repetition, and while it does review some of what is covered in Chapter 1, it digs into slightly more detail to cover only what you need to know for the exam.

Appendix C consists of a comprehensive Glossary, containing all of the terms you may encounter in your journey, and then some.

The final element of this book actually doesn't appear in the book at all. It is the companion Web site, and it is located at:

`http://www.phptr.com/phptrinteractive/`

This companion Web site is closely integrated with the content of this book, and we encourage you to visit often. It is designed to provide a unique interactive online experience that will enhance you're A+ education. As mentioned, you will find guidance and solutions that will help you complete the projects found in the Test Your Thinking section of each chapter.

You will also find additional Self-Review Questions for each chapter, which are meant to give you more experience in preparing for the actual exam, with instant results for each quiz. Take these quizzes after you have completed the Lab work in the book, taken the book's quizzes, and completed the Test Your Thinking sections. These online quizzes will help you gauge exactly how prepared you are for the exam, and what areas you may need to revisit in the book.

In the Author's Corner, you will find additional information that we think will interest you, such as CompTIA news, professional advice for preparing for the exam, and any errata that didn't make it into the book before publication.

Finally, you will find a Message Board, which you can think of as a virtual study lounge. Here, you can interact with other *A+ Certification Interactive Workbook* readers, share and discuss your projects, and perhaps even pick up a tip or two about the current exam.

WHAT YOU WILL NEED

First and foremost, you will need a **PC**, running some form of **Windows**, on which to work. Ideally, this will be a spare PC, as you will be taking it apart and putting it back together again in several Labs throughout this book. In addition, it should have as many peripherals as possible, including a printer, keyboard, mouse, monitor, and CD-ROM drive. (Don't worry, you will only be disassembling the box, not the peripherals.) If you're worried about doing this with your primary PC, we urge you to invest in an inexpensive system—a used system should work just fine. While you can follow along with this book without actually performing the Exercises, this learning system works best if you get your hands dirty.

The next thing you will need is a **workspace**. Chapter 1 offers advice on the best type of workspace for working on a PC; just make sure that you have enough space to lay out and examine your PC's components.

You will also need a **laptop system** to complete the Exercises in Chapter 5, "Portable Systems." If you do not have access to a laptop, you can still follow along with the Exercises and learn what you need for the exam, but once again it will work best if you participate in some way. Try to borrow a portable system if you don't have one of your own.

You'll need a **fresh notebook** in which to jot the answers to the Exercise questions, and to take notes about what you observe as you work through the Exercises. Yes, there are answer rules provided in the book, and they will suffice for some questions, but owing to space limitations, they are primarily meant for quick notes to yourself as well as study points, not for comprehensive discussion. Of course, an electronic notebook will work just as nicely as a traditional notebook.

Finally, you'll need an **Internet connection** to gain access to the companion Web site and to visit some of the other Web sites referenced in the book. Again, we encourage you to visit the companion site frequently to share and discuss your experiences with the virtual community.

In addition to these items, every good technician has a well-stocked **toolkit**, and you will need one as you progress through this book. The following checklist should serve you well in preparing yours:

- ❏ Screwdrivers (flat blade and Phillips #2). Ideally, you can get a double-headed one with Phillips on one end, flat blade on the other. Two sets, one each medium and small, will cover most bases.
- ❏ Chip puller
- ❏ Needle-nose pliers
- ❏ Soldering iron
- ❏ Compressed air canister
- ❏ Rubbing alcohol
- ❏ Flashlight
- ❏ Multimeter
- ❏ Wire stripper
- ❏ Cable crimping tool
- ❏ Anti-static wristband and/or mats

 At the very least, you will always need your screwdrivers. Everything else is nice, but not absolutely necessary. Then again, most good technicians will have most of these items handy. This list is repeated in Chapter 1 for your convenience.

CONVENTIONS USED IN THIS BOOK

There are several conventions that we've used in this book to try and make your learning experience easier. These are explained here.

tThis icon is used to flag tips or especially helpful tricks that will save you time or trouble. For instance, if there is a shortcut for performing a particular task or a method that the authors have found useful, you will find it set off from the main text like this.

Computers are delicate creatures and can be easily damaged. Likewise, they can be dangerous to work on if you're not careful. This icon is used to flag information and precautions that will not only save you headaches in the long run, they may even save you from harm.

This icon is used to flag passages in which there is a reference to the book's companion Web site, which once again is located at:

`http://www.phptr.com/phptrinteractive/`

THE WHOLE TRUTH

Sometimes owing to the Interactive Workbook format, some information gets watered down for efficiency sake. Also, in some cases, certain information will not necessarily apply for the A+ exam, but we feel that it's important to give you the bigger picture anyway. When that's the case, we have used this sidebar element to alert you that "it's not exactly as simple as that," and to offer a more detailed explanation.

SOME SEASONED ADVICE

Anybody may take the A+ Certification exam, but not everybody will pass. Those who are serious about passing will dedicate whatever time is required to properly prepare for the exam. In all cases, you will find that the discovery method employed by the *A+ Certification Interactive Work-*

book will surely enlighten and educate you unlike any other resource. However clever or comprehensive another resource might be, the discovery method is a proven training technique that is employed in classrooms and training centers around the world. This hands-on approach is the cornerstone of the International Workbook series, and we are sure that you will find it an engaging and productive way to learn. *There is no better way!*

ABOUT THE AUTHORS

EMMETT DULANEY

Emmett Dulaney is an MCSE, MCP+Internet, NetWare CNA, OS/2 Engineer, LAN Server Engineer, and A+ Service Technician. The <u>Certification Corner</u> columnist for *NT Systems Magazine*, he is the author or coauthor of over a dozen certification titles including seven of the MCSE Fast Track titles for Macmillan Computer Publishing, CNE Short Course, and Sam's Teach Yourself MCSE NT Workstation in 14 Days. He has also written over one hundred magazine articles in such magazines as System Administrator, UNIX Companion, Network Administrator, and NT Magazine.

As a shareware developer, his certification test engines are distributed through http://www.ds-technical.com, and are widely accepted by users as being among the best available in the marketplace. A continuing education instructor at Indiana University\Purdue University of Fort Wayne for nine years, he also teaches for a national training company and has presented technical papers at a number of seminars.

He can be reached at edulaney@iquest.net.

ROBERT L. BOGUE

Robert L. Bogue is the Chief Operating Officer of AvailTek, Inc. AvailTek is a software development and systems integration company headquartered in Carmel, IN. Robert has contributed to over 100 book projects and numerous magazine articles and reviews. He has experience with IBM compatible machines, AS/400, Macintosh, VAX/VMS, and several flavors of Unix running on various platforms. Robert can be reached at Rob.Bogue@AvailTek.com.

C H A P T E R 1

INSTALLATION, CONFIGURATION, AND UPGRADING

The time to stop a revolution is at the beginning, not the end.

—Adlai Stevenson

CHAPTER OBJECTIVES

In this chapter, you will learn about:

This chapter will be reviewing the fundamental concepts of the PC itself. We'll be discussing what the major components are and how they are installed, removed, and configured.

We'll also be talking about ports, interrrupt lines, and direct memory access channels, as well as basic peripherals and systems optimization. This chapter will cover what amounts to 30 percent of the overall score for the Core Objectives test so we've got a lot of ground to cover, but don't be intimidated; we're going to break everything down into simple, easy to understand concepts.

L A B   1.1

BASIC COMPONENTS

LAB OBJECTIVES

After this Lab, you will be able to:

✓ Prepare to Remove the Cover

✓ Remove the Cover

✓ Detach Power Supply Cables and Remove Ribbon Cables

✓ Detach Case Connector Cables

✓ Remove Add-In Cards

✓ Remove Storage Devices

✓ Remove the Power Supply

✓ Remove Memory from the Motherboard

✓ Remove the CPU

✓ Remove the Motherboard

This is perhaps the most complex Lab in this book. As a part of this Lab, we'll be completely disassembling and reassembling your PC, identifying each part along the way. You'll want to make sure that you document each of the locations of the cables and cards carefully; and you may even want to take pictures. If you don't get everything connected back together, your PC may not work. Be sure to give yourself plenty of time to walk through each step slowly and carefully. By the time you are finished, you will be fully versed on the inner workings of a PC.

In this Lab, we'll be taking your PC apart and talking about some of the basic components of the modern PC. Some of these components are listed as follows:

- Motherboard (or system board)
- Power supply
- CPU
- Memory
- Add-in cards
- Storage devices
- ROM, BIOS, Firmware, and CMOS

As we go through the following exercises, you'll learn about each of the components of your system by peeling back layers like you would an onion. Each component is covered in the order in which you will see it as you disassemble your PC. This is in many ways a backward approach to the topic; however, you're more likely to take apart your system than you are to build one from scratch. The following exercises are specifically designed to do this—to walk you through the process of disassembling your PC. So let's get started.

DON'T FORGET YOUR TOOLKIT

As outlined in the Introduction to this book, you should at least have the first of the following items in your toolkit (but it's nice to be prepared with everything listed here):

- ❑ Screwdrivers (flat blade and Phillips #2). Ideally, you can get a double-headed one with Phillips on one end, flat blade on the other. Two sets, one each medium and small, will cover most bases.
- ❑ Chip puller
- ❑ Needle-nose pliers
- ❑ Soldering iron
- ❑ Compressed air canister
- ❑ Rubbing alcohol
- ❑ Flashlight
- ❑ Multimeter
- ❑ Wire stripper
- ❑ Cable crimping tool
- ❑ Anti-static wristband and/or mats

LAB 1.1 EXERCISES

1.1.1 PREPARE TO REMOVE THE COVER

When disassembling a PC, there are a series of steps you must go through just to get past the outer case. The first of these steps is to prepare to open the case by finding a location to do the disassembly.

Finding a space to perform the disassembly is important because machines take up more space when they are disassembled than when they are put together. So you must have sufficient places to put all of the separated components. You should also have a space where screws, jumpers, and other small parts won't be easily lost by falling down into crevices.

It's also important to <u>manage the risk of static electricity, or electrostatic discharge</u>, to the components of the PC. In order to do that, you'll want pick a place that has no high-pile or shag carpet. Tile is best. You'll learn all about electrostatic discharge in Chapter 3, Lab 3.5. You can see an optimal workspace in Figure 1.1.

 a) What does your workspace look like?

 _____

 _____

Once you've found the place to do the disassembly, you'll want to shut down the PC. This should be done via the Shutdown command if you're running Windows 9x or Windows NT. If you're running DOS or Windows 3.x you'll want to shut down from a DOS command prompt. This will minimize the chance of data loss because of activity during the exact moment you attempt to shut down the PC.

Finally, you'll want to remove the power cables and the cables for each of the peripherals. Before removing these cables you may want to write down where each of these cables is connected, or take a picture of the cable connections. Even though we discuss all of the connectors in Lab 1.2, there are some times when it's not easy to tell where precisely a cable should go.

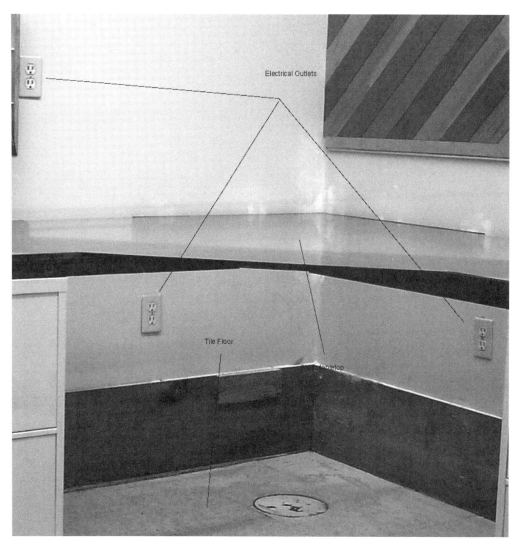

Electrical Outlets

Tile Floor

Figure 1.1 ■ This is my workspace. You'll notice that it's glass with a small recess for screws to get captured (but not lost), over a tile flooring, and it has electrical outlets within easy reach.

b) How many cables did you have to remove?

_____

_____

c) Why do we remove the power cord before working on a PC?

_____

_____

1.1.2 REMOVE THE COVER

Once you've got your machine moved to a new place, you'll want to remove its cover. Most newer machines have special tabs or handles that you pull on to remove the cover, although some still have screws in the back that must be removed.

 Most PCs have some screws exposed on the back panel that remove the power supply or fan. Figure 1.2 shows you which screws you should not attempt to unscrew when opening a case.

a) How can you tell which screws go to the case, which go to the power supply, and which go to the fan?

_____

_____

b) How many screws must you remove to remove your case?

_____

_____

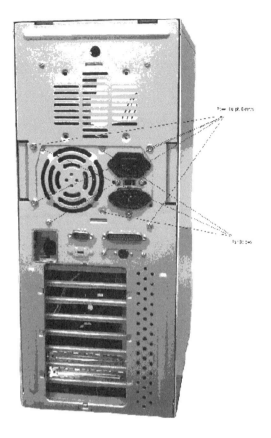

Figure 1.2 ■ There are some screws that you must avoid when removing a cover. Most of the time they will be easy to identify as a part of the power supply.

1.1.3 DETACH POWER SUPPLY CABLES AND REMOVE RIBBON CABLES

Figure 1.3 shows a dual Pentium 166 MMX system, with its cover removed. It is out-of-date by today's standards, but a good system in which to show the basic components.

The first thing that you will notice after removing the cover will be the extensive number of cables running between the different devices. Removing them is

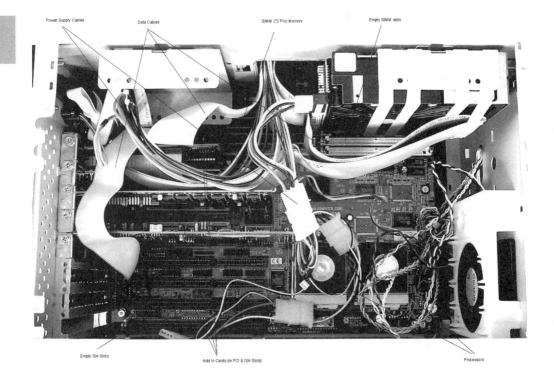

Power Supply Cables   Data Cables   SIMM (72 Pin) Memory   Empty SIMM slots

Empty ISA Slots   Add In Cards (In PCI & ISA Slots)   Processors

Figure 1.3 ■ You'll be able to determine quickly what kind of a system you're looking at by looking for the largest chip, usually with a heat sink on it. That will generally be the CPU.

the objective of this Exercise. Perhaps the most prevalent are the power cables. They take power from the power supply and conduct it to the motherboard and other devices that need it.

Disconnect and bundle the power supply cables. Pay attention to the orientation of the power supply connectors on the motherboard. You'll need to put them back on the same way. Older, AT-style systems use two power supply connectors that are physically identical but electrically different. You'll want to put the connectors back on with the black wires to the middle. Because both connectors are identical, it is possible to put them back on so that the wires are furthest away from one another. This will probably result in damage to the motherboard.

On newer, ATX-style systems, there is one connector and it can only fit on a certain way. I'll elaborate on this difference later in this Exercise when we talk about replacing power supplies. The system pictured in Figure 1.3 has an older, AT-style power supply. For more on this, see Appendix B, "Motherboards, Processors, and Memory."

    a) What type of power supply do you have?

_____

_____

 You may want to use a rubber band to bundle the power supply cables to keep them out of your way while performing the rest of the disassembly process.

It is at this point that you should plug the PC back in. Because the power supply physically connects the outlet ground to the case of the system, you want to provide a constant ground to which you can drain off potentially harmful static electric charges. To make this effective, you'll want to maintain frequent contact with the case during the rest of these exercises. The reason we told you to remove the power supply initially was so that you could get the cover off, and to prevent you from accidentally causing damage to your PC by turning it on. Another reason is because in ATX-based systems, there's always a small amount of power going to the motherboard that you don't want to accidentally tap into.

After reconnecting the power cable, you will begin to notice another set of cables connecting different devices. In this case, we have a ribbon cable for the parallel port, a serial port, floppy disk drive, and one for the hard disk drive. Ribbon cables are cables where all of the conductors are molded (or extruded) side by side. A conductor is simply a wire, or strip of metal, that conducts electricity. You can see that the power cables are not ribbon cables because they have four separate wires bound together at the ends by connectors.

It's important to know the correct orientation of the connector on each end of most cables, including ribbon cables, so signals don't get crossed. There are three techniques that are used to identify which way a cable is supposed to be installed for pin-based connectors, thus preventing the connector from being put on backward.

A different colored stripe—Most ribbon cables are blue or gray but have one conductor, on one or the other side of the cable, which has another color on it—typically red. This conductor is supposed to be oriented toward pin 1 on the component the cable plugs in to. Pin 1 may be indicated on the component either by the number '1' or a small triangle on the connector itself, or close by. Figure 1.4 shows this kind of indication of how to install the cable.

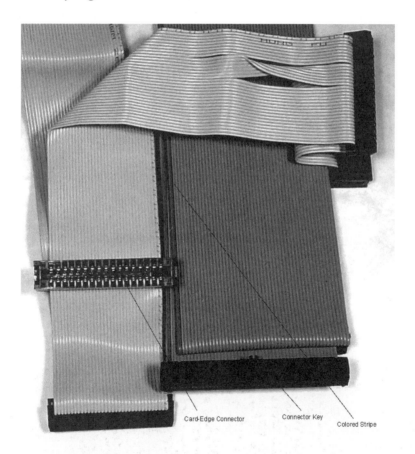

Card-Edge Connector   Connector Key   Colored Stripe

Figure 1.4 ■ Keyed connectors and colored stripes are by far the most popular way to indicate which way a cable should be installed.

A "keyed" connector—The connector on the component that the cable attaches to has a small opening of about 1/8" in the middle of one side of the plastic housing for the connector. The cable has a corresponding tab on the edge of its connector. Because of the tab on the cable, and the opening being required to be in the same location for the cable to be plugged in, it is physically impossible to install the cable incorrectly. Figure 1.4 shows this kind of indication of how to install the cable.

A blocked opening—Sometimes an unused pin in a connector is broken off on the component end. The corresponding pin hole is blocked on the connector so that the only way the connector can be physically installed is to align the blocked hole with the missing pin. Figure 1.5 shows this indication of how to install the cable.

> **b)** What method(s) of identifying the correct orientations of ribbon cables does your PC use?
>
> _____
>
> _____

Computers sometimes use Card-Edge connectors as well. These were primarily used for connecting 5.25" floppy drives and have fallen out of favor. They were designed with a small slot in the card and a corresponding plastic piece in the cable's connector so that it was physically impossible to install the cable

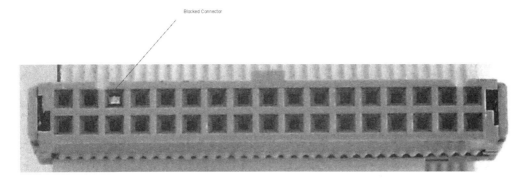

Blocked Connector

**Figure 1.5 ■ Some older cables will block out pins that match places
on the add-in card, or motherboard, where a pin is missing.**

backward. Figure 1.4 shows a floppy cable that has both the card-edge type connector and the pin-type connector.

c) Does your PC use any Card-Edge connectors on your ribbon cables?

_____

_____

It should be noted that some components indicate their pin 1 location and have a "keyed" connector, and others just indicate pin 1. Using a "keyed" cable with a connector on the component side that doesn't have the corresponding "keyed" plastic around it will mean that your "keyed" cable won't insure that the cable is plugged in correctly.

Disconnect all of the ribbon cables in your system, taking note of which way the connector is installed on each component. Remove each ribbon cable that is no longer connected to anything. Although you can use the guidelines above to determine which way they go when you put them back on, it's generally just easier to take a picture or write down the orientations.

You must remember the correct orientation of the ribbon cables, or your PC won't work when you put it back together. Depending on the system, it may even cause damage (although this is rare.)

After you've disconnected all of the ribbon cables and removed the ones that you can, you'll be left with a few dangling ribbon cables and a few small cables. Next, we're going to remove the small case connector cables before removing any of the dangling ribbon cables.

d) What were the ribbon cables in your system connected to?

_____

_____

1.1.4 DETACH CASE CONNECTOR CABLES

In addition to the cables listed below, which all attach the motherboard to the case (except possibly for the hard disk LED, which might connect the hard disk controller to the case), you may have an audio cable that connects your CD-ROM drive to your audio card. This allows you to hear audio CDs through speakers attached to your sound card. This connector is keyed, so you can remove it without worry of it's orientation.

The little cables that connect the motherboard to the case are:

Turbo LED (if present)—This LED (light emitting diode) shows you visibly from the outside of the computer whether the computer is in "turbo mode." This means that the PC is running at it's maximum rate. It used to be common to want to slow a processor down, either to run old games or to simulate how something would run on a slower computer, but it's rarely used anymore. Some cases use this lead to determine what to show on the front panel if they show a speed rating.

Turbo switch (if present)—This switch controls whether the PC is in fast or slow mode.

Speaker—This is the little 2" speaker that's inside the PC's case that is used to beep if you don't have a sound card, and to let you know when there's a problem that prevents the video display from operating. We'll discuss this in more detail in Chapter 2.

Power LED and keyboard lock—This is generally one connector, but some cases have two separate connectors for the power LED and keyboard lock. The power LED gives the user a visual indication that the PC is powered on, even if the monitor isn't, and the keyboard lock allows the keyboard to be disabled.

Hard disk LED—This allows you to see, on the front panel, whether a hard disk, or hard disk controller in actuality, is active in your PC.

Reset button—This allows you to reset your computer without physically turning the power off. Some PCs don't have or use this connector.

Figure 1.6 ■ Each of the leads is connected to a small area of the motherboard.

You need to be aware of the orientation of the connectors for the LEDs as you pull them off. LEDs only allow current to flow in one direction, and so if they are installed in reverse there won't be any damage, but they won't work.

a) Does it matter which way a reset switch connector is installed?

_____

_____

b) Does it matter which way the speaker connector is installed?

_____

_____

1.1.5 REMOVING ADD-IN CARDS

Once you've disconnected all of the case connection wires, you're ready to start removing add-in cards. The most frequently installed add-in card is a video card. It's one of those things that is seldom built into the motherboard, but is necessary for every machine. You'll also find hard disk controllers, serial cards, modems, and other types of cards in your system (see Figure 1.7)

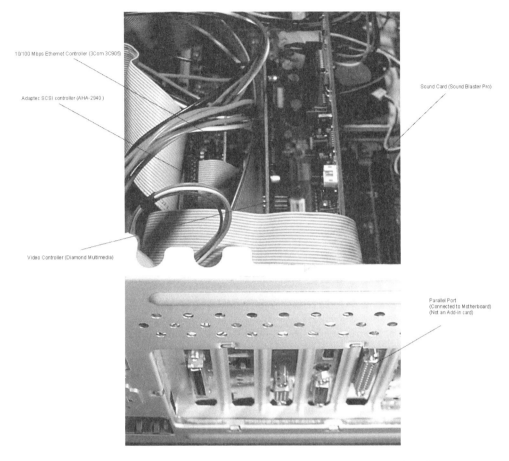

10/100 Mbps Ethernet Controller (3Com 3C905)

Adaptec SCSI controller (AHA-2940)

Sound Card (Sound Blaster Pro)

Video Controller (Diamond Multimedia)

Parallel Port
(Connected to Motherboard)
(Not an Add-in card)

Figure 1.7 ■ Add-in cards go into the slots on the motherboard, and most systems will have several.

To remove any of the add-in cards, you'll need to remove the screw on the back plate, or slat, which is holding the card in place. There are some systems that use other mechanisms for holding cards in place, such as a single bar that goes over the top of all of the cards, but it is most common for each card to be installed with a screw.

Remove all of the screws that are holding the add-in cards in place. You'll also want to make sure that a screw holding in a blank plate, or slat, is not going to interfere with removing the add-in card, as they sometimes do.

This is also a good time to remove the screws holding in any slats that have external ports on them, such as a printer port or a serial port. You should have disconnected their cables from the motherboard earlier in Exercise 1.1.3, so as soon as you remove the screw holding them in place they will drop out of the system.

Once you've removed all of the screws, you'll want to pull out each card slowly. When pulling the card out, you want to make sure that you're pulling it out as straight as possible. By that we mean that you should be bringing the front and back of the card toward you at about the same rate. Getting the card a little askew won't cause damage, but getting it far out of alignment can cause damage to the slot.

As you're removing cards, take note of the slots that the cards are coming from. There are six major slot types that are in use today. They are listed in their order of prevalence:

PCI (Peripheral Component Interconnect)—This slot type, developed by Intel, is a high-speed general-purpose bus that supports plug-and-play in native mode. Normally, a machine will have PCI and ISA slots at a minimum. PCI slots are most often white on the motherboard.

ISA (Industry Standard Architecture)—The original bus type in a PC. It's very slow by today's standards. ISA slots are generally black on the motherboard.

AGP (Advanced Graphics Port)—A special purpose port that is used for video cards to give them the quickest possible access to the rest of the PC. Generally found with PCI and ISA slots. This port is generally a brown connector on the motherboard.

VESA (Video Electronics Standards Association)/Video Localbus—An older bus design that used an ISA slot with an extra connector to allow faster access to the processor. It was originally designed for video cards, but hard disk controllers were another add-in card that used this bus architecture. This bus was tied closely to the 80486 processor architecture and all but died when Intel introduced the PCI bus and the Pentium processor. This extension to the ISA connector will generally be brown on the motherboard.

EISA (Extended Industry Standard Architecture)—An extension to the standard ISA bus architecture that allowed for 4 times the data rate and 32-bit communications instead of the maximum 16 that ISA could support. EISA slots would accept either ISA cards or EISA cards. EISA cards were plug-and-play compatible. These slots don't appear much anymore since the PCI bus is much faster. These slots are also generally brown on the motherboard. You'll be able to distinguish them because they are exactly the same length as an ISA slot, but have twice as many connectors in them.

Microchannel (MCA)—Microchannel is the slot architecture that never was. It was an IBM proprietary format that the company refused to give to the open market. As a result, very few third-party vendors developed cards for Microchannel, which eventually lead to its demise. Most machines with Microchannel slots only had microchannel slots. Microchannel does support plug-and-play.

There's another big difference between ISA/EISA/VESA/MCA cards and PCI/AGP cards: determining on which side of the card the chips are installed and to which side of the slat the card is connected. With an ISA, EISA, VESA, or MCA card, if you set the card down with the connectors toward you and the chips up, the slat, or holding bracket, will be on your right. Doing the same procedure with either a PCI or an AGP card will have the slat on the left. This is another way to help you identify what kind of a card you have.

Figure 1.8 ■ **This motherboard has PCI as well as ISA slots.**

Figure 1.9 ■ This 486-based motherboard has VESA slots as well as ISA slots.

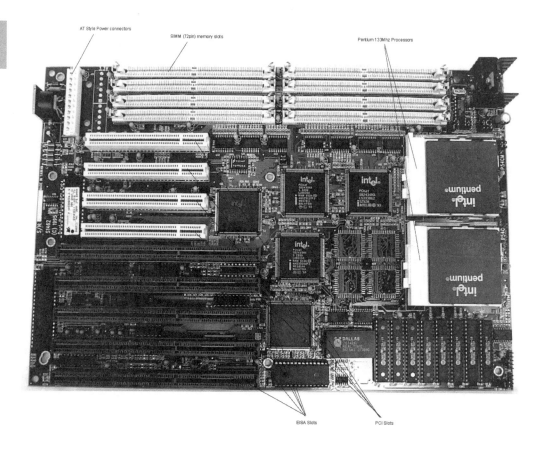

AT Style Power connectors

SIMM (72pin) memory slots

Pentium 133Mhz Processors

EISA Slots

PCI Slots

Figure 1.10 ■ **This motherboard has EISA slots in addition to PCI slots. It's truly a rare motherboard.**

a) What type of bus is your video card connected to?

_____

_____

b) What other add-in cards does your PC have?

_____

_____

c) What bus architectures does your PC support?

_____

_____

d) Do you have a PCI and ISA slot so close together that they don't look like they will both fit?

_____

_____

1.1.6 REMOVE STORAGE DEVICES

Now that you've got all of the option cards removed, it's time to turn our focus to the physical removal (and installation) of storage devices, including hard drives, CD-ROMs, DVD-ROMs, removable disks, and floppy drives.

There are two basic widths for storage devices. They are 3.5" and 5.25" Most hard drives and 3.5" floppy disks fit in the 3.5" width, while CD-ROMs, DVDs, and removable disks generally fall into the category of 5.25" devices.

Take a look at Figures 1.11 and 1.12 as you evaluate the bays in your case and remove these storage devices per the instructions provided to you by the device's manufacturer.

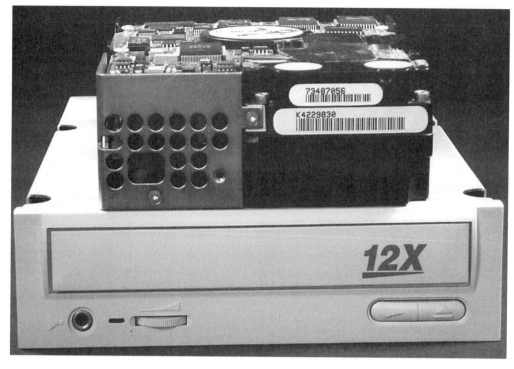

Figure 1.11 ■ 3.5" drives, such as the Seagate Barracuda shown here (on top of a 5.25" CD-ROM), can be adapted to use 5.25" bays, so 5.25" bays are most common.

a) How many bays does your case support?

_____

_____

b) How many accessible bays does it have?

_____

_____

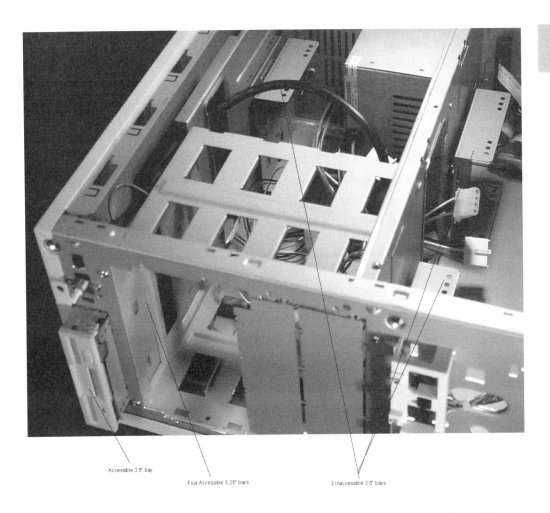

Accessible 3.5" bay

Four Accessible 5.25" bays

3 Inaccessible 3.5" bays

**Figure 1.12 ■ This case has one accessable 3.5" drive bay, three inac-
cessible 3.5" drive bays, and four accessible 5.25" bays.**

    c) How many 3.5" drives do you have?

_____

_____

d) How many 5.25" drives do you have?

_____

_____

1.1.7 REMOVE THE POWER SUPPLY

Once you've removed all of the option cards, floppy drives, and hard drives, you're now in position to remove the power supply. Although you can remove the power supply without removing the other components on most systems, it often makes removal easier when there is more room in the system.

Before attempting to remove the power supply, it's once again time to remove the power cord from the system. This is because of the voltages that could exist by leaving the power supply plugged into the wall socket.

Removing the power supply is as easy as unscrewing the screws that attach the power supply to the case and disconnecting any leads to the power switch (see Figures 1.13 and 1.14).

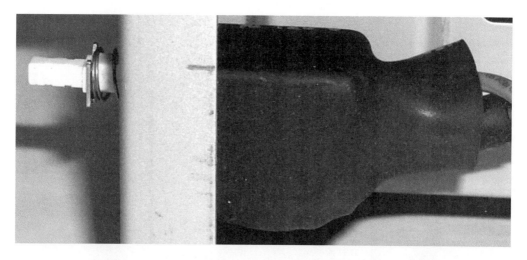

Figure 1.13 ■ The remote power switch leads, or the entire switch, should be removed before removing the power supply retaining screws.

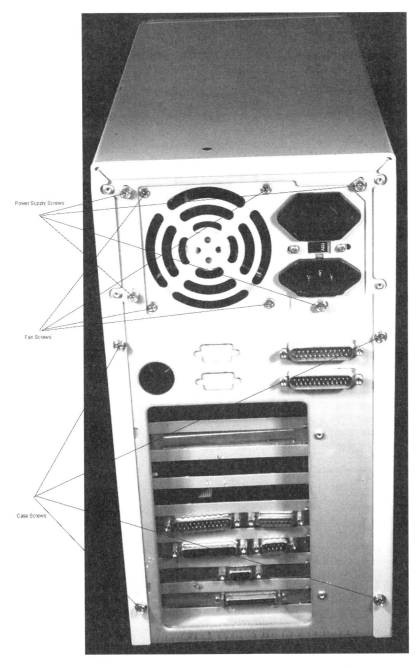

Power Supply Screws

Fan Screws

Case Screws

Figure 1.14 ■ The power supply can generally be removed by remov-ing the four screws holding it to the case.

Do not ever disconnect a power switch while the power supply is plugged in. The power supply switch always has power to it when the power supply is plugged in. You can suffer serious injury by disconnecting a power supply switch while there is power to it.

You should pay special attention to how the power leads are connected to the power switch. If power leads are connected incorrectly to a power supply switch, you can cause a short that will trip the breaker on your power strip or on your entire circuit. It might even cause a fire if the circuit breaker is defective or doesn't trip quickly enough. I've never met anyone who has ever reconnected these leads incorrectly twice. Most people get quite scared by the sparks (literally) that fly if it's done wrong.

Should it become necessary, replacing the power supply is easy. The only difficulty is making sure that you get exactly the same kind, size, and wattage rating of power supply.

Power supplies come in two basic types, defined by how they connect with the motherboard and fan direction. The first type, AT-style power supply, uses two connectors that are keyed to be plugged in only in one direction.

The other style of power supply is an ATX power supply, which uses a single integrated motherboard connector that can only be installed one way.

In Exercise 1.1.2, where we talked about how to remove the cover, we were careful to avoid the screws that held the power supply in place and those that attached the fan to the power supply. To remove the power supply, remove the four screws that hold it in place. Once the screws have been removed, the power supply can be slid out. Remember that the screws holding the fan in place do not need to be removed to remove the power supply.

a) What kind of a power supply does your PC have?

_____

_____

b) Which way does air flow through the power supply?

_____

_____

c) Where is the switch mounted?

_____

_____

1.1.8 REMOVE MEMORY FROM THE MOTHERBOARD

Once you have all of the cards removed, and you've removed the power supply, you should have an unimpeded view of the motherboard, or as CompTIA calls it, the system board. As you can see in Figure 1.15, the motherboard contains a variety of major components. They are:

- Slots
- Memory slots
- Processor(s)
- BIOS
- CMOS
- Integrated ports

In this Exercise, we'll focus on the memory found on the motherboard.

Memory in a PC comes in five basic flavors. They're listed here in descending chronological order, not necessarily in the order in which you'll run into them.

DIMMs—DIMMs are Dual Inline Memory Modules. The term *memory module* implies that the memory is installed on a mini-PC board that connects to the system via a card-edge connector. They are 168 pins wide and are used in the newest machines for two reasons. The first is that the wide nature of the data they hold reduces the amount of time that the CPU must wait to access data from them. Second, because the bits in the memory are arranged in such a wide manner (there are several bytes strung together), the ECC process becomes as efficient as using parity (see 1.1.8 Answers), and thus most DIMMs

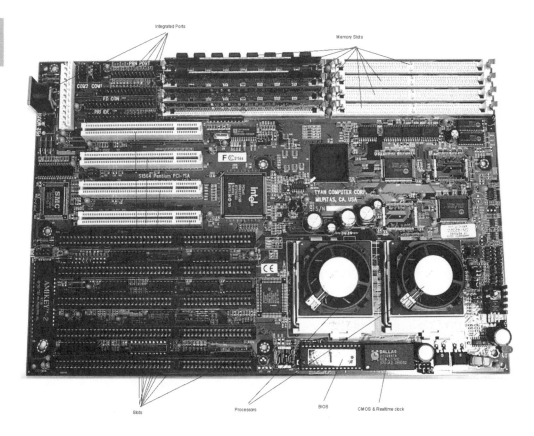

**Figure 1.15 ■ The motherboard, or system board as it referred to by
CompTIA and the A+ exam, contains a variety of components
as identified here.**

have ECC built in. DIMMs normally do not need to be installed in pairs, or
banks, as SIMMs often are. A DIMM is shown in Figure 1.16.

SIMMs (72 pin)—The newer Single Inline Memory Module format. It is twice
as wide as its 36-pin sibling. It's still common in PCs today, particularly Pentium
and Pentium Pro machines. Often required to be installed in pairs. Figure 1.17
shows a 72-pin SIMM.

SIMMs (36 pin)—The older Single Inline Memory Module format that is in
use on some 486 machines. It often required to be installed in sets of four. A
36-pin SIMM is shown in Figure 1.18.

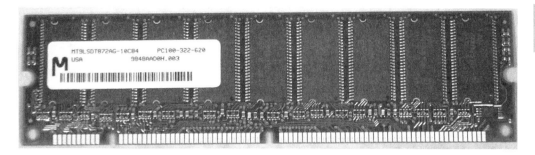

Figure 1.16 ■ The DIMM Module is the largest memory module and has the most pins on it.

Figure 1.17 ■ The 72-pin SIMM is what most people think of when they think of memory today.

Figure 1.18 ■ The older 36-pin SIMM is rarely used any longer, except perhaps on add-in cards.

SIPPs—Single Inline Pin Package, an alternative to SIMMs that used pins instead of a card-edge type connector. They were used on some 386 and 486 machines, but fell out of favor because they were so delicate and were often damaged by inexperienced technicians.

DRAM—Dynamic Random Access Memory, a truly old way to install memory, which is still sometimes used for cache memory (although cache memory is generally SRAM, Static Random Access Memory). This is memory whereby each individual memory chip is installed directly onto the motherboard.

    a) What type of memory is in your PC?

_____

_____

I mentioned cache memory and SRAM in the preceding list. This is a special optimization that PC designers devised a long time ago to improve the performance of a PC.

You can generally determine if you have cache by looking at and identifying a series of chips that are located in sockets on the motherboard. Cache memory normally has at least three chips, and can have several more. Also, motherboards with cache memory have jumpers to specify the size.

    b) Does your PC have cache memory?

_____

_____

    c) Can you explain what cache memory is used for?

_____

_____

Most often you'll run into SIMMs of some sort when working on a PC. Both types of SIMM use the same type of method for attaching to the motherboard. They are installed in a memory slot that contains a place to seat the card, a series of pins to make contact with the card's edge, and two locking clips that hold the memory against the pins. Figure 1.19 shows traditional SIMM memory slots.

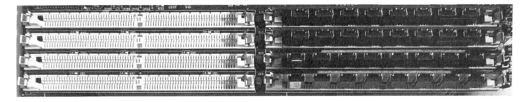

Figure 1.19 ■ SIMM memory is installed in slots that contain retaining, or locking, clips on the side to hold them in place.

To release a memory module, simply pull both clips away from the memory card. The card will spring away from the pins, end up at roughly a 45-degree angle, and can then be removed.

Installing memory is just as simple. Insert the memory card (SIMM) into the memory slot at a 45-degree angle. Gently push the card back until the locking clips grab hold of it.

Some SIMMs have memory chips only on one side, and others have memory chips on both sides. This can make it difficult to decide which way the memory should be inserted. (Remember our earlier discussion about determining which way to connect cables?)

If you carefully insert the SIMM, you'll notice a notch in the card and a plastic piece in the slot. If these don't line up, turn the SIMM around to insert it.

DIMMs are even easier to remove and install. DIMMs go directly into their slot. To remove them, just open the locking clamps by pressing them directly off the ends of the DIMMs. Not only will this remove the locking clamps, it will eject the DIMM.

Inserting a new DIMM is just as easy as removing the old one. Just line up the new DIMM with a slot, making sure that you have the notches matching. (If they don't appear to be matching up, flip the DIMM over and try it again.) Then just press the DIMM into position and pull the locks toward the DIMM to secure it in place.

Should the need arise to install DRAM or SRAM chips, the following will make your life much easier, but you won't need to know this for the A+ Exam.

To install a DRAM or SRAM chip, start by first putting one side of the chip (the set of pins) into the socket on the motherboard. (You'll need to line up the dimple in the chip with the dimple in the socket before starting.) Press slowly, evenly, and constantly on the chip so that the pins are bent slightly under the chip, then slowly tilt the chip into position. If you do this with the right amount of force, the pins for the other side of the chip will line up with the holes in the socket and it will be a simple matter to complete the installation of the chip by forcing it all them way down into the socket.

1.1.9 REMOVE THE CPU

To remove a Pentium, Pentium Pro, or 486 processor, you'll need to first locate the processor sockets. On almost every motherboard made in the past several years, processors have been installed into what is called a Zero Insertion Force (ZIF) socket. A ZIF socket allows you to set the chip in place, and then lower and lock a bar which pulls the chip into the socket and locks it in place. You can see an example of a populated and unpopulated ZIF socket in figure 1.20.

If your processor isn't installed in one of these sockets, don't bother removing it or trying to upgrade the motherboard. It's not worth the hassle.

    a) Is your processor installed in a ZIF socket?

_____

_____

To remove a processor, you only need to unlock the bar on the ZIF. This is normally done by pushing the bar away from the socket. Then lift up on the bar. The processor will be extracted from it's socket and you can pick it up.

While you have your processor out, look at the numbers on the bottom of the CPU. Figure 1.21 shows the bottom of a Pentium MMX 166Mhz chip.

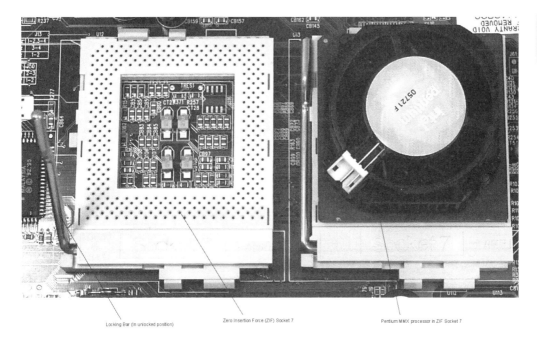

Locking Bar (In unlocked position)   Zero Insertion Force (ZIF) Socket 7   Pentium MMX processor in ZIF Socket 7

Figure 1.20 ■ **The introduction of ZIF sockets on motherboards made replacing or removing processors a trivial task that has almost no potential for damage, where standard sockets almost always caused damage when attempting to remove the processor.**

Figure 1.21 ■ **The numbers found on the bottom of a processor not only tell you what kind of processor it is, but can also tell you the exact revision of the processor that it is.**

b) What numbers are written on the bottom of your CPU?

_____

_____

Replacing the processor is as easy as setting it back on the ZIF, lowering the bar, and locking it in place.

c) Does your system have sockets to allow multiple processors?

_____

_____

1.1.10 REMOVE THE MOTHERBOARD

In most older systems the motherboard, or system board, is held in place by one to three screws and a series of spacers.

Some newer systems have eliminated plastic spacers and hold the motherboard in place with all screws. This could mean as many as 10 screws holding the motherboard in place.

Sometimes cases allow you to remove the area of the case where the motherboard attaches. This is either done with a handle type release, or with screws that hold the area that the motherboard is attached to to the rest of the case.

If your system doesn't allow you to do this, and if your system is in a tower case, lay the case down so the motherboard is parallel with the floor.

Locate all of the screws that are holding the motherboard in place and remove them.

If your motherboard is only affixed to the case by screws, you can remove the motherboard directly; however, if it's held in place with plastic spacers and screws, you'll need to slide the motherboard out. Generally, you slide the motherboard back toward the very back of the case to get it to come out. You'll want to be very careful when sliding the motherboard because the posts that the screws were attached to are now working their way across the back of the motherboard and they may do damage if too much force is used. Figure 1.22 shows a case that uses only screws to hold the motherboard in place. Figure 1.23 shows a case that uses screws and plastic standoffs to hold the motherboard in place.

Once you've slid the motherboard to the very back of the case, you should be able to wiggle it and then pick it up. The motherboard will have a series of plastic posts in it still, and you'll see that the case has a series of slots that the plastic standoffs were sliding in.

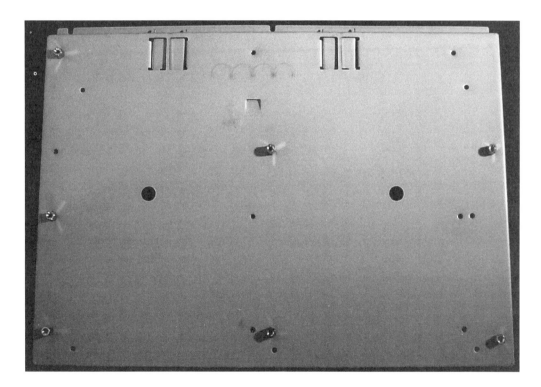

Figure 1.22 ■ A case backplane where the motherboard attaches, which uses only screws to hold the motherboard in place.

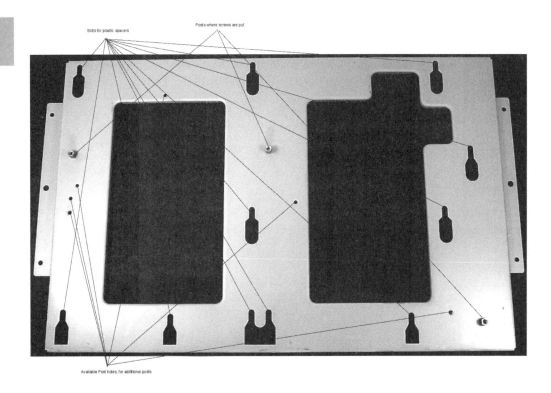

Figure 1.23 ■ A case where the motherboard is attached with a series of screws and plastic standoffs.

a) Record the steps you followed to remove your motherboard.

_____

_____

b) Will you be reinstalling the same motherboard that you just removed or will you be installing a new motherboard at this time?

_____

_____

LAB 1.1 EXERCISE ANSWERS

1.1.1 ANSWERS

a) What does your workspace look like?

Answer: It depends.

Minimally it should be in a static resistant area and should have few, or no, places for screws and cables to get lost. You may also want to have electrical outlets close by so that you can bench test the PC after you made your changes.

b) How many cables did you have to remove?

Answer: Again, it depends.

However, there will always be at least 3 cables that must be removed: the power cable, the keyboard cable, and the monitor cable. Often you'll also have had to unplug the mouse cable, modem cable, and printer cable.

c) Why do we remove the power cord before working on a PC?

Answer: So that we minimize the risk of electric shock.

Although most voltages within a PC aren't enough to hurt you, the power conducted directly to the power supply switch can cause harm. It also prevents the power cord from becoming entangled in the cover.

1.1.2 ANSWERS

a) How can you tell which screws go to the case, which go to the power supply, and which go to the fan?

Answer: The case screws generally go through the cover of the case on the outside. You can clearly see that they go through the case, while neither a power supply nor a fan screw will. However, sometimes, particularly with desktop systems, you'll find case screws that go through the cover, but internally to the PC. The older AT- and XT-style desktop cases worked this way. Your only indication here is that the screws weren't near the power supply.

Power supply screws surround the fan and power cord connectors on the back of the PC and go through the back of the case, but not through the cover.

Fan screws immediately surround the fan and do not appear to hold anything to the outer case or cover.

b)   How many screws must you remove to remove your case?

Answer: It depends on the case.

Some cases don't require any screws be removed. Others require as many as six screws be removed. Remember not to remove the screws holding the power supply and fan in place.

1.1.3 ANSWERS

a)   What type of power supply do you have?

Answer: It will depend on the case, but it will either be an AT-style power supply with two motherboard connectors, or an ATX-style power supply with a single motherboard connector.

b)   What method(s) of identifying the correct orientations of ribbon cables does your PC use?

Answer: It will depend on your PC, but most typically it will include a different colored stripe and a keyed connector. It may also include a blocked-out pin.

c)   Does your PC use any Card-Edge connectors on your ribbon cables?

Answer: Unless your PC has a 5.25" floppy drive, the answer is probably no.

In some cases, even if the PC doesn't have a 5.25" drive in it, the floppy drive cable will have a Card-Edge connector on it, just in case you want to add one in the future.

d)   What were the ribbon cables in your system connected to?

Answer: It depends.

Typically, you'll have a ribbon cable connected to your hard drive, CD-ROM or DVD drive, parallel port, serial ports, and floppy disk drives.

1.1.4 ANSWERS

a)   Does it matter which way a reset switch connector is installed?

Answer: No, the reset switch is a simple on/off connector. It doesn't matter which way current flows through the circuit.

b)   Does it matter which way the speaker connector is installed?

Answer: Technically yes, but practically no.

I say technically yes, because speakers are designed to take current in a certain direction, to allow the speaker to move in a particular direction. However, because of the low quality, and relatively low demands put on the reproduction of sound from the PC's speaker, it's not important which way the speaker is connected.

1.1.5 ANSWERS

a)   What type of bus is your video card connected to?

Answer: It depends on your PC, but most typically the video card will be installed on the PCI bus, with newer systems having them connected to the AGP bus, and older systems having video cards on the VESA bus, or perhaps even on the ISA bus.

Performance will be best with cards connected to the AGP bus, the PCI bus, VESA bus, and ISA bus, respectively.

b)   What other add-in cards does your PC have?

Answer: Most likely, your PC will have a hard disk controller and a serial and parallel controller, if there aren't integrated I/O ports. Or you may have a single card that controls the hard disk, floppy controller, serial ports, parallel port, and game port, all on one card. It may also have an internal modem, network card, and/or sound card.

c)   What bus architectures does your PC support?

Answer: If your PC is newer, it will probably have an AGP bus, PCI bus, and an ISA bus. Some newer systems are forgoing the ISA bus altogether, but they are still rare in today's market.

THE WHOLE TRUTH

The inclusion of an ISA bus for compatibility has been the secret to gaining market acceptance. Microchannel didn't include ISA support and flopped. Each other bus technology has either allowed ISA slots to coexist with the new technology, or has allowed an ISA card to be plugged into one of the newer slots.

Both VESA and EISA allowed ISA cards to be directly plugged into the new slot architectures. PCI and AGP almost always appear in systems in conjunction with ISA slots.

One of the key reasons for this is the need to be able to purchase add-in cards. If you have an ISA or ISA-friendly bus, you know that you can get an add-in card to do whatever you want. That isn't always the case with other bus types. For instance, there are very few PCI-based modems.

Microsoft and Intel, among others, are attempting to change that. The so-called "PC99" specification requires that there be no ISA slots in a computer. They feel that they can do this by including support for the PCI, USB, and other external bus technologies.

Only time will tell how successful Microsoft and Intel will be in their endeavor to remove ISA from the PC.

d) Do you have a PCI and ISA slot so close together that they don't look like they will both fit?

Answer: Sometimes PC manufacturers will create what is called a shared slot, where you can install either an ISA card or a PCI card. Because the electronics are mounted differently on a PCI card than they are on an ISA card, it is possible to create a slot (or slots) that can accept either kind of card.

1.1.6 ANSWERS

a) How many bays does your case support?

Answer: It depends upon the case, but typically a case will have two or three 3.5" bays, and three or four 5.25" bays?

b) How many accessible bays does it have?

Answer: Most likely you'll have at least one accessible 3.5" bay, and at least two accessible 5.25" bays.

c) How many 3.5" drives do you have?

Answer: Most people will have two 3.5" drives: one floppy disk drive and one hard drive.

d) How many 5.25" drives do you have?

Answer: Most people will have one 5.25" drive, such as a DVD-ROM or CD-ROM drive.

In addition to the width of the device, there are three potential heights. The most common is half-height, which is what people think of as a standard bay. CD-ROM and DVD-ROM drives are all half-height devices. In the past, it was common to have full-height hard drives. These would require what today would be considered two bays, and were generally reserved for hard drives, except for the original PC, which came with a full-height 5.25" floppy.

Finally, we come to what is called low-profile. Generally reserved for hard drives, this is supposed to mean that the drive takes up 1/3 of the size of a full-height drive. Theoretically this would mean that you could get three hard drives in two bays; however, in practice, this rarely ever works. More frequently, however, they are used in special locations within the case that couldn't fit a regular size device.

This brings us to our next issue. When looking at a case, you want to pay attention to both the total number of bays (of each width) and those that are accessible. By that we mean that the user could get to the front of the bay to access it. Accessible bays are required by any device, such as a floppy drive, where the reader will need to change the media.

Each case has a different attachment mechanism for holding storage devices in place. Some allow you to directly screw the drives in place, while others require the use of rails, which are then inserted and secured to the case. Some even use a combination of the two. The use of rails is declining because it's seen as another step that must be completed in installing a device, and because most people can never find a place to put the extra rails until they need them.

Most drive bays are located at the front of the case. Some may also have other areas, under the power supply in a tower, or next to it in a desktop unit, that can be used to attach storage devices. Utilizing these spaces that might otherwise be empty allows the manufacturer to get just a few more bays, albeit inaccessible bays, in an otherwise crowded case. Most of these secondary bays are designed for 3.5" half-height hard drives (as the three shown in Figure 1.12), since they are obviously not accessible.

Just because you can cram devices in a case doesn't mean that you should. Some case designers weren't too careful about how big a fan they put in their systems to dissipate the heat generated by all of these devices. You'll want to be cognizant of the fact that it is physically possible to put more drives in a system than can be adequately cooled.

1.1.7 ANSWERS

a) What kind of a power supply does your PC have?

Answer: It will depend. Most modern PCs use the ATX design, while older systems use the AT-style power connectors. There is one quick way to determine this even if you have the system closed.

Place your hand over the fan on the back of the power supply while the PC is on. If you feel a suction on your hand, the power supply is an ATX-style power supply. If you feel pressure against your hand, the power supply is an AT-style power supply.

One problem with AT-style power supplies is that the two power leads can be swapped into the opposite places on the motherboard. If the power supply has two connectors that connect to the motherboard, make sure that the black colored wires are toward the middle.

The other problem with AT-style power supplies is that there is little standardization on the size and workings of the switch. Some power supplies have the switch physically on the side of them; others have the switch hardwired to the power supply, and still others have removable remote switches. These issues mean that you must be very careful when selecting a power supply to replace an existing AT-style power supply.

Although ATX-type power supplies can come in different sizes and variations to accommodate other case styles, there are relatively few choices, and most of them are clearly differentiated from one another, so there's little chance of confusion when selecting this type of power supply.

b) Which way does air flow through the power supply?

Answer: It flows in different directions based on whether you've got an ATX-style or AT-style power supply. AT-style power supplies suck air through the PC; ATX-style power supplies force air through it.

THE WHOLE TRUTH

There are actually several power supply variations that I've lumped into these two basic power supply types, the reason being they differ largely by size, not by how they operate or how they connect to the motherboard.

For instance, AT-style power supplies suck air through the computer, while ATX-style power supplies push air through the case.

The same is true for the NTX and WTX variants of the ATX style. They push air through the case and use the single connector for the motherboard. They just differ in their physical dimensions. For our purposes, size will be pretty easy to determine.

c) Where is the switch mounted?

Answer: It depends. Most PCs will have their switch mounted on the front for easy access; however, some systems still have them mounted on the side, or back.

1.1.8 ANSWERS

a) What type of memory is in your PC?

Answer: If your PC is a Pentium II or better, it's probably using DIMMs, or 72-pin SIMMs, or both. Most Pentium and Pentium Pro machines use 72-pin SIMMS, with older machines generally using 36-pin SIMMS.

Every PC has memory in it. Memory holds the things that the PC is doing. When the PC is turned off, the information contained in memory is lost. One of the best ways to think about memory and how it is different from a hard disk is to think of memory as working memory, or as desk space. Hard disks, and other permanent storage media, are for storage, more like your file drawers. The more space you have on your desk (memory) to lay things down on, the more things you can do at once, and the larger the projects you can work on.

Before we talk about the different types of memory that might be in your PC, you need to understand a few things about how memory works. The PC has settled on an 8-bit byte. This means that each byte of PC memory requires at least 8 bits to represent it.

Many PCs use 9 bits to store a single byte of information. One of those bits of information is called a parity bit. This bit of information allows the PC to detect if there has been a failure in an area of memory. Notice that I said it would allow the PC to detect the problem, not correct it. That is critical. Parity-based memory can lead to those nasty non-maskable interrupt errors that halt a PC in its tracks. If you've never seen the results of a non-maskable interrupt, it is just what it sounds like. It's an interrupt that can't be delayed or ignored by the CPU. Most frequently these types of errors are fatal.

A few PCs, originally high-end servers and other critical systems, took this one step farther and used 12 bits to represent one single byte of information. This method allows for not only the detection of a memory failure but also allows for the memory error to be corrected. This is called Error Checking and Correcting (ECC) memory. It has been expensive in the past because it required so many additional bits of storage, and because of its niche market. However, the introduction of DIMMs has made ECC more or less standard in newer systems.

THE WHOLE TRUTH

I mentioned previously the number of bits that were required to represent a single byte of information for a PC. That information only is true if the memory isn't paged across multiple banks within a single memory chip. Essentially this means that the numbers are correct if the memory is arranged in single-byte lengths. Very little memory today is organized in single-byte lengths.

Multiple bytes are stored together utilizing a single parity bit to detect an error in one or the other of the bytes. (It doesn't really matter where the failure is, just that there is a failure.)

The end result is that these detection and correction schemes for memory might not require as much overhead as stated. So having an ECC memory SIMM or DIMM doesn't necessarily mean that there's 33 percent of the total storage being used for potential error correction.

b) Does your PC have cache memory?

Answer: More than likely not on the motherboard if your system is newer; however, there will probably be some on the processor card, or the processor itself.

c) Can you explain what cache memory is used for?

Answer: To improve performance by minimizing the amount of time that the processor must wait on memory.

The problem is that most PC RAM is so slow that the CPU must wait for the RAM to return information. Typical RAM might require 60ns (nanoseconds) to respond to a request (a nanosecond is one billionth of a second). SRAM might be able to respond within 10ns. This can greatly improve performance.

So why not use all SRAM in a PC? Because it's much more expensive than regular RAM. So the PC designers put a small amount of SRAM on the motherboard and put a specialized memory controller between the processor and the memory of a system. This memory controller made copies of the information in the slower DRAM anytime the CPU needed it. Then if the CPU needed the same information again, the memory controller would attempt to get the information from the SRAM instead of the slower DRAM. The problem is that there's a limited amount of cache RAM (SRAM) available, so the memory controller is constantly throwing out information in the cache to make room for new information.

So the larger the cache size, the greater the probability that the memory controller can return the requested information from the cache RAM rather than having to wait until the regular RAM (whether it be a DIMM, SIMM, or SIPP) could provide it. Intel has taken this idea to heart and is now putting more and more cache memory in the CPU, and on the CPU module.

1.1.9 ANSWERS

a) Is your processor installed in a ZIF socket?

Answer: Your answer will vary.

Traditionally, CPUs have been small squares of ceramic, which set them apart from other components in the system because most weren't square, and almost none of them were encased in ceramic. Most were encased in plastic.

Each different type of CPU was installed into a slightly different socket on the motherboard because there were a different number of pins on each processor. This has lead to a series of standardized sockets for the different CPUs.

Recently, however, Intel has been providing CPUs on a card that plugs into the motherboard, rather than a single CPU chip that plugs into a socket. The Pentium II and Pentium III are examples of this kind of packaging for the CPU.

The ZIF socket was created to allow motherboards to be sold separately from the processor. This allowed motherboard manufacturers to build stock motherboards that could support several different speeds of processor without having to build dedicated motherboards for each processor and stock them based on the processor they had installed on them. Suddenly with the ZIF socket, almost anyone could install their processor.

b) What numbers are written on the bottom of your CPU?

Answer: Your answer will vary.

c) Does your system have sockets that allow multiple processors?

Answer: Your answer will vary.

Some systems have sockets that allow multiple processors. To use these systems with two processors you'll need two identical processors. This means that they must be of the same "stepping" level. The stepping level is what Intel uses to determine which minor changes are done to the processor during its life. It's common for a processor to have a few different stepping levels over its life. Normally you can't tell the difference between processors of different stepping levels, but they can sometimes change subtle things that multiprocessor systems might get hung up on. The other thing that you'll need to use multiple processors for is in a multiprocessor operating system, Windows NT being most popular.

You can't always directly determine the stepping level of a processor, although sometimes you can feed the numbers on the bottom of the chip to Intel's Web site and receive back the exact processor stepping level. It's really only important that the CPUs be identical. The easiest way to ensure that is to make sure that the numbers on the CPUs match exactly. Intel also provides a CPU identification utility which can be used to determine the stepping level of the processor.

BIOS, FIRMWARE, AND CMOS

Once you've replaced your processor, we can start talking about where the CPU gets its instructions from. We described the CPU as the office administrator—the person who keeps everything running. But who tells the office adminstrator (CPU) what to do? The boss tells the administrator what to do. In the PC, that's the job of BIOS and other firmware. That is at least until control is passed over to software installed on the PC.

The first thing that a CPU does when it boots, the only thing it knows to do, is to go to a specific memory location to look for something to do. That location is occupied by the PC's BIOS. The BIOS is the Basic Input/Output Service. BIOS contains all of the commands that the CPU needs to perform useful functions, such as displaying text on the monitor or reading information from the hard disk.

BIOS is a special kind of firmware. Firmware is software—instructions how to utilize hardware—that is installed directly in the hardware. Sometimes firmware is burned into ROM and can't be replaced without physically removing and replacing the ROM. Other times firmware is contained on EEPROM, or FlashROM, which can be reprogrammed by the use of a special set of instructions.

It is important to understand that firmware and BIOS are just special software, and, as such, may have bugs in it. If firmware is included on a ROM chip, the ROM chip must be physically replaced. If, however, the firmware is in FlashROM, a new version can be downloaded using special software.

THE WHOLE TRUTH

Just because you can upgrade your BIOS (or firmware) doesn't mean that you should. There are certain risks attached.

The first is that the new version of the BIOS may break something that's currently working. It sounds strange, but new software frequently fixes one problem only to cause another one.

The second risk is that you'll have a problem in the process of downloading the new firmware. This could easily render the motherboard useless until it's sent back to the manufacturer. What could go wrong while downloading the new firmware? A power failure as one example.

When you're considering updating BIOS or firmware, consider whether you need to do it. If you're not experiencing a problem, there's no real need to upgrade.

One other thing that you need to be aware of is that almost every add-in card has its own firmware which, like the motherboard BIOS, can be either ROM-based or FlashROM-based. Each of these add-in card's firmware is linked into the boot process by BIOS so that each card gets an opportunity to initialize itself.

Initializing all of the add-in cards and integrated devices is just one critical part of the boot-up process that all PCs go through (at least once). The boot-up process can be broken into a few basic stages:

- Power-On Self-Test (POST)
- Initialization
- Configuration (Plug and Play)
- Bootstrap

The Power-On Self-Test (POST) process is one that most PC users are familiar with. They immediately recognize that (sometimes annoying) memory count that happens each time the PC is booted, or the series of clicks and whirs that the PC makes during start up. The job of the POST process is to make sure that all of the devices that are reported as being present (by CMOS, discussed in a moment) are truly there and are functioning.

POST checks all the memory to make sure that it can be accessed. It also checks to make sure that the floppy drive will respond, and that a few other of the PC's vital functions are working correctly. Although some or all of these tests can be turned off with newer versions of BIOS, it's important to note that the classical PC performs the complete set of tests each time it is powered up.

One interesting note about POST that most people don't realize is that it does NOT require a video card be present to report information back to the user on the state and health of the system. Information can be conveyed via a series of beeps from the PC speaker. However, if you get such a series of beeps, you're probably going to need the manufacturer's help because each BIOS manufacturer has a slightly different meaning for each pattern of beeps.

Once the POST process has finished, the next step is initialization of each of the add-in cards and devices. Although technically they have the option of initializing themselves before or during POST, most devices wait until after POST is completed to do their initialization. This ensures that they can use certain basic services, such as the video display.

Once all of the devices have initialized, the BIOS, if Plug and Play compliant, will do a little configuration cleanup and housekeeping to move conflicting Plug and Play cards out of the way so that the boot up can be completed.

Finally, a bootstrap program is run, which is designed to fetch the next set of instructions from a floppy, hard disk, or CD-ROM. This bootstrap program is very small and just tries to run whatever it finds on the first available device for booting. (I'm being somewhat vague here because most modern BIOSs let you specify in which order potential boot devices should be attempted.)

We've now talked about BIOS, the boot process, and how BIOS tells the processor what to do. But we've probably left you wondering why we weren't talking about the BIOS screens—those setup screens that you use to configure your computer to tell it what hardware is attached and how you want it to behave. The reason is because the BIOS setup screens not only utilize BIOS to do their job, but also use some semi-permanent memory, referred to as CMOS. CMOS is really the technology behind the memory storage. CMOS is a low power consumption technology that can be used to maintain the same values over a long period of time with very minimal power.

CMOS is why most PCs have a place for batteries, and/or have a lithium battery on the motherboard. It's these batteries that keep the information in CMOS even after the power has been turned off to the PC. It's also why you'll sometimes receive a message from BIOS saying that the CMOS battery is low. If the battery completely fails you may even get a message from BIOS that the CMOS checksum is invalid.

CMOS has the job of holding the values that you use to configure the PC and storing them until the next time the PC is booted up so that BIOS can read them and use them to control how the PC boots up.

A few key things to remember about CMOS:

- It does require some small amount of power.
- It doesn't have much storage space.
- It is used by BIOS to hold critical information on the hardware that has been installed and how you want your PC to work.

CMOS can be cleared easiest by removing power from it for a few minutes. Depending on the device, it may take a while to clear the memory.

Some motherboards provide a special jumper that can be used to clear CMOS memory.

A reason you might want to clear CMOS memory is if there's been a password established on a computer that you don't know, and you need to gain access to the computer. The only problem with clearing the CMOS memory is that in addition to clearing the password you'll clear all the settings, so you'll have to set up the hardware again.

Almost all systems today use a Dallas Semiconductor RealTime clock module with integrated CMOS and lithium battery to keep track of real time going by so that whenever a PC is booted it can get the current time without prompting the user. (The original PC had to do just that—prompt the user every time it was booted to get the current time.)

1.1.10 ANSWERS

a) Record the steps you followed to remove your motherboard.

Answer: Your answers will vary.

b) Will you be reinstalling the same motherboard that you just removed or will you be installing a new motherboard at this time?

Answer: Your answers will vary.

If you are replacing the motherboard, the easiest thing to do is use new plastic standoffs. Plastic standoffs are designed so that they cannot be easily removed from the motherboard once they've been inserted through a hole. The only way to get them back out is to squeeze the tops with a pair of needle nose pliers and wiggle them out. This is a difficult process and may take some time. There are motherboards and plastic standoffs that I've not been able to separate in some circumstances. My only resort was to use a pair of diagonal clippers to clip the plastic standoff into pieces.

Once you've removed the plastic standoffs you will notice the metal posts that were holding the motherboard in place are visible. These posts can be unscrewed from the case as well. This might be necessary if you're installing a new motherboard with holes in different places.

You'll probably find the rare circumstance where your new motherboard you get won't fit the case you have. That is an unfortunate side effect of only having pseudo-standards for motherboard and case mounting. You'll probably not find this to be a problem for ATX-style cases (one sporting ATX-style power supplies) and ATX motherboards because a well-defined standard exists, but sometimes older AT-style cases and AT-style motherboards don't fit together well. Figure 1.24 shows a perfect example of a way that motherboard manufacturers have attempted to adapt to the lack of standards.

When looking for a place to put screws on a motherboard, you'll want to stick to only those areas that have a circle of solder on the top of them. This is because these holes are specifically designed to be grounding points, places on the motherboard where there should be no current. If you place a screw in a hole that does not have a ring of solder around the hole, you may accidentally come in contact with a place on the motherboard that is supposed to have power, and end up grounding it out. This will most likely make the system not function and has been known to cause many hard to diagnose problems.

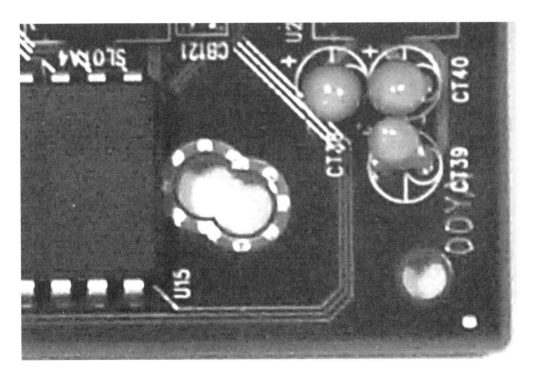

**Figure 1.24 ■ This is a sort of double hole to accommodate the lack
of standards in motherboard mounting.**

**LAB
1.1**

In attempting to prepare this chapter we were unable to locate a motherboard that didn't have solder around every hole; however, this doesn't mean that there aren't motherboards out there that don't have this problem. It's just that they are becoming more rare.

Before proceeding to the next Lab, you'll want to reassemble your PC by reversing the process that we went through here to take it apart. We'll need your system running in the next Lab to perform some of the Exercises.

LAB 1.1 SELF-REVIEW QUESTIONS

In order to test your progress, you should be able to answer the following questions.

1) Most PCs have some screws exposed on the back panel that remove the power supply or fan. You must remove these screws before opening the case.
   a) _____True
   b) _____False

2) Of the three techniques that are used to identify which way a cable is supposed to be installed for pin-based connectors, what is the technique that corresponds a tab on the cable's connector to a small 1/8" opening on the connector?
   a) _____A keyed connector on the component.
   b) _____A blocked opening on the component.
   c) _____A red conductor on the cable indicates the orientation of the connection.
   d) _____All ribbon cables operate this way.

3) How many bays does a typical case support?
   a) _____One or two 3.5" bays and three or four 5.25" bays
   b) _____Two or three 3.5" bays and three or four 5.25" bays
   c) _____Two or three 5.25" bays and three or four 3.5" bays
   d) _____Two or three 3.5" bays and three or four 5.5" bays

4) Power Supply screws can be identified because they immediately surround the fan and power cord connectors and do not appear to hold anything to the outer case or cover.
   a) _____True
   b) _____False

5) Which of the following is the most prevalent of the six major add-in card slot types?
   a) _____VESA (Video Electronics Standards Association)/Video Localbus
   b) _____EISA (Extended Industry Standard Architecture)
   c) _____PCI (Peripheral Component Interconnect)
   d) _____AGP (Advanced Graphics Port)
   e) _____Microchannel (MCA)
   f) _____ISA (Industry Standard Architecture)

6) What kind of integrated port is a modem most likely to be connected to?
   a) _____IDE/EIDE
   b) _____SCSI
   c) _____Serial
   d) _____IEEE

   Sometimes newer modems will be connected via USB.

7) Which of the following is not a memory type commonly found on a system board?
   a) _____SIMM
   b) _____SIPP
   c) _____cache
   d) _____DRAM
   e) _____These are all types of memory found on the system board.

8) Some SIMMs have memory chips only on one side, and others have memory chips on both sides. SIMMs with chips on both sides may be inserted either way.
   a) _____True
   b) _____False

9) Which of the following is not a problem with AT-style power supplies?
   a) _____The two power leads can be swapped into the opposite place on the motherboard, making it difficult to know the orientation by which to connect them.
   b) _____They have the switch hardwired to the power supply, making it difficult to maneuver when trying to remove it.
   c) _____They come in so many different sizes and variations that it makes it difficult to select a replacement power supply of this type.
   d) _____There are no problems with AT-style power supplies.

10) The introduction of which type of memory has made Error Checking and Correcting (ECC) more or less standard in newer systems?
   a) _____SIMM
   b) _____DRAM
   c) _____SIPP
   d) _____DIMM

11) Typical RAM might require how many nanoseconds to respond to a request?
   a) _____10
   b) _____30
   c) _____50
   d) _____60

12) Which of the four basic stages of the boot-up process is responsible for ensuring that all of the devices that are reported as being present by CMOS are truly there and are functioning?
   a) _____Initialization
   b) _____POST
   c) _____CMOS Checksum Test
   d) _____Bootstrap

13) What kinds of integrated ports are hard drives connected to?
   a) _____IDE/EIDE
   b) _____Parallel
   c) _____Serial
   d) _____SCSI
   e) _____Both a and d are correct
   f) _____Both c and d are correct

Quiz answers appear in Appendix A, Section 1.1.

L A B   1.2

IRQS, DMAS, AND I/O ADDRESSES

LAB OBJECTIVES

After this Lab, you will be able to:

✓ Review Resources That Are in Use on Your System

✓ Change the IRQ of a Jumper-Based Add-In Card

✓ Change the IRQ of a Software-Configured Card

✓ Change the IRQ of a Plug and Play Device

Understanding how a PC is physically put together is a good start in understanding how the PC works. However, it doesn't illuminate how it works, or what might be the cause of a problem, when something goes wrong.

In this Lab, we'll review how the PC communicates and what things can go wrong with those communications. We'll also see how add-in cards set their I/O addresses, IRQs, and DMA channels, and what they are.

UNDERSTANDING IRQs

Normally, the CPU of a PC continues executing instructions, one at a time, following the path that was set by the programmer. This works well when the PC is calculating a number, sorting a list, or updating a database, but what happens when the PC needs to get some input from the user?

The first way that the PC can respond to input from the user is to continually look for it. Every few seconds, the PC would go out and *poll* for input. The problem with this is that it is a waste of time, because the PC is constantly wasting cycles that it could be using to get work done.

Think of a typical office supply room in your company. There are all kinds of supplies around that people in the company come and get as they need them.

If we were using the polling method, every day, or every few hours we, as the office supplies manager, would walk back into the supply room and check to see that there are enough supplies to last for another day or two. If there are, we would go back to our normal work.

There's a better way to handle this. What would happen if we had the people who are checking out the supplies interrupt us when they had taken the supplies? That way we wouldn't need to go back and check the supply room to make sure that there were supplies, because we would always know how much we had, because we would know when any were taken. (We're ignoring for the moment that people forget to do this.)

This is similar to the way that your PC handles input. It responds to interrupts. Interrupts are special lines in the computer that chips, other than the CPU and add-in cards, can get the CPU's attention to do something. In this way, you can eliminate the need to constantly poll to see if there is input.

In the PC, these interrupt lines are called IRQs, or Interrupt Request Lines. Each PC, since the AT, has had 16 IRQ lines that can be used to signal the CPU that something needs attention. Although this may sound like a lot, it's really not that many, because several are used for internal functions, and others have defined functions.

In some cases, IRQs can be shared, but this only works if the devices are PCI, Microchannel, or EISA devices, and isn't recommended even then.

UNDERSTANDING DMA

Just getting the CPU's attention, rather than forcing it to poll for input, is a good start, but it's not the final answer. The CPU must still stop what it's doing and focus its attention on the data that's coming in.

Think back to our office supply analogy from the preceding section. What if you could convince your office supply vendor to come in and check the room for you. They could write the order for the things you need and then all you would need to do would be to sign the order. This is similar to how DMA works. It does the work, then the CPU is notified that the work has been completed.

Using DMA, the device that has the input transfers it directly to a location in memory from which the CPU can access it. This is because the CPU can operate much quicker with information that's stored in memory than it can use input and outputs through the bus.

A method was devised to allow devices on the peripheral buses to have direct memory access. Direct memory access allows the peripheral to transfer information to memory without the involvement of the CPU. This can dramatically reduce the CPU utilization necessary to process input, or to transfer information to a card. Unfortunately, there are only a few generally available DMA channels that can be used in the modern PC, and they can't be shared. The end result is that they are even more precious than IRQs.

Luckily, there are very few add-in cards that need DMA channels, as you will see in the Exercises.

UNDERSTANDING I/O PORTS

I said in the last section that utilizing information in memory was much more efficient than going to I/O ports to get information. This is true because memory is attached via a much faster bus structure, and is often cached with even faster memory. Therefore, accesses to I/O ports are generally much slower than memory.

I/O ports have addresses, just like memory, although the addresses don't go as high. They allow for a single byte to be read or written at a time. I/O ports cannot be shared between devices. Each I/O port must identify one unique location within the system. For that reason, certain standards have been defined for what will exist at which I/O ports.

LAB 1.2 EXERCISES

1.2.1 REVIEW RESOURCES THAT ARE IN USE ON YOUR SYSTEM

The first thing that we're going to do is review the current IRQs that are used in your PC. We're going to do this by utilizing the inventory of devices and resources that Windows 95/98 keeps for you.

Follow these steps to identify what IRQs, DMAs, and I/O ports are in use on your PC:

1. Click on the Start button, select Settings, then Control Panel.
2. Double-click the System control panel applet.
3. Click the Device Manager tab.
4. Double-click the Computer object.

a) Which IRQ resources are in use on your system and what uses them?

_____

_____

5. Click on the Direct Memory Access (DMA) radio button.

b) Which DMA channels are in use on your system and what uses them?

_____

_____

6. Click on the Input/Output (I/O) radio button.

c) Which I/O addresses are used on your system and what uses them?

_____

_____

    7. Press OK to close the Computer properties dialog box.
    8. Press OK to close the System applet dialog box.
    9. Close the control panel by clicking the close window (x) icon in the upper right-hand corner of the window.

d) Why are IRQs so scarce?

_____

_____

e) Why do you want to use IRQs?

_____

_____

f) When can two devices use the same IRQ?

_____

_____

g) Why are DMA channels better than IRQs?

_____

_____

h) Can two devices use the same DMA channel?

_____

_____

i) Why are I/O ports used without IRQs or DMAs?

j) Can two devices use the same I/O port?

1.2.2 CHANGE THE IRQ OF A JUMPER-BASED ADD-IN CARD

Most modern add-in cards utilize plug and play or software configuration to configure themselves. This is true of every PCI card and an increasing number of ISA cards. However, sometimes you'll run into cards, such as the ones in Figures 1.25 and 1.26, that use jumpers to control their settings.

Looking at Figure 1.25, it may be fairly obvious what each jumper is designed to do. Looking at Figure 1.26, it may not be so obvious. You'll find situations like

Figure 1.25 ■ A ISA serial/parallel I/O card with good silk screening to show you which jumpers do what.

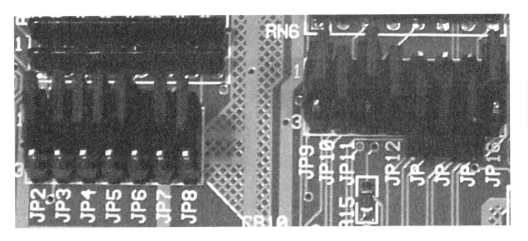

**Figure 1.26 ■ Another ISA Serial/Parallel I/O card with poor silk
screening leaving you to wonder what jumpers do what.**

this all the time. Some add-in cards clearly indicate what the jumpers do on the
card itself, while others require that you read and review the manual to get the
correct settings.

Each jumper is a small plastic box that contains a small wire, or strap, that connects the two pins over which it's placed.

In the case of the card in Figure 1.25, you can see that Serial A is assigned to
COM3 (or at least its I/O address) by looking at the first jumper (working left
to right) on the bottom row. If you continue on down the row, you'll see that
Serial A is assigned to IRQ4. Looking at the row of jumpers immediately above
this row, you'll see that Serial B is assigned to COM4 (or at least its I/O
address) and looking further you'll see that it's assigned to IRQ3.

   a) How many jumpers does your card have?

   _____

   _____

   b) Can you determine the function of the jumpers without the manual?

   _____

   _____

In the Lab text, you saw that IRQs can't be shared between ISA cards, and that COM1 and COM2 already use IRQs 3 and 4. Sometimes settings like this will work because they are serial ports and because some BIOSs actually handle the checking of both the COM1 and COM3 serial ports whenever an IRQ4 is received, but it's still not recommended.

Figure 1.27 shows a more complicated I/O card that supports a joystick (game) port, a floppy and IDE hard disk controller, and the serial and parallel ports on the last I/O card we were looking at.

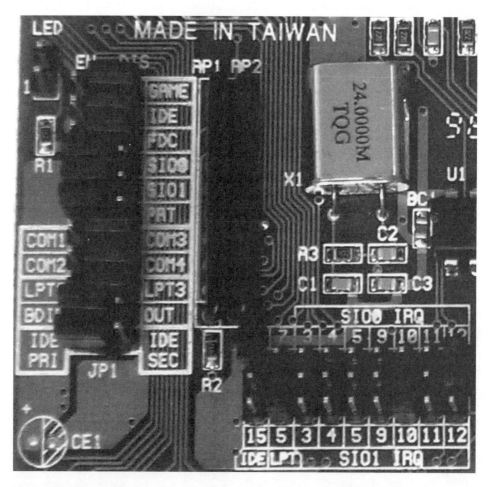

Figure 1.27 ■ A 16-bit ISA I/O card with Serial, Parallel, Game, Floppy, and IDE controllers onboard.

You'll notice that you have a great deal more options with this card, including the ability to assign either Serial 0 or Serial 1 to any IRQ in the range of 3, 4, 5, 9, 10, 11, or 12. This could potentially allow you to set up COM3 and COM4 to work correctly (albeit on nonstandard IRQs.) In this figure, the controller is configured to disable the internal game controller, IDE controller, floppy disk controller, and to enable both serial ports and the printer port. (Note that on this card SIO0 and SIO1 are the serial ports.) You'll also notice that the Serial I/O ports are assigned to COM3 and COM4. The LPT port is assigned to LPT3 and set to bidirectional mode (rather than output only.) Although IDE is set to Primary (meaning the 1F0 I/O address), it's being ignored because it's jumpered to be ignored above.

You'll also notice that I've set the jumper for the IDE interrupt off the jumper row that it should normally be in. It's only over one pin. This is a useful technique for keeping a jumper on the card, but preventing it from connecting anything. It's often used, as it is here, to prevent a connection that might cause adverse effects.

Finally, you'll see that the printer port (LPT port) is set to IRQ 5. The first serial port is set to IRQ 12, and the second to IRQ 10. This is because these were free in the system from which this card came.

So far we've talked about jumpered cards, but there are also some cards that use DIP switches to configure the card. These work the same way in that you set the switches to the way you want the card to behave. You'll frequently find these kinds of arrays of switches on older VGA video cards.

All you need to do to change the IRQ of a jumper-based add-in card is to remove the card (with the PC power off) and change the appropriate jumper. The booklet or manual that came with the card will provide you with the instructions on how to do this. As soon as you replace the card and turn the power back on, the change will have been made; however, you'll probably have to reconfigure your Windows (or DOS) software to see the new IRQ.

c) What is a jumper—really?

_____

_____

d) Why would you use a jumpered card today?

_____

_____

1.2.3 CHANGE THE IRQ OF A SOFTWARE-CONFIGURED CARD

In this section, we'll talk about transitional cards, which were developed as jumper-based cards were falling out of favor, and before Plug and Play really came to the fore.

These cards utilize a configuration utility to configure the card. It's better than a jumper-based card because you can change the configuration without removing the cover, or the card, but still not quite as good as a plug and play card because the operating system can't automatically set the card to the best settings for you.

If you have one of these cards that you can test with, locate or download the configuration program from the software that came with the card and run it. Change the IRQ setting of the card using the procedure the software walks you through. Once you've made the change, exit the configuration utility and turn off the power to the PC. Then turn the power back on after a few seconds. The IRQ of the card will be changed. Now all you have to do is update your Windows configuration.

a) How big was the configuration utility that you used to configure your add-in card?

_____

_____

b) How many add-in cards do you have that can be configured via a software program?

_____

_____

In order to determine the answer use Control Panel – System – Device Manager and examine each device's Properties.

1.2.4 CHANGE THE IRQ OF A PLUG AND PLAY DEVICE

LAB
1.2

Plug and Play devices are the answer to every technician's prayers—at least those who've ever spent hours trying to get the right set of IRQs, DMAs, and I/O ports to allow all of the add-in cards to work without killing each other. (If you don't believe that this can make you old very quickly, go find an old machine running Windows 3.1 and try to change **anything**!)

To change the IRQ, or other resource, of a plug and play device, all you have to do is go into the device manager and change the resource it's using. The following shows the series of steps that you must follow:

1. Click on the Start button, select Settings, and Control Panel.
2. Double-click the System control panel applet.
3. Click the Device Manager tab.
4. Expand a device tree and double-click a plug and play device.
5. Click the Resources tab.
6. Uncheck the Use automatic settings checkbox.

a) What happens when you uncheck this box?

_____

_____

7. Double-click the resource usage that you want to change.

b) What happens at this point?

_____

_____

8. Use the up and down arrows, or edit box, to change the value.

9. STOP! It is NOT recommended that you continue with this process, especially just for purposes of this Exercise. Instead, click the Cancel button in each of the currently opened dialog boxes to quit this procedure.

Although I've shown you how to do this, it's not recommended that you do this kind of manual configuration unless you're having problems with a device, or you know something that Windows doesn't know—such as the device driver has a bug that doesn't allow it to work well on IRQ 9.

c) Why do you suppose you shouldn't change IRQ settings of a plug and play device?

_____

_____

That said, if you really did want to continue on, you'd simply follow the remaining steps (picking up from Step 8 in the preceding procedure), as follows:

1. Click OK to close the Resource dialog.
2. Click OK again to close the Device dialog.
3. You may be prompted to insert Windows media, or to reboot your system, depending on the change you made and the device on which you made it.

Windows will take care of making the change to the device and will update the driver to reflect the new resource.

LAB 1.2 EXERCISE ANSWERS

1.2.1 ANSWERS

a) Which IRQ resources are in use on your system and what uses them?

Answer: It really depends on your individual system.

However, IRQs 3 & 4 are more than likely used by COM2 and COM1 respectively. IRQ 7 is more than likely in use by LPT1. IRQ 14 is probably in use by the primary IDE controller. Other IRQs are probably in use in your system because of audio cards and other add-ins.

Figure 1.28 shows the computer properties dialog for my notebook system.

**LAB
1.2**

Table 1.1 shows the IRQs of a PC, what they are used for, and whether they are hardcoded (and thus cannot be changed).

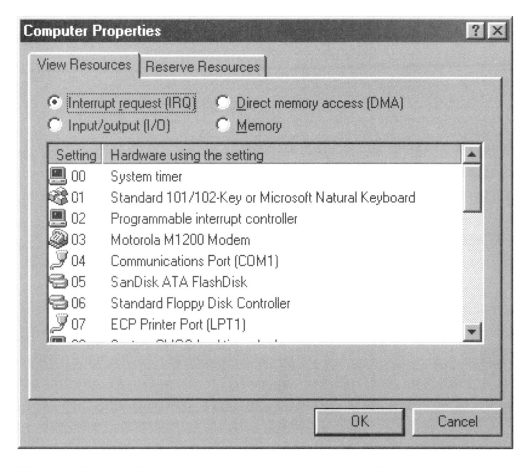

**Figure 1.28 ■ Although you cannot see the whole list, this computer
properties dialog shows that I have many IRQs in use, with only
a few still available.**

Table 1.1 ■ IRQs Explained

IRQ	Use	Hardwired
0	System Timer	Yes
1	Keyboard Controller	Yes
2	2nd Interrupt Controller Cascade	Yes
3	COM2	No
4	COM1	No
5	LPT2/Sound	No
6	Floppy Controller	Yes
7	LPT1	No
8	Real-Time Clock	Yes
9	Available	No
10	Available	No
11	Available	No
12	PS/2 Mouse/Available	No
13	Math Coprocessor	Yes
14	Primary Hard Disk Controller (AT)	No
15	Secondary Hard Disk Controller (AT)	No

You can see from the table that every IRQ has something that normally uses it, and this doesn't even include network adapters, video capture cards, and some of the other add-in cards that might want to use an IRQ. What makes IRQs so difficult is that there are too many devices that are battling for the few IRQs that are available.

b) Which DMA channels are in use on your system and what uses them?

Answer: Again, this depends on your system.

More than likely you'll have DMA 2 in use by the floppy drive controller and DMA 3 in use by an ECP/EPP parallel port. You will probably also have DMA 1 and DMA 5 in use by a sound card. Table 1.2 lists the DMA channels and their assigned uses.

Table 1.2 ■ DMA Channels Explained

DMA	Use	Transfer	Hardwired
0	Available	8-bit	No
1	Sound/Available	8-bit	No
2	Floppy Disk Controller	8-bit	Yes
3	ECP/EPP Parallel/Available	8-bit	No
4	1st DMA Controller		Yes
5	Sound Card/Available	16-bit	No
6	Available	16-bit	No
7	Available	16-bit	No

**LAB
1.2**

   c) Which I/O addresses are used on your system and what uses them?

   Answer: This also depends on your system, although certain standards do exist.

More than likely you'll have IF0 in use by an IDE controller. 3F8 and 2F8 are probably in use by COM1 and COM2, respectively. 378 is probably reserved by the LPT1 port. You may also have a joystick port at 200, and other I/O ports in use by audio cards and network cards. Table 1.3 shows some of the common I/O ports and what you'll find at them.

Table 1.3 ■ I/O Ports Explained

Port	Use
1F0	Primary Hard Disk Controller
170	Secondary Hard Disk Controller
3F8	COM1
2F8	COM2
3E8	COM3
2E8	COM4
378	LPT1

Table 1.3 ■ I/O Ports Explained (continued)

Port	Use
278	LPT2
200	Joystick Port
0F0	Math Coprocessor
070	CMOS/Real-Time Clock
330	MPU-401 MIDI

d) Why are IRQs so scarce?

Answer: Because there are so many devices in the PC but only 16 IRQs available. Many of those are already in use for internal system functions, as you saw in Table 1.1.

e) Why do you want to use IRQs?

Answer: Because it prevents the CPU from having to poll an I/O port, and thus makes the computer quicker.

f) When can two devices use the same IRQ?

Answer: When the devices are both on a single bus and the bus is one of the following: PCI, EISA, or Microchannel.

g) Why are DMA channels better than IRQs?

Answer: Because information can be transferred into memory, which is faster than I/O ports on the bus, without the CPU being required.

This means the CPU can be doing other, more productive tasks while information is being retrieved, or sent, from a device.

h) Can two devices use the same DMA channel?

Answer: No, each device must have it's own DMA channel.

i) Why are I/O ports used without IRQs or DMAs?

Answer: To conserve IRQ lines and DMA channels for devices with higher I/O requirements.

For instance, CMOS only has an I/O port address; it doesn't have an IRQ line or DMA channel because the data transferred to/from the device is so small that it doesn't need it. Another reason is because the device itself never needs to initiate communication, as in the case of CMOS.

j) Can two devices use the same I/O port?

Answer: No, each device must have a unique I/O port.

1.2.2 ANSWERS

a) How many jumpers does your card have?

Answer: It depends on your card.

However, most cards that do have jumpers have several—often more than half a dozen. The end result is that it's often confusing to determine which jumper does what without a manual. Some manufacturers did catch on to this difficulty and have subsequently put descriptions of a jumper's function directly on the card, so no manual is required for such cards.

b) Can you determine the function of the jumpers without the manual?

Answer: It depends on your card.

Older cards rarely tell you what the jumpers do. However, most new cards that use jumpers (and jumpers are getting rarer by the day) screen into the card short descriptions of what each jumper does. This greatly simplifies configuration.

c) What is a jumper—really?

Answer: It's just a short piece of wire encased in plastic. It makes a connection between one pin and another, exactly identical to how a wire or cable works, only over a much shorter distance.

d) Why would you use a jumpered card today?

Answer: Because they are cheap!

Because they are just simple pieces of metal, jumpers can be put on a card without anything special and aren't expensive to make. The end result is that they are so easy to make that we keep making them even when there are better methods of handling the need to have jumpers.

1.2.3 ANSWERS

a) How big was the configuration utility that you used to configure your add-in card?

Answer: Most often these programs are less than 50K, although some grow to be over 100K in size. They are designed with a simple purpose: to configure their card. So even if they get fancy, they won't be much more than 100K.

Why is this important? Because you can keep all of the software configuration utilities on one set of configuration disks that you can carry with you. (This assumes, of course, that your PCs don't all have CD-ROMs; the amount of storage available on a CD, or a couple of CDs anyway, would make the preceding point moot.)

b) How many add-in cards do you have that can be configured via a software program?

Answer: It will depend on your system, but this is also partially a trick question. Device Manager doesn't differentiate between devices that are add-ins and those that are integrated into the motherboard, so you have to start with a list of the devices you know are add-ins first. It's not uncommon to have NO cards that support software configuration, except perhaps those that also support Plug and Play.

This is because there was such a short span of time that software configuration was practical before cards started supporting plug and play. Finding a card that is configured via software is pretty hard to do.

1.2.4 ANSWERS

a) What happens when you uncheck this box?

Answer: Figure 1.29 shows an example resource dialog that you should see at this point.

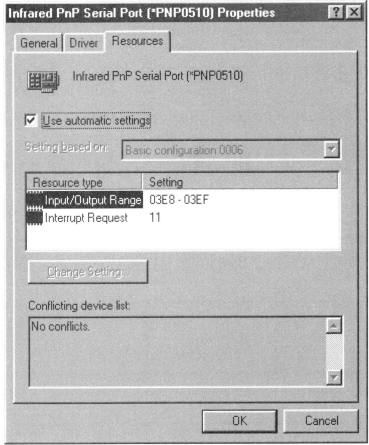

Figure 1.29 ■ **Every Plug and Play device should have a resources tab that shows the resources it uses, while allowing you to override the automatic settings.**

b) What happens at this point?

Answer: You will either get No Modifications Allowed message or an Edit dialog box opens, enabling you to change the setting manually.

There are some devices that even if you turn off the Use automatic settings you can't change the settings. System motherboard devices are examples. If you encounter this, try the procedure on a COM port and it will work.

c) Why do you suppose you shouldn't change IRQ settings of a plug and play device?

Answer: Because once you set the IRQ of a plug and play device, Windows 9x can no longer change it's setting. This means that as you add new hardware, Windows will have a hard time working around your manual IRQ settings, and potentially you'll get the message that some of your new hardware can't be installed because you don't have enough of the right kind of resources.

LAB 1.2 SELF-REVIEW QUESTIONS

In order to test your progress, you should be able to answer the following questions.

1) How many IRQ lines does every PC have?
   a) _____7
   b) _____12
   c) _____16
   d) _____20

2) What is the purpose of IRQs?
   a) _____They are used by devices that receive input to transfer that input directly to a location in memory from which the CPU can use it.
   b) _____They signal the CPU that something needs attention.
   c) _____They provide information from the user to the computer and from the computer back to the user.
   d) _____They are used by drivers to communicate with each other.

3) What is IRQ0 usually reserved for?
   a) _____Keyboard controller
   b) _____COM2
   c) _____LPT1
   d) _____System timer
   e) _____IRQ0 is not a reserved line

4) Which IRQ line is usually reserved for a primary IDE controller?
   a) _____7
   b) _____12
   c) _____14
   d) _____20

5) How many DMAs does every PC have?
   a) _____7
   b) _____12
   c) _____16
   d) _____20

LAB
1.2

6) What is the purpose of DMAs?
   a) _____They are used by devices that receive input to transfer it directly to a location in memory from which the CPU can use it.
   b) _____They signal the CPU that something needs attention.
   c) _____They provide information from the user to the computer and from the computer back to the user.
   d) _____They are used by drivers to communicate with each other.

7) What DMA channel is usually reserved for the floppy drive controller?
   a) _____2
   b) _____6
   c) _____14
   d) _____20

8) What is DMA7 usually reserved for?
   a) _____Sound card
   b) _____ECP/EPP parallel port
   c) _____1st DMA Controller
   d) _____DMA7 is not a reserved channel

9) What is the I/O port 378 usually reserved for?
   a) _____COM1
   b) _____COM2
   c) _____LPT1
   d) _____LPT2
   e) _____I/O ports are not reserved

10) Two devices can share the same DMA channel when the devices are both on a single bus and the bus is one of the following: PCI, EISA, or Microchannel.
   a) _____True
   b) _____False

Quiz answers appear in Appendix A, Section 1.2.

L A B   1.3

CABLING, CONNECTORS, AND PORTS

LAB OBJECTIVES

After this Lab, you will be able to:

✓ Identify DB-Type Connectors

✓ Understand Phone Connectors

✓ Identify Centronics Connectors

✓ Identify Miscellaneous Connectors

The modern PC has a great deal of connectors and ports. With the proliferation of devices to connect to a PC, it's become common for a single PC to have 10–20 different connectors.

The goal of this Lab is to explain the different connectors and identify the common uses.

DETERMINING GENDER

Most of this discussion of gender may seem obvious to you; however, connector gender is a source of great confusion to a great many technicians working on PCs today.

All connectors are gendered or gender neutral. Gender-neutral connectors can be connected to themselves. Gendered connectors require that they be connected with the connector of the same type but of opposite gender. Most connectors on the modern PC are gendered connectors.

The gender names are very easy to determine. Male connectors have pins, or circuit cards poking out of them; female connectors have holes or receptacles for the corresponding pins or circuit cards on the male connectors.

For those gender-neutral connectors, you'll find both a receptacle and a protrusion on the same connector. They are connected by pairing them with the receptacle on one matched with the protrusion on the other. The most notable example of this type of connector is an IBM Type A connector, which is about a 1.25" square connector containing four conductors that is used for token ring. Other than that, almost no connectors in the PC world are gender neutral.

Although the idea of a receptacle being female and protrusions being male is a simple rule, it applies to all connectors, so don't forget it. It's key to identifying what type of connection a connector is.

LAB 1.3

LAB 1.3 EXERCISES

1.3.1 IDENTIFY DB-TYPE CONNECTORS

The best exercise for learning the basic connector types and what they are used for is to remove all of the cables from the back of your computer and reconnect them one at a time. That's what you will be doing in this Exercise.

One of the most common types of connector in use in the PC today is the DB family of connectors. These connectors are a simple male-female pin-based connector that is D-shaped. Typically, they come in 9-pin (DB-9), 25-pin (DB-25), and two 15-pin (DB-15, HDDB-15) varieties.

To begin, unplug your system, then go ahead and disconnect every cable from the back of your computer, including any telephone lines.

If you have a serial mouse and/or an external modem, retrieve them and examine their connectors now.

If your mouse is a newer mouse, chances are that it's a PS/2 connector (that is, a round connector with 6 pins), and not a serial DB-type connector. If that's the case, hold off on reconnecting your mouse until Exercise 1.3.4.

**LAB
1.3**

a) How many holes/pins does the connector attached to the mouse or external modem have in it?

_____

_____

Go ahead and reconnect those now. If you have a printer, examine it's connector next.

b) Looking at your printer's connector, is it a male or a female? How many pins/holes does it have?

_____

_____

Go ahead and reconnect your printer to your computer now. If you have a joystick or MIDI device, retrieve them now and examine their connectors.

c) How many holes/pins does the connector attached to the joystick or MIDI device have in it?

_____

_____

Reconnect those devices if you have them. Retrieve your monitor's connector and examine it now.

d) Is your monitor's connector different from the connectors you've seen so far? If so, how?

_____

_____

Go ahead and reconnect your monitor now. For the purposes of the remaining Exercises, though, do not make any more connections at this time.

1.3.2 UNDERSTAND PHONE CONNECTORS

Before plugging your phone line back into your PC, carefully examine the connector. Compare it to the connector in your telephone's line. If you have other telephone wires around, examine them as well.

LAB
1.3

a) Do you see any differences in the connectors that you examined?

_____

_____

If you have other devices that you haven't reconnected to your PC yet, hold off a bit as we'll explore these miscellaneous connectors in Exercise 1.3.4.

1.3.3 IDENTIFY CENTRONICS CONNECTORS

So far, we've talked about the two most popular connectors that are directly on a PC, but there are other connectors that are important in the PC arena. One of those is the Centronics connector.

For this Exercise, disconnect your printer's cable from the printer itself and examine its connector.

a) What difference do you notice about this printer connector?

_____

_____

You can reconnect this connector to your printer now.

1.3.4 IDENTIFY MISCELLANEOUS CONNECTORS

By now, just about every device should be reconnected to your PC as a result of the previous Exercises. But, there are several other devices that we haven't mentioned yet that you may still have lying around waiting to be connected. These devices are addressed in this Exercise.

a) What devices do you have yet to connect at this point?

_____

_____

As you reconnect these devices, take note of their connectors, their characteristics, and to what devices they belong.

b) What are the differences that you note about these various connectors?

_____

_____

LAB 1.3 EXERCISE ANSWERS

1.3.1 ANSWERS

a) How many holes/pins does the connector attached to the mouse or external modem have in it?

Answer: It is most likely a DB-9 connector, which means it would have 9 pins if it's male or 9 holes if it's female.

The DB-9 format is primarily used for asynchronous serial communications. This is one possibility for the COM ports that you'll hear reference to. A modem or older style serial mouse might be connected to a DB-9 port. The DB-9 port will, in turn, be connected to either the motherboard via an integrated I/O controller, or to an add-in card with an I/O controller on it.

There are also other uses for a DB-9 port on a PC. It can be used for a token ring connection, or for older style monitor connections (pre-VGA). Serial connections from a PC always have a male connector on the PC itself, whereas both token ring and monitor connections use female connectors on the PC.

b) Looking at your printer's connector, is it a male or a female? How many pins/holes does it have?

Answer: If it is a serial version of this connector, it will be a female connector, with the male counterpart being attached to the PC. More common, however, is the parallel connection, which is the male version. It is most likely a DB-25 connector, with 25 pins.

The DB-25 format is used for both serial communications (both asynchronous and synchronous) and parallel communications, and to confuse things more, it's often used to connect to multi-port serial breakout boxes, SCSI, and a host of other types of devices.

As above, the serial version of this connector on a PC has historically been a male connector. Parallel connections, which are by far the most common other use for this connector, use a female connector on the back of the PC. Both the serial and parallel versions of this port will be connected to the motherboard via an integrated I/O chip or an add-in card. You'll also be able to determine which port is which when the case is open because parallel ports have much wider ribbon cables connecting them.

However, you do need to be careful when installing a cable to a DB-25 port on the back of a PC; because of its large number of pins (25) and low cost, many devices use this connector format. Unfortunately, sometimes the voltage and signaling differences between the various uses for this port can make it dangerous if you plug the wrong device into a DB-25 port.

c) How many holes/pins does the connector attached to the joystick or MIDI device have in it?

Answer: It's most likely a male DB-15 connector, with 15 pins.

The DB-15 connector is most often used for joystick and MIDI connections. It almost always appears as a female connector on the back of the PC. If the connector occurs on a sound card, it most often does double duty as a MIDI interface and a joystick port; otherwise, it's probably just a joystick port (without the MIDI capabilities). This port is almost universally found on an add-in I/O card or on a sound card. Although there are exceptions, this port is rarely integrated into the motherboard.

d) Is your monitor's connector different from the connectors you've seen so far? If so, how?

Answer: If your monitor is VGA-quality or higher, the connector will have 15 pins, but unlike the DB-15 connector, which is a two-row connector, this is a three-row connector called the HDDB-15 connector.

Up until this point, all of the DB connectors that I've been talking about are of the two-row variety. That is, they have two rows of pins. The DB-9 has a row of 5 pins over a row of 4 pins. The DB-25 has a row of 13 pins over a row of 12 pins, and the DB-15 has a row of 8 pins over 7 pins. This changes with the HDDB-15.

The HDDB-15, or High Density DB-15, is a three-row DB connector that uses smaller pins, and thus smaller holes, to cram in 15 pins in the same space as a DB-9 connector. This connector is used almost exclusively for connecting to monitors (VGA and above) in the PC market.

As connectors go, it's not that sturdy because of the smaller pins and is known to have a problem with pins bending fairly easily. You're advised to use caution when plugging in HDDB-15 connectors. You should also make sure that you visually inspect the number of pins and holes when attempting to make a connection. Many male HDDB-15 connectors have been damaged by trying to plug them into a DB-9 female connector by accident.

DB connectors are held in place by screws or thumb screws. One is on each end. This provides a very stable connection and is another reason for the popularity of the format.

1.3.2 ANSWERS

a) Do you see any differences in the connectors that you examined?

Answer: Chances are, you did, but you may not have depending on how many you examined.

What you probably noticed was that the telephone connector had either two or four conductors. If there are two conductors, which is an RJ-11 connector, they are probably attached to a pair of red and green wires. The four-conductor connector, the RJ-14, has four wires: red, green, black, and yellow.

In all, there are basically four types of phone connectors, or jacks. They are known as RJ-11, RJ-14, RJ-36, and RJ-45 connectors, with the RJ-11 and the RJ-14 being the most popular. The RJ-11 is most commonly found in the PC in the form of a modem connection, although some systems, particularly those deployed for telephony applications, may have RJ-14 or RJ-36 connectors.

Most people think of these connectors as a single type because they use the same form factor (size) and can be used interchangeably; however, they are slightly different. The RJ-11 only has two conductors, and thus can only complete one circuit. The RJ-14 has four conductors and can complete two circuits, thereby allowing you to have multiple lines using only one jack. The RJ-36 contains the maximum number of connectors, six, and can be used to complete three circuits.

RJ-45 is the bigger cousin of RJ-11, RJ-14, and RJ-36. It uses a slightly bigger connector, which can hold eight conductors, and thus four complete circuits. In addition to being used in most digital phone systems, in a PC it's used for Ethernet (both 10Base-T and 100Base-T) and Type 3 Token Ring.

The RJ series of connectors is held in place by the plastic tab that is found on the top of the connector. It is released by pressing down on the tab. The most common problem with RJ-type connectors is that the plastic tab breaks off because it's pulled too far back. Some RJ cables place plastic hoods over the connector to prevent this from happening. Still, it's quick to attach and stays connected relatively easily.

1.3.3 ANSWERS

a) What difference do you notice about this printer connector?

Answer: This should be obvious as you try to remove the connector. This is a Centronics connector, which is a Card-Edge type connector, held in place with wire clips.

A Centronics connector (often abbreviated as C) is most frequently used in printer connections. The standard printer connector (defined as a IEEE 1284 Type C connector) is a Centronics-36 connector.

You'll also find 50-pin Centronics connectors on SCSI devices. This type of connector is popular in the PC because it's easy to connect and disconnect without tools. The wire clips can be quickly pried off of the connector, freeing it to be removed. When the clips are in place, they hold the cable in place quite well.

Which way do we go? WHICH WAY DO WE GO?

Although I mentioned that the DB connector was D shaped, I didn't indicate why. Back in the first Lab, we talked about all of the different ways that internal cable manufacturers identified which way the internal ribbon cables were supposed to be attached to one another. These different methods were required because the connectors that were being used (pin grid arrays) didn't require a specific orientation of the connector.

With connections that were external to the PC and thus potentially handled by a greater variety of people, this wasn't acceptable, so a type of connector was used that could be installed only one way. The DB connector is perfect for this because it cannot physically be inserted the wrong way, although many have tried. It's also good because someone with average dexterity can feel the connector in the dark and orient the cable correctly.

Likewise, Centronics connectors are D-shaped and can be attached only one way. Phone connectors are shaped so that they, too, can only be attached one way.

1.3.4 ANSWERS

a)   What devices do you have yet to connect at this point?

Answer: This answer, of course, will vary depending on your system. The two most obvious devices are probably your keyboard and your mouse (if you didn't connect it back in Exercise 1.3.1). Some other possibilities include an Ethernet cable, a microphone, desktop speakers, and some sort of video device.

So far we've been talking about families of connectors—connectors that appear in the PC in several different sizes. However, there are a few connectors that don't fit these guidelines and are discussed here.

b)   What are the differences that you note about these various connectors?

Answer: What follows is a list of the common miscellaneous connectors that you'll find on a PC, and a description of them and their uses.

- **BNC (Bayonet Connector/British Naval Connector)**—The BNC connector is most often used to connect a PC to an Ethernet 10Base-2 (Thinnet) network. The BNC connector is a locking connector with a barrel that surrounds the female connector. That barrel is rotated around the male connector until it locks the connectors in place by grabbing hold of small metal tabs on the male connector. It's also used for composite video and other non-computer-related applications, so you may run into the connector being used for other purposes. Figure 1.30 shows Ethernet 10Base-2 T connectors that have both male and female BNC connectors on them.

- **Stereo Mini-Plug (1/8")**—Most PCs today include sound capabilities. To be able to use these capabilities, speakers or headphones must be attached to the system. The most compact connector that was in general use in the audio industry was a 1/8" inch mini-plug that allows for three conductors to be connected. This is enough to drive two speakers, or get input from a stereo mike. (This is because they can both use the same ground line in the case of speakers, or power line in the case of a stereo microphone.) Most sound cards use

Figure 1.30 ■ The Ethernet 10Base-2 (Thinnet) connector is the BNC connector that locks in place to prevent accidental separation. It requires no tools to install or remove.

this connector because of its compact size and acceptance in the audio market. The connector snaps in place; it doesn't lock in place so it's possible that it may accidentally disconnect. Figure 1.31 shows an 1/8" Stereo Mini-Plug to dual-RCA cable.

- **RCA Connector**—In addition to audio capabilities, many systems are coming with video capture and output capabilities. Most of the time, the RCA connector is chosen for input and output of video signals because it's compact and widely accepted. The RCA connector is also used in most home audio systems for audio, in addition to its use for video signals. Figure 1.31 shows what the RCA connector looks like.

- **PS/2 Connector**—This type of connector is used for both keyboards and mice in most systems today. It's a 6-pin mini-DIN format with is a small round connector. There's also a small plastic rectangle that is offset from the center of the connector to ensure that the connector is plugged in with the correct orientation.

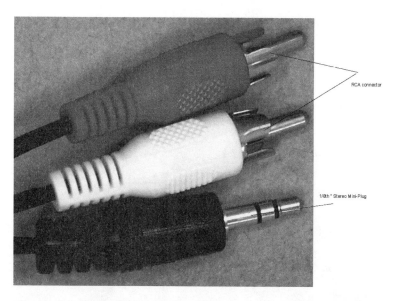

RCA connector

1/8th " Stereo Mini-Plug

Figure 1.31 ■ **Most sound cards come with a cable like this one to allow you to connect your sound card's 1/8" Stereo Mini-Plug port to your home stereo system, which probably uses individual RCA connectors.**

- **S-Video Connector**—On some systems you may find an S-Video connector, which is similar to the PS/2 connector except that it has four conductors. It is used to carry video signals with a higher degree of clarity than is possible on an RCA connector. This is because the signal is broken down into its luminance and chrominence components instead of being combined into one signal.

We haven't covered every conceivable connector that might be contained on the back of the PC; however, we've covered all the ones that are on the A+ exam, and all of the ones that you'll routinely run into in the course of working on PCs.

**LAB
1.3**

LAB 1.3 SELF-REVIEW QUESTIONS

In order to test your progress, you should be able to answer the following questions.

1) How many pins does a PS/2 connector have?
    a) _____2
    b) _____4
    c) _____6
    d) _____8

2) Gendered connectors require that they be connected with the connector of the same type but of opposite gender.
    a) _____True
    b) _____False

3) The DB-9 format is primarily used for which of the following purposes?
    a) _____synchronous serial communications
    b) _____asynchronous serial communications
    c) _____any serial communications
    d) _____parallel communications

4) The High Density DB-15 connector is a two-row DB connector used almost exclusively for connecting monitors to the PC.
    a) _____True
    b) _____False

Trick question. It's a three-row connector.

5) What's the difference between the RJ-11 and RJ-14 telephone connectors?

a) _____There is no difference. They use the same form factor and can be used interchangeably.

b) _____The RJ-11 connector contains only two conductors, enabling only one complete circuit, whereas the RJ-14 contains four conductors, enabling two complete circuits.

c) _____The RJ-11 connector contains only two conductors, enabling only two complete circuits, whereas the RJ-14 contains four conductors, enabling four complete circuits.

d) _____The RJ-14 connector contains only two conductors, enabling only one complete circuit, whereas the RJ-11 contains four conductors, enabling two complete circuits.

6) What is the standard printer connector defined as?

a) _____IEEE 1248 Type C connector
b) _____IEEE 1284 Type DB connector
c) _____IEEE 1248 Type DB connector
d) _____IEEE 1284 Type C connector

7) What are the two possible types of mouse connections?

a) _____Serial and parallel
b) _____Serial and PS/2
c) _____Serial and PS/3
d) _____Serial and RCA

Quiz answers appear in Appendix A, Section 1.3.

L A B   1.4

IDE AND EIDE DEVICES

LAB OBJECTIVES

After this Lab, you will be able to:

✓ Install an IDE/EIDE Device

✓ Explain Performance Issues with IDE/EIDE

**LAB
1.4**

The most common type of drive that you will run into when working on a PC is an IDE drive. It is most prevalent because of its low cost and ease of installation. IDE stands for Integrated Drive Electronics. I'll use IDE here to refer to both IDE and EIDE drives because from a configuration standpoint they are identical, although EIDE drives can have a significant performance advantage and can accommodate larger drives. EIDE stands for Enhanced Integrated Drive Electronics.

IDE drives have an integrated controller, just as SCSI (Small Computer Systems Interface) drives do, but the controllers on IDE drives were specifically designed to easily interface to PCs and the ISA bus. Although IDE drives are more commonly connected to a PCI interface these days, their cost-effective controller and ease of installation have made them the most popular drive type for several years.

It may seem strange to have a controller on the hard drive itself and another controller in the computer. However, the controller in the computer is really just a simple interface (more like a bridge) that allows the drives to be connected. The controller on the drive is the one that has all of the intelligence in it. It allows the computer to treat all of the drives the same.

PERFORMANCE ISSUES WITH IDE/EIDE

When IDE devices first came out, PCs weren't all that fast. We were still working with 80386 processors, with a maximum speed well under 50Mhz. Because of this, the original IDE specification didn't require that drives be able to transfer at rates that today would be considered fast. EIDE devices added additional transfer modes that allowed for faster communications.

Today's EIDE devices can transfer up to 16.6 MB/Sec, a huge leap over the original IDE devices, which communicated at a mere 3.2 MB/Sec. These transfer rates are for Programmed I/O transfers, which are essentially IRQ initiated, CPU-driven communications. This means that the CPU is involved with the transfer of data to and from the drive.

EIDE devices also support DMA, allowing them to transfer data to and from the drive without the intervention of the CPU, which can improve overall performance yet again.

One problem with the enhancements provided by EIDE devices is that they require that the IDE interface be on the PCI (or VESA) bus. Some motherboards that have two IDE connections only have the first one connected to the PCI bus; the other is connected to the ISA bus. The end result is that you'll get better performance from your EIDE devices if they are on the first controller on these motherboards. You'll want to review the motherboard documentation, or call the manufacturer, to determine how the second IDE interface is connected.

**LAB
1.4**

LAB 1.4 EXERCISES

1.4.1 INSTALL AN *IDE/EIDE* DEVICE

The best way to see how to install a drive, or a second drive, is to do it. In this Exercise, we'll install a second hard drive.

First, remove the case as described in Lab 1.1. As you'll remember, this varies slightly between different case manufacturers. Remember to unplug the PC and disconnect any peripheral cables that are connected to it.

Once the case is removed, you'll need to identify a place to install the new hard drive. More than likely you'll be looking for a 3.5" drive bay in which to put your IDE drive, as it will probably be a 3.5" drive.

If you don't have any available 3.5" drive bays (assuming your drive is 3.5"), you'll need a drive mounting kit. A drive mounting kit allows you to install a 3.5" device in a 5.25" bay. This, of course, assumes that you've got at least one bay available in which to install the drive.

If you get a drive mounting kit (which are inexpensive), you'll want to secure the kit to the drive before proceeding. This will essentially change the form factor of the drive into a 5.25" form factor.

Installing IDE devices is easy because the controllers generally have just two settings (if a controller is even needed, since most motherboards are coming with one or two EIDE controllers on them): the I/O port and the interrupt. Each of these has only two settings, making only four total (and two practical) settings for the controller.

> **LAB 1.4**

    a) Is a controller needed on your system?

    _____

    _____

    b) What type of cable is used to attach the drive to the computer controller?

    _____

    _____

The first step before physically installing the drive is to set the slave jumper and remove the jumper from the master pins, if it's present. This will allow the drive to be seen as the slave IDE drive when it's properly connected. In order to do this properly, you should refer to your drive's manual since in some cases, the jumpers are clearly labeled, but in others they are not.

c) How many jumpers does your drive have?

_____

_____

The next step is to take note of the orientation that the IDE cable and power cable will need to have when plugged into the drive. This will make it easier to perform the connections once you've physically installed the drive.

You're now ready to physically install the drive in the case. In most cases, this is done by sliding the drive in place and securing it with a series of screws; however, your case may require the use of rails.

Once the drive is secured, you need to connect it to the IDE cable, remembering that pin 1 of the cable should match pin 1 on the drive. Your existing IDE cable, which the existing hard drive is plugged into, should have another connector for your new drive. You may have to unplug your existing drive and rearrange the connections to make the cable fit. Don't worry about doing this. Cable position does not change anything with IDE drives.

Once the IDE cable is connected, you need only replace the case, connect the power, and reconnect all of the cables.

Go ahead now and start up the machine.

d) What happens when your machine first boots?

_____

_____

e) How many IDE/EIDE devices does your PC have?

_____

_____

1.4.2 EXPLAIN PERFORMANCE ISSUES WITH *IDE/EIDE*

It's important to understand performance issues associated with IDE/EIDE. To test your understanding of this, this non-interactive Exercise asks one simple question.

a) How do you get the best performance out of EIDE drives?

_____

_____

LAB 1.4 EXERCISE ANSWERS

1.4.1 ANSWERS

a) Is a controller needed on your system?

Answer: This depends on your system. Newer systems probably don't require an external controller. To be sure, you need to check your system/external device documentation to REALLY know.

For each controller, there can be one or two drives connected. The first drive is referred to as the master drive; the second drive, if attached, is referred to as the slave drive.

b) What type of cable is used to attach the drive to the computer controller?

Answer: The cable that attaches the computer controller or interface to the drive is a 36-pin ribbon cable. It doesn't require any kind of special termination.

c) How many jumpers does your drive have?

Answer: Most IDE drives only have three sets of jumpers.

d) What must you do when your machine first boots?

Answer: The first time you boot up, you'll need to go into BIOS and tell it that you have a new IDE drive.

In most cases, you can have BIOS automatically detect the second drive to get its geometry from the drive rather than having to key it in; however, be prepared to enter the number of heads, cylinders, and sectors. If you have to enter the information, you should get that from the documentation that comes with the drive. Although these are probably not the real numbers used in the manufacture of the drive, they are what the drive will report to the PC. Accessing the BIOS will differ from system to system, so consult your PC's manual for the specific method.

The final step is to partition and format the drive. That's beyond our scope for now, but when we start talking about DOS and Windows, we'll cover how to partition and format your new drive.

e) How many IDE/EIDE devices does your PC have?

*Answer: It will vary based on your machine, but typically machines will have one IDE/
EIDE hard drive and one IDE/EIDE CD-ROM drive.*

1.4.2 ANSWERS

a) How do you get the best performance out of EIDE drives?

*Answer: Connect it to an EIDE controller that is connected via the PCI bus, either via a
PCI add-in card, or attached on the motherboard via the PCI bus interface.*

LAB 1.4 SELF-REVIEW QUESTIONS

In order to test your progress, you should be able to answer the following questions.

1) IDE drives can have a significant performance advantage over EIDE drives and can accommodate larger drives.
    a) _____True
    b) _____False

2) The two settings for an IDE device are the I/O port and the interrupt.
    a) _____True
    b) _____False

3) What type of cable connects a PC's controller (interface) to an IDE drive?

a) _____A card-edge ribbon cable
b) _____A 48-pin ribbon cable
c) _____A hard disk LED cable
d) _____A 36-pin ribbon cable

4) How fast can today's EIDE devices transfer data?

a) _____Up to 3.2 MB/Sec
b) _____Up to 16.6 MB/Sec
c) _____Up to 26.6 MB/Sec
d) _____Up to 50 MB/Sec

5) How many jumpers do most IDE drives have?

a) _____2
b) _____3
c) _____4
d) _____5

**LAB
1.4**

6) A 3.5" device can easily be installed into a 5.25" bay.

a) _____True
b) _____False

Quiz answers appear in Appendix A, Section 1.4.

L A B   1.5

SCSI DEVICES

SCSI (Small Computer System Interface) drives are the older brother of IDE drives. They were around before IDE drives, but still are not as popular in the PC market, primarily because they are more expensive than their IDE siblings.

SCSI drives are faster performers, on the whole, and support commands that make them even better suited to multitasking applications. However, the extra performance and extra features mean extra price.

DIFFERENT TYPES OF SCSI

There are now several different versions of SCSI, each with their own properties. The following list talks about the basic standards.

- **SCSI-1**—The original SCSI interface that called for a 50-pin interface running at 5 MBps.
- **SCSI-2**—An extension that increased the speed to 10MBps.
- **Ultra-SCSI**—A vendor-sponsored extension to SCSI that increased the transfer rate to 20 MBps.
- **Wide-SCSI/SCSI-3**—Wide SCSI doubled the data width that could be transferred in a single cycle, effectively doubling the performance of the interface without requiring twice the bus speed.

- **Ultra-Wide SCSI**—The combination of the Ultra SCSI initiative and the Wide SCSI initiative. The speed limit of an Ultra-Wide SCSI bus is 40 MBps.

IDENTIFYING SCSI CONNECTORS

SCSI devices can be identified by their two types of connectors, both of which are wider than the connectors used by IDE devices. SCSI-1, SCSI-2, and Ultra-SCSI devices are referred to as narrow SCSI devices, and use a 50-pin connector, similar to the 36-pin connector used for IDE drives. Wide SCSI, or SCSI-3 devices, are referred to as wide devices and use a 68-pin connector that is D shaped to prevent accidental reversal of the cable, which sometimes happens with narrow SCSI devices.

In external devices, there are four types of connectors that are used. They are:

- **DB-25**—Used for older, narrow SCSI devices, often confused with a printer connection and was susceptible to grounding issues, so is no longer in widespread use.
- **Centronics-50**—Often referred to as the SCSI-1 connector, and by far the most popular external interface. However, because of its large size, it's not often used as an external interface on the PC itself.
- **HD-50**—Often referred to as the SCSI-2 connector, it's the most popular connector on the PC itself because of its smaller size. It's beginning to be used more on external drives, particularly tape drives. Sometimes this connector is secured with thumb screws, and sometimes with clips. This has been somewhat of a problem with locating the appropriate cable to go with a device.
- **HD-68**—Often referred to as the SCSI-3 connector, it's the only connector for wide devices. It's becoming more popular as wider SCSI devices come on the market.

LAB 1.5

UNDERSTANDING IDs

Where IDE devices have a Master/Slave relationship, SCSI devices have IDs. Every SCSI device, including the controller has a unique ID. The ID allows each command on the SCSI chain to have a specific target; thus, devices can communicate directly with one another—they don't necessarily have to communicate with the controller.

In SCSI-1 and SCSI-2, or narrow SCSI, the IDs have a range of 0-7. Wide SCSI, or SCSI-3, doubles this range to 0-15. On both, the controller is typically ID 7, although it can be any ID.

RESOLVING CONFLICTS

If, for any reason, two devices are using the same ID, one of two things will happen. First, neither device will work. Each device will shut itself down.

Second, one of the devices will shut down and the other will function. Most of the time the device that didn't shut down will function properly, but sometimes not. It is always advisable to resolve ID conflicts immediately.

To resolve the conflict, simply change the ID of one of the devices by changing the jumpers or using the external SCSI ID selector.

TERMINATION

One of the most troubling things about SCSI device chains is the need for proper termination. It's not that termination is particularly complicated, but rather it's rarely explained well in technical documentation, so people often get confused.

First, termination is related to where devices are located on the SCSI chain. It's totally unrelated to the SCSI ID, or whether the device is internal or external. Second, there are two and only two places that a SCSI chain should be terminated, and those are the ends of the bus that connects the devices. If there are no other devices connected on the other side of a device, then the device should be terminated.

LAB 1.5 EXERCISES

1.5.1 INSTALL A SCSI DRIVE

In this series of Exercises, we're going to perform roughly the same steps here as we did in an earlier Lab, except that we'll be doing it for an internal SCSI device. This distinction is important because we're going to talk about the differences between installing an IDE device and installing the SCSI device.

1. To start, we're going to perform the same case cover removal steps as described earlier, following the tips from Lab 1.1, making sure that all devices and cables are disconnected, and that the PC is powered off via the mechanism in Windows 95, or at least all programs are stopped in DOS. Once the case is opened, we have the same physical issues that we had with the IDE drive. We need to find an available drive bay to install the new drive. This means that we might need to install a mounting kit on the drive if it's a 3.5" drive and we only have 5.25" bays available.

> **a)** How many devices (excluding the controller) can your SCSI bus support?

> _____

> _____

2. The next step in installing a SCSI drive is to determine where this device will be plugged into the internal cable. This is done by examining the location of the adapter in relation to the previously installed SCSI devices, and the bay that you intend to install the new drive in. If the new SCSI drive will be on the end of the SCSI chain, the device must be configured to have termination, and the drive that is currently on the end of the SCSI chain must have its termination removed.

LAB 1.5

> **b)** Where is your SCSI bus terminated?

> _____

> _____

3. The next step is to configure the SCSI ID of the new drive. You'll want to take care that it doesn't conflict with any other devices. This includes internal devices such as existing CD-ROM drives, hard drives, and tape drives, as well as the controller itself and any external devices that may be present.

> **c)** How many devices may be used with your SCSI ID?

> _____

> _____

4. Once you've set the termination and SCSI ID, and before you physically install the drive, you'll want to determine the correct orientation of the SCSI cable and the power cable that need to be connected to the drive.

5. The next step is to physically install the drive. As with the IDE drive, this may mean using rails or other specialized mounting methods, as required by your specific case.

6. Once the drive has been physically installed, it's time to connect the SCSI cable. Unlike the IDE drive, you can't just decide at the last minute to change the arrangement of the cable (unless you keep the end drive the same). You'll also need to attach the power cable and close the case.

> **d)** Do you need to do anything further in order for the system to recognize the new device?

_____

_____

LAB 1.5 EXERCISE ANSWERS

1.5.1 ANSWERS

a) How many devices (excluding the controller) can your SCSI bus support?

Answer: If your device is of type SCSI-1, the answer will be 7. SCSI (Narrow) supports a total of 8 devices, including the controller. If you are using Wide SCSI, the answer will be 15. Wide SCSI supports a total of 16 devices, including the controller.

b) Where is your SCSI bus terminated?

Answer: Hopefully, on both ends of the bus, and only on both ends of the bus. If only internal or only external devices are present on a bus, then the controller will be terminated; however, if devices exist both on the external and internal interfaces, the controller will not be terminated.

If you have only two devices—the controller and a hard drive—then both devices should be terminated. If, on the other hand, you have an internal hard drive, an internal CD-ROM, and a controller, then you will have the controller and either the hard drive or CD-ROM, but not both, terminated.

If the new SCSI drive will be on the end of the SCSI chain, the device must be configured to have termination, and the drive that is currently on the end of the SCSI chain must have its termination removed.

THE WHOLE TRUTH

Almost every digital circuit needs termination; it's just that sometimes it's handled in a special way that you're not aware of.

SCSI, because of its speed and early design, uses a single terminator on the end of the chain to stop electrical signals from being reflected back off the end of the cable and appearing as noise.

Other drive types, like floppy and IDE drives, use distributed termination, where each device provides a small amount of termination to prevent the signals from bouncing off the ends of the cables.

Terminators are really resistors that absorb small amounts of current before they can be reflected. That's why SCSI terminators can't be in the middle of the chain, they'll absorb too much of the signal for other devices to understand what is happening on the bus.

LAB 1.5

c)   How many devices may be used with your SCSI ID?

   Answer: One. Each SCSI device must have it's own unique ID so that it can be uniquely addressed.

THE WHOLE TRUTH

The SCSI standard (from the original SCSI-1 specification) has defined a logical unit number that is used to identify specific units within a master connection to the SCSI bus. These LUNs (Logical Unit Numbers) are used when there are multiple parts to a connected device, which you may want to refer to individually. One such case is a CD-ROM changer. Each CD is given it's own logical unit number so that it can be referred to individually by the computer.

Most of the time you will not need to worry about logical unit numbers, because SCSI hard drives don't use them, nor do most SCSI devices, such as tape drives or scanners.

d) Do you need to do anything further in order for the system to recognize the new device?

Answer: With a SCSI drive, you don't have to go into the BIOS to tell it that the new drive is there. Almost all SCSI devices are detected as part of the boot-up process and are automatically made accessible via the SCSI BIOS. You should see your new drive listed as a device when the SCSI adapter polls the SCSI bus looking for devices.

As with the IDE drive, you'll still need to partition the hard drive and format it in Windows, which we'll discuss in a later chapter.

As you complete this Exercise, know that each SCSI standard is backwards compatible, except that Wide (or Ultra-Wide) SCSI devices can't be connected to a Narrow (SCSI-1, SCSI-2, or Ultra SCSI) controller. This has been very useful to the industry in protecting the investment in drives while allowing upgrades to faster technologies.

THE WHOLE TRUTH

SCSI is a parallel standard. It transfers more than one bit of information during a single cycle of the bus. This was originally thought to be the best way to communicate large amounts of information quickly. However, we've found out that it's not always the best way.

There are a bunch of serious electrical issues with making sure that signals all reach the other end of the cable at the same time (or close enough to not be confused). That has caused SCSI's cable length limitations to be quite short, and has lead to an effective stall in the overall speed the bus can be pushed to.

Newer high-speed technologies such as USB and IEEE 1384/Firewire are based on serial communications that don't have this synchronization problem. As it turns out, it's much easier to push information serially over one line than it is to manage the electrical issues of synchronizing a series of conductors.

When you think of SCSI and all of the performance, understand that it comes at a cost of flexibility.

LAB 1.5 SELF-REVIEW QUESTIONS

In order to test your progress, you should be able to answer the following questions.

1) SCSI drives are not commonly used because they are not as equipped as IDE drives to support multitasking applications.
   a) _____True
   b) _____False

2) What is the speed of an Ultra-Wide SCSI?
   a) _____45 MBps
   b) _____40 MBps
   c) _____20 MBps
   d) _____10 MBps

3) What is the ID range of narrow SCSI?
   a) _____0-7
   b) _____1-7
   c) _____0-15
   d) _____1-15

4) SCSI termination is totally unrelated to the SCSI ID.
   a) _____True
   b) _____False

5) How many devices does Wide SCSI support?
   a) _____7
   b) _____8
   c) _____15
   d) _____16

   Quiz answers appear in Appendix A, Section 1.5.

LAB
1.5

L A B   1.6

SYSTEM OPTIMIZATION

LAB OBJECTIVES

After this Lab, you will be able to:

✓ Troubleshoot Performance Issues and Optimization

LAB
1.6

The fundamental thing about PCs is that they will be too slow. Not every day, not every minute, and maybe not even the first day that it's installed, but at some point, it will be too slow. The key to cost-effective upgrades is understanding what the problem is that you're trying to solve.

UNDERSTANDING THE PERFORMANCE ISSUE

It's absolutely critical that you understand what the problem is before you try to solve it. Never has this been so true as in system optimization. I've seen technicians, even seasoned technicians, routinely "throw hardware" at a problem as they attempt in vain to resolve performance issues.

The problem isn't that these technicians are not skilled, that they can't install the upgrades or find faster performing components. They can and do install faster components in people's systems; however, it doesn't matter, because that wasn't the part of the computer that they were waiting on.

Think for a moment about when you were growing up (particularly if you lived in a large family). The rush to get everyone out the door in the morning and off to school or work was often one of the busiest and most stressful times of the day. Why was that? Because each person wanted to use the house resources (shower, bathroom) at the same time.

If you were the parents in this situation, you could have made the situation slightly better by having everyone select their clothes for the next day the previous night. This would allow them to do any necessary mending or ironing that often got saved for the morning.

This surely would have made life a little smoother in the morning. It would have perhaps eliminated competition for the iron, or just by having less to do would have contributed to a less hectic morning. But wouldn't it have helped immensely if the family structured time in the bathroom (or, if they could have afforded it, added another bathroom?) Think of how much more effective that would have made getting out in the morning. You would have doubled capacity in exactly the area that needed it the most.

This is the kind of thinking that you have to keep in the back of your mind when trying to optimize a PC. Work on the big issues first, and worry about the little ones when you can no longer do anything about the big ones.

TOOLS FOR DETERMINING BOTTLENECKS

**LAB
1.6**

A bottleneck is a part of the process that becomes overwhelmed too quickly. It's the limiting factor that prevents the process from completing quicker, just as a bottle's neck prevents the soda from flowing out any faster.

In the previous paragraphs, I stressed the importance of identifying the problem, or bottleneck, before attempting to solve the problem. That's fine, but how do you do it?

There are a few tricks that you can use to determine what the bottleneck is, and a few tools that most operating systems have that will help you understand what it is.

Let's start with the tools first, then proceed to the tricks—because the tools are the way to go when at all possible.

Windows 95/98 includes a tool called System Monitor, which allows you to see what parts of the PC are being exercised. This tool should run while you're doing the activities that prompted your desire to upgrade or remove the bottleneck.

By tracking the CPU utilization, memory utilization, and disk utilization, you'll be able to determine which area you should focus your attention on. In the Lab Exercise, we'll start the system monitor, and talk about how to read the graphs.

HOW TO KNOW WHEN TO UPGRADE A CPU

As you should recall, the CPU is what makes everything happen in the PC. As such, it is often the target for upgrading. When most people talk about their PC, they almost always refer to the CPU and its speed, sometimes exclusively.

Rarely do I find that the CPU is the appropriate upgrade. Most of the time it's just not being used to its fullest capacity.

HOW TO KNOW WHEN TO UPGRADE MEMORY

We're talking here about memory beyond the CPU because it's often mistaken for a disk bottleneck in modern operating systems, since modern operating systems will start using disk space if they run out of memory. In this way, the operating system transfers a great deal of load to the disk drive that it shouldn't, so its usage goes through the roof and shows up as a bottleneck.

The best indicator of whether memory is an issue or not is to look at unused physical memory and disk cache size. Both of these two values exist in physical RAM, so they can't be confused with virtual memory that may, and often does, include disk space.

When unused memory drops below 4-8 MB (on average) on a personal PC, or when doing the normal things that you would do on the PC are perceived as being too slow, it's probably time to add RAM.

■ *FOR EXAMPLE*

My notebook (which I'm using to write this Lab) has a total of 160 MB of RAM, much more than what a normal system would need. There's almost 100 MB of RAM between the disk cache and the available physical RAM. This is a clear indication that I don't need more RAM for writing chapters of a book. In the case of this system, even if I load the programming development environments and databases into memory, I still have over 40 MB of available RAM. So upgrading the RAM in this system isn't necessary. This may seem like a silly example, but I've seen systems that are RAM-starved with 512 MB of RAM in them. Those machines were running databases, or complex finite element analysis software, which needed as much RAM as they could get their hands on.

HOW TO KNOW WHEN TO UPGRADE DISK

Upgrading disks is a bit more difficult to understand than the other options we've been talking about, for a few reasons. First, most people think about adding disk capacity when they think of upgrading disks. This is because disk performance is so hard to quantify.

Second, there's no single performance indicator that can tell you that your drive is being overworked. It's a function of watching the reads and writes to and from the disk to determine if it appears that the drive is working over 80 percent of the time.

Third, and finally, hard drive performance is rarely quoted anymore. It used to be that the access times, rotational latency, track-to-track seek times, and other metrics were all important to hard disk users as they were looking for storage. However, today it seems that the raw capacity is much more of an issue.

As a result of these three factors, you may find it difficult to quantify the need for a new, faster, hard disk drive to improve performance, and you may find it difficult to actually utilize the new drive in a way that will truly improve performance. That is at least until you replace your existing hard drive.

LAB 1.6

TRICKS OF THE TRADE

Earlier, I mentioned that there were a couple of tricks that you could use to determine what needed to be upgraded. They are listed in no particular order as follows:

- **Try it**—If we're talking about an upgrade that doesn't take long to do, and you can find a way to try, perhaps by borrowing from another machine or friend, go ahead and do it. It's an easy way to test what kind of an improvement you'll get. I wouldn't recommend this for hard disk upgrades, but often you can find some memory you can borrow to see if that will help.

- **Leave other applications open**—If you suspect that memory is an issue, you can amplify the problem on purpose by opening a bunch of applications that you don't need to use. If memory is an issue and you do this, then your performance should substantially suffer. If it doesn't, you've probably got another problem.
- **Run long calculation-intense macros**—If you think CPU utilization might be an issue, create a long running macro to run in the background while you test your applications. If the macro completes in anywhere near the same amount of time as it would if nothing else was running, then you're probably not CPU-bound.
- **Watch the lights**—Most systems and hard drives have activity lights. If those activity lights are constantly on or are steadily flickering, you may need another, faster, hard disk.

LAB 1.6 EXERCISES

1.6.1 TROUBLESHOOT PERFORMANCE ISSUES AND OPTIMIZATION

**LAB
1.6**

In this Exercise, we will use the System Monitor to try to figure out what the bottleneck is in your system and investigate potential solutions.

To open the System Monitor utility, select Start – Programs – Accessories – System Tools – System Monitor.

a) What items, if any, are being monitored on your machine currently?

_____

_____

The System Monitor isn't installed in the typical installation, so you may need to install it now to complete this Exercise. To do so, go to the Add/ Remove Programs dialog, select Windows Setup, then System Tools and Details. You'll see System Monitor in the list of programs that can be installed. When you check this box and close these dialogs, you'll be prompted for your Windows media to install the program.

Once the System Monitor is running, you'll need to add some counters to it to be able to determine which component of your system is performing slowest. To do so, choose Add Item from the Edit menu. You will see a dialog like the one in Figure 1.32.

Click on the various categories in the left panel of the Add Item dialog box and scan the Item panel on the right to see what items are stored in each category. You should select the following counters to be monitored:

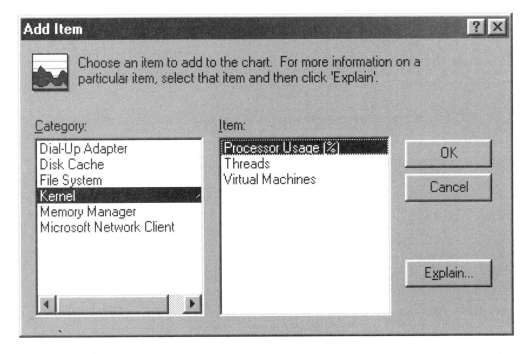

LAB
1.6

Figure 1.32 ■ The Add Item dialog allows you to add new counters to be monitored.

- Kernel: Processor usage
- File System: Reads/second
- File system: Writes/second
- File System: Dirty data
- Memory Manager: Disk cache size
- Memory Manager: Unused physical memory

 You can select multiple items in any particular category by pressing the Ctrl or Shift key and choosing multiple items.

b) How does your display change when you select these items and click the OK button?

_____

_____

c) Based on what you see, what area of your PC needs to be upgraded first? Why?

_____

_____

LAB 1.6

d) If your system reports a high number of disk writes and reads, but low available physical memory, what would you upgrade first?

_____

_____

e) You notice that the disk light seems to be busy a great deal lately. Would this lead you to expect an upgrade? Why or why not?

_____

_____

f) If your CPU utilization is high, and there is plenty of free RAM, what would you upgrade? Why?

_____

_____

You will revisit the System Monitor again in Chapter 9, "Memory Management."

LAB 1.6 EXERCISE ANSWERS

1.6.1 ANSWERS

a) What items, if any, are being monitored on your machine currently?

Answer: Your answer will vary according to your system.

Each item that is currently active in the System Monitor is clearly labeled. If you have more than one item active, you may click on it in the main window and view the status bar at the bottom of the window to see details of that item, including its current value and its peak value.

**LAB
1.6**

b) How does your display change when you select these items and click the OK button?

Answer: Your display should change to accommodate whatever new items you've added.

Depending on what View you are in, Figure 1.33 shows what your System Monitor should look like after you've added all of the counters in this list.

You can change the View in the System Monitor using the View menu. There are three choices: Line Charts, Bar Charts, and Numeric Charts. The display in Figure 1.33 uses the Line Charts View.

Looking at the graph for the system in Figure 1.33, you'll see that there's no real performance issue, at least with what I'm doing. There's plenty of

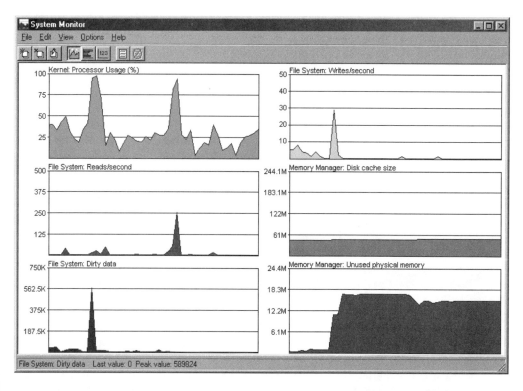

Figure 1.33 ■ The System Monitor display with all of the basic counters to determine which area should be upgraded.

free RAM. The processor isn't particularly taxed, and even all of the disk performance indicators are low. This system is probably a little oversized for what I'm doing with it (that is, writing a book).

c) Based on what you see, what area of your PC needs to be upgraded first? Why?

Answer: This will depend on the numbers that System Monitor gives you. Often I find that people RAM-starve their systems. I find that RAM is one of the best upgrades you can do for your PC. It's cheap and easy.

d) If your system reports a high number of disk writes and reads, but low available physical memory, what would you upgrade first?

Answer: RAM. This is generally a sign that you don't have enough RAM, so the system is forced to use the hard disk drive as if it were memory.

e) You notice that the disk light seems to be busy a great deal lately. Would this lead you to expect an upgrade? Why or why not?

Answer: If you're trying to determine if your hard drive is overtaxed and needs replacing, you'll first want to look at the number of bytes that are being written and the number of bytes that are being read in a given second. This will give you an idea of the overall performance that you are getting. Unfortunately, Windows 95/98 only allows you to look at bytes read and written on a file system level so there's no way to isolate activity to any one drive.

In addition to looking at the number of bytes read or written from the drive, you'll want to look at the "dirty data" counter, which shows the data that hasn't been able to be written back to disk yet because the drive is busy. If that number climbs at any point to over a few hundred K (a few MB), then your hard drive, or at least one of them, is probably overworked.

There are two approaches to resolving this issue. The first is to add a new hard drive and move some data or applications to the new drive. The second is to replace your hard drive with a new one. Both cases have their downfalls.

In the case of adding the drive, you may find that you can't move enough activity off the busy drive to help much. In the case of replacing the drive, you'll have to spend a great deal of time copying the data from the old drive onto the new one.

Unlike all of the other upgrades, adding a disk can be a time-consuming process, so it should probably only be done when it's very clear that it will help.

**LAB
1.6**

Before you jump directly into replacing the drive, you may also want to run a defragmentation program to see if performance improves.

THE WHOLE TRUTH

When you add a second IDE hard disk, you'll probably only marginally improve performance because most of the time the CPU's attention is required to handle IDE devices. (With some newer EIDE drives this is not the case, but it's most often true.)

This is not necessarily the case with SCSI drives, particularly running Windows NT. This is because SCSI hard drives support disconnecting from the bus while they fetch the information, then reconnect when they have data to return. When running Windows NT the operating system takes advantage of this to be able to submit multiple requests to different drives all at the same time (presumably to service different processes or programs running on the system).

When considering how to improve hard disk performance, consider the impact that changing to SCSI can make if you need to move to multiple drives.

f) If your CPU utilization is high, and there is plenty of free RAM, what would you upgrade? Why?

Answer: The CPU. High utilization on the CPU usually means it should be upgraded – unless there's something more pressing, and if there's plenty of available RAM it's not likely that there's anything more pressing.

It's generally accepted that a processor that is more than about 80 percent busy on average is a candidate for an upgrade. I say candidate because it may not be the most bottlenecked item on the PC, and thus may not be the first upgrade that you should perform.

It's easy to determine CPU usage because System Monitor and most other performance monitoring utilities show you overall CPU utilization as a single number.

THE WHOLE TRUTH

There's a whole series of things that may show up as a CPU issue but that may not be improved if you upgrade your CPU. Some controllers require more of the CPU's attention than others. And sometimes you can offload some processing on to video cards, or other devices, if you purchase more intelligent add-in cards. Fortunately, the A+ exam doesn't drill into this level of detail. You just need to be able to identify the major component areas that can be upgraded.

LAB 1.6

LAB 1.6 SELF-REVIEW QUESTIONS

In order to test your progress, you should be able to answer the following questions.

1) When you first encounter a problem with your PC's performance, what's the first thing you should do?
   a) _____Run the System Monitor while you are working.
   b) _____Reboot the machine.
   c) _____Upgrade RAM.
   d) _____Reinstall the program that you think is causing the bottleneck.
   e) _____Upgrade the CPU.

2) The best indicator of whether memory is an issue or not is to look at unused physical memory and disk cache size.
   a) _____True
   b) _____False

3) Using the System Monitor, what's a good indicator that you probably need to upgrade RAM?

   a) _____ The processor is more than 80 percent busy, indicating that it's overcompensating for lack of RAM.

   b) _____A large amount of data that hasn't been able to be written back to disk yet.

   c) _____A high number of disk writes and reads and a low amount of available physical memory.

   d) _____None of these is a good indicator that RAM needs upgrading.

4) hat needs to be upgraded if your "dirty data" number climbs to over a few MB?

   a) _____Hard disk

   b) _____RAM

   c) _____CPU

   d) _____Nothing. It just means that you need to defrag your hard drive.

5) Joe calls you to complain that his system is running too slowly and he wants a new CPU. What should your initial reaction be?

   a) _____That it's more likely RAM that needs to be upgraded, as most systems are RAM-starved.

   b) _____That before upgrading, you'll first need to install your own CPU into his machine to determine if that's really the problem.

   c) _____That you'd like to try offloading some processing onto video cards or other devices first.

   d) _____That you'll need to perform some analysis of his problem.

   e) _____That he's probably right and you should order that CPU right away.

Quiz answers appear in Appendix A, Section 1.6.

LAB
1.6

C H A P T E R 1

TEST YOUR THINKING

In this chapter, we learned all of the basics of tearing down a PC and replacing parts of it, and with that knowledge you should have a complete understanding of how a PC is built, and the pieces you need.

1) To test your thinking of what you have learned, purchase all of the individual components that you need to build a PC and build one from scratch. This may sound silly at first, but this is absolutely the best way to test your understanding of this chapter and puts you well on your way to becoming an excellent technician.

CHAPTER 2

DIAGNOSING AND TROUBLESHOOTING

 It's hard to find the solution if you can't see the problem...

—Anonymous

One of the most difficult things to do in any line of work is to identify problems. Whether you're an automobile mechanic, a TV repairman, or a computer technician, identifying the problem generally takes all of your resources and skills.

Before we get to discussing how to solve specific hardware problems, I want to reiterate just how difficult troubleshooting really is. A gentleman by the name of Benjamin Bloom developed a system of identifying the level of knowledge required to complete specific tasks, and the task of identifying the cause of a problem is well up on this list.

The A+ Certification Exam is going to ask you particulars about how certain things react when installed incorrectly, or when a failure occurs. Some or perhaps most of these things will be beyond your experience. The way to answer the questions best is generally to remember some of the fundamentals of how to diagnose a problem, and to make an educated guess at the correct answers.

Our goal here is to show you some of the basic failures on which you're likely to be tested, as well as develop an understanding so you can make those educated guesses for problems that appear on the exam and in the field.

L A B   2.1

BASIC TROUBLESHOOTING PROCEDURES

LAB OBJECTIVES

After this Lab, you will be able to:

✓ Localize the Cause of the Problem

✓ Test Line Voltages with a Multimeter

✓ Test Internal PC Voltages

This Lab is the foundation for troubleshooting and diagnosing problems. It shows you a time-honored way of approaching problems, and focuses on understanding the problem so that you can consistently solve problems.

APPROACHING TROUBLESHOOTING IN A UNIFORM WAY

There once was a time when we thought the world was flat. Why? Because when you looked to the horizon, you could see that it was almost level with you, which naturally meant that it had to be flat. We also once believed that the earth was the center of the universe. We based this on the fact that it appeared that everything moved around us. Everything moved in circles across our sky. Both of the preceding are dramatic examples of how our understanding of the world we live in was wrong. They are shining examples of what happened before people began to utilize the scientific method to discover the world around them.

The scientific method was developed to help humanity avoid such large mistakes as those just mentioned, but it can also be applied to how we approach any problem. The scientific method is, simply:

1. Identify and understand the problem.
2. Hypothesize a solution.
3. Test the hypothesis.
4. If the test fails, go to step 1.

A few steps repeated iteratively lead to a better understanding of the problem, until the problem is understood well enough that a correct solution can be formed. At this point I want to caution you to truly identify the problem whenever you start trying to diagnose or troubleshoot it. This is the step that people so often scurry by in their quest to reach the solution. Failure to understand the problem often leads people to try solutions that cannot possibly work.

LOCALIZE THE CAUSE OF THE PROBLEM

Once you've developed a process for trying to solve a problem, it's important to understand how to identify and understand the problem. Saying that you understand the problem is quite easy; actually understanding the problem can be quite hard. The Exercises in this Lab will challenge you to try to localize the cause of some common hardware problems before trying to solve them.

**LAB
2.1**

TOOLS OF THE TRADE

Most technicians carry with them at least a Phillips and flatblade screwdriver, or at least a combination screwdriver, but there are a few other tools that you should consider carrying. Although not all of these tools fit in with our overall goal of troubleshooting, they are covered here to give you one place to go to find the tools you need.

MULTIMETER

Although I find in practice few people actually carry multimeters with them, or even know how to use them, the A+ exam requires that you have a basic understanding of them. This is a good requirement, because a multimeter can isolate a variety of voltage-based problems within and between system components.

A multimeter is a multifunction device designed to measure voltage, amperage, and resistance. In practice in a PC environment (and in most environments), you'll only use the voltage and ohms measurement portions of the meter.

Before continuing, we'll review what voltage, amperage, and resistance are.

Voltage is the amount of power on a line. It's how tall the power wave is. It's what most people think of when they talk about power. Voltage is measured in volts.

Amperage is the strength of the power being output at a given voltage. It tells you how strong the current is at a given power amount. Amperage is measured in amperes.

Resistance is the amount of opposition to current flowing through it that a line or circuit has; in other words, how much "negative push" against the free-flowing current does a line have. Resistance is measured in ohms, and is generally not used directly by technicians. Resistance can also indicate continuity—whether a wire on one end is connected with a wire on the other.

Voltage, amperage, and resistance are analogous to how a river flows. The voltage is how tall the river is flowing. It is the amount of water (or electricity) that's flowing every second. Amperage is current flow or volume that is flowing. Resistance is any rocks, trees, or other debris that is preventing the water from flowing faster.

Radio Shack sells a variety of inexpensive multimeters that are appropriate for your needs. I personally have a small digital multimeter that travels in my tool kit with me. Its Radio Shack Catalog # is 22-802. It costs about $20.

A multimeter is a useful tool because you can measure the voltage coming in from the wall outlet to the PC ensuring that it has sufficient voltage to properly drive the PC's power supply.

 Using a multimeter can be potentially dangerous if you use it to test the power coming out of a wall outlet. If you have to test a voltage that is potentially high (more than about 25 volts), either only hold on to one lead, or hold on to both leads with one hand. This prevents the power from taking a path across your heart, potentially killing you.

A multimeter can also be used to test the output voltage of a power supply to make sure that it is functioning correctly.

The Exercises that follow walk you through testing the outlet voltage and the PC power supplies output.

SPECIALIZED POST TEST CARDS

Using the diagnostics built into the PC is the best way to handle most problems because they work on every machine, and it's free. However, there are times when a problem gets to be too much. There are too many things that can go wrong in a Power-On Self-Test (POST) routine, and many of them are so subtle that you may never fully understand what's wrong without some specialized testing gear.

Luckily, there are cards designed specifically to help you troubleshoot hardware problems. These cards start at about $150 in price and go up from there. They're certainly not something that you'll want to buy unless you have a good reason.

LAB 2.1

These POST test cards provide a detailed readout, mostly on a two-cell, eight-segment LED display that can be looked up in the accompanying manual. Because of rapidly falling hardware prices, only the largest Information Services/Information Technology, commonly abbreviated as IS and IT, shops or repair companies can make effective use of POST test cards in "assembly line" repair facilities. This is because the value of a technician's time often makes it less expensive to simply discard malfunctioning hardware rather than take the time to diagnose it.

LAB 2.1 EXERCISES

2.1.1 LOCALIZE THE CAUSE OF THE PROBLEM

Try your luck on trying to determine the true cause of the following problems. The first two are clearly hardware problems; the third appears to be a hardware problem on the surface, but it may not truly be a hardware problem.

a) There's no display on the monitor.

_____

_____

b) The PC won't start at all. No lights, no sounds, or anything else.

_____

_____

c) Windows NT won't start. It responds with a message about a boot disk failure.

_____

_____

**LAB
2.1**

2.1.2 TEST LINE VOLTAGES WITH A MULTIMETER

In this Exercise, we're going to use a multimeter to test the output voltage of the wall circuit that your computer is connected to.

To do so, follow these steps:

1. Set your multimeter to read AC volts.
2. Take both leads in one hand.
3. Insert one lead into one of the rectangular openings of the electrical outlet.
4. Insert the other lead into the other side.

a) What is the line voltage at your PC now?

_____

_____

b) Is this voltage fluctuating at all?

_____

_____

c) What happens if you connect one of the leads to the round hole instead?

_____

_____

d) What happens if you set the multimeter to DC volts rather than AC volts?

_____

_____

2.1.3 TEST INTERNAL PC VOLTAGES

Now that you've tested the wall outlet's voltage, let's test the power supply's output voltages. Follow these steps to do so:

1. Switch your multimeter to read DC voltages.
2. Turn your PC off and open the case.
3. Insert the black lead of your multimeter into one of the two center holes of a free drive connector. It doesn't matter which one.
4. Turn on your PC.
5. Insert the red lead of your multimeter into the hole connected to the red wire and observe the readings.
6. Insert the red lead of your multimeter into the hole connected to the yellow wire and observe the readings.

a) What voltage did you read on the Red wire?

_____

_____

b) What voltage did you read on the Yellow wire?

_____

_____

c) What happens if you set the multimeter to AC volts?

_____

_____

LAB 2.1 EXERCISE ANSWERS

2.1.1 ANSWERS

a) There's no display on the monitor.

Answer: There are many possible solutions to this one, because there's not a specific enough definition of the problem. The following is a list of questions that should be asked about this problem:

- **Is the monitor turned on? (i.e., is the light on the front of the monitor on?)** As simple as it seems, there's been a fair amount of calls that have been solved by turning the monitor on.

BUT WAIT A MINUTE

Before you decide that all users are stupid, remember that computers aren't their life. Most users use the computer as a tool, and they're used to it behaving the same way each day. If their monitor automatically goes black via a screen saver, or because the machine is turned off, they will never think about having to turn the monitor on. It will just "magically" come on when they turn the computer on or when they move the mouse.

- **If the monitor won't turn on, is there power to the wall outlet?** Simple question, but people often plug their monitors into different outlets than their PC, because the monitors are on their desks but the PC itself may be under the desk. This is particularly common in cubicles. Sometimes you'll find that there's an outlet, or entire electrical circuit, out that is preventing the monitor from being turned on.

- **Are the contrast and brightness turned up high enough? (i.e., turn the contrast and brightness to their maximum setting)** Again, this seems simple, but it's also a very frequent call that corporate help desks get. Why? Because some people like to play pranks and most users never mess with these controls.

- **Does another working monitor work on the PC? Does the monitor work on a different PC?** Finally, we get to an isolation question. We are trying to determine if the problem is in the video card or the monitor. If you match a known good component, another monitor for instance, with a suspect component, such as a video card, you can determine if the video card is really bad.

I find most cases can be solved with just this list of questions. By the time you're verifying whether the monitor or the video card works with a known good component (which takes some time), you will have exhausted all of the simple solutions.

b) The PC won't start at all. No lights, no sounds, or anything else.

Answer: Most people faithfully expect their PC to turn on when they press the power button, or press a key on the keyboard. The concept that there's a problem so severe, or that a problem can occur so early on in the process that the PC won't even make it's familiar "hello" beep, is unthinkable.

Unfortunately, this does happen, and will happen to you. So what are the potential causes for the problem?

The first, somewhat obvious, cause is that there is no power. I'll break this down in a moment, but for now, just remember the somewhat obvious: the PC requires power to work.

The second, less obvious, answer is that the motherboard or CPU is defective.

Okay, let's discuss power for a second, because it is the one that is most likely to be the problem. The following is a list of questions that I would ask to see if there's a power problem.

LAB 2.1

- **Is the PC power supply's fan running?** Sometimes people say nothing is happening, when something small really is happening. If the PC power supply's fan is running, you can skip down to testing the output of the power supply, because you know that you've got power coming into the power supply.
- **Is the PC plugged in?** Simple, but always a good place to start.
- **Is there power to the outlet the PC is plugged into?** Normally I would ask specifically if the power strip's circuit breaker has been tripped, if it is on, and if the complete circuit is functioning. Sometimes I suggest that the user test the circuit and the outlet with a lamp (that they know works).
- **Is the power switch really turning on?** Sometimes with these newer fancy cases with remote power switches, even the slightest change in the positioning of the case can make the power switch not work. The answer to this question may require your direct intervention where the preceding questions may have been able to have been answered by the user themselves without you having to go to see them.
- **Is there enough voltage flowing through the power supply?** This will require that you test the output of the power supply with a multimeter, which we'll get into in the next exercise.

If you've truly ruled out that it's a power problem, and you've verified that power is correctly flowing to the motherboard but nothing is happening, then your problem gets a lot harder.

In this case I was talking about a failure, and suggested that if you had power it had to be a motherboard or CPU. Strictly speaking, this is not necessarily the case—you can have a problem with an add-in card or with memory. You should certainly test this case by removing all memory and add-in cards and attempting to boot. At the very least, you should get a light on the power indicator, and a beep, or more likely a series of beeps if there's a problem that's not on the motherboard. If this is the case, that the motherboard works with no memory or add-in cards, step-by-step add memory and add-in cards one at a time until the PC no longer works. The card that you added last is the defective card.

**LAB
2.1**

BUT WAIT, HOW CAN A PC WORK WITHOUT MEMORY?

The answer is that it can't in the more general sense; however, for troubleshooting the case, all we need is for the POST (Power-On Self-Test) to start. POST, as you'll remember from Chapter 1, is contained in BIOS (in ROM), so even without memory it will be able to test certain core components, like the CPU, before determining that there's no memory and sending you an audible message of a series of beeps via the internal speaker.

c)   Windows NT won't start. It responds with a message about a boot disk failure.

Answer: First, I want to make it clear that you won't be asked about Windows NT on the A+ Exam. This problem is designed to illustrate some concepts and how problems can appear to be hardware problems, but might be software.

When Windows NT starts, it loads itself from the hard disk in a rather specific way. If something goes wrong with that boot process, Windows NT will fail to load, as would DOS or Windows 9x.

Windows NT is generally good about telling you what the problem is. It calls out in this case that there's a boot disk failure, something that's not particularly hard to understand. At first glance, this would appear to be a hard drive failure of the first hard drive. However, if you were to test the hard drive with any utility software, it would report that the drive is completely okay. So what gives?

The answer, in this case, is that it can be one of a limited set of things: 1) there's a virus that has infected the boot sector (most likely), 2) there's been a subtle change in the settings on the SCSI card, 3) incorrect settings in NT's boot.ini. Also, if a user has set the active partition to a non-system partition, either through FDISK or Disk Administrator, similar disk failure messages are likely.

LAB 2.1

The first one is clearly a software problem. Because most viruses assume that DOS/Windows is installed on a system, and know nothing about NT, they go changing things on the boot sector, like they know what they are doing, and mess it up. The end result is that NT refuses to start.

The second one is a hardware problem, but not the one pointed to by the software; nor is it going to be easy to locate because the changes can be quite subtle.

The reason that I took the time here to show this example is because it shows clearly how software can say it's one problem, but it can really be quite a different problem. It's important to realize as you're troubleshooting that the message you're getting back can be misleading.

CAPTURE INFORMATION ON THE PROBLEM

We've talked about using a standard method to troubleshoot problems, and about localizing the cause of the problem, but there will be some problems that you just can't fix. Problems that you just don't have the experience with. Problems that you'll need someone else's help with.

We're lucky in the computer industry that most people are willing to help you if you've "done your homework." If you've shown that you're willing to solve the problem, and you've put effort into solving the problem, almost anyone with the knowledge to help you will.

Capturing information on a problem is your way of showing that you've done your homework. It's a way of being able to share with someone else what you've done and tried, and what didn't work, or what changed.

In addition to being helpful when asking peers for help, it's imperative to have the information when working with technical support departments or when you call in consultants for help.

When you contact a technical support department for a piece of hardware or software that you're using, they'll probably ask for some of the basics, such as what version of software or hardware revision you're using, as well as your computer operating system (and revision or patch level). You'll want to make sure that you document these kinds of things when working on the problem so that you'll have the answers right at hand when you are asked.

Having all of the information together will also help when you have a consultant come in to help. They won't have to spend their time tracking down all of this information because you'll already have it.

**LAB
2.1**

The final reason for capturing information on a problem is so that you can refer back to your notes on the problem in the future when you encounter a similar problem.

Get a spiral bound notebook in which to record your activities. Keep a daily log of what you work on and when. Include any details about the problem as well as contact phone numbers, version numbers, and any other details that seem relevant.

This will pay off tenfold when you don't have to track down where you left that technical support person's number, or when trying to figure out what day you worked on a particular problem.

2.1.2 ANSWERS

a) What is the line voltage at your PC now?

Answer: Your answer will vary, but a typical line voltage in North America is somewhere between 110 and 125 volts.

b) Is this voltage fluctuating at all?

Answer: It shouldn't be. Fluctuating voltage, usually caused by high-load equipment such as air-conditioning or industrial equipment, can interfere with the proper functioning of PCs, causing a wide range of symptoms, such as spontaneous rebooting, locking up, and memory and disk errors.

c) What happens if you connect one of the leads to the round hole instead?

Answer: Depending upon which lead is moved to the round hole (the ground connection), either the voltage will remain the same or go to zero.

d) What happens if you set the multimeter to DC volts rather than AC volts?

Answer: The multimeter will read zero volts DC. This is because the DC measuring circuits in the multimeter do not "see" the rapidly oscillating AC voltage.

2.1.3 ANSWERS

a) What voltage did you read on the Red wire?

Answer: About +5 volts

b) What voltage did you read on the Yellow wire?

Answer: About +12 volts

c) What happens if you set the multimeter to AC volts?

Answer: The multimeter will read about 25 volts AC. This is because the multimeter's circuitry thinks it is measuring AC voltage.

**LAB
2.1**

LAB 2.1 SELF-REVIEW QUESTIONS

In order to test your progress, you should be able to answer the following questions.

1) The four steps to the scientific method are: i) Identify and understand the problem; ii) Hypothesize a solution; iii) Test the hypothesis; and iv) If the test fails, hypothesize another solution.
   a) _____True
   b) _____False

2) Which of the following is a multimeter designed to test?
   a) _____Voltage, amperage, and ohms
   b) _____Voltage and amperage
   c) _____Voltage, amperage, and resistance
   d) _____Voltage, amperage, and wattage

3) When using a multimeter to test the power coming out of a wall outlet, the proper procedure to avoid danger is which of the following?
   a) _____Hold both leads with one hand.
   b) _____Hold one lead in each hand.
   c) _____Never handle the leads under any circumstances.
   d) _____There is no danger in handling a multimeter's leads.

4) Testing a known working monitor on a malfunctioning PC is an example of which of the following?
   a) _____The scientific method
   b) _____Hypothesizing a solution
   c) _____The blind leading the blind
   d) _____An isolation strategy

5) A computer can run without memory long enough for you to be able to test certain core components.
   a) _____True
   b) _____False

Quiz answers appear in Appendix A, Section 2.1.

LAB 2.1

L A B   2.2

SYMPTOMS AND PROBLEMS WITH MODULES

LAB OBJECTIVES

After this Lab, you will be able to:

✓ Identify and Troubleshoot Types of Keyboard Errors

✓ Identify and Troubleshoot Mouse Errors

✓ Test and Troubleshoot Modems

✓ Test and Troubleshoot Problems with the Audio Subsystem

✓ Identify Common Problems with Floppy Drives

LAB 2.2

In this Lab, we'll discuss common problems with PCs and how they are resolved. Even as we talk about these common problems, you should be thinking back to Lab 2.1 and the lessons learned there.

MOTHERBOARD PROBLEMS

Motherboard problems are by far the hardest problems to diagnose, and the ones that cause the most frustration. If there's a problem on the motherboard, whether it be a problem with the CPU, memory, BIOS, or whatever, it's going to affect your whole experience with the PC.

Motherboard problems manifest themselves in a variety of ways, but most often they are the source of unexplained lockups. Lockups occur when there is no activity, even after the operating system has been reloaded.

 Many people are quick to jump on the idea that a problem is automatically a motherboard problem. This is rarely the case; generally, a related system, such as a power supply, is the true source of the problem. Don't jump to conclusions.

The best suggestion when dealing with intermittent lockup problems is to rule out other problems first. If you determine that there are no other potential causes, then the best solution is to replace the processor to determine if that makes the problem go away. Finally, replace the motherboard only when no other alternatives appear to be available.

If there's a problem with the motherboard, you'll not be able to isolate whether it's the processor or the motherboard itself. So the easiest solution is to replace the processor, because removing the motherboard, as you discovered in Chapter 1, almost always requires that the entire system be torn down. Processor replacements can generally be done quickly and easily; but carefully read and follow the removal and replacement instructions that come with the replacement CPU.

In addition to mysterious lockups, you may receive errors on boot-up about the CMOS battery being low, or that the CMOS checksum has failed. These errors are usually caused by a failure in the battery that keeps the CMOS chip running. This can either be depletion of the batteries if the motherboard uses an external battery pack to power the CMOS chip, or a depletion of the internal rechargeable battery if the CMOS chip has one.

In the case of external batteries that power the CMOS's chip, it's easy enough just to replace them. Most computer stores will sell either an integrated battery pack designed for this purpose, or a holder that will house four AA batteries.

If the CMOS chip has an internal battery, then the best thing to do is leave the computer on for a long time (a few days). This should recharge the internal batteries and allow you to turn the computer off without fear that the CMOS circuit will lose power again.

If you do one of these steps, or both, and you still have problems, you more than likely have a defect that's severe enough to warrant replacing the CMOS chip, which because it's soldered onto most motherboards, means that you'll probably have to replace the motherboard.

POWER SUPPLY/SLOT COVERS

It may seem reasonable for a faulty power supply to cause problems, but it may not be so obvious what a slot cover might do to cause problems, or how it might be faulty.

The answer is simply that the power supply in your system performs two functions. The first, most obvious, function is to provide the correct power to the rest of the computer. The non-obvious answer is that it performs a cooling function. The fan in a power supply is designed to not only provide cooling for the power supply itself, but for the complete PC as well.

The fan requires that the airflow inside the PC be carefully considered; if slot covers are missing from the back, airflow can be compromised, and it's possible that the fan won't be able to keep the PC as cool as it should.

HEAT IS A LONG-TERM KILLER

Like many professionals who've been in the business for a long time, I've seen lots of machines that haven't had proper maintenance, and I've seen a lot of PCs that shouldn't be running that are.

One of the most common causes of flaky behavior, and ultimate demise, of a PC is a fan in the power supply that has failed. Because of the fan failure, the inside of the computer is allowed to reach incredibly high temperatures – temperatures well in excess of what the components were designed for.

The problem is that when a fan fails, it doesn't notify you of a problem unless you have a fancy high-end server, and because there aren't any short-term effects when a fan fails you don't know it until it's too late—until you've sufficiently heated the inside of your computer to a point that the chips are no longer stable, that is. The machine will probably never be the same again.

The moral of this story: Check your power supply fan from time to time; it won't tell you that it's broken until it's too late. Make sure you hear it running regularly, and be sure to keep it clean. Fans attract a lot of dust, so cleaning it by vacuuming on a regular basis is your best insurance policy against fan failure and system overheating.

LAB 2.2

KEYBOARD

By far the most popular input device on PCs today is the keyboard. Even though there are a multitude of different input choices, there are none of them that are as widely available or have the flexibility as a keyboard.

Although mice and their cousins are quite impressive input devices, they don't offer the same ability to enter textual information that the keyboard does. (Conversely, try moving a pointer around with the keyboard.)

Keyboards are the only peripheral input device natively detected on every PC. As a result, most keyboard errors are displayed when the PC starts. They either appear as a keyboard missing error, or a stuck key error.

THE WHOLE TRUTH

You've probably heard about the Universal Serial Bus (USB) by now. It's the standard that Microsoft, Intel, and other mainstream PC manufacturers have been pushing for a while to get away from the older serial and parallel ports. Well, at least some devices are supporting USB, including keyboards.

Most older PC BIOSs don't support USB-connected keyboards natively. This means that the keyboard may not be detected by BIOS if you plug in a USB keyboard. Normally that's not a problem because you don't often do much before the operating system is running, but it can make it difficult when fixing system settings.

SERIAL DEVICES—OF MICE AND MODEMS

Although not all mice are serial devices, there are still many of them out in the world that are, so we're going to treat them as a serial device.

Mice and their cousins are notorious for having problems, skipping around, causing trouble. But the truth is that there are two basic causes for mice problems. There are physical problems—problems with the way that the mouse is translating your movements. Other problems are caused by the computer or the driver that is being used to convert the mice's signals into something the computer can recognize.

In the case of mice, more often than not the problem is dirt in the rollers that translate the motion into the electrical signals. Cleaning these rollers, and the mouse ball itself, is very easy and applies to both trackballs and mice. More on cleaning is covered in the Exercises later in this chapter.

THE WHOLE TRUTH

There are some mice, called Optical Mice, which position themselves by watching the reflection of light from a special mouse pad. These mice never need internal cleaning. Just cleaning the bottom of the mouse and the pad itself should eliminate any weird behavior (that is, if it's a problem with the mouse itself, and not the driver).

Mice aren't the only cause of problems with serial devices; modems can also be problematic. Like their rodent counterparts, there are two basic problems with modems. The first is with the modem itself. For some reason, it can't pick up the phone and dial another modem, but it still communicates with the PC. On the other side, it can suffer from the same driver and IRQ problems that a mouse can. More information on modems, testing, and communications is covered in this Lab's Exercises.

PARALLEL PORTS

Parallel ports are a hardy component of your PC as components go. They rarely fail, although from time to time you may find that they don't quite work like you might want them to.

The most common problem that people have with parallel ports is that they install a new parallel port device, such as a scanner, and find that it doesn't work. This can be caused by three things.

The first potential cause, and the most likely one, is that the cable that you're using to connect the two devices can't handle the high rate of data that the device is trying to send. This is true of unusually long printer cables (greater than 15 feet), or cables that have been plugged and unplugged numerous times. Where a printer might print out an occasional garbled character, devices such as Zip drives and scanners just fail to operate. It might be a good idea to try a known good parallel cable. If this doesn't do the trick, see the following two reasons.

**LAB
2.2**

The second potential cause is that your parallel port is an older port that doesn't support the necessary communications methods that the device requires. There are several variations in parallel port design, from the original unidirectional parallel port used on the PC XT to the ECP (Enhanced Capabilities Port) and EPP (Enhanced Printer Port) most often installed today. Most parallel devices will work with most ports in use today, but there may be the occasion where a device won't work because the port is too old.

The final cause is that the device that you're trying to attach doesn't work because of some kind of hardware defect, or software bug. In these cases, of course, the only solution is to replace the affected hardware.

FLOPPY DRIVE

Although people are using floppy drives less and less these days, they are still the most prevalent removable media for PCs, and as such are often used to exchange data. Although other removable media, such as Zip and Jaz drives, have reduced the need to use floppies because of their greater storage capacity, and the Internet has allowed the transmission of most files through e-mail, there are still organizations that do not have these alternatives.

Although there are a wide variety of problems that can occur when installing the floppy drive, such as installing the control cable on the drive backwards, there are relatively few things that can go wrong with a floppy drive, and a relatively narrow number of solutions. Read on for some things to try.

First, if you are having trouble reading or writing a floppy disk, try another disk, or try the disk on another computer. Try reading known good disks on the suspected drive.

Dirt can be a problem, so cleaning the floppy drive may help. There are commercial drive cleaner kits available that you can use for this purpose.

It's also worth checking the CMOS settings—they may have been accidentally changed.

HARD DRIVES

Nothing strikes fear into the hearts and minds of users and technicians alike as the sound of a hard drive failing. If you've ever experienced a problem where the heads have flown off the disk arms (or even just one), you'll know the raspy, scratchy, snow-plow-going-down-the-street sound that assures you that you're not going to get your data back.

Hard drives are probably the one component in your PC that will most often fail. Hard drives are on constantly, heating up, and taking little jolts of energy, from the wall, and from the user kicking the machine (accidentally). The physical parts of a computer, those that move—such as your hard drive—are much more likely to fail because they are manipulating the physical world, rather than just small amounts of electric current.

Hard drives spin at as little as 3,600 RPM and up to 10,000 RPM or more. It's no wonder they sometimes break down. Contrast this with the number of RPM that your car engine goes through and it's even easier to see. Most of the time your car's engine is revolving at less than 2,500 RPM, and most cars top out at 7,000 RPM or less, or less than the average speed of a hard drive.

Although the most fearful sound may be the sound that is made when a head flies off the drive arm, it's certainly not the only problem that can occur with a hard drive. Hard drive problems break down into two basic categories. The first category, which is far more likely, is data problems— problems where the data stored on the drive is wrong, but physically and logically the drive is working fine. These are problems where the user has deleted a file, or a virus had deleted the partition table, or someone installed some bad drivers and the computer won't boot, and the like. This section doesn't address these types of problems, as they are not hardware related.

The other category of problems is hardware-related: the drive won't spin up at all, or it won't spin up reliably, or it spins up for a moment then shuts itself down, or the data can't be read from the drive. These are the kinds of problems we will be discussing.

Hard drives work by spinning magnetic media, called platters, under a set of read-write heads—the electromagnetic devices that convert the information read into electrical pulses the computer can interpret—that are suspended by an arm over the platters. Every time the hard drive is powered up, the media starts spinning. The hard drive attempts to get the media spinning under the read-write heads at a constant rate, within the tolerances of the drive. Getting the media up to that speed is the most stressful event a hard drive has to endure. As a result, it is one of the most likely causes of failure.

It's important that the media spin at a precise and consistent speed so that the read-write head will be able to accurately interpret the information on the drive, and write new information on the drive. If the hard drive cannot spin the media up to the required speed, dictated by the hard drive design, one of two things will happen. The first is that the drive won't spin up at all; the other is that the drive will attempt to spin up and will shortly stop trying to spin up because it realizes that it can't get the speed within tolerances.

**LAB
2.2**

THE WHOLE TRUTH

SCSI hard drives may not automatically start spinning up as soon as they are powered on. Whether they do this or not is determined by their jumper settings.

In addition to startup on power up, SCSI drives have the ability to only spin up when ordered to by the controller. This allows the SCSI controller to slowly bring drives up to speed one at a time so as not to overburden a power supply or trip a circuit breaker.

Some drives also allow you to set the drive to wait 10 seconds per SCSI ID before spinning up, which will also distribute the load of startup and accomplish the same thing as allowing the controller to spin the drives up.

If you have a hard drive that won't spin up, you can usually retrieve the data, or have the data retrieved, should that become necessary. We, of course, recommend that you backup your hard drive periodically, so that retrieval won't become necessary.

If you have that wonderful scratchy sound coming out of your hard drive, you may have a head crash. This is where, for some reason or another, the head that was perched on the hard drive arm just nanometers from the surface of the hard drive platters (or media) became dislodged from the arm and is now floating around scratching the surface of the media it used to be comfortably floating above.

There are two problems with this precarious position. The first is that the media that once held precious data is being scraped off the platter that held it in such a neat order. It's not going to be there to read even if the head was reattached to the arm.

The second problem is that this loose media is now floating around on the inside of what amounts to a huge tornado going on inside the hard drive. These particles that were scraped off are now impacting other parts of the disk, potentially causing more damage, and potentially causing even more media to be scraped off the platters, making the situation worse.

If you have a head crash, the prognosis for hard drive repair is not good. Although data recovery centers can work miracles sometimes, you have to be a skeptic if this kind of a crash occurs.

Another type of problem you can have with a hard drive is that you start getting bad sectors. Bad sectors are a normal part of life with hard drives.

What may seem like a simple bump into your computer may send shock waves through your hard drive as the heads make contact with the surface of the media.

The drive heads are almost literally resting on a cushion of air. The heads have air whizzing past them at roughly the same speed the media is spinning. This creates a small amount of air that the heads fly over. If the hard drive media moves into the way of the heads because of a bump, your head will crash, or bump into the media itself. This may dislodge some of the media on the platters, causing a small bad area on the hard drive.

Bad sectors may also be caused by the media just getting sucked off the platter, or from a defect in manufacturing, but they are quite rare in today's market.

THE WHOLE TRUTH

It used to be that drives came with defect tables on them, areas that the factory knew were bad. You entered these defects into a low-level formatting program that masked them off from the operating system.

Today, hard drives come with their low-level formats already on them. They already have any defects masked out of them. However, most new drives are manufactured in such tightly controlled environments that they rarely have ANY defects anymore.

Finally, what may be perceived as a hard drive problem could be a controller problem. All hard drives are connected to the PC by a controller of some kind. SCSI drives have a somewhat complex controller. IDE drives have a much less complicated controller, much more of a bridge between two different interfaces than a true controller. In either case, however, there are problems that can occur in either controller.

Generally when a controller fails, it will fail completely. There won't be any in between; it will just not work. The easiest way to isolate a problem to a controller failure is when the drive will spin up and act fine, but it will not be accessible from the PC. The PC may even indicate a hard drive failure in a message during POST.

**LAB
2.2**

AUDIO AND VIDEO

In all of the other parts of this Lab, we've been talking about how to identify the cause of a problem. We've been talking primarily about how a system shows you errors that occur via messages on your screen. And in the case of motherboard problems, we've been talking about how the motherboard beeps to indicate problems.

But what happens when your video card fails, or when the speaker doesn't work? How do you determine what is wrong with a PC?

When video cards fail, a PC may act much as it would if there's a motherboard failure. It attempts to identify the problem to you by means of beep codes, which are determined by the BIOS and motherboard manufacturers. It may also behave as though it weren't even installed in the machine.

If you determine that you have a bad video card, you can easily swap it out with another. Or if the video card is built into the motherboard, you can plug in another video card and disable the one on the motherboard. This will either be done automatically for you, or you may need to change a jumper on the motherboard itself. The motherboard manual will tell you for sure what you need to do.

Audio is a bit of a different story, however, because PCs weren't originally designed with much in the way of audio hardware. In fact, all there used to be was a small cheap speaker that was connected directly to the motherboard. It's good for producing beeps, but little else.

Because the internal audio capabilities were so limited, several add-in cards have emerged that provide for more robust sound. These range from a simple 8-bit mono card to the 16+ bit stereo cards of today. These cards are most likely to fail because they are more complex and often receive input from other systems, such as your home stereo.

It is important to be sure that the PC's software drivers match the installed hardware, and that the software driver's settings match the hardware configuration.

Finally, consider whether a given audio card has *ever* worked in the system. A software or hardware conflict can prevent some brands or models (or configurations) of cards from working in some PC makes or models.

LAB 2.2 EXERCISES

2.2.1 IDENTIFY AND TROUBLESHOOT TYPES OF KEYBOARD ERRORS

In this Exercise, you will simulate some of the types of keyboard problems you may encounter. For the first problem, disconnect the keyboard on your PC before you boot the machine.

a) What happens when you boot up the system?

_____

_____

Now, shut down the PC and reboot it, this time holding down a key from the keyboard.

b) What behavior do you observe?

_____

_____

2.2.2 IDENTIFY AND TROUBLESHOOT MOUSE ERRORS

For the next few Exercises, try to determine how you would troubleshoot the given scenarios.

a) You notice the mouse on your PC is acting erratically—moving in a jerky fashion, skipping across the page. What would you do to fix this behavior?

_____

_____

b) After booting your PC, you observe that the mouse is no longer responding. You suspect a problem with the connection. You verify

**LAB
2.2**

that the cable plugging the mouse into the PC is connected tightly; what else should you check?

_____

_____

2.2.3 TEST AND TROUBLESHOOT MODEMS

a) You try to connect to the Internet through your usual connection program, and get no response from your modem. How would you test it to isolate the problem?

_____

_____

2.2.4 TEST AND TROUBLESHOOT PROBLEMS WITH THE AUDIO SUBSYSTEM

a) You receive a phone call from a user who complains that his system is no longer playing the music CD he had put into the drive. When you arrive, you notice there seems to be none of the usual "noises," such as error beeps and notification sounds. How would you go about isolating the problem?

_____

_____

2.2.5 IDENTIFY COMMON PROBLEMS WITH FLOPPY DRIVES

a) If you are experiencing problems with your floppy drive, what steps would you go through to determine the source of the problem and move to a solution?

_____

_____

LAB 2.2 EXERCISE ANSWERS

2.2.1 ANSWERS

In this Exercise, you simulated some of the types of keyboard problems you may encounter. For the first problem, you disconnected the keyboard on your PC before you booted the machine.

a) What happens when you boot up the system?

Answer: A missing keyboard error is one where the PC cannot detect the keyboard. When a PC starts, it sends a series of messages to the keyboard's controller and waits for a short period of time for the controller to respond. If it doesn't, it generates a "Missing Keyboard – Press F2 to Continue" message .

This can literally mean that the keyboard is missing to the PC. In other words, it's not connected. The other possibility is that the controller on the keyboard is either locked up or faulty.

The easiest way to resolve the issue is to connect the keyboard, or to replace the keyboard with another.

In this second Exercise, you shut down the PC and rebooted it, this time holding down a key from the keyboard.

b) What behavior do you observe?

Answer: The other type of keyboard error that the PC can detect when starting up is a stuck key message. This message means that the keyboard's controller is continuously sending a message to the PC that a key is being pressed (or in essence it's being held down.) If you're not holding down a key, then it may be hard to identify the cause of the failure because most PC BIOSs do not report which key is being held down.

LAB 2.2

You may also have a keyboard that the PC thinks is fine, but has keys on it that just won't register, or don't register to the PC easily. In either of these cases, you're going to have to attempt to clean the keyboard, or replace it. Cleaning a keyboard is best taken in stages. The more involved you get in attempting to clean a keyboard to make it work, the more likely you are to destroy it in the process.

The first step that I recommend to clean a keyboard is to take a business card, or other stiff piece of paper, and slide it between all of the edges. This will generally bring up some dust bunnies. These dust bunnies are usually comprised partially of hairs. Sometimes these hairs will get caught in the mechanism of the keyboard and will prevent a key from returning to its "home" position.

After doing this, you should attempt to test the keyboard again. If it hasn't started working at this point, the best course of action is to replace the keyboard. If that isn't possible, you may be able try the following steps and procedures.

It's important to understand how the keyboards work in most systems today. Most use a small spring underneath the keys to help push them up. Inside (or outside) the spring is a mechanism that allows the key to release quickly at a certain point, thus allowing the user to feel that the key has registered to the PC.

The problem is that it's possible to have the mechanism lock up. Generally, debris has become lodged in the mechanism. So in order to fix the keyboard, it will be necessary to remove the top of the keyboard and review each key's operation, making sure that it feels like the mechanism is working. For any keys that are questionable, you can visually inspect the key and attempt to remove any debris. Another effective way of cleaning dust from keys is by using pressurized air, dispensed through special cleaner cans, to blast out the dust from between keyboard components.

If this doesn't work, your last choice is to try to wash off the keyboard either via **distilled** water or isopropyl alcohol. Notice that I didn't say tap water, or even spring water. Both have so many contaminants in them that they will cause more harm than good. When cleaning the keyboard using this method, you want to make sure that you wash off any debris without soaking the keyboard. If you're careful to pressure wash the keyboard and not soak it, you may be able to repair it.

LAB 2.2

2.2.2 ANSWERS

a) You notice the mouse on your PC is acting erratically—moving in a jerky fashion, skipping across the page. What would you do to fix this behavior?

Answer: The first step in cleaning a mouse is to remove the ball. In the case of a trackball, sometimes this is possible and sometimes it isn't. Once the ball is removed, it should be washed thoroughly with warm soapy water. This will get all of the dirt, hairs, and other particles off the mouse ball before you put it back.

Next, remove the screws that hold the mouse itself together. Don't worry about parts springing all over the place; they are all attached to a central circuit board and won't come out when you open the mouse.

The next step is to separate the two halves of the mouse housing. Generally, there's at least one plastic retaining clip that must be pushed aside to allow the housing to come apart.

Once the two halves are apart, you'll see a circuit board that contains all of the circuitry for the mouse, including the sensors that "see" the movement. Most of the time, there will be a small plastic roller that makes contact with the ball when the mouse ball is in the mouse.

Sometimes that plastic roller will have a small rubber coating on it, or a rubber band around it. However, rollers are almost always flat; if you see a ridge on the roller, it's most likely "gunk" and not part of the original design. You'll want to scrape off any "gunk" that has become attached to the roller. Normally, I do this with a small Exacto knife. I simply scrape the material off by holding the roller in place and scraping in a diagonal motion. The reason for the diagonal motion is because the knife will cause small grooves in the roller. I try to make sure that these will add grip between the mouse ball and the roller, not take away from it.

Once all of the "gunk" has been removed from both rollers, you'll want to remove any remaining debris by blowing or swabbing it out with a cotton swab. Once the residual dirt has been removed, you need to reassemble the mouse. You'll want to make sure that the cord is in its appropriate spot within the case. Once the halves have been reassembled, you need to put the screws back in and reinstall the mouse ball.

Running through this process will reasonably guarantee that the mechanical operation of the mouse is in working order, but sometimes there are IRQ or driver problems that aren't related to the mechanical operation that cause trouble with the mouse.

b)   After booting your PC, you observe that the mouse is no longer responding. You suspect a problem with the connection. You verify that the cable plugging the mouse into the PC is connected tightly; what else should you check?

**LAB
2.2**

Answer: Besides just moving the mouse around in circles, you may want to right- or left-click a button to see if any response—such as getting the pulldown menu to appear—occurs. If you do get a response, it is likely that the problem isn't with the mouse drivers or connections, but rather a mechanical problem similar to that encountered in Question a of this Exercise.

There are three ways that mice can be connected to the PC. The first is serially, via a COM port. They may also be connected to a special mouse card, or a card that has a bus mouse port on it. Finally, they may be connected via a PS/2 port.

The serial mice historically have been the most popular because they are easy to connect. As long as the COM ports are configured correctly, each with their own IRQ and I/O port, there should be no problems. You can review the IRQ and I/O port settings given in Chapter 1 to verify that the COM port is configured correctly.

Bus mice, or those connected to a special card, are rarely in use today because they take an additional slot. Most machines today come with integrated PS/2 ports and Serial ports, so it's rarely a good option to add a special card to handle a mouse. However, when they are used, they require a special mouse driver that is able to detect the presence of a bus mouse and is usually provided with them. There's also the potential issue of having the correct IRQ. Bus mouse cards do allow their IRQ to be set, IRQ 5 being a standard setting.

PS/2-connected mice are becoming more prevalent, which is making mouse problems even rarer. PS/2 ports are almost never configurable; they are installed on the motherboard and are hardwired. This means that there's no potential trouble with IRQs and I/O ports like there are with serial mice.

2.2.3 ANSWERS

a) You try to connect to the Internet through your usual connection program, and get no response from your modem. How would you test it to isolate the problem?

Answer: The best way to test a modem is to load a simple communications program, such as Terminal in Windows 3.1 or Hyperterminal in Windows 95. This will allow you to get a direct connection with the modem.

Once you have loaded the program, any commands you type in communicate directly with the modem. At the program's command prompt, type in ATE1Q0V1 followed by Return. The letters that you type may or may not show up on the screen. It will depend in which state the modem was last left. You may have to do this a few times for the modem to synchronize its speed with the speed that the terminal program is using to communicate to the modem.

LAB
2.2

This command should result in the modem responding with OK. The command first gets the modem's attention (AT). Then it tells it to start echoing characters back (E1). Then it tells the modem to not be quiet (Q0). Finally, it tells the modem to give back verbose responses (V1).

If you get an ERROR back from the modem at any point, the modem is bad and must be replaced. If the modem responds with OK, the first part of the testing is complete. You know that the COM port is working and that the modem's internal circuitry is working as well.

If you get NO response, then you may still have a bad modem, or the communications settings for the PC and the modem don't match.

The next step is to tell the modem to do an internal diagnostic. This is done by typing ATI and pressing Return. The modem should either return an identification string identifying itself, or more likely it will return two OKs separated by two returns.

The final step in making sure the modem is okay is to type ATDT. It should respond with NO CARRIER after a minute or so. If it responds with NO DIAL TONE, you'll need to make sure that the phone line is connected to the modem's line or telecommunications port.

The best way to test the line is to plug a phone directly into the back of the modem in the jack labeled Phone. Even if the line works there, it may still be a cabling problem and not a modem problem.

The telephone line must come into the modem in the line or telco jack to work. This is because the modem automatically disconnects the phone jack when it makes a call. If the phone line is plugged into the phone port, it will be disconnected when the modem attempts to pick up the line to make an outbound call.

If you've made sure that the line is plugged into the correct port and the modem still responds with NO DIAL TONE, then the modem must be replaced as the analog-to-digital circuitry within the modem itself has become damaged.

If the modem is working at this point, any remaining problems must be related to the driver that you're using to communicate with the modem.

**LAB
2.2**

2.2.4 ANSWERS

a) You receive a phone call from a user who complains that his system is no longer playing the music CD he had put into the drive. When you arrive, you notice there seems to be none of the usual "noises," such as error beeps and notification sounds. How would you go about isolating the problem?

Answer: Determining if you have an audio system problem is fairly easy. You can simply hold down a key during boot-up. Every PC should make some kind of noise when you do this, both because it will generate an error and because it should overflow the keyboard buffer, responding with a beep.

If there's another audio subsystem in your PC, it's a bit harder to test because it's not activated in any way by the PC's BIOS. To test the hardware, you'll need to utilize the test programs provided by the card. Most of the time, they offer a DOS-based testing utility to verify that it's working.

When testing your audio system, you should adjust all levels to their maximum setting. Oftentimes people believe their audio systems have failed when really a small external volume control had been turned down while they were making other adjustments on their computer, such as plugging in a joystick.

The next thing to check is to make sure that any external speakers that you have installed are actually plugged into the speaker jack—not the microphone or line in jack. These simple solutions generally fix most problems.

2.2.5 ANSWERS

a) If you are experiencing problems with your floppy drive, what steps would you go through to determine the source of the problem and move to a solution?

Answer: Essentially there are only four problems that can occur with a floppy drive, as overviewed in the following discussion.

The first is that the cable will become disconnected or damaged in some way. This occurs if the case was removed or replaced. It may also occur if the machine is moved or shipped. The solution is simply to reconnect or replace the floppy drive cable.

With the rest of the problems that you might have, you'll more than likely want to just replace the drive because the cost of floppy drives are so cheap. Also, for all intents and purposes, floppy drives are complete units, which don't have components that you can easily replace.

The second possible problem is that the drive motor failed. In this case, you insert the disk, or you try to access the disk and the disk activity light comes on, but the disk doesn't spin or you don't hear it spin. The solution is just to replace the drive.

The third possible problem is that the read-write heads have become so dirty or misaligned as to not be able to properly read or write data from/to the disk. When this happens, there'll usually be a slow process where disks become more and more unreliable. Although you can clean disk read-write heads with alcohol or with specialized cleaning diskettes, this almost never returns the drive to the same level of efficiency that it originally had, so it's often best to replace the drive.

The final possible problem is a component failure on the drive itself. This is very unlikely, but could cause the drive to constantly run, or to exhibit some other erratic behavior besides those specific symptoms discussed here. In these cases, you'll definitely want to replace the drive.

There are two potential problems that you should be aware of. The first is the issue of a Disk Change Indicator. The original floppy drive specification didn't have a way for the drive to tell the PC that the disk had changed. As a result of the caching that would occur on the PC, some strange and damaging results would happen.

Most of the time the problem shows itself as a floppy having the same files on it just after the disk is changed. However, serious data loss can occur if DOS caches information for the FAT table, or a directory, and it doesn't get a chance to write it to the diskette.

Disk change indicators are standard on most drives today, but you may run into a drive that doesn't have a functioning disk change indicator. In those cases, the easiest thing to do is simply replace the drive.

The second potential problem that you don't want to overlook is that the disk itself is corrupt, unreadable, or otherwise damaged. Sometimes the drive that wrote the floppy disk will be so misaligned that no other drive will be able to read the disk back except for the one that wrote it. In those cases, you'll want to first read those disks back into the PC, then replace the drive. There are also cases where the disk itself is bad and just needs to be discarded.

**LAB
2.2**

LAB 2.2 SELF-REVIEW QUESTIONS

In order to test your progress, you should be able to answer the following questions.

1) If after testing all other possibilities you suspect that there is a problem between either the processor or the motherboard, your best bet is to simply replace the motherboard because replacing the processor is an arduous process.
   a) _____True
   b) _____False

2) If you suspect that the internal battery of the CMOS chip is low on power, what's the best thing to do?
   a) _____Replace the battery, as they are fairly inexpensive.
   b) _____Power down the system for a few days to let the battery recharge.
   c) _____Leave the system up and running for a few days to let the battery recharge.
   d) _____Replace both the CMOS and the battery should this occur.

3) Aside from simply supplying power to your machine, what other function does the power supply in your system provide?
   a) _____It recharges any internal batteries in the system.
   b) _____It performs the cooling function.
   c) _____It protects the hard drive from erosion.
   d) _____There is no other function provided by the power supply other than providing power to the system.

4) Keyboards and mice are the only peripheral input devices natively detected on every PC.
   a) _____True
   b) _____False

5) Two types of keyboard errors are missing key and stuck key.
   a) _____True
   b) _____False

6) Which of the following is not a way for a mouse to be connected to a machine?
   a) _____Via a SCSI port.
   b) _____Via a special mouse card.
   c) _____Via a PS/2 port.
   d) _____Serially, via a COM port.

LAB
2.2

7) Both modems and mice can suffer from the same types of driver and IRQ problems.
   a) _____True
   b) _____False

8) Which command do you send to a modem to determine if it is okay?
   a) _____ATE1Q0V1
   b) _____ATI
   c) _____ATDT
   d) _____ATT1Q0V2

9) The audio and video system will always fail together.
   a) _____True
   b) _____False

10) What is a normal RPM range for a hard drive to spin?
   a) _____Between 7,500 and 10,000
   b) _____Between 2,600 and 5,000
   c) _____Between 3,600 and 10,000
   d) _____Between 2,500 and 7,000

11) Heat is a common cause of floppy drive problems.
   a) _____True
   b) _____False

Quiz answers appear in Appendix A, Section 2.2.

LAB 2.2

C H A P T E R   2

TEST YOUR THINKING

In this chapter, we learned all about diagnosing problems and proper troubleshooting procedures.

1) To test your thinking, have a friend change some of the settings in your computer (they need to write down the "before" and "after" settings). Try and diagnose the problem to the point of being able to identify which settings were changed. For instance, your friend might change the IRQ settings on the modem to render it inoperative or loosen the video monitor cable a bit. Any changes made should be non-destructive unless you really don't care about the data on the PC.

CHAPTER 3

SAFETY AND PREVENTIVE MAINTENANCE

As if there were safety in stupidity alone.

—Thoreau

This is the chapter where we discuss those areas of the test that most people have difficulty with. It's not because the material is particularly hard, it's just that most people don't think about this area of the test in their daily jobs. Most of us are focused on getting the job done, and often that leads to little time to think about how to keep things going, or the impact we're having on the environment.

L A B   3.1

PREVENTIVE MAINTENANCE

LAB OBJECTIVES

After this Lab, you will be able to:

✓ Remove Harmful Dust, Dirt, and Debris from the Inside of PCs

✓ Secure Chips in Place

✓ Clean Floppy and Tape Heads

✓ Identify Components and Cables for Replacement

REMOVE HARMFUL DUST, DIRT, AND DEBRIS FROM THE INSIDE OF PCS

LAB 3.1

If you've ever had the fortune of opening the case of a computer that's been deployed for very long, you've learned that dust bunnies, and dust in general, love computers. It seems like dust and dirt (not to mention food particles) are attracted to PCs.

Actually, dust, dirt, hair, and just about any other form of airborne contaminant is literally attracted to the inside of PCs. The reason is really quite simple when you think about it.

All PCs have power supplies that force air through the system to cool the power supply and the rest of the computer. You'll remember from Chapter 1 that these fans generally suck air through the case and out the power supply, but the reverse can be true.

So we have the first part of the trap. We move a large amount of air through a small space. In other words, we have lots of floating contaminants running through the PC.

The second part of the trap is an electromagnetic field. This magnetic field is caused by the electricity flowing through the computer and has a tendency to attract dirt and other debris. By now some of you are probably thinking back to seventh-grade science class where you learned about magnetism and magnets.

Even if your seventh grade science class didn't cover this, you've probably had enough experience to know that magnets don't attract anything but metal. That's not precisely true, however; it's just a convenient explanation. In truth, almost everything, including dirt, is attracted by magnets and by static electric fields. (We'll talk about static electric fields in the final Lab of this chapter when we talk about static electric discharge.) I'm not saying that you can run a magnet through your house collecting all of your dust; however, I am suggesting that if you applied a static electric field in the air intake of your furnace, you could capture dirt. In fact, my home has just such a device that helps to remove the dust from the air. In practice it works okay, but still leaves enough dust that I still have to dust things off from time to time.

So, now we know what causes dust to get inside a PC; the next question is why it's important that we remove the dust from a PC.

To answer that I go back to describing the function of the fan inside the PC—the fan forces air to flow over the components inside the PC to cool them. When dust builds up on the components, or when the fan can't push as much air through the PC as it should, the components will get hot. Perhaps too hot.

The other problem with dirt in PCs is that the floppy drive has an exposed, albeit protected, read-write head. Dirt and debris building up on this read-write head will eventually prevent the floppy drive from functioning.

LAB 3.1

SECURE CHIPS IN PLACE

Despite the power supply's best efforts, the PC does heat up when it's turned on. And when it's turned off, it will cool off. Even if the environment is well within the tolerances of the chips, it may cause a subtle problem—the chips may walk out of their sockets.

Most chips today are surface mounted on the motherboard. Some chips, such as the CPU, may be in a ZIF socket, as we discussed in Chapter 1. But there are still a few chips that are in standard sockets. Standard sockets will allow a chip to walk up until it's no longer in good contact with the socket. BIOS chips are the most common chips today that still use standard sockets, although you may find other chips in a standard socket, such as cache SRAM chips.

CLEAN FLOPPY AND TAPE HEADS

With the exception of removable media, most read-write heads in a computer are hidden from the dust and debris that we are always battling with. However, with removable media, the read-write heads must be at least somewhat exposed to the elements.

The two most removable drives you'll probably have are a floppy drive and a tape drive. Both use read-write heads that are at some point exposed to the air flowing through the PC. Both must remain clean to operate correctly. You will learn how to clean them in this Lab's Exercises.

LAB 3.1 EXERCISES

3.1.1 REMOVE HARMFUL DUST, DIRT, AND DEBRIS FROM THE INSIDE OF PCs

LAB
3.1

Now that we know how dirt is attracted to our PC, and why it's important to remove it, we can talk about how to remove it safely.

Follow the procedures outlined in Chapter 1 for removing the cover from your PC.

When you clean the inside of a PC, the first thing is to accumulate any dust or dust bunnies by hand and get them out of there.

a) Why do you suppose you should bother with this step?

_____

_____

Once you've removed the dust that you can remove on your own, take a source of compressed air. It can either be a can of compressed air, or compressed air from an air compressor with a hose. In either case, you'll want to be cognizant of the moisture in the air. If the air is too moist, it will actually cause damage to the PC.

The best way to minimize moisture is to hold cans of compressed air upright; decompress, drain, and recompress any air compressor that you might be using. You'll also want to make sure that you're careful about the amount of pressure that you use if you are using a regular air compressor. You don't want to use more than about 40 PSI (Pounds per Square Inch) of pressure through the nozzle.

Start blowing dirt out of the PC around the power supply in short bursts. Using short bursts will minimize the distance that the dust can travel and will help to prevent your area from becoming a huge dust cloud.

b) What area appears to have the most dirt?

_____

_____

Next you'll want to blow off floppy drives and hard drives. Floppy drives have exposed read-write heads, and since they are generally in close proximity to hard drives, they have a tendency to collect more than their share of dust. It doesn't help that floppies have an opening through which air can flow.

Finally, you should blow off all add-in cards and the motherboard. Remember to be cautious of blowing dust back onto the components you've already blown the dust off of. The goal here is to get the PC 80-90 percent dust free, not 100 percent dust free. That's not realistic. So we do what we can do to improve the situation.

**LAB
3.1**

3.1.2 SECURE CHIPS IN PLACE

Whenever you clean the inside of the PC, it's a good idea to make sure your chips haven't "walked" by pushing on them firmly with your thumb to secure them in place. By firmly I mean hard enough that you can feel the board beginning to bow, but not so hard that you think it will break.

If you hear a crack or a snap, don't worry; it's probably just the chip breaking loose from it's current position and bottoming out in the bottom of the socket. It's a disconcerting sound at first, but you get used to it.

a) Discuss what causes chips to "walk."

_____

_____

3.1.3 CLEAN FLOPPY AND TAPE HEADS

For this Exercise, you will need either a cleaning diskette or tape that is specifically designed to clean the tape or floppy heads. If you do not have this type of item, you will need isopropyl alcohol or a similar cleaning solution and a clean piece of foam sponge on the head of a small dowel. These are the two basic methods of cleaning floppy and tape heads.

 You can usually find the foam sponge item in an art supply or crafts store.

By far the best way to clean a floppy drive or tape drive is to use a diskette or tape designed specifically for that purpose, because any special considerations for the tape or floppy drive are taken into account by these special purpose cleaners.

a) If you're using a special-purpose cleaner for this Exercise, is it a wet or a dry cleaning type?

_____

_____

 It is very important when using a wet cleaning system not to overapply the cleaning solution. You don't want to apply so much fluid that it gets thrown off the cleaning diskette. The cleaning fluid could work it's way into other areas of the drive or PC and cause trouble.

If you are using this type of product, go ahead and follow its specific instructions to clean your heads.

The other way to clean a tape or floppy drive is to do it manually. Although this process is harder to do, it can do a better job of cleaning if you do it well.

Apply small amounts of the cleaning solution to the foam sponge. As we talked about before, you must be careful to not overdo it. You don't want to have excess fluid that can get squeezed out of the sponge while cleaning.

Once you've got your sponge prepared, you need to locate the read-write heads. It's easy enough to do this with a small flashlight. You're looking for a small ceramic-looking square that has two or more small lines in it. You probably won't be able to see the lines, but if you can they are the actual read and write heads.

Rub the sponge repeatedly across the read-write heads, making sure to scrub every part of the heads at least three times. Once you've done that you just need to let the drive dry for a few moments before trying to use it. This will prevent media from sticking to the heads.

b) Why do you suppose it is recommended that you use a special-purpose cleaner instead of the manual method?

_____

_____

**LAB
3.1**

Every component has a finite life. Sometimes those lives can be measured in dozens of our lifetimes, but other times components can fail after very little use.

a) What are two ways that you can think of to determine visually if a component should be replaced?

_____

_____

LAB 3.1 ANSWERS

3.1.1 ANSWERS

When you clean the inside of a PC, the first thing is to accumulate any dust or dust bunnies by hand and get them out of there.

a) Why do you suppose you should bother with this step?

Answer: You want to pick out what you can by hand to minimize the amount of dust that you scatter around your work area.

We've all seen people with cans of compressed air blowing out the insides of a computer, only to cause this huge dust cloud in their area. What they don't realize is that cleaning a computer is a delicate operation that should be approached with the care of a gentle breeze, not the force of a tornado.

b) What area appears to have the most dirt?

Answer: The power supply, because it's the point of entry for air and because it's got the highest level of power and thus the largest static electric and magnetic fields. It's best to get as much dirt out as quickly as possible.

LAB
3.1

3.1.2 ANSWERS

a) Discuss what causes chips to "walk."

Answer: A chip walking out of its socket is caused by the continual heating and cooling of the leads on the chips. This heating and cooling causes them to expand and contract slightly. That slight expansion and contraction can, over time, move the chip further and further up in the socket until the chip is no longer firmly housed in the socket.

LEARNING THE STRENGTH OF A PC BOARD

The time I really learned what a PC board is capable of taking in terms of pressure was when I had to get a chip back in its socket on a Thomas-Conrad TC4045 token ring card. (Thomas-Conrad was purchased by Compaq some years ago.)

The chip in question was a square chip about an inch in each direction. It was a Texas Instruments chip—and the core of that particular card. As I remember it, they had changed their manufacturing practice from a handmade process to an automated machine, and the machine didn't always apply enough pressure to snap the chip into position.

I couldn't get the chip to sit in the socket, and I'm on the phone with their technical support who told me I wasn't applying enough pressure. With their assurances that they would take the card back even if I cracked it in half trying to get the chip in it, I put both of my thumbs on top of the chip and literally picked myself up off the ground pushing down on the chip.

I heard a loud pop as the chip landed in it's socket. The card worked fine, and continued to work fine for at least the next two years. (I left the department and couldn't track the card any longer.)

The moral of the story is that you're probably not going to give the PC board that your add-in cards or motherboard are attached to enough credit for the pressure that it can take without breaking.

3.1.3 ANSWERS

a) If you're using a special-purpose cleaner for this Exercise, is it a wet or a dry cleaning type?

Answer: This answer will vary.

**LAB
3.1**

Some special-purpose cleaners use a dry cleaning method—they don't require that you add any fluid to the tape prior to putting it in the drive. Most tape drive cleaning cartridges are this type. Most floppy drive cleaning diskettes are not dry cleaning, but rather a wet cleaning system.

With a wet cleaning system, a small amount of a cleaning solution, usually isopropyl alcohol, is applied to the cleaning diskette (or tape). This solution helps to remove dirt and dust from the read-write heads.

b)   Why do you suppose it is recommended that you use a special-purpose cleaner instead of the manual method?

Answer: Because special-purpose cleaners are designed specifically for this function, and it is harder to do it manually.

Because it takes some skill to clean drives well doing it manually, most tape drive manufacturers require that their cleaning tapes be used, and some will even void the warranty if you try to clean the heads manually.

It used to be that we cleaned heads with cotton swabs. Generally they had a longer, wooden handle than the ones you might use for home personal use, but other than that they were almost identical. However, we've learned that sometimes the cotton can get caught in the drive making things worse rather than better.

Today, if we try to manually clean a tape drive we use a small foam sponge on the end of a wooden stick, because the foam doesn't have a tendency to come apart when cleaning the heads, although it does happen on occasion.

3.1.4 ANSWERS

a)   What are two ways that you can think of to determine visually if a component should be replaced?

Answer: One indicator that a component should be replaced is an indication that it's gone through excessive heat stress. Another is a frayed or bare cable.

LAB 3.1

Heat stress may appear as a discoloration on the component or the surrounding components. Any item that has been severely heat stressed should be considered suspect, and is a candidate for replacement.

All cables should have complete coatings around them and should appear without kinks or breaks of any kind. If there appear to be any kinks or breaks in the cable, replace it immediately.

LAB 3.1 SELF-REVIEW QUESTIONS

In order to test your progress, you should be able to answer the following questions.

1) The PC fan forces air to flow over the components inside the PC to cool them. Dust causes the components within a PC to get hotter.
   a) _____True
   b) _____False

2) ZIF-type chip sockets will allow a chip to walk up until it's no longer in good contact with the socket.
   a) _____True
   b) _____False

3) BIOS chips are the only type of chips that still use standard sockets.
   a) _____True
   b) _____False

4) What is the recommended amount of pressure for an air compressor when cleaning the inside of your computer?
   a) _____20 psi
   b) _____30 psi
   c) _____40 psi
   d) _____50 psi
   e) _____You should never use an air compressor to clean the inside of your PC.

5) How could you tell if a PC component has suffered severe heat stress?
   a) _____It feels excessively hot
   b) _____Its cables are frayed
   c) _____It, or a surrounding component, has a discoloration
   d) _____It has failed to work

   Quiz answers appear in Appendix A, Section 3.1.

**LAB
3.1**

L A B   3.2

POWER ISSUES

The A+ Certification exam includes this topic in a section called "environmental hazards." Whenever I think of environmental hazards, I consider disposing of batteries and other potentially toxic substances, and controlling their disposal so they don't leach into the environment. However, the test is referring to the inevitable damage that can be brought down on an unprotected PC.

IDENTIFY POWER PROBLEMS

Before you learn the remedies for power problems, it's important to understand what they are and why your computer can't handle too many of them. And before understanding power problems, you have to understand some of the basics of power itself. (Remember our discussion in Chapter 2 about understanding the problem before attempting to understand the solution?)

First, there are two kinds of power. Ordinary household power, or current, is an AC voltage. AC means Alternating Current. It is called this because the direction that the current is flowing changes. If you were to graph the

**LAB
3.2**

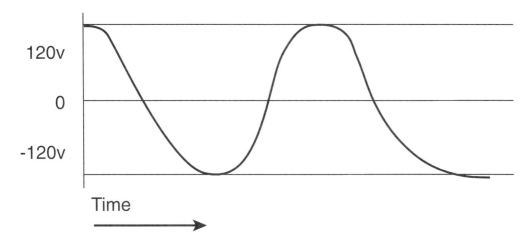

Figure 3.1 ▪ The alternating current from the wall looks like this when there is no problem.

voltage of an AC circuit it will look like a sine wave. It rises and falls in a predefined pattern, as illustrated in Figure 3.1.

There are a lot of reasons why power from the wall is alternating current, but the best reason is that it allows power to be transferred more efficiently from the power-generating plants to your home.

The second type of power is called DC, or direct current. DC current is what you find in batteries. Direct current is so named because it doesn't change its direction. It's direct, always flowing in a specific direction, as illustrated in Figure 3.2.

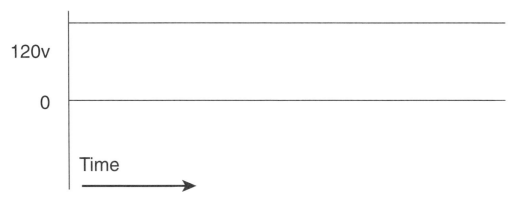

Figure 3.2 ▪ Direct current looks like this—i.e., it never changes.

LAB
3.2

The PC's power supply has the job of converting the AC current from the wall into the DC current that the PC needs to operate. To accomplish that job, it uses a series of specialized circuits and transformers. Each of these components has a finite life and a safe operating range.

The power supply in a typical PC is a switching power supply, or possibly a linear power supply. Linear power supplies are an older design methodology that results in significantly more wasted energy, so all but a few antique power supplies will be switching.

The switching power supply utilizes digital circuitry to accomplish its efficiency and as a result of its usage of digital circuitry is more susceptible to the kinds of problems that we're going to be talking about here.

The primary enemy of a power supply is a spike. This occurs when the AC current from the wall makes an unexplained, unpredictable jump in voltage. This spike is in effect more energy impacting the power supply. That's something that it needs to compensate for quickly so it's not passed on to the computer. In practice, many of these spikes are transferred to the components, but in a sufficiently diminished way so as not to damage them.

However, the continual bombardment of a power supply, and a computer, by these spikes can eventually lead to power supply failure, or failure of one of the internal components of the computer. Almost always, power supplies are designed like secret service men—to get in the way of spikes

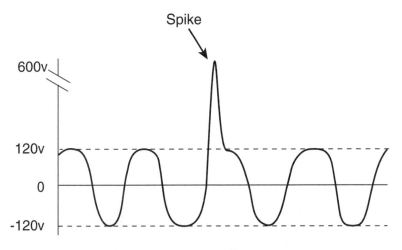

Figure 3.3 ■ Spikes are an unexpected increase in voltage that can be as much as 6000 volts.

and sacrifice themselves before allowing the PC to absorb them. As a result, they are most likely to have problems, or to die, if your power is particularly poor.

You'll probably never notice spikes, but if you do it will be a momentary flickering in the lights as they receive a slightly larger burst of energy. This is particularly pronounced with incandescent bulbs, and not so much with fluorescent bulbs because of their design.

Another enemy of a power supply is over-voltage, which occurs when the AC current is above the range that it's supposed to be operating at. This is destructive because the power supply may need to continue to operate beyond its rated range to keep from "dropping" the internal components. Dropping the internal components would be stopping the output of power, thus dropping the output voltage to 0. In the United States, over-voltage is rarely a problem because we all consume so much energy. However, if you have an over-voltage situation, your computer may suddenly stop operating, despite all of your lights being on.

Over-voltage will be hard to spot, but you may notice that your lights are brighter than they should be, or that your clock is running a little fast. For the most part, you'll have to get your multimeter out to see this problem.

Yet another enemy of a power supply is a sag. That is an unexplained, unpredictable loss in energy from the AC power line (see Figure 3.4). This isn't that much of a problem for the power supply itself, because it's not dealing with excess power that has to go somewhere; it's more of an issue that the power supply has a finite amount of stored energy within it and if the sag takes too long, it's possible that the power supply may not be able to "carry the load," or maintain the proper voltage to the PC.

Sags are going to show themselves as momentary blips in the lights, where all of the lights go out for a short period of time, less than ¼ of a second. You may also see the lights just dim for a short period of time, but rarely can someone perceive that the power just went down, and not off.

The final enemy of a power supply is a brownout. This is a long sag. In other words, the voltage coming in is below the amount that it should be. Brownouts are named because they tend to make light bulbs glow dimmer, giving them a more brownish tint. In the United States, brownouts are all too common. They most often occur in the middle of summer when everyone is running air conditioners to keep cool. Brownouts, like sags, are not so much the problem for the power supply as the components that the power supply is trying to power. If the brownout causes the

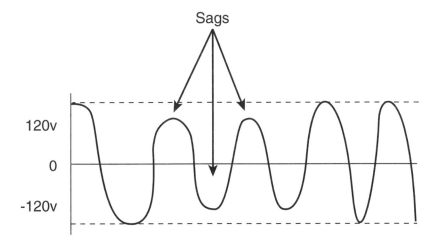

Figure 3.4 ■ A sag occurs when the AC power does alternate between the +120 and –120 volts.

voltage to drop beyond the operating range of a power supply, the load will be dropped (the PC will shut off).

Something that's not an enemy to power supplies, but is certainly a problem for PCs, is a blackout—the complete loss of power. While to the power supply it's much like being turned off, it can be a very frustrating moment if you forgot to save your work.

THE WHOLE TRUTH

Not all power supplies are created equal. Not all of them have the same safe operating range for under- and over-voltages, nor do they suppress spikes and fill in sags the same way.

It has been the author's experience that PC Power & Cooling makes some of the best power supplies on the market. They have the greatest operating input voltage range, the tightest regulation of output voltage, and the highest capacitance. If you're building a system from scratch, or need to replace a power supply, check them out. Their Web address is www.pcpowercooling.com.

LAB
3.2

DETERMINE APPROPRIATE SOLUTIONS TO POWER PROBLEMS

There are three basic lines of defense to prevent your power supply from being eaten by the problems we talked about so far. Table 3.1 lists these options and shows you which problems they can help resolve.

Table 3.1 ■ Defenses Against Power Supply Problems

Solution	Spike	Over-Voltage	Sag	Brownout	Blackout
Surge suppresser	✓				
Line conditioner	✓*	✓*	✓*	✓*	
SPS/UPS**	✓*	✓	✓	✓	✓

* There are some limits to the capabilities that may prevent it from being able to handle extreme cases.

** SPS is a Standby Power Supply; UPS is an Uninterruptable Power Supply. They can be functionally equivalent in most environments.

If you look carefully at the preceding table, you'll notice that there's not a single solution to the power problem that will address all of your problems. Each device has things that it can and cannot do. In many cases, you'll use a surge suppresser and a SPS/UPS to completely protect your PC from unwanted power problems.

The most basic form of protection for your PC, and the one that should be deployed in every office, is a surge suppressor. From the table, you'll see that surge suppressors are only helpful in controlling spikes. However, spikes are by far the most potentially damaging kind of power problem that can occur.

Surge suppressers work by shunting, or diverting, excess energy away from the PC before it gets there. Surge suppressers have a variety of ways in which they can do that, but by far the most popular method for surge suppression is metal-oxide varistors (MOVs). MOVs work well for surge suppression because below a certain voltage threshold they have a very high resistance, and thus little or no current slips through.

However, once power exceeds a certain threshold, they begin to lose their resistance. The result is that the excess voltage, in this case a spike, is clipped, or drawn down, to the resistance threshold of the MOV.

MOVs are typically placed between all three lines of a power circuit so that a spike may occur on any line within the circuit and the surge sup-

LAB 3.2

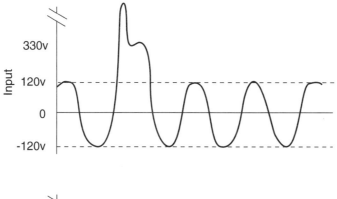

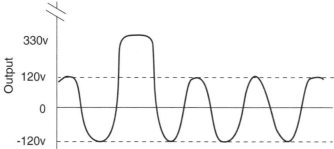

Figure 3.5 ■ A surge suppressor prevents surges from getting out of hand.

pressor will still be effective. Although spikes occur primarily on the hot line (where the power comes from), they are also known to occur on the neutral and ground legs of a circuit as well.

This all sounds good until you learn that MOVs eventually do damage to themselves internally as they shunt the power off. Pathways form in the inside of the MOV making it less and less capable of diverting energy until eventually it fails to be of any value at all.

The amount of power that a MOV can shunt off before becoming ineffective is measured in joules. Joules are used because they are a measure that accounts for both level (voltage) and duration (amperage). The higher the joules rating, the better the surge suppressor.

The other critical number that you should be aware of is clamping voltage. This is the voltage where the MOV activates and starts diverting energy. The lower this number is, the better. Typically the clamping voltage will be 330, 400, or 600 volts.

Units with higher joules ratings and voltage ratings are most often found protecting entire buildings and are often called transient voltage surge suppressors (TVSS) and are directly wired into the electrical system of the building.

Now that we understand the basic workings of a surge suppressor and the values that determine their length of service and effectiveness, it's time to talk about how they should be used.

One thing about surge suppressors that isn't obvious to most people is that they work in parallel with the circuit they are protecting. They don't have to be positioned directly between the path of the spike and the computer they are protecting. They just have to be relatively close to it. This means that you don't need to physically plug in computers and other electronics directly to a surge suppressor. Plugging them into the same outlet, or in fact even the same circuit within the home or office, will have the same effect.

This is a powerful thing. It means that if you have two computers on opposite sides in the same office, you need not have a surge suppressor for each computer, if they are on the same electrical circuit. In practice, however, we often use a surge suppressor at each electronic device so that we distribute the amount of power that must be shunted between multiple surge suppressors, increasing the overall life of each single suppressor.

The proximity to the electronic device is important because causes of spikes that occur after the surge suppressor will still impact the computer. If you have a surge suppressor at the entrance from the power company and you have an internal air compressor or air conditioner that starts up and causes a spike, it will still hit the electronics.

The way that most people combat this is to place larger, higher clamping voltage surge suppressors at the entrance of power to the building and then place smaller, lower clamping voltage surge suppressors at each PC. This works well because a higher clamping voltage means a higher joule rating and a lower cost. In that way, the largest spikes are clipped by the cheapest surge suppression equipment.

Line conditioners are different. They are essentially a power supply that outputs the same voltage on output as on input. This means that they are designed to take 120 volts of power in and put 120 volts of power out.

This seems silly at first. Why waste the effort to build a device that does nothing? The answer is that it doesn't do nothing. Because of the process that is used to convert the power, it has the ability to adjust how it works to smooth out sags, to soften spikes, and to bump up brownouts, or bump down over-voltages.

**LAB
3.2**

When working with electricity, you'll remember that are two numbers of which you need to be aware: amperage and voltage. Because of the relationship between voltage and amperage, it is possible to increase or decrease voltage by altering the way to convert the power. For instance, we've been talking about a power supply, which converts AC current into DC current a PC can use. It requires a relatively low amperage of 120-volt AC current to produce several amps of 12- and 5-volt DC current. A high voltage at low amperage is the same as a low voltage circuit at high amperage.

There are limits to how much you can translate the power, but all you need to know is that you can get more voltage out of a circuit if you're willing to sacrifice amperage.

A line conditioner works to increase or decrease voltage slightly to keep it within a narrow range that it expects the power supply can handle. It does this by using a large transformer to manipulate how it outputs power. Because line conditioners use transformers at their base, they have a certain amount of capacitance and as a result will smooth off a spike or a sag, making it look more like regular current; however, they don't eliminate them, they just soften them a bit (see Figure 3.6). They still make it through to the power supply or other electronic equipment.

There are certain power events that occur that only a SPS/UPS can handle. The one most familiar to everyone is a blackout, or power outage. The ability to keep a computer running during a power outage is the primary selling point for a SPS/UPS in today's market.

Before we talk about the role that an SPS/UPS plays in protecting your computer, we need to first understand how they work differently and what is sold most often in today's market.

An SPS, or Standby Power Supply, is little more than a battery, a charger, and an inverter, which is designed to turn on whenever the power coming from the wall isn't suitable to continue operating the PC. This is the most common type of power backup device sold today, although most vendors utilize the UPS moniker for these devices, despite the fact that it's technically incorrect.

A UPS, or Uninterruptable Power Supply, is the same combination of charger, battery, and inverter as an SPS, except that the UPS always operates on the battery power. There is no switching between the line voltage and the battery. This is an important difference for several reasons.

First, a UPS will consume more power than an SPS. Because there's some inefficiencies in the conversion of AC current to DC current and back to AC current, there will be more power consumed for the same amount of

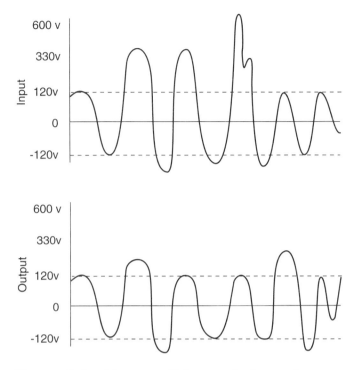

Figure 3.6 ■ Line conditioners help to dampen power problems.

load. Because an SPS doesn't incur these inefficiencies unless it has to transfer power to the batteries, the overhead is lower.

Second, a UPS will completely filter out all disturbances from the outside. Because the inverter is completely separate from the input power supply and there's a very high capacitance device (called a battery) between the incoming power and the inverter, almost none of the power problems can be passed through.

Third, because there's no switchover, devices that require constant power don't have any problems using a UPS where they might have problems with an SPS. When an SPS transfers load to the batteries in the event of a blackout or brownout, there's a few milliseconds where there is no power flowing. During this time, it's necessary for the capacitance of the device to carry it through. If there's not enough capacitance, the device will shut down, and the whole point of the SPS will have been defeated.

An SPS or a UPS will protect your computer from brownouts, blackouts, and over-voltage conditions. Whenever these problems occur, the battery is engaged and will output the correct voltage. However, an SPS will not

**LAB
3.2**

address problems with spikes. Nor will an SPS address sags – unless it decides that it is a brownout.

For high-end implementations, it is most often recommended that you have a building-level surge suppressor, followed by a UPS device and power strip type surge suppressor. This provides the best cost of ownership, and a complete power solution. However, that's the high end. Most PCs are recommended to have at least a surge suppressor on them. Line conditioners are rarely used in today's environment except in limited, specialized cases.

LAB 3.2 EXERCISES

3.2.1 IDENTIFY POWER PROBLEMS AND DETERMINE APPROPRIATE SOLUTIONS

Because of the nature of this topic, this Exercise will depart slightly from the interactive format of many of the other Exercises in this workbook.

a) For this Exercise, use your understanding of the types of problems and solutions discussed in this Lab to fill in the following table. This table will become a good reference to use when studying for this portion of the exam.

Power Problems and Solutions

Problem	Description	Detection	Potential Solutions
Spike			
Over-Voltage			
Sag			
Brown-Out			
Black-Out			

b) The next table lists the potential solutions to power problems that were discussed in this Lab. Your assignment here is to briefly describe how each solution operates and what its limitations are, if any.

Solutions and Descriptions

Solution	Description	Limitations
Surge Suppressor		
Line Conditioner		
Standby Power Supply		
Uninterruptible Power Supply		

LAB 3.2 EXERCISE ANSWERS

3.2.1 ANSWERS

a) For this Exercise, use your understanding of the types of problems and solutions discussed in this Lab to fill in the following table. This table will become a good reference to use when studying for this portion of the exam.

Table 3.2 ■ Power Problems and Solution

Problem	Description	Detection	Potential Solutions
Spike	Spikes are an unexpected increase in voltage that can be as much as 6000 volts. The PC's power supply compensates by distributing the excess power to the PC's components.	Hardly noticeable, but it may be a momentary flickering in the lights as they receive a slightly larger burst of energy.	Surge suppressor, line conditioner (except in extreme cases), UPS (except in extreme cases).
Over-Voltage	This occurs when the AC current is above the range that it's supposed to be operating at. This is destructive because the power supply may need to continue to operate beyond its rated range to keep from "dropping" the internal components.	Over-voltage will be hard to spot, but you may notice that your lights are brighter than they should be, or that a clock that you have is running a little fast. For the most part, you'll have to get your multimeter out to see this problem. The computer may stop working.	Line conditioner (except in extreme cases), SPS/UPS.

LAB 3.2

Table 3.2 ■ Power Problems and Solution (continued)

Problem	Description	Detection	Potential Solutions
Sag	A sag occurs when the AC power does alternate between the +120 and -120 volts. It's possible that the power supply may not be able to "carry the load" or maintain the proper voltage to the PC.	Sags show themselves as momentary blips in the lights, You may also see the lights just dim for a short period of time.	Line conditioner (except in extreme cases), SPS/UPS.
Brownout	Brownouts are simply log sags during which voltage coming in is below the amount that it should be.	They usually make light bulbs glow dimmer. If the brownout causes the voltage to drop beyond the operating range of a power supply, the PC will shut off.	Line conditioner (except in extreme cases), SPS/UPS.
Blackout	A complete loss of power. This is not in and of itself damaging to the power supply.	A complete loss of power.	SPS/UPS.

b) The next table lists the potential solutions to power problems that were discussed in this Lab. Your assignment here is to briefly describe how each solution operates.

Table 3.3 ■ Solutions and Descriptions

Solution	Description	Limitations
Surge Suppressor	Surge Suppressors work by shunting, or diverting, energy away from the PC before it gets there.	Once power exceeds a certain threshold, they begin to lose their resistance. Each hit reduces the life of the suppressor.
Line Conditioner	Line conditioners are a power supply is designed to take 120 volts of power in and put out 120 volts of power. This enables it to adjust how it works to smooth out sags, to soften spikes, and to bump up brown outs, or bump down over-voltages.	While they can smooth out sags or soften spikes, they cannot eliminate them entirely, resulting still in some effect on the power supply.

**LAB
3.2**

Table 3.3 ▪ Solutions and Descriptions (continued)

Solution	Description	Limitations
Standby Power Supply	An SPS is little more than a battery, a charger, and an inverter, which is designed to turn on whenever the power coming from the wall isn't suitable to continue operating the PC.	An SPS does not address spikes or sags (unless it thinks the sag is a brown out). Also, when an SPS transfers load to the batteries, there's a few milliseconds where there is no power flowing. If there's not enough capacitance in the device itself to get through the transfer, it will shut down for lack of power.
Uninterruptible Power Supply	A UPS is the same combination of charger, battery, and inverter as an SPS, except that the UPS always operates on the battery power. There is no switching between the line voltage and the battery.	The only drawback with a UPS is that it will consume more power than an SPS. There are no real limitations to a UPS.

LAB 3.2 SELF-REVIEW QUESTIONS

1) DC stands for Direct Current, which means that it never changes its direction.
    a) _____True
    b) _____False

2) A PC requires which type of current in order to operate?
    a) _____AC
    b) _____DC
    c) _____Switching

3) Which type of power supply uses digital circuitry, making it more susceptible to a wider range of problems?
    a) _____Linear
    b) _____Switching
    c) _____Alternating
    d) _____All power supplies use digital circuitry

LAB
3.2

4) Which of the following is not a problem for the power supply?
    a) _____Spike
    b) _____Sag
    c) _____Brownout
    d) _____Blackout
    e) _____These are all problems for the power supply.

5) Which of the following is the most potentially damaging power problem?
    a) _____Spike
    b) _____Sag
    c) _____Over-voltage
    d) _____Brownout
    e) _____Blackout

6) Which of the following best describes a joule?
    a) _____ The unit of measurement used to determine the amperage at which a surge suppressor's MOV becomes ineffective.
    b) _____The voltage at which the MOV activates and starts diverting energy.
    c) _____The unit of measurement used to determine the amount of power, both voltage and amperage, that a surge suppressor's MOV can effectively shunt.
    d) _____The unit of measurement used to determine the voltage at which a surge suppressor's MOV becomes ineffective.

7) An MOV's clamping voltage is typically which of the following?
    a) _____300, 400, or 600 volts
    b) _____330, 440, or 660 volts
    c) _____330, 430, or 630 volts
    d) _____330, 400, or 600 volts

Quiz answers appear in Appendix A, Section 3.2.

LAB
3.2

L A B   3.3

LASER AND HIGH-VOLTAGE HAZARDS

LAB OBJECTIVES

After this Lab, you will be able to:

✓ Discuss Risks Associated with Power Components

An important part of working on a system is knowing what not to work on. This section discusses potentially dangerous devices within a computer that require special care and, sometimes, specialized tools.

IDENTIFY HAZARDS WITH LASER DEVICES

Human eyes are amazing things. They allow us to see in a wide variety of lighting conditions. They allow us to see on the brightest summer day, and into very dark nights. Our eyes are remarkable because they can focus on something very close, or very far away, and everything in between.

However, our eyes can be permanently damaged by excessively bright lights. Whenever you hear about a solar eclipse, the newscasters are constantly warning you not to view the sun directly because looking directly at it for very long will cause permanent eye damage. The same issue applies to bright lights here on earth.

Most of us wouldn't stare directly into a floodlight for any length of time, or stare at the lights in a football stadium. We recognize that the lights are very bright and might cause eye damage, or we simply recognize that staring into them causes us pain.

Lasers are another kind of light that shouldn't be looked directly into. Lasers emit light similar to a bright spotlight, or the sun as viewed from earth, but in a very narrow beam, and in a very narrow area of the spectrum of light that we are capable of seeing (usually red).

Lasers are really just a special kind of light-emitting device, like a flashlight, or candle, or a floodlight. They put off a certain amount of photons per second. In the case of a candle, the number of photons emitted is fairly small, and they are not at all focused. They go off in all directions. That's why a candle is not particularly harmful if viewed directly.

NEVER STARE INTO ANY LIGHT

It's important to realize that the destructive effects of staring into light are still there even if the light is smaller; it's just that your eye can better compensate for the problem.

In your eye there are two types of light receptors. There are the rods, which are spread out throughout the eye that allow you to see black and white. They are more sensitive to light, and that's why you can see some things when there's not much light. They are also able to handle greater amounts of light.

The other type of light receptor, cones, are concentrated in the center of the eye. They work in a much smaller range of light, but allow us to see color.

Because of the limited range of light that our cones can tolerate, the eye has an aperture mechanism, much like a camera. The aperture mechanism of our eye is our iris. It controls how big the opening into the eye is and thus how much light gets in.

With small light sources, the iris can close the aperture enough that damage can be reduced or eliminated, but the larger the light source, the less effective this closing down of the aperture is.

No matter what the light source, never look directly into it. Always look 30 degrees to any side of it. This will have the light primarily falling on your rods, which can better tolerate the light source.

A laser has a relatively low photon output count, however, those photons are very focused and operate on a very tight frequency. These two combinations are potentially dangerous to our human eyes because there's a high concentration of photons in a small area.

If lasers are so hazardous to our eyes, why do we use them?

Well, because there are certain things that lasers are very good at. The first, which we've all probably heard of, is surgery. A laser, being a very tight beam, can cut through (or actually burn through) flesh with great precision. Because the laser burns its way through (rather than cut as a blade) blood vessels automatically seal. This can be critical to certain types of medical operations.

Lasers are also used for cutting through metal, burning or melting their way through with great speed and accuracy. This also results in less waste because the traditional saw method would remove some of the metal and deposit it on the floor as metal shavings.

In a PC, lasers are very good at burning information onto a special disk, but are most often used to read information that has been stored on a CD or DVD-ROM. This is done by shining a low-power laser at the disk and reading whether the light is absorbed or reflected. Being absorbed or reflected communicates the basic binary (1/0) information that the computer needs to store and retrieve information.

Lasers are also used in printers to activate a photoreactive drum that the toner adheres to. It's the process of using a laser to define the pattern of toner in a laser printer that gave the laser printer its name.

IDENTIFY NON-SERVICABLE, HAZARDOUS, HIGH-VOLTAGE EQUIPMENT

We've been working with things through the course of the last few chapters that you can replace, that you can fix, or that you can work on. This section is specifically reserved for those things that you can replace, but shouldn't attempt to fix or work on.

There's a reason for this. The parts that we're discussing here contain hazardous materials, or more likely, high voltages, which can be harmful, or in rare cases fatal, if you should come in contact with them.

THE WHOLE TRUTH

Our bodies are basically huge electrochemical machines that work on minute chemical changes and electrical impulses. When our bodies come in contact with a huge source of power, we overload. Our nervous and our muscular systems don't know how to handle such high voltages so they shut down momentarily, or permanently. Even a momentary shutdown may cause damage, however. Our heart and lungs will be momentarily interrupted in their continuous job of making sure that we have the oxygen we need to live. Even a relatively small pause in the oxygen we get can cause our brain or muscles to be permanently damaged.

Remember in our previous discussion of power protection devices that we mentioned the concept of capacitance—the amount of power held by a device or component. In the case of the devices that we're going to talk about here, there's a very high capacitance at a very high voltage. These two characteristics mean that hazardous levels of power can be maintained in the devices for a long time after the power is turned off.

There are two primary devices that are of concern for high voltages. They are the power supply and the monitor, or CRT (Cathode Ray Tube). The power supply converts the AC voltage from the wall into the DC voltage that the PC needs and as a part of that process has a high-voltage, high-capacitance property, meaning that it holds the 120 volt input current for a long time after the power has been removed. It is for this reason that you should **never** open a power supply. If the power supply is bad, replace it; don't open it up.

THE WHOLE TRUTH

There's a temptation to replace a power supply fan that has gone bad with a new fan. Resist this urge. If the fan has gone bad, there are generally two things you can infer. The first is that the power supply wasn't put together all that well in the first place. Second, the power supply, at some point, has become excessively hot.

Replacing the fan may solve that problem, but the power supply is very likely to fail in time, so it's best to replace it as soon as you can.

The other potentially hazardous component is the monitor. Monitors work by directing electrons at the screen under the guide of a powerful magnet. Electrons are essentially pure electric energy. When they strike the front of the screen, they are really hitting a coating applied to the inside of the monitor called a phosphor. The phosphor glows for a short period of time when struck by the electrons. The different colors that can be displayed on a monitor come from a very tight grouping of the additive primary colors red, green, and blue. By striking the appropriate phosphors with a controlled amount of electrons, any color can be made.

All of these electrons flying around and the huge magnets needed to deflect them cause a need for very high voltage, high capacitance components. As a result, a monitor can maintain a high voltage for a long time after power is removed.

As with power supplies, never ever open a monitor, even to retrieve something dropped in it. The risks of electrocution are much greater than the chances that you'll retrieve anything.

LAB 3.3 EXERCISES

3.3.1 DISCUSS RISKS ASSOCIATED WITH POWER COMPONENTS

Because of the nature of this topic, this Exercise will depart slightly from the interactive format of many of the other Exercises in this workbook.

a) Which of the following PC components can be serviced in the field and why? Discuss risks associated with high voltages and other hazards.
- PC power supply
- Laptop battery
- CMOS battery
- PC motherboard
- Laptop display
- Color (or monochrome) monitor
- Disk drive
- CD-ROM or DVD drive
- Floppy drive

_____

_____

b) What precautions must one take before attempting to work on a PC or component removed from a PC?

_____

_____

LAB 3.3 EXERCISE ANSWERS

3.3.1 ANSWERS

a) Which of the following PC components can be serviced in the field and why? Discuss risks associated with high voltages and other hazards.

Answer: Power supplies are generally not field serviceable.

Because of the risk of exposure to dangerous chemicals, batteries should not be serviced (they can be replaced, however).

A PC motherboard can be serviced to the extent that removable components (such as memory, CPU, ROM chips) can be replaced.

Laptop displays are not considered field serviceable.

Because of their high voltages and large capacitors, monitors should only be serviced at qualified factory repair depots.

Disk drives are not field serviceable.

Be very careful with CD and DVD drives, as they contain lasers that can permanently damage eyesight.

Floppy drives are serviceable, but not worth the effort.

b) What precautions must one take before attempting to work on a PC or component removed from a PC?

Answer: Before working on a PC, it must be switched off and disconnected from any power supply (power cords must be unplugged; laptop batteries must be removed). Metallic jewelry should be removed. The PC chassis should be grounded. Finally, the PC should be serviced as though it is "hot" (powered up). Be very careful with metal tools, particularly those without insulated handles. To be absolutely sure, before touching a metallic component, measure its voltage with a voltmeter.

LAB 3.3 SELF-REVIEW QUESTIONS

1) Which of the following components is it okay to repair by yourself?
    a) _____Mouse
    b) _____Power Supply
    c) _____Monitor
    d) _____Fan
    e) _____You should not attempt to repair any of these components
    by yourself.

2) An ESD strap will prevent electrocution when working on a computer
    monitor.
    a) _____True
    b) _____False

3) Sunglasses are an effective means of protecting yourself against injury
    from lasers.
    a) _____True
    b) _____False

4) The risk of electrocution can be eliminated by turning off the computer
    and disconnecting the power cord.
    a) _____True
    b) _____False

    Quiz answers appear in Appendix A, Section 3.3.

L A B 3.4

ENVIRONMENTAL DISPOSAL PROCEDURES

LAB OBJECTIVES

After this Lab, you will be able to:

✓ Investigate Sources of Recycle and Disposal Information

One of the often-overlooked areas of PC maintenance is the need to manage the refuse that we generate. You've heard through the first three chapters of this book that it's often more economical to replace an item rather than try to repair it. This leaves the question of what to do with the original component when it needs to be discarded.

If we were talking about paper or biodegradable materials, there wouldn't be an issue; you would simply throw it into the nearest trash receptacle and that would be the end of it. However, we're talking about computer components that can break down into chemicals and metals that are harmful to the environment.

PROPERLY DISPOSE OF BATTERIES

Batteries often contain rare earth metals that can be harmful to the environment. Mercury is one element commonly used in the manufacture of batteries. It's also an element that's extremely toxic to humans. It's been carefully controlled in the manufacture of batteries over the last few years, but batteries still contain the element. There's also the issue of lead that is used in the manufacture of the batteries. It's not as harmful as mercury, but it still can cause problems with the environment.

LAB 3.4

Because of these metals, the disposal of batteries is tightly controlled. In fact, there are regulations that control the disposal of even household batteries, such as AA batteries. In addition to the federal guidelines on disposal of batteries and other potentially harmful materials into the environment, several states have enacted laws designed to further limit where batteries can be disposed of.

All batteries, including lithium-ion, nickel-cadmium, nickel-metal hydride, and lead-acid are subject to these disposal requirements. Because the regulations vary from state to state, it's best to contact the people who handle trash removal for your company for more information. They can generally either arrange for special disposal facilities for you, or put you in contact with a supplier that can remove batteries safely.

PROPERLY DISPOSE OF TONER KITS, CARTRIDGES, AND DEVELOPER

There is almost no way to recycle batteries. Once the charges have been expended and they can no longer be recharged, they must be disposed of because there is no effective way of recycling batteries today.

However, batteries represent a relatively small amount of waste when compared with the amount of waste generated by laser printers (and copiers). Laser printer supplies, both toner and developer, can be destructive to the environment and their sheer volume necessitates that we be cautious of how they are handled.

In most cases, when you buy a toner cartridge you can exchange your old cartridges for a small credit. At the very least, the vendor will accept the old cartridges for processing. This is how you should dispose of cartridges that you no longer want.

These cartridges are recycled and reloaded with toner and developer so that they can be resold. This not only prevents them from being a burden to dispose of, but also helps ensure that more are not made to fill a need.

PROPERLY DISPOSE OF CHEMICAL SOLVENTS AND CANS

Another source of environmental problems is the chemicals and solvents that we use to clean computers to keep them running. When leached into the environment, these chemicals can cause significant damage.

As with batteries, you should contact your sanitation provider to find out how and where to dispose of these chemicals. You should never dump them down the sink or dispose of them in any drain that connects to the public sewers. Any cans or bottles that the solvents came in must also be specially treated. You need to make sure that they are identified and treated as special hazardous waste.

READ MATERIAL SAFETY DATA SHEETS

In addition to the solvents and chemicals that you can safely identify by yourself, OSHA (Occupational Safety and Health Administration) has developed a series of data sheets on hazardous materials indicating hazards and their handling. These sheets are required, by OSHA, to be posted prominently in those organizations that work directly with these materials. Your organization probably doesn't work directly enough with these materials to be required to post these sheets, but you should be aware that they exist, and that they describe the handling of materials.

LAB 3.4 EXERCISES

3.4.1 INVESTIGATE SOURCES OF RECYCLE AND DISPOSAL INFORMATION

Because of the nature of this topic, this Exercise will depart slightly from the interactive format of many of the other Exercises in this workbook.

In this Lab, we have discussed the proper methods of handling and disposing of used computer consumables and equipment. For this Exercise, you should investigate and be aware of the following Web sites and see what their guidelines are for disposal and recycling.

```
www.epa.gov
www.recycles.com
www.educate.com/crc_webpage/index.html
```

LAB
3.4

Visit the Environmental Protection Agency's Web site (www.epa.gov) and perform a search for the words "computer monitor disposal."

a) What is the concern about recycling computer monitors?

_____

_____

Visit the Recycles Web site (www.recycles.com) and poke around a bit.

b) What is the primary purpose of the Recycles Web site?

_____

_____

Visit the Computer Recycling Center's Web site (www.educate.com/crc_webpage/index.html).

c) What is the primary purpose of the Computer Recycling Center?

_____

_____

LAB 3.4 EXERCISE ANSWERS

3.4.1 ANSWERS

For Question a, you visited the EPA's Web site.

a) What is the concern about recycling computer monitors?

Answer: This answer may vary depending on when you visit the EPA's site.

At the time this book is going to press, the current EPA regulations inhibit responsible recycling of CRT tubes because they contain the toxic lead oxide element. These requirements mean that recycled CRT glass must be transported and processed as a hazardous waste, which would impose non-trivial legal and economic burdens on such recycling. The EPA is currently trying to find a compromise on this issue, however.

b) What is the primary purpose of the Recycles Web site?

Answer: The Computer Recycle Center is an international resource for trading and recycling computer equipment and materials. At this site, you can purchase refurbished equipment or sell your old equipment, as well as buy new equipment and learn more about recycling computer parts.

c) What is the primary purpose of the Computer Recycling Center?

Answer: The Computer Recycling Center focuses on reusing computers in America's education system.

The Center accepts donations of all types of computer equipment, working or not (except for monitors, which must be working to be accepted). The Center then funnels this equipment through the educational system to provide high-school and college students with computers and computer parts.

LAB 3.4 SELF-REVIEW QUESTIONS

In order to test your progress, you should be able to answer the following questions.

1) When a laptop battery loses its charging capacity, you should throw it away.
   a) _____True
   b) _____False

2) Most solvents can be safely poured down a drain.
   a) _____True
   b) _____False

3) Mercury, an element that is generally non-toxic to humans but extremely toxic to animals and other wildlife, is one element commonly used to manufacture batteries.
   a) _____True
   b) _____False

4) Unlike laptop batteries, toner cartridges can be recycled.
   a) _____True
   b) _____False

5) What toxic element does CRT glass contain, making it an environmental hazard to dispose of and/or recycle?
   a) _____Mercury
   b) _____Lead
   c) _____Lead oxide
   d) _____Iron

Quiz answers appear in Appendix A, Section 3.4.

L A B   3.5

ELECTROSTATIC DISCHARGE

> ## LAB OBJECTIVES
>
> After this Lab, you will be able to:
>
> ✓ Recognize ESD Factors and Preventive Measures

Static electricity is a powerful thing. Normally, electricity flows in a slow, relatively stable current, moving from one point to another. But static electricity is different. Static electricity doesn't flow until a triggering event causes it to discharge.

HOW ESD WORKS

Static electricity pools up until it's discharged; when it does get discharged, it's discharged at a huge voltage. The static electric discharges that you're probably most familiar with is the little electric shocks that you get when you touch something metal after walking through a dry room with a shag carpet. We've all had that little spark run from our finger to that metal file cabinet, or the VCR, or computer.

That electric charge was probably in excess of 10,000 volts. However, there's very little amperage in the charge so it can't do you any harm. However, the electric circuits that operate at 5 volts are not very happy about getting 20,000 volts dumped into them.

Sometimes this rapid influx of energy will do something very obvious. It might blow the plastic molding off of a chip, or visibly char it. While these are two possibilities, they are not likely. The more frequent occurrence is that you have a small amount of static electricity built up that discharges into the chip and it appears that nothing bad has happened.

However, it is rarely the case that nothing bad has happened. What generally happens is the chip is "weakened." By that I mean it becomes more prone to failure, particularly to intermittent failure. The reason this is a cause of great concern is because intermittent failures can be the most costly failures to identify, and thus to correct.

If you have a component that's just acting "weird" or is randomly failing, it's possible that it's been exposed to electrostatic discharge at some point in its life and should be replaced.

**LAB
3.5**

WHAT CAUSES ESD?

We've now talked about what static electricity is and does, and how a static electric charge can build up, but we've not talked about what causes it to form, and how we can design workspaces to minimize its build up.

First, carpet is the father of static electricity. Although you can on occasion build up a static electric charge just from normal fabrics, carpets are by far the greatest cause of static electricity. In Chapter 1, we saw my workspace—it didn't have carpeting around where I worked. It·was completely devoid of this killer.

Second, in order for static electricity to form, it must be fairly dry. A relative humidity below 30 percent is particularly conducive to generating static electricity. This is why you most often see static electricity in the winter. In the winter, your furnace heats the air, reducing the relative humidity. The colder it is outside, the more heating the furnace must do on the inside and consequently the dryer the air gets.

PROTECTING YOUR PC

Even when you make your environment as static-resistant as possible, it will still build up. It will be in smaller quantities, perhaps even so small that you don't recognize it, but it will be there. That's why it's important to have ways of safely eliminating the electricity before it can reach the sensitive PC components that you'll be working on.

Probably the most common protection device is an antistatic wrist band. Sometimes disposable versions of these come with memory chips or components. They're disposable because they're not designed to hold up to continued use. They basically amount to a fabric (TyVek) over a conductive wire. You attach one end of the wire to an earth ground (or large metal object such as a file cabinet), and put the other end around your wrist. The earth ground will drain away the harmful static electricity.

If you frequently work on components, a permanent static electricity wrist strap is a good investment. Generally, they look like expandable wrist bands that have a wire coming off them. This wire can be clipped to an earth ground just as the disposable ones can.

LAB 3.5

THE WHOLE TRUTH

The best place to connect any ESD prevention tool is to the ground in your electrical outlets. Generally there's a good patch back to a real earth ground that will drain away any potentially dangerous static electricity.

However, before you do this make sure that your ground is both connected and is connected to ground. On rare occasions, electricians have misconnected the ground wire in an outlet, and thus may have accidentally put power on the ground.

You can test for this with a surge suppressor that has a ground indicator, a simple household wiring tester, or by checking the voltage differential between ground and neutral with your multimeter. (Neutral is the larger of the two blade holes, and ground is the round hole.)

There are also other protection options available to you including antistatic pads that you can either touch, or set the computer housing directly on, then touch the computer housing. There are antistatic sprays that can be used to reduce the amount of static built up in the area, and a wide variety of more exotic devices that you won't be asked about on the exam.

However, before you invest in any ESD protection tools, ask yourself how frequently you work with memory, or directly on the motherboard of a PC. If the answer is not often, you may be best served to follow a few simple rules.

First, when working on a PC, disconnect the power, then unplug the power supply from the motherboard, then plug the PC back in. From this point, try to maintain contact with the PC case at all times. Rest an arm on it, or in some other way maintain contact with it. This will prevent static electric charges from having the opportunity to build.

It's important that the motherboard be unplugged because ATX power supplies still supply power to the motherboard whenever they are plugged in. It's important that the PC be plugged in so that the case is connected to ground.

Second, whenever working outside of a PC, such as handling memory, try to maintain contact with a plugged in, metal case. This will drain away any static electricity.

 If the device is plugged in via an AC/DC transformer, it won't help drain static electric charges. You need something that's directly plugged into the wall.

This works because all devices with metal housings are required to connect that housing to ground. This is to protect people from unintentional electrocution because of a failure or manufacturing defect in the unit. However, it is a great help in controlling static electric charges.

LAB 3.5 EXERCISES

3.5.1 RECOGNIZE *ESD* FACTORS AND PREVENTIVE MEASURES

Because of the nature of this topic, this Exercise will depart slightly from the question/answer format of many of the other Exercises in this workbook.

Buy or borrow a hygrometer (a device used to measure relative humidity) and measure the humidity in your office (and computer room if there is one).

> **a)** Are there any differences between the humidity you measure and the acceptable range discussed in this Lab? If the humidity is below the acceptable range, are you noticing any static shocks and/or [otherwise] unexplainable equipment failures?

_____

_____

Record your readings; measure once a month throughout the year.

b) What, if any, antistatic safeguards are in use in your workplace?

_____

_____

LAB 3.5 EXERCISE ANSWERS

3.5.1 ANSWERS

a) Are there any differences between the humidity you measure and the acceptable range discussed in this Lab? If the humidity is below the acceptable range, are you noticing any static shocks and/or [otherwise] unexplainable equipment failures?

Answer: Your findings will vary, naturally, with your environment, but you will likely find that the relative humidity will fluctuate over the course of the year, along with the seasons and conditions outside your building.

THE WHOLE TRUTH

Relative humidity is just that—relative. But relative to what? To the temperature of the air.

Air can hold only so much water. It can hold less than its maximum, but not more. However, that's only half the picture. The amount of water that air can contain is directly relative to the air's temperature. Warmer air can hold more water than cooler air.

When air is heated, its relative humidity goes down because the air can hold more water. There's the same amount of water in the air, but there's a greater capacity so the ratio, or relative humidity, goes down.

b) What, if any, antistatic safeguards are in use in your workplace?

Answer: Again, your answers will vary, but see if any of the following are in use:
- Grounded antistatic mats
- Grounded wrist straps
- Antistatic carpet
- Antistatic tile floor

For each device that you have in use, be sure you know how to use it properly.

LAB 3.5 SELF-REVIEW QUESTIONS

In order to test your progress, you should be able to answer the following questions.

1) To prevent ESD, to what should the relative humidity in the room be kept?
   a) _____100%
   b) _____65%
   c) _____20%

2) ESD can be prevented by unplugging the computer before working on it.
   a) _____True
   b) _____False

3) Static electricity doesn't flow until a triggering event causes it to discharge.
   a) _____True
   b) _____False

4) Which of the following is not considered a protection option against ESD?
   a) _____Static electricity wrist strap
   b) _____Antistatic pads
   c) _____Antistatic sprays
   d) _____Antistatic tile floor
   e) _____All of these are protection options.

5) An AC/DC transformer is a convenient alternative to having a wall outlet in which to ground a device you are working on.
   a) _____True
   b) _____False

Quiz answers appear in Appendix A, Section 3.5.

LAB
3.5

C H A P T E R   3

TEST YOUR THINKING

The best way to really learn how to do something is often to just go ahead and do it. In this chapter, we covered cleaning and preventive maintenance procedures and techniques. For this project, select two systems on which to try your hand: one should be relatively clean—perhaps a new system or one where the user generally cares for it well; the second should be an older system or one that is exposed to a less computer-friendly environment.

You may want to move them both to a lab area or an open space where you can place them side by side with ample room for work space.

Once you have them in your work area, begin to follow the procedures for preventive maintenance and cleaning, one step at a time—first on the one system, then on the second system—completing each step on both machines before progressing to the next procedure.

1) In each case, note any differences in the appearance or condition of the "clean" vs. "dirty" system. This will give you a good understanding of the types of environmental influences systems are subjected to and their effects on the systems' components and performance.

2) Also, as you proceed through your preventive maintenance routine, keep in mind the other topics in this chapter on hazards and safety measures, and examine your components to see if any meet the criteria for disposal. If so, follow the recommendations set forth here for properly dealing with expired components.

CHAPTER 4

PRINTERS

You can have an entire network up and running on Monday, then spend the rest of the week trying to get the printers working.

—William Mark Steen

The printers section of the core exam expects you to know the different types of printers in use today, the major components of each, and how they work. You should know how to troubleshoot problems as well as pro-actively perform preventive maintenance. Lastly, you should be familiar with ways printers are connected to computers, through parallel, serial, and network connections.

L A B   4.1

BASIC PRINTING CONCEPTS AND COMPONENTS

LAB 4.1

LAB OBJECTIVES

After this Lab, you will be able to:

✓ Identify the Components of an Inkjet Printer

✓ Identify the Differences Between Printer Types

✓ Replace a Laser Printer's Toner

At the risk of sounding overly simplistic, a printer is any device that can take the data output generated by a user or application and put it on paper in the form intended. The types of printers in use today fall under the following categories:

- Daisy Wheel
- Dot Matrix
- Inkjet
- Laser

DAISY WHEEL

A daisy wheel printer is a carry-over from the days of typewriters. An actual wheel with characters on it is rotated to the appropriate position and the character is struck against the ribbon that deposits the inked character image on the paper. The printer is considered to be an "impact" printer because the paper must be struck. Daisy wheel printers are rarely used anymore, primarily because of the limitations they impose, namely, graphics are not possible, and the wheel can hold only one font.

The only components of the printer are the daisy wheel, an inked ribbon, the platen (against which the paper rests), and paper guides that advance it.

DOT MATRIX

Dot matrix printers work by creating an image or character out of a series of dots—each dot produced by a pin on a print head that pushes through a ribbon and strikes the paper. Like daisy wheel printers, dot matrix printers are considered to be "impact" printers, making them perfect choices when working with multipart forms.

Unlike daisy wheel printers, graphics can be produced because the pins can be manipulated to create almost any image. Lesser-quality printers typically have 9-pins, while those of higher quality have 24-pins. Besides the ribbon and print head, other components of the printer include the platen (the cylinder against which the paper moves) and some sort of traverse assembly to move the print head back and forth. Figure 4.1 shows a dot matrix printer.

Due to the activity involved, the print head can become quite hot and care must be taken when servicing the printer to avoid burning.

INKJET

Inkjet printers work by heating ink to a boiling point. The ink vaporizes through microscopic holes (jets) onto a print head. The hot ink is then sprayed onto the paper and forms the image. At no point in time does the print head come into contact with the paper, and thus inkjet printers utilize "impact-less" printing.

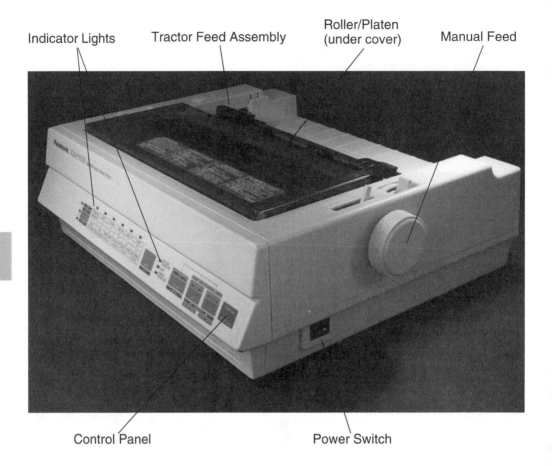

Indicator Lights   Tractor Feed Assembly   Roller/Platen (under cover)   Manual Feed

Control Panel   Power Switch

LAB 4.1

Figure 4.1 ■ **The dot matrix printer creates a series of dots to reproduce an image, be it a graphic or text.**

In addition to the inkjets and print head, other components of the printer include the cartridge (which holds the ink), the heating transistors (which heat the ink), a traverse assembly, and a "storage" area. The storage area, also known as the park position, is where the print head moves and "parks" itself to keep the ink from drying out while the printer is not in use.

Paper typically feeds from the top or side of the printer and comes out the front.

Figure 4.2 shows an example of an Inkjet printer with the cover opened so you can see the components.

Roller/Platen   Ink Cartridges and Print Head   Control Panel

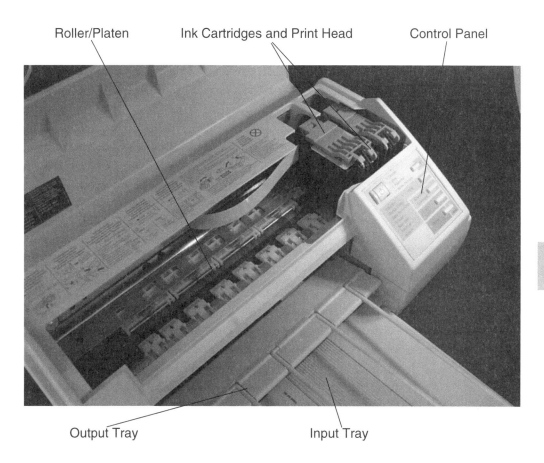

Output Tray   Input Tray

Figure 4.2 ■ Inkjet printers can deliver higher quality than dot matrix printers and are less expensive than laser printers.

Bubble jet printers are an advanced form of ink jet printer, and they function similarly. The vaporizing ink is pushed out through the hole, forming a bubble of ink, until it gets so large that it breaks off into a droplet. The remainder of the ink drops back into the ink chamber.

LASER

Laser printers are complicated beasts. Created by Xerox and Canon in the late 1980s, they are "impact-less" and work by transferring toner to paper and are more expensive than the other printers. Figure 4.3 shows a laser printer intended for a home user.

**LAB
4.1**

Indicator Lights   Power Switch   Paper Input Tray   Top Paper Output Tray

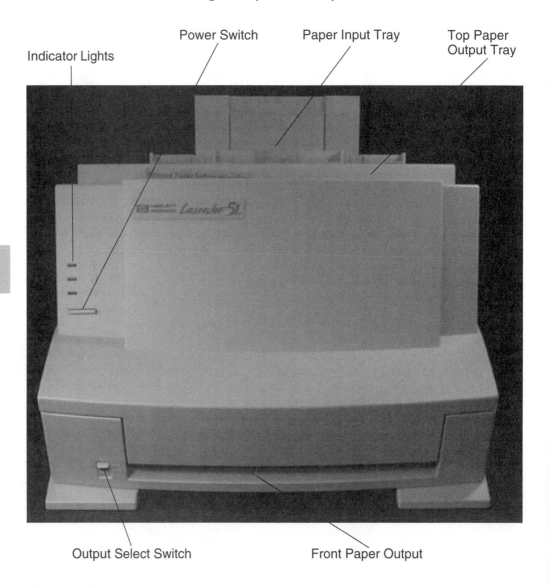

Output Select Switch   Front Paper Output

Figure 4.3 ■ Laser printer intended for a home user.

Regardless of the size or capacity, all laser printers work by following these principles:

1. A photosensitive drum is cleaned (electrically and physically)—this is known as the cleaning phase. It must be

cleaned before every page is printed so that it can generate the image. This is accomplished by a cleaning blade and a sweeping blade removing any residual toner. An erase lamp is then turned on the drum and neutralizes any charge that may be remaining from a previous operation.

2. The drum is charged to a high voltage (around 600 to 1000 volts) using an electrically charged wire called the primary corona wire. This wire never touches the drum but uses an electric field to charge the surface particles. The drum is negatively charged and loses this charge when light hits it (the negative charge has made it photo-conductive).

3. A laser beam reflects off a fixed mirror to write the image to the drum by changing the charge of the particles needed to create the image. The laser strikes the particles and they release some of their negative charge into the drum, making them more positive than those particles around them. How big is the area the laser strikes? It depends upon the dpi (dots per inch) rating of the printer. If the printer is rated at 300dpi, then the laser fires 300 individual times for every inch of the drum. If it is a 600dpi printer, then it fires 600 times per inch.

4. Known as the developing stage, toner is put on the drum where the charge indicates it is needed. A cylinder within the toner releases it so it can fall against a control blade. The control blade, also known as a restricting blade, keeps all the toner from dumping onto the drum. Instead, it holds it microscopically away from the drum and toner leaps from it to the drum where it is attracted by the more positively charged particles.

5. A transfer corona charges the paper with a positive charge (remember, the drum received a negative charge) and the drum transfers its image to the paper. This is accomplished by the toner particles moving from the drum to the paper. A static eliminator, or eliminator comb, now removes the positive charge from the paper.

6. The toner particles on the paper are only there because of the charge that was going on. They now must be made to stay there and this is done by the "fusing process." The paper is rolled between a heated roller and a pressure roller, and the toner is heated to the point where it melts into the paper.

LAB 4.1

7. The paper comes out of the printer and the process begins again. If the printer prints 17 pages per minute, this entire process is taking place every four seconds.

For the exam, memorize, memorize, memorize the steps as:

1. Cleaning

2. Charging or Conditioning

3. Writing

4. Developing

5. Transferring

6. Fusing

Memorize, as well, the differences between printer types, which you will overview as part of an Exercise.

**LAB
4.1**

THE WHOLE TRUTH

The term *duplexing*, in relation to printing, is used to indicate the ability to print on both sides of a sheet of paper. This is accomplished by a "duplexer," which takes the paper as it is ejected from the machine, turns it over, and feeds it back through again with the other side up.

LAB 4.1 EXERCISES

4.1.1 IDENTIFY THE COMPONENTS OF AN INKJET PRINTER

In the main Lab text, you saw a photo of an Inkjet printer with its cover opened and its components identified.

For this Exercise, you will physically remove the case from your inkjet printer and identify the various components within. Take another look at Figure 4.2 before beginning so you have an idea of what you'll find.

To begin, first power off your printer and unplug the power supply from the wall.

Next, disassemble the exterior components of the printer, such as the dust cover, paper tray, and outer panels. Check your printer's documentation as to where the screws for removal are located.

Once you have the exterior components removed, compare your printer to the one shown in Figure 4.2.

Identify the print head unit in your printer.

> **a)** What is the primary purpose of the print head unit on an inkjet printer?

_____

_____

LAB 4.1

Next, continue to identify the other components of your inkjet printer, including the storage area, the paper feed mechanism, and the traverse assembly. Take special note of the traverse assembly's components.

Finally, remove your ink cartridge or cartridges carefully and examine them and the print head unit to visualize how the process works.

> **b)** Briefly describe the process that an inkjet printer goes through to print a page.

_____

_____

4.1.2 IDENTIFY THE DIFFERENCES BETWEEN PRINTER TYPES

Something you will need to be able to do for the exam is know the differences between the different types of printers. The features and drawbacks of each type of printer were discussed in the main Lab text, but try to do this Exercise without peeking.

a) Complete the following table, which overviews the differences between printer types, by inserting Yes or No into the appropriate cell:

Table 4.1 ■ Differences in Printer Types

Printer	Impact	Letter Quality	Multiple Fonts	Graphics-Capable
Daisy wheel				
Dot matrix				
Inkjet				
Laser				

4.1.3 REPLACE A LASER PRINTER'S TONER

You saw in the Lab text that there are four types of printers currently in use, with a laser printer being one of the most popular. Replace the toner cartridge in a laser printer per the manufacturer's instructions. We will use an HP LaserJet 4000 as the example here.

Open the top cover and find the handle built into the toner cartridge.

Remove the toner by pulling up and out. A spring built on the cartridge will move to cover the opening and prevent spillage.

Place the toner in a sealable bag or container and unpack the new cartridge. Always turn the new cartridge clockwise and counterclockwise several times to loosen the toner.

Remove the strip of tape across the opening and install the new cartridge. The spring should flip back to indicate proper insertion.

a) What should be done with the old toner cartridge?

_____

_____

b) In the event of a toner spill, what should be used to clean it up?

_____

_____

LAB 4.1 EXERCISE ANSWERS

4.1.1 ANSWERS

a) What is the primary purpose of the print head unit on an inkjet printer?

Answer: The print head unit houses the print head nozzles. It extracts the ink from the cartridges and ejects onto the page.

b) Briefly describe the process that an inkjet printer goes through to print a page.

Answer: As explained earlier, inkjet printers work by heating ink to the boiling point and releasing the vaporized ink through a microscopic hole on the print head. As the paper is pulled through the printer rollers, the traverse assembly moves the print head unit back and forth while hot ink drops onto the paper and forms an image.

Inkjet printers can be either *unidirectional* or *bidirectional*. Unidirectional means that as the print head unit traverses the page back and forth, it prints in only one direction: left to right. Bidirectional means that it prints both left to right and right to left as it traverses the page. Bidirectional printers print every other line on the way back, which means twice as many lines can be printed during a print job, cutting the time of printing an entire page in half.

4.1.2 ANSWERS

a) Complete the following table, which overviews the differences between printer types, by inserting Yes or No into the appropriate cell:

Table 4.2 ■ Differences in Printer Types

Printer	Impact	Letter Quality	Multiple Fonts	Graphics-Capable
Daisy wheel	Yes	Yes	No	No
Dot matrix	Yes	No—"near letter quality"*	Yes	Yes
Inkjet	No	Yes	Yes	Yes
Laser	No	Yes	Yes	Yes

*The term "near letter quality" is used to describe a quality of printing that is not quite as good as that produced by a typewriter. A dot matrix printer, because of the dots used to make up the character, will create printed text that, although it may be adequate for its purpose, is not as high a quality as that created by a typewriter—or by other types of "letter quality"-designated printers, such as laser jets or daisy wheels.

4.1.3 ANSWERS

a) What should be done with the old toner cartridge?

Answer: NEVER discard it. It can be returned to the manufacturer for recycling, or refilled for additional use by a qualified company.

b) In the event of a toner spill, what should be used to clean it up?

Answer: Liquids should be avoided at all costs as they will make a mess of the fine toner. The best solution is to use a vacuum cleaner designed for toner spills. The design does not allow the toner to escape the sealed bag and thus does not present a safety hazard.

LAB 4.1 SELF-REVIEW QUESTIONS

In order to test your progress, you should be able to answer the following questions.

1) Which of the following produces a high-voltage negative charge in a laser printer?
    a) ___Primary corona wire
    b) ___Transfer corona
    c) ___Laser
    d) ___Drum

2) Against which of the following components of a dot matrix printer does the paper rest?
    a) ___Drum
    b) ___Plenum
    c) ___Print head
    d) ___Platen

3) Which of the following printers is not capable of producing graphics?
    a) ___Laser
    b) ___Inkjet
    c) ___Dot matrix
    d) ___Daisy wheel

4) Which of the following printers cannot be used to print multipart forms?
    a) ___Laser
    b) ___Inkjet
    c) ___Dot matrix
    d) ___Daisy wheel

5) When an inkjet printer is not in use, in what position should the print head be?
    a) ___Starting
    b) ___Park
    c) ___Medial
    d) ___Platen

    Quiz answers appear in Appendix A, Section 4.1.

**LAB
4.1**

L A B   4.2

CARE AND SERVICE OF COMMON PROBLEMS

LAB OBJECTIVES

After this Lab, you will be able to:

✓ Troubleshoot Dot Matrix Printer Problems

✓ Troubleshoot Inkjet Printer Problems

✓ Troubleshoot Laser Printer Problems

✓ Clean the Platen

Printers are wonderful devices when they work as they should. As with every other mechanical component, problems can and do occur. In this section, we will look at common problems with the different types of printers and in this Lab's Exercises, we'll explore preventive maintenance steps that should keep them from breaking down and help them last longer.

DAISY WHEEL

The biggest problem with a daisy wheel printer is its limited printing ability. Because it can do only one font and is incapable of producing graphics, you must make certain the output being sent to it can be printed by it.

An additional problem can be the paper feed. The paper can become jammed going into or out of the printer and care should be taken to line up the paper precisely.

 Because daisy wheel printers are much less common today than they once were, there is not much about them on the exam.

DOT MATRIX

A dot matrix print head reaches high temperatures and care must be taken to avoid touching it and getting burned. Most dot matrix printers include a temperature sensor to tell if the print head is getting too hot. The sensor will interrupt the printing to let the print head cool down, then allow the printing to start again. If this sensor becomes faulty, it can cause the printer to print a few lines, stop for a while, print more, stop, and so forth.

**LAB
4.2**

Some other common problems associated with dot matrix printers include:

- Incomplete images or characters, or white lines running through the text
- Print head not printing or moving
- Paper not feeding correctly
- Smudged or light output
- Paper jams
- Incorrect printer driver

INKJET

Inkjet printers have few problems that can be encountered. Among them are:

- Ink goops up on the paper
- Ink dries out too frequently
- Incomplete images or characters, or white lines running through the text
- Paper not feeding correctly

- Smudged or light output
- Blank pages printing or paper jamming
- Print head not printing or moving

LASER

Just as laser printers are the most complicated of the types (and offer the most capabilities), they also have the most that can go awry. A thermal fuse is included to keep the system from overheating, and if it becomes faulty, it can prevent the printer from printing. Many high-capacity laser printers also include an ozone filter to prevent the ozone output from the coronas reaching too high a level. On these printers, the filter should be changed as part of regular maintenance. This is different for every printer, so check the particular printer's manual for instructions.

Other common problems are:

- Blank pages print
- Dark spots print
- Garbled pages print
- Print quality problems

 It's important to note that we are only exploring hardware-related printing problems and solutions in this chapter. Software-related printing problems are covered in Chapter 11, "Diagnosing and Troubleshooting."

LAB 4.2 EXERCISES

4.2.1 TROUBLESHOOT DOT MATRIX PRINTER PROBLEMS

In the main Lab text, you saw a series of potential problems that could occur with dot matrix printers. In this Exercise, you will be asked to troubleshoot some of these problems on your own.

For each of the following problems, offer some troubleshooting techniques.

a) Incomplete images or characters, or white lines running through the text.

_____

_____

b) Smudged or light output.

_____

_____

c) What are some preventive maintenance techniques for dot matrix printers?

_____

_____

4.2.2 TROUBLESHOOT INKJET PRINTER PROBLEMS

In the main Lab text, you saw a series of potential problems that could occur with inkjet printers. In this Exercise, you will be asked to troubleshoot some of these problems on your own.

For each of the following problems, offer some troubleshooting techniques.

a) Ink goops up on the paper.

_____

_____

b) Print head not printing.

_____

_____

c) Ink dries out too frequently.

_____

_____

d) Characters are all complete, but appear faded, smudged, or display other problems.

_____

_____

e) Ink takes too long to dry.

_____

_____

f) What are some preventive maintenance techniques for inkjet printers?

_____

_____

4.2.3 TROUBLESHOOT LASER PRINTER PROBLEMS

In the main Lab text, you saw a series of potential problems that could occur with laser printers. In this Exercise, you will be asked to troubleshoot some of these problems on your own.

For each of the following problems, offer some troubleshooting techniques.

a) Blank pages print.

_____

_____

b) Dark spots print on the paper.

_____

_____

c) Garbled pages print.

_____

_____

d) Print quality problems.

_____

_____

e) What are some preventive maintenance techniques for laser printers?

_____

_____

LAB
4.2

4.2.4 CLEAN THE PLATEN

The paper in dot matrix and daisy wheel printers rests against a platen. The platen holds the paper in place and guides it through the printer. The platen can become dirty from the environment (dust and other particles) as well as from use (ink off the ribbon, paper shredding, and the like).

Find a dot matrix printer and clean the platen, thereby prolonging its life and increasing the quality of paper output.

a) What should be done before you begin cleaning the platen?

_____

_____

b) What should you clean the platen with?

_____

_____

LAB 4.2 EXERCISE ANSWERS

4.2.1 ANSWERS

For each of the following problems, offer some troubleshooting techniques.

a) Incomplete images or characters, or white lines running through the text.

Answer: For some reason, ink is not reaching the paper. Either there is something keeping the head from reaching the ribbon or the ribbon is not delivering ink to the paper.

The first measure is to try cleaning the print head. The print head should never be lubricated, but can be cleaned of debris with a cotton swab and denatured alcohol.

If this doesn't remedy the problem, it's possible that print pins are missing from the print head. The only remedy is to replace the print head.

If the print head is not at fault, make certain it is close enough to the platen to make the right image. The print head can be moved closer or further from the platen depending upon the thickness of the paper and other considerations.

b) Smudged or light output.

Answer: Here, ink is reaching the ribbon, but not in the correct amount.

The most common culprit is the ribbon. A tight ribbon or one that is not advancing properly will cause smudges or overly light printout. Where do I fix it? Check your owner's manual for specifics on tightening or loosening a gear for ribbon tension.

c) What are some preventive maintenance techniques for dot matrix printers?

Answer: Preventive maintenance includes keeping the print head dry and clean and vacuuming paper shreds from inside the machine.

4.2.2 ANSWERS

For each of the following problems, offer some troubleshooting techniques.

a) Ink goops up on the paper.

Answer: Ink is not being delivered to the paper in the correct amount.

If the ink becomes goopy on the paper, make certain the nozzles are clean and the heating transistors are working properly. Check the manufacturer's manual for cleaning and testing procedures.

b) Print head not printing.

Answer: If the print head unit moves but nothing is printed on the page, it's possible that your ink cartridge is empty or not installed properly. Check the cartridge(s) to make sure that they are not empty and that they are seated in place properly. Perform the cleaning technique outlined in the owner's manual, and try printing again.

Another problem that frequently occurs is that the tape that initially covers the ink nozzles when the cartridge is first removed from its package has not been removed prior to installing it in the printer. Remove the cartridge from the printer and make sure no tape covers the nozzles. Also, take care when installing printer cartridges; damage to the cartridge contacts can keep the printer from properly reading the status of the cartridge, resulting in improper printing.

LAB 4.2

c) Ink dries out too frequently.

Answer: This problem is most commonly due to the print head not parking itself properly in the storage area. Be sure that the head reaches the park position after print jobs are completed.

d) Characters are all complete, but appear faded, smudged, or display other problems.

Answer: The culprit behind this behavior is frequently the use of an incorrect paper type. If the paper bond or weight used is too light or too heavy for the type of printer, this kind of behavior can occur. Also, use of inexpensive "glossy" or lacquered paper can lead to smudged ink because the ink cannot properly bond to the glossy surface of the paper.

e) Ink takes too long to dry.

Answer: This can be the result of too high a water content in the ink. This frequently occurs when you buy a "generic" cartridge and not one from printer vendor or manufacturer.

f) What are some preventive maintenance techniques for inkjet printers?

Answer: Routinely perform head cleaning procedures, replace ink cartridges that are empty, and routinely clean the paper feed area of all dust, paper shreds, and other foreign items.

Never use oil or any kind of cleanser inside the printer. Instead, use a soft, dry cloth to remove any ink or paper debris.

Also, use caution when using ink cartridge refill kits, which are popular alternatives to buying completely new cartridges. Some of these refill kits use different types of ink than cartridges that come complete and ready to install. Furthermore, the ink refill kits can be messy!

4.2.3 ANSWERS

For each of the following problems, offer some troubleshooting techniques.

a) Blank pages print.

Answer: Verify that there is toner in the cartridge. If it is an old cartridge, you can often shake it slightly to free up toner before replacing. If it is a new cartridge, make sure the sealing tape has been removed from the cartridge prior to placing it in the printer.

Check also that the printer isn't feeding too many pages at one time. This can happen with paper stock that is too light for the rating of the printer.

Another reason for this behavior has nothing to do with the printer itself, but rather that the actual file being printed contains blank pages, either intentionally or inadvertently. This can happen when document revision cycles fail to weed out extra page breaks.

b) Dark spots print on the paper.

Answer: The most likely culprit here is too much toner. Run blank pages through the printer to clean it. Run a test pattern through the printer to verify that the problem is fixed before returning the printer to active service.

c) Garbled pages print.

Answer: Make sure you are using the right printer driver in your application.

d) Print quality problems.

Answer: See if your printer has the ability to turn RET (Resolution Enhancement Technology) on and off. This is what allows the printer to use partial-size dots for images that are rounded. If it is turned off, turn it back on. You can find whether your printer is RET-capable or not in the owner's manual. Also, check the printer's software interface—it might be operating at a different print quality level than you are expecting, whether that is "best", "medium", or "draft."

e) What are some preventive maintenance techniques for laser printers?

Answer: Preventive maintenance, in addition to the ozone filter, includes:

- Never reuse paper that has been through the printer once. Although it may look as if there is nothing on it, you are repeating the charging and fusing process on a piece of paper that most likely has *something* already on it.
- Change the toner when needed. **Never** under any circumstances throw away a laser cartridge—they are to be recycled, and most toner manufacturers participate in a recycling program of some type. The toner cartridge which usually comes shipped sealed in a black plastic light-resistant bag, should never be exposed to light for longer than a few minutes. Figure 4.4 shows a common toner cartridge.
- Clean any toner that accidentally spills into the printer with a dry, lint-free cloth. Bear in mind that spilled toner in the paper path should clear after running a few blank pages through. If toner gets on

LAB 4.2

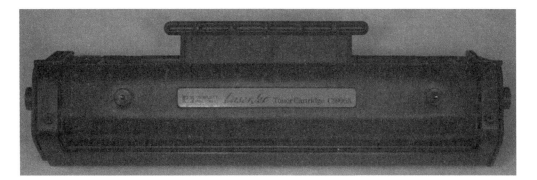

Figure 4.4 ■ Laser toner cartridges are shipped in a black plastic light-resistant bag to prevent exposure to light.

your clothes, wipe them with a dry cloth and wash them with cold water (hot water works like the fusing process to set ink into the material).

*   Clean any paper shreds/dust/dander that find themselves deposited in the printer. Pressurized air is the most effective method of removal. Vacuuming is another accepted alternative.
*   Keep the drum in good working order. If it develops lines, replace the drum.

GENERAL PROBLEMS

Other printing problems that can occur include:

*   Computer won't work while printer is printing—If your operating system supports background printing (such as spooling), make certain those features are turned on.
*   Print job being clobbered by another—If you are sharing a network printer, check the printer timeout settings on your workstation. If the number of seconds there is too low, a printer can think it has received all of a print job when it has not, and accept the next incoming job.
*   Printing stops before it is done—Check the power being delivered to the printer, particularly if it is a laser printer. Because of the high charges and other operations going on, the laser printer will pull a lot of power. If you are sharing a circuit with a number of other things, problems will occur. A typical workgroup laser printer consumes 330 watts when printing, requires a minimum of 8 amps circuit capacity, and has a line voltage requirement of 50-60 Hz.
*   Print job doesn't appear when/where expected—First, check to see if the printer cable is properly seated into the computer interface; if you're printing across a network, check to see if your network cable is properly plugged in. Next, check to make sure you have the right printer selected through your application. If you don't select a specific printer, the computer will use the "default" printer, which may be different from the one you intended to use. If you are printing to a network printer, can other computers print to that printer? If they can, then the problem is specific to the computer; if no one can print to the printer, then the problem is at the printer or at the print server. Can you print from

other applications other than this one that seems to be having the problem? If so, then the problem is application specific.

4.2.4 ANSWERS

a) What should be done before you clean the platen?

Answer: Always turn the printer off and disconnect it from power. Failing to do so could cause considerable harm to you or the printer.

b) What should you clean the platen with?

Answer: Denatured alcohol is the all-purpose cleaner in the technician's toolkit for just such a purpose.

LAB 4.2 SELF-REVIEW QUESTIONS

1) Which of the following is the part of a dot matrix printer that reaches high temperatures?
    a) ___Platen
    b) ___Print head
    c) ___Pins
    d) ___Corona

2) The print head of a dot matrix printer should be lubricated with which of the following?
    a) ___Machine oil
    b) ___Denatured alcohol
    c) ___WD-40
    d) ___It should not be lubricated

3) Dark spots are appearing on the pages produced by a laser printer. How can this be corrected?
    a) ___Change the drum
    b) ___Run blank pages
    c) ___Change toner
    d) ___Replace drivers

4) RET technology is used for which of the following?
   a) ___To spool print jobs to a queue
   b) ___To remove excess toner from the drum
   c) ___To create partial-sized dot output
   d) ___To reduce ozone output

5) When servicing a laser printer, which of the following should you replace?
   a) ___ozone filter
   b) ___drum
   c) ___transfer corona
   d) ___primary corona

Quiz answers appear in Appendix A, Section 4.2.

**LAB
4.2**

L A B   4.3

CONNECTIONS AND CONFIGURATIONS

LAB OBJECTIVES

After this Lab, you will be able to:

✓ Set Up a Network Printer

There are three basic ways that a printer can be connected:

1. Directly connected to a PC via the parallel port (the most popular method).
2. Directly connected to a PC via the serial port.
3. Connected to a network.

PARALLEL

Parallel ports allow eight bits at a time to be sent from the computer to the printer. This allows for sending all the bits for one byte of data at one time (eight bits making a byte).

The standard connection on the back of the computer is a 25-pin female DB. A 25-pin male connector exists on one end of most cables, and a 36-pin Centronics connector on the printer end. Figure 4.5 shows a cable with a Centronics connection on one end and a DB-25 on the other.

Centronics (Male) Connector

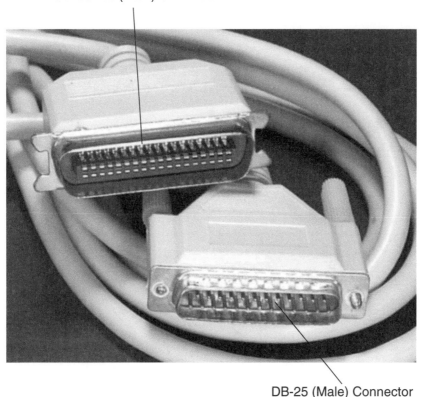

DB-25 (Male) Connector

Figure 4.5 ■ Centronics connection on one end and a DB-25 on the other.

A parallel cable can be 10 feet long without needing something to boost the signal. The most common length is six feet, severely limiting the distance between the PC and where the printer can be placed.

Several enhancements to parallel ports and printing have appeared over the years, including Enhanced Parallel Ports (EPP) and Extended Capability Ports (ECP). For the exam, know that much of the functionality these provided were rolled into the standard IEEE 1284. In its simplest form, IEEE 1284 is a specification for bi-directional printing. Rather than data flowing only to the printer from the computer, data (often unsolicited) can also flow from the printer to the computer. This is useful for sending messages to the user, such as being out paper or low on toner, for example.

SERIAL

Serial communications exchange one bit at a time, and thus printing is much slower than with a parallel connection. The benefit is that the cable length has now grown to 25 feet, giving you more flexibility in where the printer can be placed in relation to the computer.

NETWORK

A printer can be added to a network in two ways:

1.   It can be connected to the serial or parallel port of a PC or server that is then shared with the network.
2.   It can be directly connected to the network.

The benefit of the latter method is that it does not require a direct connection to a particular computer and can function independently. A network interface card (NIC) is installed in the printer, allowing a network cable to connect it directly to a hub or outlet port. By using a hub, which has a parallel port on one side and a network interface on the other, any printer can be shared by any computer on the network. Most network printers are hosts running TCP/IP or DLC (Data Link Control) networking protocols—both of which are addressed in the next chapter.

 For the exam, learn and remember the differences between the printer configuration types, as shown in Table 4.2.

LAB 4.3

Table 4.3 ■ Printer Configuration Types

	Parallel	Serial	Network
Number of bits simultaneously sent	8	1	N/A
Cable length	10 feet	25 feet	unlimited
Connectors	DB-25, 36-pin Centronics	DB-9, DB-25	Network Interface Card, serial or parallel

LAB 4.3 EXERCISES

4.3.1 SET UP A NETWORK PRINTER

Your task for this Exercise is to create a network printer on a Windows 95 or Windows 98 network.

To do so, you must first enable printer sharing on the computer to which the printer is attached (if you are unfamiliar with how to do this, it is covered in detail in Chapter 12, "Networks").

On the remote computer that will be printing to the shared printer, choose the My Computer icon from the Desktop. Next, select the Printers icon and Add Printer.

Choose for the location to be network (versus local) and click the Browse button to find the printer on the network.

Finish the steps in the wizard; the remote client is now using the network printer.

LAB 4.3

a) What is the last step of the process?

_____

_____

b) How many users can share this printer?

_____

_____

c) Where will print jobs go on the remote client if the network is down?

_____

_____

LAB 4.3 EXERCISE ANSWERS

4.3.1 ANSWERS

a) What is the last step of the process?

Answer: Always print a test page to make certain the configuration is correct.

b) How many users can share this printer?

Answer: There is no theoretical limitation.

As with all devices, the printer will get too busy if too many people try to print to it. Worse, the user using the client machine to which it is attached will notice a decrease in local performance as his hard drive services everyone else's print jobs.

c) Where will print jobs go on the remote client if the network is down?

Answer: They will spool to the local hard drive until the connection can be reestablished.

This is known as *deferred printing* and is used quite often on laptops – a user chooses print after finishing a letter while sitting in a hotel room and the job sits in the spool until the user gets back to the office and connects his laptop to a printer. This is also called working *offline*.

LAB 4.3

LAB 4.3 SELF-REVIEW QUESTIONS

1) What is the maximum distance a parallel port network printer connected to a server can be from that server?
   a) ____10 feet
   b) ____25 feet
   c) ____50 feet
   d) ____unlimited

2) When connected to a serial port on the server, the same printer in Question 1 can now be how far from the server?
   a) ____10 feet
   b) ____25 feet
   c) ____50 feet
   d) ____unlimited

3) When connected as a network printer, the same printer in the previous two questions can now be how far from the server?
   a) ___10 feet
   b) ___25 feet
   c) ___50 feet
   d) ___unlimited

4) A serial cable sends data to the printer by how many bits simultaneously?
   a) ___1
   b) ___2
   c) ___4
   d) ___8

5) A parallel cable sends data to the printer by how many bits simultaneously?
   a) ___1
   b) ___2
   c) ___4
   d) ___8

Quiz answers appear in Appendix A, Section 4.3.

**LAB
4.3**

C H A P T E R   4

TEST YOUR THINKING

This section is intended to provide you with an opportunity for additional self-study. The projects in this section are not part of the actual exam, but rather are included to give you a chance to further apply what you have learned in this chapter.

In the projects that follow, you are expected to test your knowledge using your own computing environment. For this reason, there is not necessarily one set of "right" or "wrong" answers—the solutions are highly dependent on the type of environment you have to work with. The "answers" that you will find at the companion Web site are more likely to include suggested results, and will include further references to help you.

SCENARIO: SET UP AND TROUBLESHOOT NEW PRINTER

1) You are the administrator for the ABC Company. You need to perform the following tasks:

   a) Install a printer on your Windows 95 computer.

   b) Share out the printer for use on the network.

   c) Assign permissions to the printer to enable its use.

   d) After sharing, the printer is malfunctioning so you need to clean the printer.

   e) After cleaning the printer, you need to test connectivity to it from another Microsoft Windows 95 machine on the network.

As you perform these tasks, document the necessary steps you take to complete this project.

SCENARIO: IDENTIFY AND LIST PRINTERS

1) Identify the different types of printers in use at your company.

2) Find the handbooks or service manuals for the printers in your company and investigate the procedures for cleaning, changing cartridges, and other basic maintenance functions.

CHAPTER 5

PORTABLE SYSTEMS

The explosion and diversity of the laptop market has created a demand that technicians get up to speed quickly with new and emerging technologies.

—Emmett

The Portable Systems section of the core exam expects you to know all you can about laptop computers, their components, and their problems. While portable systems represent a quickly growing segment of the marketplace, only about 5 percent of the A+ exam is dedicated to them. However, a broad understanding of portable systems will greatly enhance your strengths as a technician. Much of the discussion in this chapter builds upon the basic knowledge of traditional desktop systems that you have already obtained. When you finish with the Labs and Exercises in this chapter, you'll be a whiz at identifying and troubleshooting the many different components and component types available for a variety of portable systems.

For the exam, know that 1) portable systems are generally harder to repair than desktop machines, 2) size is a big factor, and 3) dead batteries are a very common problem.

L A B   5.1

BASIC PORTABLE SYSTEM COMPONENTS

LAB OBJECTIVES

After this Lab, you will be able to:

✓ Identify and Replace a Portable's Battery

✓ Understand Power Management Software

✓ Replace Hard Drives

✓ Upgrade Memory

LAB 5.1

A portable computer must provide all the functionality of a desktop counterpart, yet be more compact, able to withstand travel, and run in the absence of AC power. The two components that enable much of this are batteries and liquid crystal displays (LCDs). Aside from those two items, laptop computers contain many of the same components as desktops. Some of the objectives of this Lab may seem silly—sure, we've all seen a laptop; we know what a keyboard is; we know there's a hard drive and memory. But as is common in our industry, the only thing we can rely on is that technology will change. You are bound to be called upon to service laptops of various types and from various stages of technological evolution. Armed with the information in this Lab, you should have no problem telling the difference between a NiMH and a NiCad, active and passive matrix displays, or memory types.

BATTERIES AND ADAPTERS

AC adapters enable laptop computers to run off regular current when it is available by converting the power to DC. But the essence of a portable machine is that it should be able to run anywhere, anytime—with or without an AC power source. Batteries enable laptops to continue to operate when regular current is not available. AC adapters also serve a secondary purpose of charging the DC batteries when plugged in.

Laptops require continuous voltage to be supplied to them, and cannot run when the power strength begins to diminish. Contrast this with a child's toy. When the batteries begin to run low (diminishment in voltage) in the toy, the toy just talks slower, flashes its lights less, or otherwise behaves in ways that would be unacceptable in a laptop. When the power strength begins to diminish in a laptop, it must cease operation—so the batteries it uses must be able to provide continuous voltage. One advantage in the laptop is that it can be configured to warn you when battery capacity reaches a certain percentage so you can plug in a new battery or switch to AC power before the PC shuts down.

There are basically three types of laptop batteries in use today. The characteristics of each are shown in Table 5.1.

Table 5.1 ■ Portable Battery Types

Battery Type	Memory Problems	Number of Charges
Nickel-Cadmium (NiCad)	Yes	1000
Nickel-Metal Hydride (NiMH)	Yes	~1000
Lithium Ion	No	~500

LAB 5.1

Many operating systems include power management features to take better advantage of the capabilities of the laptop. In Windows 95, for example, the Power applet in Control Panel (shown in Figure 5.1) allows you to configure the battery-sensing components of the operating system. In DOS, the power.exe utility was used to configure similar settings.

LCD DISPLAYS

When designing portable machines, one of the biggest problems the engineers faced was how to supply enough current to power the monitor. The

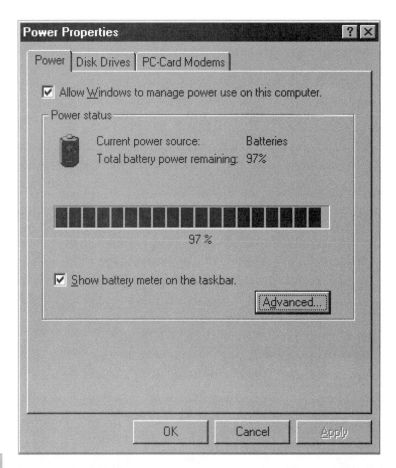

**Figure 5.1 ■ To access the Power Properties dialog box in Windows
9x, select Settings, then Control Panel from the Start menu and
double-click on the Power icon.**

solution they arrived at was the Liquid Crystal Display (LCD). Instead of
using the traditional vacuum tube to create the display, liquid crystals are
employed. This reduces the power consumption, and has the added benefit of reducing the size of the monitor to a flat panel (made from two
polarized glass panes with liquid between them).

The panels themselves are made of columns and rows called a matrix.
Most panels fall into one of two categories: *active matrix* or *passive matrix*.
The primary differences between the two types of display are that passive
matrix displays require less power and also offer far less in terms of qual-

ity. With a passive matrix, the display is controlled and essentially created at one time by two rows of transitors, and changes take place over a matter of a millisecond or two; whereas with an active matrix, a transistor behind each single liquid crystal (pixel) causes the change to the pixel from light to dark.

Because of the way the screen is refreshed, you typically cannot run LCD projectors, LCD panels, or other similar devices from passive matrix laptops.

HARD DRIVES AND MEMORY

The portable system being what it is, you'll be happy to note that hard drives and memory are much simpler to remove and install than their desktop counterparts. Usually, in most models, it's a simple matter of turning a few screws, popping out the old device, and snapping in the new. You'll get a better feel for this in this Lab's Exercises.

LAB 5.1 EXERCISES

5.1.1 IDENTIFY AND REPLACE A PORTABLE'S BATTERY

You saw in the Lab text that there are three types of batteries used in laptop computers. For this Exercise, you will remove the battery from your laptop, identify which type it is, and replace the battery.

Power down and unplug your laptop and remove any peripheral devices. Remember, never remove the battery from your laptop while the power is still on.

Locate the battery compartment on your laptop and remove the battery according to the manufacturer's instructions. All models are different, so be sure not to force the battery free. It should be removed smoothly.

a) Which type of battery is used in your laptop?

_____

_____

LAB 5.1

Next, examine your laptop's battery and note its characteristics. There should be a row or two of contact points that connect to the inside of the battery compartment.

If your battery does not seem to be charging correctly, the contact points may need to be cleaned. A standard computer keyboard vacuum should do the trick on the battery itself.

Examine the battery compartment and identify the contact points.

Reinsert the battery into the compartment and lock it back in place.

Reconnect the AC supply and any peripheral devices.

   b) Can you replace one type of laptop battery with a different type?

_____

_____

5.1.2 UNDERSTAND POWER MANAGEMENT SOFTWARE

You will need Windows 9x to perform this Exercise.

For this Exercise, you will fire up the power management software that is included with Windows 95 and take a quick tour of its features.

Open your Control Panel and double-click the icon for Power. The Power Properties window opens, much like the one shown in Figure 5.1. It may differ in the amount of tab choices you have, though, as these options vary from computer to computer.

a) What tab options are available in your Power Properties window?

_____

_____

Click on each tab in the Power Properties window and explore the available configurations that can be made to your laptop.

b) What are the default times for Windows to wait before switching the disk drive to low power mode?

_____

_____

5.1.3 REPLACE HARD DRIVES

For this Exercise, you will simply remove the hard drive from your laptop and reinstall it.

 Before you begin, be sure to take all proper precautions to avoid static discharge (ESD). These precautions were discussed in detail in Chapter 3.

LAB
5.1

Power down and unplug your laptop and remove any peripheral devices. It's a sure bet that you're getting used to doing this by now!

Remove the battery from the battery compartment before proceeding (see Exercise 5.1.1).

Locate the hard drive compartment, usually located underneath your laptop. It is usually protected by a cover.

Go ahead and unscrew the plastic cover. Again, all models are different, so consult the manufacturer's instructions if you're unsure.

Once the hard drive is exposed, it can be removed. In some models, it will simply lift out; in others, there may be a screw or tab or lever that is used to keep the disk from falling out that needs to be removed before the hard drive itself can be removed. Examine it when you remove it.

> **a)** What are the physical characteristics of your hard drive? Does it indicate anything about its size or other features?

_____

_____

Reinstalling the hard drive is simply a matter of performing these steps in reverse.

> **b)** Is it okay to install the hard drive from one laptop system into another laptop system?

_____

_____

5.1.4 UPGRADE MEMORY

For this Exercise, you will simply remove the existing memory chip from your laptop, examine it, and replace it. If you really do want to upgrade your memory, however, feel free.

Remember, memory specifications are different for all types of computers. Be sure you are installing the correct type.

Go ahead and power down and unplug your laptop and remove any peripheral devices.

Remove the battery from the battery compartment before proceeding (see Exercise 5.1.1).

Locate the memory compartment on your laptop (usually located on the underside of the machine) and remove the compartment door according to the manufacturer's instructions.

a) How many memory modules are present in your laptop?

_____

_____

Next, GENTLY lift the outer edge of the memory module away from the machine, and pull it upward until it frees.

 Do not force the memory module out as you could damage it and the compartment permanently! It should slide out with just a little resistance.

Examine the memory module and the memory compartment.

b) Is there any indication on the module itself as to what type of memory this is?

_____

_____

Reinsert the module by sliding it back into place until it locks in.

Replace the memory compartment door.

Replace the battery, reconnect the AC supply and any peripheral devices, and power up your system.

If you're using Windows 9x, open the System Properties box from the Control Panel and click on the Performance tab.

c) How much memory is installed on your system?

_____

_____

LAB
5.1

LAB 5.1 EXERCISE ANSWERS

5.1.1 ANSWERS

a) Which type of battery is used in your laptop?

Answer: Obviously, this will vary from machine to machine. Each battery type is discussed in more detail below.

NiCad batteries were the first engineered for laptop use to provide continuous voltage. When fully charged, most provide about 30 minutes of power. Over time, however, the batteries develop a "memory" and each time you recharge them, the length of time they can provide power diminishes. For example, if you recharge a NiCad battery while it is still 30 percent charged, you will lose that 30 percent off the life of your battery. It will only ever run at 70 percent capacity again. The only way to prevent the development of this "memory" is to fully discharge the batteries—down to 0 percent—before charging them. The disadvantages of doing this are obvious. Even still, this gives them the ability to last for only about 1000 charges before failing to be useful. When they do fail and must be tossed, you cannot throw them in with regular trash. They must be disposed of in accordance with local regulations. For obvious reasons, NiCad batteries are not used as commonly today as they were when there were no alternatives.

Nickel-Metal Hydride (*NiMH*) batteries are an improvement over NiCad, and today are supplied with most laptop purchases as your first battery. They still develop a memory with recharging, though not to the same extent as NiCad, and must be disposed of properly. To quote from the back of a popular model:

- Do not put in fire or mutilate; may burst or release toxic materials
- Do not crush, puncture, incinerate, or short external circuits
- Do not short circuit; may cause burns
- Do not pull out when the system is on.

While a bit redundant in wording, it stresses the importance of proper handling and use.

Lithium Ion batteries are newer and are most commonly purchased for laptop battery upgrades today. As a rule of thumb, the amount of time they can provide a charge is double that of NiMH batteries, and they do not develop memory problems. On the downside, they cannot withstand as many charges, and can explode if overcharged.

b) Can you replace one type of laptop battery with a different type?

Answer: Yes, you can.

By "type" we mean that the battery can vary in the type of battery—NiMH, NiCad, etc.—but it needs to be of a size and configuration that is intended to be used in your computer. Not all batteries are built and shaped the same; "close fits" are not allowed.

5.1.2 ANSWERS

a) What tab options are available in your Power Properties window?

Answer: This answer will vary from machine to machine.

There are several options that are available in the Power Properties window, depending on your particular laptop. Some of the more common options are explained here—these are all simply power-saving options.

- Power—This panel allows you to check the current Power Status of your machine. It also enables you to configure more advanced options for managing power, as well as troubleshoot power problems.
- Disk Drives—This panel allows you to configure how long your laptop should wait before switching your hard drive to low power mode when using AC power.
- PC-Card Modems—This panel enables you to shut down PC-Card modems when they are not being used.
- Hibernation—This panel lets you set the level of hibernation when your computer is inactive.
- Alarm—This panel gives you the option of enabling an alarm if your computer's power gets too low.

LAB 5.1

b) What are the default times for Windows to wait before switching the disk drive to low power mode?

Answer: 3 minutes for battery power and 30 minutes for AC power.

Basically, this question was intended to familiarize you with some of the options that can be set in the Power Properties window. Switching your disk drive to low power mode has the advantage of prolonging battery life. The disadvantage is that any reading or writing to the disk experiences delays, because the disk has to spin up each time a request is made. After the disk access is complete, the disk remains spinning for a period of time, anticipating another access. If it doesn't get one, the disk will finally, after a while, spin down again.

5.1.3 ANSWERS

For this Exercise, you simply removed the hard drive from your laptop and reinstalled it.

a) What are the physical characteristics of your hard drive? Does it indicate anything about its size or other features?

Answer: It varies from manufacturer to manufacturer. The only consistency is that the drive comes in a metal or plastic case, has a connector at the other end, and usually has the manufacturer's name on it. Sometimes the size information is printed on the disk, but not always. If there are screws used to open it, at least one of them will be covered with a seal because hard drives are not intended to be opened.

b) Is it okay to install the hard drive from one laptop system into another laptop system?

Answer: Absolutely not!

LAB 5.1

Never assume that an internal component from one computer can be installed into a different computer. Especially with hard drives and memory, always make sure that you are purchasing a component designed specifically for the model you wish to upgrade. Being careless in this regard can cause serious damage to your computer.

5.1.4 ANSWERS

a) How many memory modules are present in your laptop?

Answer: In many newer systems, the answer is likely to be zero, regardless of the actual amount of memory. The base memory is frequently integrated directly with the motherboard, so the slot(s) for additional memory will be empty.

b) Is there any indication on the module itself as to what type of memory this is?

Answer: Frequently, the memory modules these days are boring; there is nothing directly printed on it that provides any clue to its size or characteristics. You actually need to install it into your system and power it up to see what type of memory you have.

c) How much memory is installed on your system?

Answer: This is entirely system dependent; however, it should be the first thing you see upon power up. The system will echo the amount of memory in bytes upon power up.

Laptops and PCs do not use the same memory modules. Laptop memory modules are much more compact than those found on their PC cousins. The size and shape of memory expansion for laptops are different from manufacturer to manufacturer, unlike PCs, which have a standard size and configuration.

LAB 5.1 SELF-REVIEW QUESTIONS

In order to test your progress, you should be able to answer the following questions.

1) Which of the following should you do when disposing of a laptop battery?
   a) _____Toss it with regular waste.
   b) _____Return it to the manufacturer.
   c) _____Check with your local agency.
   d) _____Incinerate.

2) In DOS, which command is used to conserve battery power on laptops?
   a) _____Power
   b) _____Screen
   c) _____Lapt
   d) _____Intrlnk

3) A laptop's AC adapter converts power to which of the following?:
   a) _____PC
   b) _____BC
   c) _____DC
   d) _____AC

4) Which of the following was an improvement over NiCad batteries?
    a) ___Nickel Cadium
    b) ___Alkaline
    c) ___Lead-based
    d) ___Nickel-Metal Hydride

5) Which of the following controls the hibernation state of your PC?
    a) _____AUTOEXEC.BAT
    b) _____Power Properties
    c) _____Your battery type
    d) _____CONFIG.SYS

6) Which type of display is controlled by rows of transistors to light an individual pixel?
    a) _____Passive matrix
    b) _____LCD
    c) _____Active Matrix
    d) _____SVGA

7) To configure battery parameters in Windows 95, which Control Panel applet would you use?
    a) ___Battery
    b) ___Suspend
    c) ___Configuration
    d) ___Power

Quiz answers appear in Appendix A, Section 5.1.

**LAB
5.1**

L A B   5.2

PC CARDS

With the emphasis on compactness in a laptop, it is impractical to fit full-sized cards (network and other) into such a small unit. The Personal Computer Memory Card International Association (PCMCIA) developed a standard for credit-card sized devices that can be swapped in and out of a laptop to provide the additional functionality that cards provide. The original emphasis was on providing additional memory (thus the acronym), but today these cards can offer more features than just memory and have hence come to be known as PC Cards instead of the older name PCMCIA cards.

There are three types of PC Cards in use, all with a 68-pin socket connection. Regardless of the type, all are 85.6 mm × 54.0 mm in size. They all differ, however, in thickness. Table 5.2 shows their primary usage and dimensions.

Table 5.2 ■ Portable Card Types

Type	Purpose	Thickness
I	Memory	3.3 mm
II	Network cards, modems, among others	5.0 mm
III	Hard drives	10.5 mm

It is important to understand that the cards are hot swappable, meaning that under most circumstances they can be removed or inserted into a running machine. The only item they require for recognition and use is software capable of enabling them.

Advice

For the exam, know the dimensions of each card and what it is used for.

LAB 5.2 EXERCISES

5.2.1 IDENTIFY AND EXAMINE YOUR PCMCIA CARDS

Before you start this Exercise, visit the PCMCIA Web site located at http://www.pc-card.com.

Explore this site to get an idea of the many different types of cards that are available, and learn about the PCMCIA association.

a) From browsing the PCMCIA site, can you find when the first PCMCIA standard was released and what it defined?

_____

_____

Next, remove and examine the PCMCIA cards in a laptop to which you have easy access.

b) What types do you find, how many of each, and what are they used for?

_____

_____

LAB
5.2

Now, examine the slots in your laptop, even if there are no cards installed.

    c) What types can you use in these slots?

_____

_____

LAB 5.2 EXERCISE ANSWERS

5.2.1 ANSWERS

    a) From browsing the PCMCIA site, can you find when the first PCMCIA standard was released and what it defined?

    Answer: The first PCMCIA standard, release 1.0, was released in June 1990. It defined only the electrical and physical requirements for memory cards and the 68-pin interface.

    b) What types do you find, how many of each, and what are they used for?

    Answer: Your answer here will vary depending on your system.

PC cards today support a wide variety of functions and technologies. There are cards available to add memory, networking capabilities, modem, additional hard drives, parallel port interface, CD-ROM or DVD interface, even sound and video to your laptop.

    c) What types can you use in these slots?

    Answer: You can identify the types of PCMCIA slots and the cards used within them based on the thickness of the card. For reference, review Table 5.2, presented earlier in this chapter, for the types of cards and their respective configurations.

LAB 5.2

LAB 5.2 SELF-REVIEW QUESTIONS

In order to test your progress, you should be able to answer the following questions.

1) How thick is a memory PC card, typically?
    a) ___3.3 mm
    b) ___5.0 mm
    c) ___3.3 cm
    d) ___5.0 cm

2) How thick is a modem card usually?
    a) _____3.0 mm
    b) _____10.5 mm
    c) _____5.0 cm
    d) _____5.0 mm

3) You must power the computer down before removing the PCMCIA card.
    a) _____True
    b) _____False

4) What type of connection is used for all PCMCIA cards today?
    a) _____48-pin socket connection
    b) _____48-pin slot connection
    c) _____68-pin socket connection
    d) _____68-pin slot connection

Quiz answers appear in Appendix A, Section 5.2.

**LAB
5.2**

L A B   5.3

DOCKING STATIONS

LAB OBJECTIVES

After this Lab, you will be able to:

✓ Understand Docking Stations

✓ Identify Hardware Profiles

DOCKING STATIONS

Essentially, docking stations enable a laptop computer to be converted to a desktop computer. When plugged into a docking station, a laptop now has access to peripherals that it would not have as a stand-alone—such as access to the network, a workgroup printer, and so forth. The cheapest form of a docking station, if it can even be called that, is a port replicator. Typically, a laptop slides into a port replicator, which is connected to peripheral desktop devices such as a full-sized monitor, keyboard (versus the standard 84 keys on a laptop), mouse, and so on. The replicator enables your laptop to access these devices. Extended, or enhanced, replicators add other ports not found on the laptop itself, such as PC slots, sound, and so on.

The most common difference between port replicators and docking stations used to be that you could gain network access by being plugged into a docking station. Now the term "port replicator" and "docking station" are virtually synonymous as their features are becoming increasingly identical with time.

**LAB
5.3**

Laptops can support Plug and Play at three different levels, depending on how dynamically they are able to adapt to changes:

1. Cold Docking—The laptop must be turned off and back on for the change to be recognized.
2. Warm Docking—The laptop must be put in and out of suspended mode for the change to be recognized.
3. Hot Docking—The change can be made while running at normal operations and the change is recognized.

Desktop computers capable of having multiple profiles (Windows 95) should have only one profile for the system (hardware) because it cannot radically change itself from one moment to the next. Laptop computers, on the other hand, can have dramatically different capabilities based on whether they are docked or not, and thus they should have multiple hardware/system profiles.

LAB 5.3 EXERCISES

5.3.1 UNDERSTAND DOCKING STATIONS

If you have a docking station, examine it carefully and note the connections that can be made to it. Note the differences between the amount of connections on the docking station and the amount of connections on the back of your laptop.

a) What is the primary advantage to using a docking station over using your laptop stand-alone?

_____

_____

b) What's the difference between using a port replicator and using a docking station?

_____

_____

LAB
5.3

5.3.2 *IDENTIFY HARDWARE PROFILES*

To identify what hardware profiles exist on your laptop, if any, follow these simple steps.

1. Click on the Start menu and select Settings, then Control Panel.
2. From the Control Panel, double-click on the System icon.
3. In the System Properties dialog box, click on the Hardware Profiles tab.

a) What hardware profiles exist on your system?

_____

_____

LAB 5.3 EXERCISE ANSWERS

5.3.1 *ANSWERS*

a) What is the primary advantage to using a docking station over using your laptop stand-alone?

Answer: There are several advantages over using a docking station. While most laptops enable you to connect peripheral devices such as monitors and keyboards to the back of the laptop itself, connecting these devices to a docking station is far more convenient because the connections only need to be made once; you do not have to connect and disconnect each device whenever you wish to use the devices or go mobile.

b) What's the difference between using a port replicator and using a docking station?

Answer: A port replicator provides the same primary benefit as a docking station by enabling you to make peripheral device connections once and simply connecting or disconnecting your laptop whenever you need to. But the main difference between true docking stations and port replicators is that docking stations give you all of the same capabilities, including full network capabilities, as a desktop computer does.

5.3.2 ANSWERS

a) What hardware profiles exist on your system?

Answer: Of course this will vary depending on your system.

If you are not "docked" when you do this Exercise, the Hardware Profile list will simply say Undocked. A hardware profile tells Windows what drivers to load when you boot your computer. So, if you are not docked, Windows only loads the drivers that it needs for you to operate your laptop without any peripheral devices, such as a monitor or keyboard. If you are docked, Windows will need to load the correct drivers for the devices connected to your docking station. By creating hardware profiles for each situation, you are telling Windows whether or not you are docked and what device drivers you need when you boot up. Windows will prompt you to select the profile for your needs when you start your laptop.

To create a new hardware profile, you would follow these steps:

1. Open the System Properties dialog box as you did in the Exercise and click on the Hardware Profiles tab.
2. Click on the profile on which you want to base the new profile and click the Copy button.
3. Name the new profile in the Copy Profile dialog box and click the OK button. These three steps create the new profile, but now you must change the hardware configuration associated with it.
4. In the Systems Properties dialog box, click on the Device Manager tab.
5. Scroll to the hardware type that you would like to enable (or disable) for the new profile and click the plus sign to expand it.
6. Double-click the name of the hardware you wish to enable (or disable) for this profile.
7. In the new dialog box, named for that hardware's properties, click the General tab and, in the Device Usage portion at the bottom of that panel, choose the profiles in which to enable this hardware. If you wish to disable this hardware, uncheck the box next to the profile name.

LAB 5.3 SELF-REVIEW QUESTIONS

In order to test your progress, you should be able to answer the following questions.

1) For which of the following docking modes must a laptop be placed into suspend mode before it recognizes a change?
   a) ___Hot
   b) ___Warm
   c) ___Cold
   d) ___Dry

2) In order to have different hardware configurations in Windows 95 for the laptop in a docked and undocked environment, which of the following should you create?
   a) ___Multiple user profiles
   b) ___Multiple system profiles
   c) ___Multiple registries
   d) ___Multiple system policies

3) Basically, a hardware profile tells Windows what device drivers to load when you boot your computer.
   a) _____True
   b) _____False

4) What's the standard amount of keys on a laptop?
   a) _____64
   b) _____78
   c) _____84
   d) _____86

5) What is the primary difference between docking stations and port replicators?
   a) _____Docking stations give you more options for connecting devices than port replicators.
   b) _____Docking stations give you network access, whereas port replicators do not.
   c) _____Docking stations are more expensive than port replicators.
   d) _____Port replicators work with any laptop, whereas docking stations must be tailored to a specific model.

   Quiz answers appear in Appendix A, Section 5.3.

LAB
5.3

LAB 5.4

PORTABLE SYSTEM PROBLEMS

LAB OBJECTIVES

After this Lab, you will be able to:

✓ Troubleshoot Modem Problems

✓ Troubleshoot Network Connection Problems

✓ Identify External Monitor Connection and Configuration

Portable computers are subject to the same problems as their desktop counterparts as well as those specific to the technology employed in them. Areas to be aware of include:

- Adding devices
- Connectivity

ADDING DEVICES

Adding devices to a laptop is considerably more difficult than adding to a desktop. For that reason, most devices are added as external components, such as CD-ROM drives, tape backup devices, and so forth. Memory is added through the PC Card slot or proprietary expansion slots.

**LAB
5.4**

MODEM CONNECTIVITY

Most laptops come with or include the capability to add a modem and network connector.

 For the exam, you should know the command-line methods of talking to the modem. Typical commands are listed in Table 5.3.

Table 5.3 ■ AT Commands

Command	Purpose
ATA	Answer
ATD	Dial. For example, "ATD5551672" dials 555-1672.
ATDT	Dial using tone dialing—"ATDT5551672".
ATH	Hang up. Can also use the number zero or one. ATH0 just hangs up, while ATH1 enters command mode.
ATL	Sets the loudness. ATL1=low, ATL2=medium, ATL3=high.
ATM	Turns the speaker on or off. ATM0=always off. ATM1=on until carrier detect, and ATM2=always on.
ATZ	Reset modem.
ATX	Configures responses to busy and dial tones.

NETWORK CONNECTIVITY

Network connectivity problems can be difficult to diagnose. The possible sources of a network connectivity problem include:

- Misconfigured network adaptors
- Misconfigured hardware profiles

Further, network connectivity problems may involve physical wiring (patch cords, patch panels, and network jacks) and the configuration of active devices such as hubs, bridges, switches, and routers. Cooperation with site network administrators is required to successfully solve network connectivity issues.

LAB 5.4

DISPLAYS AND MONITORS

Internal displays and external monitors can be used with portable systems. External monitors can be connected to docking stations and port replicators, and they can also be directly connected to the portable systems themselves when they are undocked.

Users can become easily confused when using external monitors and projectors because many systems allow several configurations of internal and external displays:

- Internal display only
- External display only
- Both internal and external display

Different systems toggle among these settings using different hotkeys or software commands. Problems with external displays and projectors can appear to be internal to the portable system, and vice versa.

 For the exam, know that 1) portable systems are generally harder to repair than desktop machines, 2) size is a big factor, and 3) dead batteries are a very common problem. Spare parts are more difficult to find, since they are proprietary and specific to each make and model.

LAB 5.4 EXERCISES

5.4.1 TROUBLESHOOT MODEM PROBLEMS

 For more on troubleshooting modem problems, see Chapter 2, "Diagnosing and Troubleshooting," (Exercise 2.2.3).

Connect to your portable system's internal (or PCMCIA) modem using Hyperterm or Terminal and connect it to the appropriate COM: port.

Enter any basic commands, such as ATM, and hit the Enter key.

a) Does your modem answer basic commands?

_____

_____

b) What is the ATM command used for?

_____

_____

c) Can your portable system's internal (or PCMCIA) modem connect to the telephone network?

_____

_____

5.4.2 TROUBLESHOOT NETWORK CONNECTION PROBLEMS

Using Control Panel → System → Hardware Profiles, Control Panel → Network, and Control Panel → System → Device Manager, examine and document all your portable system's network adaptor and driver configurations, hardware profile, and physical connectivity characteristics. Confirm connectivity to the network.

Have a colleague "break" one of the above.

a) Attempt to isolate the cause of the problem by examining wiring and system configuration. What steps did you take to restore network connectivity?

_____

_____

LAB
5.4

5.4.3 IDENTIFY EXTERNAL MONITOR CONNECTION AND CONFIGURATION

Trace the monitor's cables from the monitor to the port replicator or docking station monitor port.

a) How many cables do you find, and what are their functions?

_____

_____

With the portable system undocked, connect the monitor cable to the portable system's monitor jack.

b) How would you configure the portable system to use the external monitor?

_____

_____

LAB 5.4 EXERCISE ANSWERS

5.4.1 ANSWERS

a) Does your modem answer basic commands?

Answer: It should have answered any basic command with OK.

If you get an ERROR back from the modem at any point, the modem is bad and must be replaced.

If the modem responds with OK, the first part of the testing is complete. You know that the COM port is working, and that the modem's internal circuitry is working as well.

If you get NO response, then you may still have a bad modem, or the communications settings for the PC and the modem don't match. Revisit Exercise 2.2.3 to continue troubleshooting your modem if you have a problem.

b)   What is the ATM command used for?

Answer: The ATM command is used to turn the speaker on or off. ATM0 means the speaker will always be off. ATM1 turns it on until a carrier is detected, and ATM2 keeps your modem speaker on at all times.

c)   Can your portable system's internal (or PCMCIA) modem connect to the telephone network?

Answer: To confirm this, first connect a telephone cord from the portable system's modem to a working phone jack. Next, use Hyperterm or Terminal to enter a dialing command (such as ATDT5551212) to see if the modem is able to attempt a dial connection. For modems (or their respective drivers) with speakers, you should be able to hear the dial tone and the phone number being dialed.

If you have a problem with this Exercise, return to Exercise 2.2.3 to complete the troubleshooting of your modem.

5.4.2 ANSWERS

a)   Attempt to isolate the cause of the problem by examining wiring and system configuration. What steps did you take to restore network connectivity?

Answer: This answer will vary depending on what was changed by your colleague. Generally, however, after observing the system's behavior, methodically check all physical and configuration settings until the cause is found. Confirm the suspected culprit with your colleague. After restoring all configurations, confirm that the system is working normally.

5.4.3 ANSWERS

a)   How many cables do you find, and what are their functions?

Answer: Monitors typically have only two cables: a power cable and a signal cable. The power cable will go to a power outlet or plug strip. The signal cable is the other cable; follow it to the port replicator or docking station.

With the portable system undocked, connect the monitor cable to the portable system's monitor jack.

**LAB
5.4**

b) How would you configure the portable system to use the external monitor?

Answer: Most portables have a monitor connection, but it may not be configured to work. Some portable systems have a keyboard "function" command used to "toggle" an external monitor on and off. On some systems, it may be necessary to activate the portable system's internal video adaptor to work in an "undocked" hardware profile. In all cases, consult the system's documentation for information as needed.

LAB 5.4 SELF-REVIEW QUESTIONS

In order to test your progress, you should be able to answer the following questions.

1) Which of the following is the command-line command to hang up a modem?
   a) ___AT
   b) ___ATM
   c) ___ATH
   d) ___ATX

2) What settings are used to configure network adaptors (choose all that apply)?
   a) _____Control Panel → System
   b) _____Control Panel → Network
   c) _____My Computer → Dial Up Networking
   d) _____PCMCIA Network Cards

3) What cables are used by a monitor?
   a) _____Network patch cord
   b) _____Infrared patch cord
   c) _____Signal and power cords
   d) _____CGI and power cords

4) Which of the following is command-line command to reset the modem?
   a) _____ATR
   b) _____ATD
   c) _____ATZ
   d) _____ATX

LAB
5.4

5) What does the command-line command ATL3 do?

   a) _____It sets the modem speaker's loudness to high.

   b) _____It sets the modem's speaker to always be on.

   c) _____It configures the response tone to busy.

   d) _____This is not a valid command.

6) The AT, which precedes each of the AT modem commands, is the part of the command that gets the modem's attention.

   a) _____True

   b) _____False

Quiz answers appear in Appendix A, Section 5.4.

**LAB
5.4**

CHAPTER 5

TEST YOUR THINKING

In this chapter, you learned all about portable systems, their features, functions, and problems. Because there are not a lot of possibilities for projects in this section, it would be a good idea to do some independent research on your own with regard to the various makes and models of laptops that are currently available. The more familiar you are with the various types of laptops that are available, the more knowledgeable you will be when it comes to troubleshooting and diagnosing problems.

1) Visit an informative consumer Web site, such as www.circuitcity.com, and research 10 different laptop makes and models. Use the following table to record the appropriate information:

Make/ Model	Suggested Price	Speed	RAM	Hard Drive	CD-ROM/ DVD	Screen Type/Size	Modem

Be sure to choose one or two models from each manufacturer rather than choosing from only one or two manufacturers. The purpose of this project is to compare the features/prices of models from different manufacturers and to get an idea of what's currently on the market.

2) Develop a complete architecture for portable systems to include two operating paradigms:

   a) running in a docking station with external keyboard, mouse, monitor, and network connection, and

   b) running out of a docking station with internal keyboard, mouse, display, and modem.

Select a high-end model portable system that offers docking stations, port replicators, and a wide array of features (such as large hard drives, high amounts of memory, CD-ROM, DVD drives), as well as a lower-priced model. In the system architecture, develop hardware device configurations so that the system will automatically sense (at boot time) whether it is docked or undocked.

Include in this architecture a provision for using an external monitor or projector (directly connected to the portable system) and a PCMCIA network adaptor.

C H A P T E R   6

BASIC NETWORKING

When you start a new venture, you'll get lucky three times. The first will be a relative that will help you, the second will be a friend that will help you, and the third will be a complete stranger that picks you out of happenstance. If you want any business at all after those three, you have to network.

—Johnny Yellow

CHAPTER OBJECTIVES

In this chapter, you will learn about:

The Basic Networking section of the core exam expects you to know the principles behind computer (and in particular, personal computer) networking. The amount of detail you must know is nowhere near as broad or inclusive as it is for other exams that focus on this topic alone (such as the Networking Essentials exam by Microsoft, or Novell's Networking Technologies exam).

267

L A B   6.1

BASIC NETWORKING CONCEPTS

LAB OBJECTIVES

After this Lab, you will be able to:

✓ Identify OSI Specifics
✓ Identify Cabling Specifics

A network is a group of two or more computer systems sharing services and interacting in some manner. In most cases, the interaction is done through a shared communications link with the shared components being data or printers. Simply put, a network is a collection of machines that have been linked together both physically and logically through software components to facilitate communication and sharing of information among them.

A physical pathway, known as the *transmission medium*, connects the systems, and a set of rules determines how they communicate. The rules are known as *protocols*. A network protocol is software installed on a machine that determines the agreed-upon set of rules for two or more machines to communicate with each other. One common metaphor used to describe different protocols is to compare them to human languages.

Think of a group of people in the same room who know nothing about each other. In order for them to communicate, this group has to determine what language to speak, how to handle identifying each other, whether to make general announcements or have private conversations, and so on. If machines are using different protocols, it is equivalent to one person speaking French and another person speaking Spanish. Machines that have different protocols installed are not able to communicate with each other. Common protocols in the Microsoft family include: NetBEUI (Net-BIOS Extended User Interface), NWlink (NDIS compliant version of Novell's IPX/SPX), DLC (Data Link Control), AFP (Appletalk File Protocol), and TCP/IP (Transmission Control Protocol/Internet Protocol).

THE OSI MODEL

The OSI (Open Systems Interconnection) model is the framework used to divide the functions of networking into seven distinct layers. Each layer has a job and responsibility that it must do in order for a network to work effectively. The seven layers are:

- Layer 7: Application
- Layer 6: Presentation
- Layer 5: Session
- Layer 4: Transport
- Layer 3: Network
- Layer 2: Data Link
- Layer 1: Physical

Many people use the mnemonic "All People Seem To Need Data Processing" to memorize the order of the layers. Another is "Please Do Not Throw Sausage Pizza Away."

All messages begin at the top layer and move down to the bottom. As the message moves down, each successive layer adds a header to it, essentially explaining the functions it has carried out. On the receiving side, headers are stripped from the message as it travels up the corresponding layers.

The top layer (application) has a great deal of intelligence built into it, and as you move down through the layers, you lose intelligence at each layer until you come to the Physical layer, which essentially has no intelligence at all. The purpose of each layer, the type of data it handles, and the hardware that can work at that layer are summarized in Table 6.1.

Table 6.1 ■ The OSI Model Layers

Layer	Purpose	Data Type	Hardware	Windows Example
Application	Interface to network services.	Message	Gateway	File sharing, printing, and/or messaging services.
Presentation	Translates between Application and all others. Determines the appearance or formatting of all data. Responsible for encoding and decoding.	Packet	Gateway	Character-set translation used by connectivity products that provide a connection to a mainframe or other server from the PC.
Session	Establishes rules for communication, synchronization, and how the system begins and ends a working session.	Packet	Gateway	An established session between an MS Mail or Exchange/Outlook client and its corresponding server.
Transport	Handles network transmission, all error checking, and end-to-end communications.	Datagram, segment (and packet)	Gateway	The network drivers in Windows that guarantee the integrity of the message traffic (i.e., packet "checksums" and order of packet delivery).
Network	Addressing; flow control; switching; translation of logical addresses into physical addresses. Routing data between network addresses.	Datagram (and packet)	Router—uses routing table; can determine best path; can be static or dynamic; can support multiple paths.	Drivers within Windows that address packets at this level—given distinct IP addresses.

Table 6.1 ■ The OSI Model Layers *(continued)*

Layer	Purpose	Data Type	Hardware	Windows Example
Data Link	Arranges data into chunks called "frames"; error checking within frames; manages link control; communicates with card.	Frame	Bridge—uses MAC addresses, can connect different media and unlike segments.	When Windows wants to send a packet to another system, it sends a request over the network to translate the IP address of the server to its MAC equivalent.
Physical	The connection, wire, cards, and so forth; what you can see and touch.	Bits and signals	Repeater—no filtering or processing, just regeneration; can connect different media.	Windows is not aware of activity at this level; handled exclusively at the NIC level.

Under no conditions must an individual protocol adhere to the structure given, as the model is only a framework of operations that must take place. The TCP/IP protocol, for example, is the most commonly used networking protocol, yet it has only five layers. It has five layers because it predates the OSI model in development; it carries out the exact same functions, but divides them into five layers instead of seven. The five layers of the TCP/IP protocol are:

- Application
- Transport
- Internet
- Network Interface
- Hardware

The first four layers are part of the TCP/IP software and, as such, often are considered to be the only portions that apply to the TCP/IP protocol. However, the hardware layer cannot be overlooked, which is why it is included here as part of the whole TCP/IP picture.

Likewise, the OSI model does not specify *any* physical specifications (only use Ethernet, only use twisted-pair wiring, and so forth)—it is a model and a model only.

The OSI Model is a complicated one and beyond the scope of this book. You may want to research more about this model on your own via the Internet or through a good networking fundamentals book, such as Douglas Comer's Internetworking with TCP/IP *(Prentice Hall PTR, 1995).*

DIFFERENT WAYS OF NETWORKING

There are two primary methods by which personal computers can be networked. The first is called a workgroup, or peer-to-peer network. The second is known as server-based, or domain.

With a workgroup, networking cards are inserted into a number of personal computers and a wire is strung between them. The only additional cost to what the company already has is that of the cards and cable. Each machine is known as a peer and able to participate in the sharing of files or resources. No server is required, thus there is no additional cost for a dedicated machine, but there is no real security. Furthermore, in a peer-to-peer environment, each machine can be a client when it connects to other computers and it can also be a server when others connect to it.

Peer-to-peer networks require an operating system (or add-on) that can understand networking to function in this way. Microsoft's Windows 3.11, Windows 95, and Windows 98 can all function well in a peer-to-peer environment.

If file and print sharing has been enabled on a Windows 95 system, for example, a share may be created by selecting a folder and choosing to share it. By default, there is no password associated with it, but you can choose to assign one that a user must give to access the resource. Access permissions can be Read-Only, Full, or Depends on Password. This is known as *share-level* security wherein the security is passed upon a user supplying the correct password to access the share.

Peer-to-peer networking works in small environments. If you grow beyond approximately 10 machines, then the administrative overhead of establishing the shares, coupled with the lack of tight security, creates an undesirable nightmare.

In the presence of a server, be it NetWare or NT, you can implement *user-level* security on your network. With user-level security, permissions are based upon how the user logged on and was authenticated by the server. Every user has an *account*. In this environment, you can assign permissions to shares based upon individual user permissions or group member-ships. In short: You must have a server on the network to have user-level security, but can have share-level security with, or without, a server.

Also known as client-server networks, server-based networking's down-side is that it requires a dedicated machine (the server); the upside is that you gain centralized administration and authentication. With centralized administration, you can add all users at one location, control logon scripts, backups, and so forth. With centralized authentication, you can identify a user to your entire network based upon their logon name and password, and not based upon each share they attempt to access.

A network utilizing a server and commonly confined to a geographic area is known as a Local Area Network, or LAN. Multiple LANs can be com-bined to form a bigger network, known as a Wide Area Network, or WAN. If the geographic area is a campus, then it becomes a CAN (Campus Area Network), or a metropolitan area, then it becomes known as a MAN (Met-ropolitan Area Network).

COMMON NETWORKING PROTOCOLS

There are a number of protocols in use for creating networks today. The most popular is the set of protocols known collectively as *TCP/IP (Trans-mission Control Protocol/Internet Protocol)*. It was originally written to pro-vide networking capabilities in the Unix operating system and is now the protocol required to connect to the Internet.

Internetwork Packet Exchange/Sequenced Packet Exchange (IPX/SPX) was developed by Novell and used as the networking protocol in its popular NetWare network operating systems series. Both TCP/IP and IPX/SPX are routable protocols (meaning they can be used to connect a number of networks together) and have the ability to service networks of all sizes—from very small to very large. *NWLink* is a protocol compatible with IPX/SPX that was developed by Microsoft to provide communications between newer Microsoft operating systems and NetWare servers.

NetBIOS Extended User Interface (NetBEUI) was used as the default network-ing protocol in Windows 3.11 (Windows for Workgroups), LAN Manager, and a number of other Microsoft operating systems. It has a very small overhead, but also cannot be routed, making it less than practical for building large networks or connecting several networks together.

AppleTalk is the protocol Macintosh computers use. It allows Mac users to access files and printers that are either shared or on a Server.

Data Link Control (DLC) is primarily used to communicate with IBM mainframes and AS400s. There is one additional use: since many HP network printers also use DLC, they can be (and often are) converted to TCP/IP with the inclusion of a JetDirect card. Like NetBEUI, it is not a routable protocol.

CABLING BASICS

The type of cabling you use, speed, length of cable run, and so forth, all determine how many computers you can connect to your network. The choices you have are:

Unshielded Twisted Pair (*UTP*) is the cheapest cable to use and easiest to install. It resembles telephone wire, and has a range of 100 meters. It can carry transmissions between 10MBps and 100MBps, but is very susceptible to electromagnetic interference (known as EMI); in fact, UTP is the most susceptible to EMI of any wire type. UTP is usually an adequate type of cable, unless your usage requires you to run it around motors and fluorescent lights, which generate a significant amount of EMI.

There are five categories of UTP that provide different cable configurations to support the different types of data transmission grade ratings. Table 6.2 summarizes the types of twisted pair cables and their configurations:

Table 6.2 ■ Twisted Pair Cables and Configurations

Category	Number of Wire Pairs	Used For
Category 1	1	Voice-only (telephone)
Category 2	4	Data at speeds up to 4Mbps
Category 3	4 (three twists per foot of cable)	Data at speeds up to 10Mbps
Category 4	4	Data at speeds up to 16Mbps
Category 5	4 pairs of copper wire	Data at speeds up to 100Mbps

Shielded Twisted Pair (STP) is less sensitive to EMI due to its shielding, but costs a bit more. Still relatively easy to install, it remains limited to 100 meters in length and can carry transmissions from 16MBps to 500MBps. With either UTP or STP, RJ-45 connectors are used to connect cables to the computer's network card or to a hub. The RJ-45 connectors resemble telephone line connectors (RJ-11 or RJ-12), except they have eight connectors versus the telephone's four.

10BaseT cable is an example of twisted pair cable. The "10" stands for the common speed—10MBps, the "Base" for baseband mode, and the "T" for twisted pair cabling. An easy way to recognize this cable type is that it resembles telephone wire, so remember that "T is for twisted."

Figure 6.1 shows a piece of 10BaseT cabling and a hub. 10BaseT cabling uses a hub, and all networked computers using the hub have a cable running from the network adapter in their computer directly to the hub. If the connection to any one computer becomes faulty, it is only that computer that is affected.

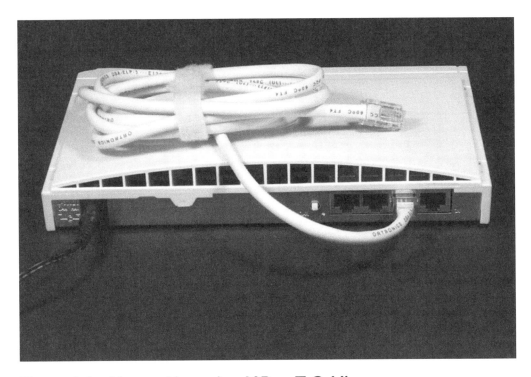

Figure 6.1 ■ Networking using 10BaseT Cabling

Thinnet cabling looks like the coaxial cable used by your television cable company. It costs less than STP, but more than UTP. It is easy to install and has a range of 185 meters. It typically carries transmissions at 10Mbps and is less sensitive than UTP to EMI. BNC (British Naval Connectors) connectors are used to connect cables together, and T-connectors must be used to connect to the network card in the computer. Both ends of the network must be terminated with a 50-ohm resistor, and one end must be grounded. 10Base2 cable is an example of thinnet. The "10" indicates speed—10MBps, the "Base" stands for baseband mode, while the "2" rounds up the number of meters it can run to 200 (whereas it is limited to 185).

Figure 6.2 shows a section of 10Base2 cabling (note the BNC connectors and T-connector). Extending to the left of the T-connector is standard BNC cabling. Extending to the right of the T-connector is a 50-ohm resistor with a ground wire running from it. With 10Base2, the cable leaving the network adapter of one computer connects to the network adapter of the next computer. If one computer goes down—by something so simple as a user disconnecting the T-connector to move his machine 3 feet—the entire network can go down.

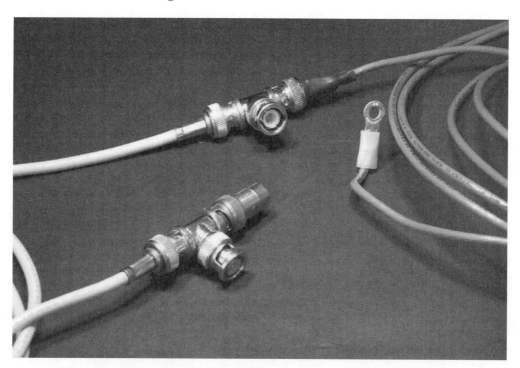

Figure 6.2 ■ 10Base2 Cable with Typical Connectors

Thicknet cabling is seldom used in new installations, but is a carryover from days gone by. Another form of coaxial cable, it costs more than the previously mentioned cable types, and is difficult to install due to its size and limited flexibility. It typically operates at 10MBps and can extend to 500 meters. Like its cousin thinnet, it is less sensitive to EMI than UTP. DIX/AUI connectors are used to connect cables together, and transceivers must be used to connect to the network card in the computer. Both ends of the network must be terminated with a 50-ohm resistor, and one end must be grounded. 10Base5 cable is an example of thicknet. The "10" indicates 10MBps speed, "Base" indicates baseband mode, while the "5" means it can go 500 meters.

Figure 6.3 shows a section of 10Base5 cabling stripped to show its components and size in relation to a quarter. There is a center conductor at the core of the cable that is wrapped in an insulator. Surrounding the insulator is the shield, or outer conductor (looks like mesh), and the actual jacket of the cable is on the outside.

Fiber Optic cabling is the most expensive of all. It is hard to install and you must be very precise in your installation. The costs and difficulties are outweighed, however, by the benefits. Fiber optic (FDDI) cabling typically runs at 100MBps and can extend for kilometers due to the fact that light is being sent down the wire, not electrical signals. It is the least sensitive of any cable type to EMI and cannot be easily tapped into or split.

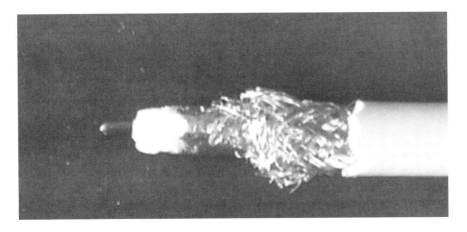

Figure 6.3 ■ Cross section of 10Base5 Cabling

Figure 6.4 shows a size comparison of the four types of cables discussed. At the top of the picture is 10Base2 (Thinnet) with a T-connector attached. Beneath it is a section of 10BaseT (Twisted Pair), followed by a small piece of Fiber Optic cabling. The 10Base5 (Thicknet) cable is at the bottom of the figure.

MISCELLANEOUS: DUPLEXING

The term *duplexing* is used to explain how communications can take place. In a full-duplex environment, both machines can communicate in both directions with each other at the same time (simultaneously). In a half-duplex environment, though they are both communicating, only one can communicate at a time (sequentially).

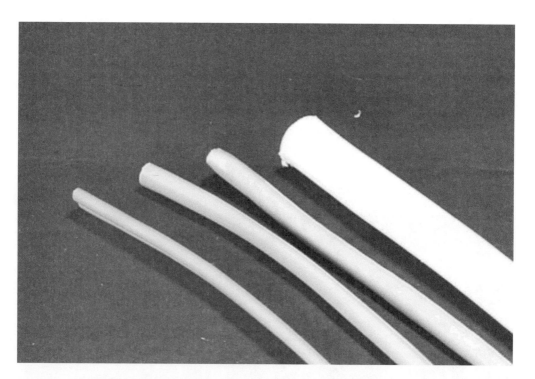

Figure 6.4 ■ **Size Comparison of the Four Primary Cables Types**

LAB 6.1 EXERCISES

6.1.1 IDENTIFY OSI SPECIFICS

a) Fill in the blanks in the following table to complete the OSI discussions.

Layer	Purpose	Data Type	Hardware
Application	Interface to network services.		Gateway
Presentation		Packet	Gateway
	Establishes rules for communication, synchronization, and how the system begins and ends a working session.	Packet	Gateway
Transport	Handles network transmission, all error checking, and end-to-end communications.	Datagram, segment (and packet)	
Network	Addressing; flow control; switching; translation of logical addresses into physical addresses.		Router—uses routing table; can determine best path; can be static or dynamic; can support multiple paths.
Data Link		Frame	Bridge—uses MAC addresses; can connect different media and unlike segments
	The connection, wire, cards, etc.; what you can see and touch.	Bits and signals	

6.1.2 IDENTIFY CABLING SPECIFICS

a) Fill in the blanks in the following table to complete the cabling specifications.

Cable	Cost	Installation	Capacity	Range	EMI
Thinnet	Less than STP and more than UTP	Easy			Less sensitive than UTP
Thicknet	More than STP and less than fiber	Not as easy as Thinnet			Less sensitive than UTP
Shielded Twisted Pair (STP)	More than UTP and less than Thicknet	Relatively easy			Less sensitive than UTP
Unshielded Twisted Pair (UTP)	Cheapest	Easy			Most sensitive of all
Fiber Optic	Most	Hard			Least sensitive of all

6.1.3 SHARING A FOLDER AND SETTING ACCESS LEVELS

For this Exercise, you will enable your My Documents folder for sharing and set access permissions to allow any user to see and read files in the folder.

1. The first step is to make sure that file sharing is enabled on your computer. To do so, open the Network control panel and select the button called File and Print Sharing. The resulting dialog box will allow you to select which services you would like to share. To enable file sharing, click on the box next to the text that reads "I Want to Be Able to Give Others Access to My Files."

    a) What effect does selecting this box have?

_____

_____

Now you must specify what type of access users may have.

    2. To set the security levels, choose the Access Control tab on the Network control panel.

    b) What options does this command give you?

_____

_____

Once you have selected the security level, you are ready to share the My Documents folder.

    3. Sharing a specific folder can be done from either the Desktop or from Windows Explorer. To share the My Documents folder, select it from either one of the programs named above.

    c) In this dialog, where do you think you would go to enable sharing?

_____

_____

    4. To start sharing the folder, click Shared As on the Sharing dialog. Supply a Share Name, which is the name you'll use to access this folder. The description is optional.

    d) When you select the access type, what options do you get for sharing?

_____

_____

5. Once you have filled in all these options, click OK to complete sharing.

e) e) What visual effect did this action have that indicates sharing is enabled?

_____

_____

LAB 6.1 EXERCISE ANSWERS

6.1.1 ANSWERS

a) Fill in the blanks in the following table to complete the OSI discussions.

Layer	Purpose	Data Type	Hardware
Application	Interface to network services.	Message	Gateway
Presentation	*Translates between Application and all others. Determines the appearance or formatting of all data. Responsible for encoding and decoding.*	Packet	Gateway
Session	Establishes rules for communication, synchronization, and how the system begins and ends a working session.	Packet	Gateway
Transport	Handles network transmission, all error checking, and end-to-end communications.	Datagram, segment (and packet)	*Gateway*

Network	Addressing; flow control; switching; translation of logical addresses into physical addresses. Routing data between network addresses.	*Datagram (and packet)*	Router—uses routing table; can determine best path; can be static or dynamic; can support multiple paths.
Data Link	*Arranges data into chunks called "frames"; error checking within frames; manages link control; communicates with card.*	Frame	Bridge—uses MAC addresses; can connect different media and unlike segments.
Physical	The connection, wire, cards, etc; what you can see and touch.	Bits and signals	*Repeater—no filtering or processing, just regeneration; can connect different media.*

6.1.2 ANSWERS

a) Fill in the blanks in the following table to complete the cabling specifications.

Cable	Cost	Installation	Capacity	Range	EMI
Thinnet	Less than STP and more than UTP	Easy	*Typically 10MBps*	*185 meters*	Less sensitive than UTP
Thicknet	More than STP and less than fiber	Not as easy as Thinnet	*Typically 10MBps*	*500 meters*	Less sensitive than UTP
Shielded Twisted Pair (STP)	More than UTP and less than Thicknet	Relatively easy	*From 16MBps to 500MBps*	*100 meters*	Less sensitive than UTP
Unshielded Twisted Pair (UTP)	Cheapest	Easy	*10MBps to 100MBps*	*100 meters*	Most sensitive of all
Fiber Optic	Most	Hard	*Typically 100MBps*	*kilometers*	Least sensitive of all

Cable length is an important factor in choosing the right cable type because certain types of cable are more susceptible to attenuation. Attenuation refers to the decrease in the power of the signal that can be transmitted over a wire. Attenuation can become a problem in local area networks where cable lengths might exceed the maximum accepted length for a particular type of cable.

6.1.3 ANSWERS

a) What effect does selecting this box have?

Answer: The File and Printer Sharing for Microsoft Networks service will appear among the list of installed services.

b) What options does this command give you?

Answer: You can select either "Share Level" access control—which requires a userid and password for each resource that you share—or User level which uses a central database to control access. Generally, share-level is sufficient.

c) In this dialog, where do you think you would go to enable sharing?

Answer: From the File menu, select Properties, then click on the "Sharing..." tab. Alternatively, you can select the folder from the program, then right click and select "Sharing..." from the pop-up menu.

d) When you select the access type, what options do you get for sharing?

Answer: There are three choices:
  - *Read Only: users will only be able to read and open files in the folder.*
  - *Full Access: users will be able to do anything with the files in the folder, including deleting them.*
  - *Depends on Password: users will need one password to access the shared folder in read-only mode and a different one to access it in "full."*

e) What visual effect did this action have that indicates sharing is enabled?

Answer: The icon next to My Documents now has changed and a hand appears under the original icon indicating it is shared.

LAB 6.1 SELF-REVIEW QUESTIONS

1) To what distance can 10Base5 cable extend?
   a) ___185 meters
   b) ___200 meters
   c) ___500 meters
   d) ___unlimited

2) The network cable most resistant to EMI would be which of the following?
   a) ___Fiber Optic
   b) ___Thicknet
   c) ___Thinnet
   d) ___STP

3) Coaxial cable must be terminated with a resistor of which of the following?
   a) ___1 ohm
   b) ___5 ohms
   c) ___10 ohms
   d) ___50 ohms

4) Which of the following are routable protocols?
   a) ___TCP/IP
   b) ___IPX/SPX
   c) ___NetBEUI
   d) ___DLC

5) To what distance can 10Base2 cable run?
   a) ___unlimited
   b) ___500 meters
   c) ___200 meters
   d) ___185 meters

Quiz answers appear in Appendix A, Section 6.1.

L A B   6.2

NETWORKING INTERFACE CARDS AND RAMIFICATION OF REPAIRS

LAB OBJECTIVES

After this Lab, you will be able to:

✓ Understand Network Interface Cards

✓ Understand Some Potential Problems When Working with Networks

✓ Install Network Interface Cards

Network adapters, also known as Network Interface Cards or NICs, are the hardware components installed into a personal computer to allow it to connect to a network. The NIC has the connections on it that the cabling needs in order to join the computer to the rest of the network. Common connections on a NIC are:

- RJ-45—for 10BaseT cabling
- BNC—for 10Base2
- Female DB—either 9- or 15-pin

The Network Driver Interface Specification (NDIS), a standard developed by Microsoft and 3Com Corp., describes the interface between the network transport protocol and the Data Link layer network adapter driver. The following list details the goals of NDIS:

- To provide a vendor-neutral boundary between the protocol and the network adapter driver so that any NDIS-compliant protocol stack can operate with any NDIS-compliant adapter driver.
- To define a method for binding multiple protocols to a single driver so that the adapter can simultaneously support communications under multiple protocols. In addition, the method enables binding of one protocol to more than one adapter.

The Open Data-Link Interface (ODI), developed by Apple and Novell, serves the same function as NDIS. Originally, ODI was written for NetWare and Macintosh environments. Like NDIS, ODI provides rules that establish a vendor-neutral interface between the protocol stack and the adapter driver. This interface also enables one or more network drivers to support one or more protocol stacks.

In the Windows 95 and Windows 98 environments, network cards are configured by the Plug and Play portion of the operating systems. In operating systems lacking Plug and Play, such as DOS, Windows 3.1*x*, or Windows NT 4.0, configuration can either be done through jumpers or the EPROM configuration switch, accomplished with software provided with the card. NICs will use an Interrupt Request (IRQ) setting, and often Input/Output (I/O) or Direct Memory Access (DMA) as well.

Figure 6.5 shows a typical Ethernet NIC for a desktop PC, while Figure 6.6 shows a PC Card NIC for a laptop computer. Notice in Figure 6.6 the adapter that converts the pin connections from the card into accepting a 10BaseT cable.

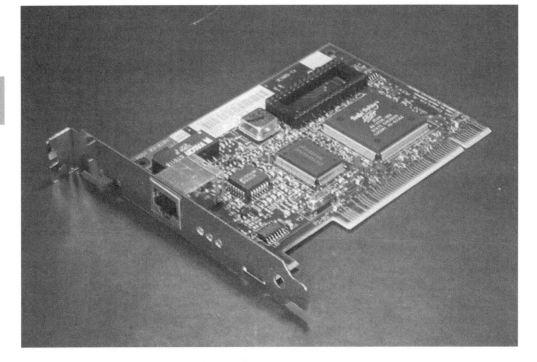

Figure 6.5 ■ **Typical Ethernet NIC for a desktop PC.**

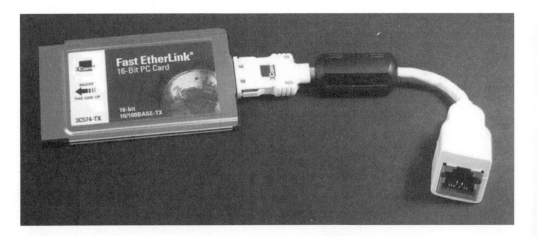

Figure 6.6 ■ **PC Card NIC for a laptop computer.**

TROUBLESHOOTING AND REPAIRS

When a personal computer must be taken off-line and worked on for some time, you are preventing a user from getting his regularly assigned work done. When the same situation exists for a network server, however, you are potentially preventing all employees of a company from getting their work done. Never underestimate the dependency that a company has on a network.

Common problems can be broken into the following categories:

- Cabling
- NICs
- Broadcast Storms

CABLING PROBLEMS

When dealing with cabling, check for the simplest solutions first. Make sure that connector pins are in the correct sockets and crimped tightly. Look for bent or broken pins. Rule out potential EMI causes: power cords, fluorescent lights, transformers, electric motors, and so forth.

Make sure that all the component cables in a segment are connected. A user who moves his client and removes the T-connector incorrectly can cause a broken segment. On networks based on coaxial Ethernet, look for missing terminators or improper impedance ratings. Impedance is described as the capability of the cable, at a given frequency, to respond to the flow of current. Mismatches in impedance along the length of a cable can lead to signal distortion.

With 10BaseT, because it is a "twisted" pair, make sure the cable used has the correct number of twists to meet the data-grade specifications. Watch out for malfunctioning transceivers with 10Base5, or T-connectors with 10Base2.

NIC PROBLEMS

When trying to troubleshoot a NIC, make sure the cable is properly connected to the card and you have the correct network adapter card driver (one that is associated with the proper transport protocol for the card's specifications). Verification of the protocol against the type of NIC is left for later in this chapter as an exercise. If the card came with any diagnostic software, run it and look for any problems that may be reported by the program.

To rule out any hardware or connection problems, pull the card and reseat it, making certain it fits properly in the slot. If that does not solve the problem, replace it with a card you know is good to verify that it is indeed the card that is the problem. If the NIC still doesn't respond, it is likely now that the slot into which the NIC is installed is the problem—you may need to move the NIC to another slot, if available, to resolve the problem.

Also, keep in mind that, even with Plug and Play, you can encounter conflicts between cards, especially if you have a lot of them installed. If this happens, you may need to disable Plug and Play on the NIC and use a hard address instead.

BROADCAST STORMS

A broadcast storm is a sudden flood of broadcast messages that clogs the transmission medium, approaching 100 percent of the bandwidth. Broadcast storms cause performance to decline and, in the worst case, prevent computers from accessing the network. The cause of a broadcast storm is often a malfunctioning network adapter, but a broadcast storm also can be caused when a device on the network attempts to contact another device that either doesn't exist or for some reason doesn't respond to the broadcast.

If the broadcast messages are viable packets (or even error-filled but partially legible packets), a network-monitoring or protocol-analysis tool often can determine the source of the storm. If the broadcast storm is caused by a malfunctioning adapter throwing illegible packets onto the line, and a protocol analyzer can't find the source, try to isolate the offending PC by removing computers from the network one at a time until the line returns to normal.

LAB 6.2 EXERCISES

6.2.1 TROUBLESHOOTING CABLING PROBLEMS

Identify the type of cabling used to connect your computer to the network.

a) Which type of cabling is in use on your system?

_____

_____

If possible, obtain a sample of this cable, strip the jacket, examine the conductors (noting the number of wires and whether they are twisted), and compare it to the cable's specification.

For the next procedure, request assistance from the network administrator in order to avoid causing any network outages.

Trace the cabling from your computer to the nearest network hub or switch.

b) How well are the connectors crimped?

_____

_____

c) Does the cabling pass near any EMI sources such as power cords, transformers, or electric motors?

_____

_____

6.2.2 VERIFYING NIC TRANSPORT PROTOCOLS

Using the NIC installed in your computer, verify that the proper protocol is in use for that card. *Tip*: You may want to have on hand the manual that came with the card.

To determine which protocol is in use with your card, go to Control Panel, then select Network. Highlight the type of card you are using from the list on the "Configuration" tab, and select Properties.

a) Where in this dialog would you expect to find protocol information?

_____

_____

6.2.3 INSTALL NETWORK INTERFACE CARDS

Using instructions as necessary from your PC's manufacturer, install a new NIC in your system.

    a) What tools were required?

_____

_____

    b) Were there any jumpers on the NIC that needed to be configured?

_____

_____

    c) Were any precautions required?

_____

_____

    d) What type of network connector is on the card?

_____

_____

LAB 6.2 EXERCISE ANSWERS

6.2.1 ANSWERS

    a) Which type of cabling is in use on your system?

    Answer: This answer will vary depending on your system.

To determine the cabling type, carefully examine the labeling along the cable jacket; every foot or so you will find writing indicating the cable manufacturer's name, part number, and specification such as Cat-3, Cat-5.

b) How well are the connectors crimped?

Answer: This answer will vary depending on your system. If it looks as though connectors are not well attached to the cable, you can possibly fix the situation with a crimping tool to crush the bottom ends of the connector pins around the cable.

Most crimping tools resemble pliers, but they are designed to allow the user to insert the cable into one portion of the tool, then "top" the wire to be crimped with its connector on the open end. When the tool is squeezed, the crimping tool compresses the connector around the cable. Note: Not all connectors are attached using this type of tool, but visual examination of the cable and its connector will quickly indicate which ones are "crushed on" and which ones might be soldered on.

LAB 6.2

c) Does the cabling pass near any EMI sources such as power cords, transformers, or electric motors?

Answer: Depending upon your specific office environment, the network wiring from your computer to the nearest hub or switch may be easy or difficult to trace. Where it is easy to trace, note its proximity to power cables and devices such as transformers and motors. As we discussed earlier in Lab 6.1, you'll want to protect against possible EMI influence from sources such as these.

6.2.2 ANSWERS

a) Where in this dialog would you expect to find protocol information?

Answer: Check the "Bindings" tab against the information provided in the manual that came with the card to see if you are using the correct one for the type of card installed.

6.2.3 ANSWERS

The procedure for installing a NIC varies from one brand and model of PC to another. Common among all models are the steps of removing the cover and one of the empty card slot blanks.

a) What tools were required?

Answer: This will usually just be a screwdriver for removing the cover and the card slot blank.

b) Were there any jumpers on the NIC that needed to be configured?

Answer: This will vary from make to make. Some NICs have jumpers, while most are software configurable.

**LAB
6.2**

c) Were any precautions required?

Answer: This is usually limited to the following: 1) powering down the PC, and 2) using anti-static mats and wrist straps.

d) What type of network connector is on the card?

Answer: Again this varies from model to model. Most will contain either a 10BaseT (which resembles a telephone jack) or a Coax (like a TV cable connector except with a twist lock instead of threads) connector.

LAB 6.2 SELF-REVIEW QUESTIONS

1) NDIS was developed by Microsoft and which other company?
   a) ___Cisco
   b) ___Novell
   c) ___IBM
   d) ___3Com

2) ODI was developed by Apple and which other company?
   a) ___Cisco
   b) ___Novell
   c) ___IBM
   d) ___3Com

3) Under NDIS, you can bind one protocol to how many adapter(s)?
   a) ___0
   b) ___1
   c) ___more than one
   d) ___protocols are not bound to adapters

4) A DB connection on the NIC card in the back of the PC would normally have how many pins?
   a) ___4
   b) ___8
   c) ___9
   d) ___12

5) The DB connection mentioned in Question 4 would normally be which of the following?

   a) ___male

   b) ___female

   c) ___either male or female

   d) ___neither male nor female

6) Which cabling type would employ transceivers?

   a) ___10BaseT

   b) ___10Base2

   c) ___10Base5

   d) ___none of the above

7) The source of a broadcast storm can often be determined by evaluating which of the following?

   a) ___a packet

   b) ___a broadcast

   c) ___a protocol

   d) ___a standard

8) Transport protocols must be compatible with which of the following? (Choose all correct answers)

   a) ___NICs

   b) ___Applications

   c) ___Operating systems

   d) ___Storms

9) Within a 10BaseT cable, the individual wires must be which of the following?

   a) ___isolated

   b) ___grounded

   c) ___twisted

   d) ___terminated

Quiz answers appear in Appendix A, Section 6.2.

C H A P T E R   6

TEST YOUR THINKING

With assistance as needed from the site network administrator, make a drawing of the organization's network. Include:

1)   Location of routers, switches, and hubs;

2)   Location of wiring closets (if any) and the type of connectors used there;

3)   Location and type of wiring between all of the above components; and

4)   Connections to phone company circuits (such as Frame Relay, ISDN, T-1, T-3, etc.).

C H A P T E R 7

CUSTOMER SATISFACTION

 Labor disgraces no man; unfortunately, you occasionally find men disgrace labor.

—Ulysses S. Grant

The Customer Satisfaction category makes up ten percent of the core exam—seven questions. Always appearing at the end of the exam, the responses you give to these questions do not factor into your pass/fail grade. They do, however, appear on the transcript and are intended to be a flag to employers indicating whether you understand the difference between what good service is and what it is not.

For all of the questions, the best rule of thumb is to use common sense. Never take actions more drastic than you need to and never involve other parties if you can solve the problem yourself.

LAB 7.1

EFFECTIVE BEHAVIOR

> ## LAB OBJECTIVES
>
> After this Lab, you will be able to:
> ✓ Understand the Keys to Effective Customer Satisfaction

Whether representing a company or yourself, you should always act in a professional manner. Your appearance and demeanor have a great deal to do with the lasting impression that stays with the customer. Always go to great lengths to instill in their minds confidence and a sense of security.

We have all been customers before, and are (hopefully) all familiar with the conduct required for effective customer service. Professional conduct includes politeness, guidance, punctuality, and accountability. Always treat customers with the same respect and empathy you would expect if the situation were reversed. Likewise, guide customers through the problem and the explanation. Tell them what has caused the problem they are currently experiencing and explain the best solution to keep it from reoccurring in the future.

The Exercises in this Lab will have you analyze some typical (and maybe not-so-typical) customer service situations and either suggest a course of action to take or decide whether or not the situation was handled successfully. If not, you will be asked to explain how you think it should have been handled.

This Lab examines customer satisfaction as it relates to effective behavior. While you may dismiss the topic as not factoring into your passing grade, know that many employers do ask to see your transcript and do take this portion very seriously. It will become painfully obvious if successful customer satisfaction is not on your agenda the first time you are on a call. Nobody likes to deal with difficult people, but if you are difficult as a technician, you will reflect poorly on yourself and the company you represent. This will not bode well for your future as a technician!

LAB 7.1 EXERCISES

7.1.1 UNDERSTAND THE KEYS TO EFFECTIVE CUSTOMER SATISFACTION

Customer C is expecting you any time between 10:30 and 11:30 am. The customer pleaded that you be there as early as possible because a critical piece of hardware isn't working and they have a deadline that must be met that afternoon. But because you had two other appointments that morning (with Customers A and B), you couldn't commit to anything earlier and couldn't be more specific in your Estimated Time of Arrival (ETA).

At 11 am, you find yourself ready to leave Customer B's shop to head to Customer C's place—about a 15-minute drive.

      a) What would you do at this point?

      _____

      _____

Technician John is called to a site to install a larger hard drive into a server. While doing so, he accidentally slips on some water that someone had spilled on the floor, loses his balance, and slams the new hard drive against a wooden cabinet.

To save face and to avoid a potential delay for the customer, John installs the now potentially damaged hard drive anyway, hoping that it still works. When it doesn't, John acts completely baffled by the faulty hard drive, apologizes profusely to the customer, who is very understanding, and promises to do everything he can to return as quickly as possible with a new hard drive. The customer ends up pleased that the delay was kept minimal and requests John the next time he calls for service.

b) Did John handle this situation successfully?

_____

_____

Technician Joan arrives at a job site expecting to do a routine repair of a malfunctioning printer, as outlined on the incident report. While repairing the printer, one of the client's employees interrupts Joan and asks her if she could take a look at his laptop, as he can't seem to get his modem to work. Joan apologizes and politely explains that she has been dispatched for a specific purpose and would get into trouble if she were to provide a service without going through the proper channels. She further explains that she would be glad to diagnose the problem, as long as the employee's supervisor filed another incident report and made an appointment for her to return.

c) Was Joan right to insist that the employee go through the proper channels before helping him?

_____

_____

While working the help desk, you receive a call from a customer who clearly has little technical skills. After spending 15 minutes calmly trying to extract the true nature of the customer's problem, he becomes irate with you, accuses you of being condescending, and demands to speak to your superior because you clearly cannot help him.

d) What would you do in this situation?

_____

_____

LAB 7.1 EXERCISE ANSWERS

7.1.1 ANSWERS

At 11 am, you find yourself ready to leave Customer B's shop to head to Customer C's place—about a 15-minute drive.

a) What would you do at this point?

Answer: You should call Customer C before leaving Customer B's shop to let them know you are on your way.

LAB 7.1

You may have answered a little differently in that you would simply head to Customer C's place content in knowing that you were going to be a little earlier than 11:30 after all, and this would have been correct. However, considering how important it was to the client that you be there as early as possible, a courtesy call just to let them know you are on your way shows that you care about the customer and his needs. This reflects well on both you and your employer.

PUNCTUALITY

Punctuality is important even before you ever arrive at the site. If you tell the customer you will be there at 10:30, you need to make every attempt to be there at that time. If you arrive late, you have given him false hope that the problem would be solved by a set time. That false hope can lead to anger when you arrive late and appear not to be taking their problem with the same seriousness as he is. Punctuality continues to be important throughout the service call and does not end with your arrival. If you need to leave to get parts, make sure that you tell the customer that you are leaving, give him the reason, and tell him when you will return. And make sure that you are there at that time. If, for some reason, you cannot return at the expected time, alert the customer and inform him of the new time.

In conjunction with time and punctuality, if a user asks how much longer the server will be down and you respond that it will up in five minutes, only to have it down for five more hours, you are creating resentment and possibly anger. When estimating downtime, always allow for more time than you think you will need just in case other problems occur. If you greatly underestimate the time, always inform the affected parties and give them a new time estimate. To use an analogy that will put it in perspective: if you take your car in to get an oil change and the clerk tells you it will be "about 15 minutes," the last thing you want is to be sitting there four hours later.

Always put yourself in your customer's shoes and treat them with the same respect you demand.

b) Did John handle this situation successfully?

Answer: Absolutely not!

Even though John was able to schmooze his way out of this situation and end up pleasing the customer in the long run, he still caused the customer an unnecessary delay by installing a potentially damaged hard drive. He also seriously jeopardized his integrity and that of his employer. An accountable technician would have admitted to the accident and explained to the customer that he could either take the chance and install it anyway or return to his office for a new hard drive.

ACCOUNTABILITY

Accountability is a trait well-respected in every technician. When problems occur, you need to be accountable for them and not attempt to pass the buck somewhere else. An instantly recognizable characteristic, you can no doubt think of people you know who have and do not have any sense of accountability. As easy as it is for you to think of such, it is equally easy for a customer to identify it in a technician. John was successful in pleasing the customer in the given example, but what if someone had seen him drop the hard drive? Never—ever, ever, ever, ever—lie to a customer!

c) Was Joan right to insist that the employee go through the proper channels before helping him?

Answer: Of course Joan was correct to suggest that he go through proper channels, but it wouldn't have hurt anything for her to at least take a look at the employee's laptop to see if the problem could be diagnosed quickly.

While it was admirable for Joan to want to follow procedure, taking five minutes to see if she could solve the problem quickly would have made the employee happy and wouldn't have set her back much at all. Flexibility is an important part of successful customer satisfaction.

FLEXIBILITY

Flexibility is another equally important trait for a service technician. While it is important you respond to service calls promptly and close them (solve them) as quickly as you can, you must also be flexible. If a customer cannot have you onsite until the afternoon, make your best attempt to work him into your schedule around the time most convenient for him. Likewise, if you are called to a site to solve a problem and the customer brings another problem to your attention while you are there, make every attempt to address that problem as well. Under no circumstances should you ever give a customer the cold shoulder or not respond to his problems because they were not on an initial incident report.

LAB
7.1

GUIDELINES FOR ONSITE SUPPORT

Customer satisfaction goes a long way toward generating repeat business. If you can meet the customers' expectations, you will almost assuredly hear from them again when another problem arises. If you can exceed the customers' expectations, you can almost guarantee that they will call you the next time a problem arises.

Customer satisfaction is important in all communication mediums—whether you are on-site, providing phone support, or communicating through e-mail or other correspondence. If you are on-site:

- When you arrive, immediately look for the person (user, manager, administrator, whoever) who is affected by the problem. Announce that you are there and assure him or her that you will do all you can to remedy the problem.
- Listen intently to what your customer is saying. Make it obvious that you are listening and respecting what he or she is telling you. If you do not understand for whatever reason, go to whatever lengths you need to in order to remedy the situation. Look for verbal and nonverbal cues that can help you isolate the problem.
- Share the customer's sense of urgency. What may seem like a small problem to you can appear as if the whole world is collapsing in around your customer. Remember that his or

her *business* is affected by the current problem he or she is experiencing.

- Be honest and fair with the customer and try to establish a personal rapport. Explain what the problem is or appears to be, what you believe is the cause of it, and what can be done in the future to prevent it from reccurring.
- Handle complaints as professionally as possible. Accept responsibility for any errors that may have occurred on your part and never try to pass the blame elsewhere. Avoid arguing with a customer as it serves no purpose; resolve any anger with as little conflict as possible. The goal is to keep him or her as a customer, not to win an argument. Remember the old saying: "The customer is always right."
- When you finish a job, notify the user that you are done. Make every attempt to find and inform the user of the resolution. If that is not possible, leave a note and/or a phone message explaining the resolution. You should also leave a means by which the user can contact you should there be a question about the resolution, or a related problem. In most cases, you should leave your business number and, when applicable, your pager number.

While working the help desk, you receive a call from a customer who clearly has little technical skills. After spending 15 minutes calmly trying to extract the true nature of the customer's problem, he becomes irate with you, accuses you of being condescending, and demands to speak to your superior because you clearly cannot help him.

d) What would you do in this situation?

Answer: This is a tough one. The best thing to do would be to apologize for appearing condescending and calmly explain that you think you know what the problem might be but you have a few more questions and would like to try and resolve the problem before handing it to someone else. If he continues to insist on speaking with your superior, provide him with that individual's name and contact information. Also, at your first opportunity, privately contact your superior directly and inform him of the possibility of an impending call from the client, along with the facts behind the situation, being as objective and accurate as possible, without making assumptions about who is right or wrong. The goal is to provide your superior with the background information that will enable him or her to adequately respond to the call from the customer if and when it occurs.

The key here is to try and calm the customer, alleviate his anger, and help him understand that you are truly concerned with his problem. Do not, under any circumstances, counter a customer's perceived insult with another. Telephone interaction is not always easy, but it's important to stay professional and focused on the customer's needs. Only if the customer becomes truly unreasonable with you should you consider handing him off to another technician.

GUIDELINES FOR TELEPHONE SUPPORT

LAB 7.1

- Always answer the telephone in a professional manner, announcing the name of the company and your own name.
- Make a concentrated effort to ascertain the customer's technical level and communicate at that level—not above or below it.
- The most important skill you can have is the ability to listen. You have to rely on the customer to tell you the problem and describe it accurately. He or she cannot do that if you are second-guessing or jumping to conclusions before the whole story is told. Ask questions that begin broadly, and then narrow down to help isolate the problem. It is your job to help guide the description of the problem from the user. For example:
  — Is the printer plugged in?
  — Is it on-line?
  — Are there any lights flashing on it?
  — When did the problem first occur?
  — Were there any other changes to the printer or the computer around the same time as the problem began?
- Complaints should be handled in the same manner as if you were on-site. Make your best effort to resolve the problem and not argue its points. Again: more than accomplish any other goal, you want to keep the customer.
- Only close the incident when the customer is satisfied that the solution you have given is the correct one and the problem has gone away.
- End the telephone call in a courteous manner. Thanking the customer for the opportunity to serve him or her is often the best way.

LAB 7.1 SELF-REVIEW QUESTIONS

In order to test your progress, you should be able to answer the following questions.

1) A customer is trying to explain a problem to you when you arrive on site, but you cannot understand the dialect. What should you do?
   a) ____ Request another technician be dispatched.
   b) ____Nod politely as if you understand and go about trying to solve the problem.
   c) ____Ignore the user and go about trying to solve the problem as contained on the incident report.
   d) ____Look for another person present who can help with the translation.

2) A customer becomes physically abusive by pushing you. What should you do?
   a) ____Push him as well to establish pecking order.
   b) ____Try to calm him down and leave if you cannot.
   c) ____Request all available technicians be dispatched.
   d) ____Call the local police.

3) The best way to show a customer you are paying attention when he or she is detailing an intermittent problem is to do which of the following?
   a) ____Nod.
   b) ____Smile to show you know just what they mean.
   c) ____Take notes.
   d) ____Arrange your tools.

4) A user in the next department has been on the phone with you for 15 minutes describing his desktop problem. No matter how many times you explain it to him, he does not understand what you are saying. What should you do?
   a) ____Suggest he call another tech.
   b) ____Suggest he get his manager.
   c) ____Suggest he call back tomorrow.
   d) ____Go to the user's machine.

5) When providing phone support and answering the call, which of the following should you do first?
   a) ____Identify yourself.
   b) ____Ask for the problem immediately.
   c) ____Ask the caller to please hold while you finish another call.
   d) ____Answer with a tech joke.

6) A customer tells you that she is really glad to see you and not Tony, the tech they had last time who she describes as a real jerk. How should you respond?

a) ___Thank her for her support and tell her how Tony screwed up another customer's site.

b) ___Call your manager and ask that Tony never be dispatched here again.

c) ___Suggest that the current perception could have been caused by Tony's drinking problem.

d) ___Thank her for her support and ask to see the system in question.

LAB 7.1

7) A customer complains that the printer on system A no longer prints after you were there working on system B. What should you do?

a) ___Adamantly tell the customer that you never touched system A.

b) ___Ask what type of network connects systems A and B.

c) ___Suggest that all printing be on system B.

d) ___Recommend that another tech address the problem.

8) While troubleshooting a customer's LAN, you determine the server must be rebooted. What should you do?

a) ___Broadcast a message to all users telling them the reboot is coming.

b) ___Reboot as quickly as you can.

c) ___Suggest the customer do the reboot after hours.

d) ___Ignore the request.

9) A customer complains that he cannot print to the workgroup laser printer. The first question you ask should be?

a) ___Have you checked the cables?

b) ___Have you rebooted the printer?

c) ___Have you ever printed to that printer?

d) ___Is the printer turned on?

10) When a customer needs to reach you quickly for troubleshooting mission-critical applications, you should provide them with which of the following?

a) ___Business phone number

b) ___Home phone number

c) ___E-mail address

d) ___Pager number

Quiz answers appear in Appendix A, Section 7.1.

C H A P T E R   7

TEST YOUR THINKING

You saw in the Lab text that there are many traits that make for good customer service. Apply this to your own world.

1) Have you ever had an experience where you were treated poorly by a salesperson? How did it make you feel—did you go back the next time you needed something and/or did you make sure someone else waited on you next time?

2) Have you ever gone to a restaurant and been told there is a 15-minute wait only to have it turn into 30, or even 45 minutes?

Observe other people in a customer service environment and consider how you might have handled both sides differently.

 The key here is to train yourself to be conscious of customer service situations. There is a lot to be learned by merely observing how various customer service interactions proceed and whether they are successful or not.

Call your local cable company, whether you are a customer or not, and tell them that you've heard a little bit about cable modems for your home PC, but you're unclear what they are or how you would get one. Ask them if this service is available in your area, and if so, ask them to explain it to you. If they tell you it's not available in your area, ask them if they have any advice for you.

(Alternatively, call your local phone company and ask them to explain your service options.)

3) Answer the following questions about your experience.

a) How long did you have to wait to speak with a representative?

b) Was the representative courteous and helpful?

c) Did the representative understand your request, and did he or she show genuine interest in your needs?

d) Were you satisfied that the representative truly tried to help you before ending the call?

e) Did the representative thank you for the opportunity to assist you?

f) How would you rate the company's customer service based on this experiment?

OPERATING SYSTEM FUNCTIONS, OPERATION, AND FILE MANAGEMENT

Something deeply hidden had to be behind things.

—Albert Einstein

CHAPTER OBJECTIVES

In this chapter, you will learn about:

This section constitutes the largest portion of the elective exam—with 30 percent of all questions coming from here. It is important to know the commands available within the operating systems and their purpose, as well as the basics of disk management.

L A B   8.1

OPERATING SYSTEM FUNCTIONS

LAB OBJECTIVES

After this Lab, you will be able to:

✓ Use DOS Commands

✓ Find and Examine a DOS System File

✓ Use Regedit.EXE

An operating system provides the user with the interface to the processor. It is the operating system that acts on the user's behalf and submits jobs that are processed. The operating system then takes the results and returns them to the user in a manner they were expecting. In most cases, the user does not interact directly with the operating system during the majority of the session, but rather interacts with applications that work between the operating system and the user.

Every operating system shares the commonality of providing the operations between the user (or their application) and the processor. How they implement it and other features they offer set one operating system apart from another. In this section, we will look at DOS, Windows 3.1, and Windows 95 and see how each is implemented and what it offers.

THE DOS OPERATING SYSTEM

Microsoft DOS (MS-DOS) is the oldest of the operating systems that you must know for the exam. As such, it is the simplest in implementation and in features. The latest version is 6.22.

In order for the operating system to boot, three files are needed:

- IO.SYS—hidden
- MSDOS.SYS—hidden
- COMMAND.COM—the command interpreter, not hidden

The first two files are used to actually start the operating system, while the third is the shell with which the user interacts. Whenever the user enters a command, COMMAND.COM checks to see if it can handle the request internally with its plethora of internal commands, or if it must look elsewhere for an executable file to handle the request. You will explore these commands in this Lab's Exercises.

LAB 8.1

In addition to the three files needed for the operating system to boot, two others—if they exist—can play an important part in the process: CONFIG.SYS and AUTOEXEC.BAT. If it exists, the CONFIG.SYS file runs before COMMAND.COM does, establishing the environment for the command interpreter. The AUTOEXEC.BAT file runs after COMMAND.COM does, setting variables and other parameters for the user. Both of these files are examined in greater detail in the next chapter.

There is one additional file you should be aware of: ANSI.SYS. This is a device driver that controls display functions, allowing you to set screen color, cursor position, display mode, and text attributes. All navigation in DOS is done through the command line (CD command).

THE WINDOWS 3.X OPERATING SYSTEM

If ever there was a misnomer, it is "Windows 3.x operating system." In reality, Windows 3.x runs on top of DOS—therefore it still utilizes IO.SYS, MSDOS.SYS, CONFIG.SYS, COMMAND.COM, and AUTOEXEC.BAT. Once booted, the user (or the AUTOEXEC.BAT file) calls the WIN.COM executable, which brings up the GUI (Graphical User Interface), that is, Windows 3.1 and Windows 3.11.

Being an extension of DOS, if you will, you have files with the same extensions that existed previously with DOS and more, as shown in Table 8.1.

Table 8.1 ■ Common File Types and Extensions for Windows 3.x

Extension	File Type
$$$	Temporary file
BMP	Bitmap picture
DLL	Dynamic Link Library
FNT	Font file
GIF	Graphics Interchange Format file
GRP	Program Manager group information
HLP	Help file
ICO	Icon
INI	Setup information for application
PIF	Program Information file
REC	Recorder macro file
TTF	Truetype Font file
WAV	Sound file

Of key importance are the INI—initialization files. These are start-up files written in ASCII text that Windows (or another application) needs to obtain parameters from in order to run. PROGRAM.INI contains information about Program Manager (PROGMAN.EXE) and restrictions that apply to its use. SYSTEM.INI holds hardware and settings information, while CONTROL.INI has "control" information such as screen saver, password, and so forth. WIN.INI is the daddy of them all, holding actual WIN.COM configuration data as well as pointers to the other files.

The operating system functions are divided into the kernel (KERN-LXXX.EXE), user (USER.EXE), and graphical component (GDI.EXE). All files are traditionally located in the Windows subdirectory (C:\WIN-DOWS).

THE WINDOWS 95 OPERATING SYSTEM

Unlike Windows 3.x, Windows 95 is a true operating system, although some people would argue this point, and have. The boot sequence is very similar to that of DOS, with the IO.SYS and MSDOS.SYS and COMMAND.COM files playing crucial rules. CONFIG.SYS and AUTOEXEC.BAT are not used, however, unless needed for compatibility with older (DOS) programs. Their functionality has now been incorporated into the Registry. The Registry consists of two files—SYSTEM.DAT and USER.DAT—that hold all configuration information. System.dat, as the name implies, holds information relevant to the hardware and the software installed upon it, while User.dat holds information relevant to the user—screen saver, wallpaper, shortcuts, and so forth. By default, all users share these two files, traditionally located in C:\Windows.

At any given time, the Registry is the combination of files currently active. For example, if Kristin logs in (username of kdulaney) on a Windows 95 machine, then the Registry is the SYSTEM.DAT file and USER.DAT file for her. If Evan logs in (username evand), then the System component remains the same, but the user portion changes to reflect his USER.DAT. The .dat files are compiled, non-ASCII files that can be edited with a tool for just such a purpose—REGEDIT.EXE—the Registry Editor. Figure 8.1 shows the editor. You will explore this program in this Lab's Exercises.

**LAB
8.1**

LAB 8.1 EXERCISES

8.1.1 USE DOS COMMANDS

For this Exercise, you will create a simple text file in a Windows program, save it to a new directory on your root directory, and then use some simple DOS commands to locate and manipulate the file. This is the first step in illustrating the nature of using the DOS operating system.

1. First, create a new folder on your C: drive and call it "aplustest."
2. Next, create a simple .txt file using any Windows word processing program.

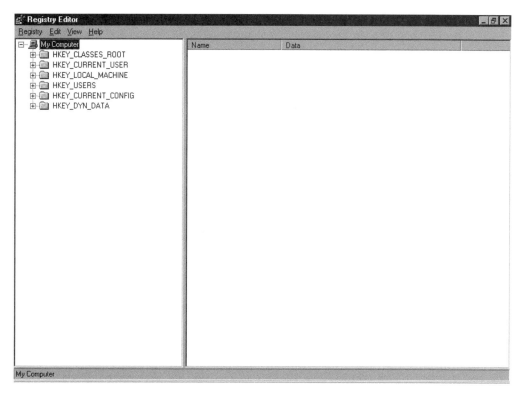

Figure 8.1 ■ This is a screen in the Registry Editor, which you will explore in Exercise 8.1.3.

3. Name the .txt file "test.txt", save it into the aplustest folder, and exit the program you used to create it.

4. To open a DOS window in which to work, click on the Start menu and choose Programs, then the MS-DOS Prompt icon.

   a) What do you see when you open the MS-DOS Prompt window?

   _____

   _____

5. As your first command, type in the command date and press the Enter key.

b) What happens when you enter the date command?

_____

_____

Press the Enter key to return to a normal prompt.

6. Type in the following command and press Enter:

    ```
    cd c:\aplustest
    ```

    c) What happens when you enter this command?

    _____

    _____

LAB 8.1

7. Type in the following command and press Enter:

    ```
    dir
    ```

    d) Do you see the file test.txt listed? What is the size of the file?

    _____

    _____

8. Type in the following command and press Enter:

    ```
    cls
    ```

    e) What happens when you enter the cls command?

    _____

    _____

9. Type in the following command and press Enter:

    ```
    ren test.txt test2.txt
    ```

10. Finally, close the DOS Prompt window to return to Windows 95. Go to the aplustest directory and take a look at the file you created.

f) What is the ren command used for?

_____

_____

8.1.2 FIND AND EXAMINE A DOS SYSTEM FILE

For this Exercise, you will locate one of the five primary DOS system files and examine it. While we can find and examine this file in Windows, we'll do it in DOS instead.

1. Open the DOS Prompt window as you did in Exercise 8.1.1. Maximize the window as you would any Windows window (it's easier to read this way).

 You can press ALT+Enter at this point for a full screen display.

2. Enter the following command:

   `cd c:\`

3. Now enter the following command:

   `dir`

   a) What happens now that's different from when you entered the dir command in Exercise 8.1.1?

_____

_____

4.   Now try this command:

`dir/p`

b) What's different?

_____

_____

5.   Examine the listed files.

c) Is the CONFIG.SYS file among those listed?

_____

LAB
8.1

_____

If not, hit any key to continue listing the contents of this directory. Continue until you have found this file.

6.   When you have spotted CONFIG.SYS, press Ctrl-C (that's the Control key and the C key simultaneously).

d) What happens when you press Ctrl-C?

_____

_____

Now we're going to examine the contents of this file.

7.   Enter the following command:

`type config.sys`

e) From the results, what does it appear that CONFIG.SYS is responsible for?

_____

_____

8.1.3 USE REGEDIT.EXE

In this Exercise, you will start REGEDIT.EXE on your system and examine some if its contents.

    1. Select Run from the Start menu.
    2. Enter REGEDIT in the Run dialog box and click the OK button. A window similar to the one shown in Figure 8.1 should open.

    a) What keys are listed in the left panel of your Registry Editor?

_____

_____

    3. Click the plus sign next to the HKEY_CURRENT_USER key to expand it.

    b) What is listed here as a result?

_____

_____

Go ahead and explore some of the items under HKEY_CURRENT_USER. Do not change any settings, however.

    c) What can you find to indicate to what this information applies?

_____

_____

LAB 8.1 EXERCISE ANSWERS

8.1.1 ANSWERS

a) What do you see when you open the MS-DOS Prompt window?

Answer: DOS is entirely a textual environment, so you should see some text similar to the following:

```
Microsoft (R) Windows 95
    (C) Copyright Microsoft Corp 1981 - 1996.


C:\Windows>
```

The last line of this display is known as the DOS prompt, or the command line. You should see a blinking cursor at the end of this line, which indicates this is where you begin typing commands.

b) What happens when you enter the `date` command?

Answer: You should see something similar to the following:

```
Current date is Sat 07-17-1999
Enter new date (mm-dd-yy):
```

Pressing the Enter key returns you to a normal prompt, as you did in the Exercise.

c) What happens when you enter this command?

Answer: The prompt changes to the directory you specified.

d) Do you see the file test.txt listed? What is the size of the file?

Answer: Yes, the file should be listed. My file is 27 bytes in size.

If you've never used DOS before, the results of this step may seem confusing, but essentially what the `dir` command does is list the contents of the specified directory, in this case aplustest. Basically the same information is displayed here as is in the detailed view of Windows Explorer.

■ FOR EXAMPLE

Let's examine the results of listing the directory:

```
Directory of C:\aplustest

.                <DIR>              07-17-99  12:56P    .

..               <DIR>              07-17-99  12:56P    ..

TEST    TXT              27         07-17-99  12:56P    test.txt

        1 file (s) 27 bytes

        2 dir (s) 120,356,864 bytes free
```

It's the fourth line of this directory that you are concerned with (the first line tells you which directory you're displaying, the second represents My Computer, and the third represents your C:\ directory). Interpreting this line from left to right, you can see the name of the file, the file type, the file size, and the date and time the file was modified. The last item is simply the file's full Windows 95 name. If you were to view the contents of this folder in Windows Explorer, you would find the same information. (Note that if there were more files in aplustest, they would be listed as well on separate lines.) The last two lines show you how many files were found, the total size of those files combined, and the number of directories with disk space free (similar to what is shown on the status bar of Windows Explorer).

The `dir` command lists the files and folders of any specified directory.

e) What happens when you enter the `cls` command?

Answer: The cls command clears the DOS screen.

9. Type in the following command and press Enter:

```
ren test.txt test2.txt
```

10. Finally, close the DOS Prompt window to return to Windows 95. Go to the aplustest directory and take a look at the file you created.

f) What is the `ren` command used for?

Answer: The `ren` command is used to rename a file.

You should see the results of renaming the file from test.txt to test2.txt in Windows Explorer. You could have used the DOS `dir` command to verify this as well.

The syntax of the `ren` command is as follows:

```
ren oldfilename newfilename
```

Commands that you enter in DOS are interpreted by the COMMAND.COM file mentioned earlier. If COMMAND.COM cannot handle the request internally, it looks elsewhere for an executable file to handle the request. Commands internal to COMMAND.COM are shown in Table 8.2.

**LAB
8.1**

Table 8.2 ■ DOS Commands

Command	Purpose
BREAK	Look for CTRL-C key combination
CALL	Provides ability to shell out to another program
CD	Changes directories
CLS	Clear the screen
COPY	Copy files
DATE	Set or show the system date
DEL	Delete files
DIR	List files in the directory
ECHO	Send back a message to the screen
ERASE	Delete files
FOR	Looping logic control
GOTO	Jump over a set of commands

Table 8.2 ■ DOS Commands *(continued)*

Command	Purpose
IF	Perform rudimentary logic control
LOADHIGH	Place a program in memory above 640K
MD	Make directories and subdirectories
PATH	Show or set the search path, separating entries with semicolons (for example, C:\;C:\DOS;C:\DATA\EDULANEY). There is no limitation on the number of directories that can be specified, but the limit on the entire statement is 128 characters.
PAUSE	Stop processing until the user presses a key
PROMPT	Change the command prompt the user interacts with
RD	Remove directories and subdirectories
REM	Remark statement
REN	Rename a file
SET	Show or add environmental variables
SHIFT	Change to the next variable
TIME	Show or set the system time
TRUENAME	Complete name for file
TYPE	Display the contents of a file to the screen
VER	Show the current DOS version
VOL	Show the volume (disk) ID

If COMMAND.COM cannot resolve the command internally, it looks in the current directory for a file with a .COM extension that can do so. If it does not find a match, it looks in the current directory for a file with a .EXE extension that can do so. If it does not find a match, it looks in the current directory for a file with a .BAT extension that can do so. Finding no matches in the current directory, it searches the first directory specified in the PATH statement for a .COM file, then a .EXE file, then a .BAT file. Finding no matches, it moves through the rest of the PATH statement, in the order given, looking for a .COM, .EXE, or .BAT file that matches the name so it can execute it. If none is found, an error message is returned to the user.

 While this book is in no way intended to be a complete DOS primer, you will explore more of these commands in Lab 8.2.

The fact that COMMAND.COM only searches for files with three extensions serves as a pointer to how important file extensions are to DOS. Table 8.3 lists the common extensions and their file types.

**LAB
8.1**

Table 8.3 ■ Common File Types and Extensions

Extension	File Type
000	DBLSPACE (compression) file
BAS	Basic language program
BAK	Backup of a BAT file
BAT	Batch program holding calls to other programs
BIN	Device driver/machine language file
COM	Small machine language program
DRV	Device driver (often used with printers)
EXE	Larger machine language program
INF	Information file used to configure an application
OVL	Program overlay file
PCX	Paintbrush picture
ME	Text file of information relevant to program or operating system (READ.ME)
SYS	Device driver/configuration file
TXT	ASCII text file

8.1.2 ANSWERS

For this Exercise, you listed the contents of the C:\ directory using the following command:

```
dir
```

a) What happens now that's different from when you entered the `dir` command in Exercise 8.1.1?

Answer: Too many files are listed too quickly to be able to see them all.

You cannot use the arrow keys in DOS to scroll up or down to view text that has scrolled off the screen. The next command should have solved this problem:

```
dir/p
```

b) What's different?

Answer: DOS pauses when the screen fills with text.

`/p` is known as a DIR parameter. This and other parameters will be explored further in Lab 8.2.

c) Is the CONFIG.SYS file among those listed?

Answer: This answer depends on your system.

d) What happens when you press Ctrl-C?

Answer: Ctrl-C acts as a break from the currently running operation.

e) From the results, what does it appear that CONFIG.SYS is responsible for?

Answer: As you may have guessed, the type *command lists the contents of the specified file. The CONFIG.SYS file will contain different drivers and settings depending on your specific environment.*

The DOS command PROMPT opens at your profile level. This also affects whether or not the CONFIG.SYS file will be viewed.

As another exercise, you may want to go to another computer and examine its CONFIG.SYS file to see where the settings may be similar and where they may differ.

The CONFIG.SYS file is examined in greater detail in Chapter 9, "Memory Management."

8.1.3 ANSWERS

In this Exercise, you started REGEDIT.EXE on your system.

a) What keys are listed in the left panel of your Registry Editor?

Answer: When first started, REGEDIT presents a series of items on the left:

HKEY_CLASSES_ROOT

HKEY_CURRENT_USER

HKEY_LOCAL_MACHINE

HKEY_USERS

HKEY_CURRENT_CONFIG

HKEY_DYN_DATA

These items are called the *root keys*, the top-level fields beneath which all other information is contained. The root keys, which are the same for all systems, are a means of presenting the information stored within the Registry.

Next, you expanded the HKEY_CURRENT_USER key.

b) What is listed here as a result?

Answer: Additional items such as those listed below are located beneath HKEY_CURRENT_USER:

- AppEvents
- Control Panel
- InstallLocationsMRU
- Keyboard Layout
- Network
- RemoveAccess
- Software

c) What can you find to indicate to what this information applies?

Answer: HKEY_CURRENT_USER is the USER.DAT file that is currently in use. It is a mirror to what is beneath one portion of HKEY_USERS (the current user must be a subset of all users who can use the system) and displays information about the current user's profile. With each new user logged on, the USER.DAT file will be loaded to reflect the preferences of the logged on user—assuming that profiles have been enabled. The other keys in REGEDIT are explained as follows.

HKEY_USERS contains the possible USER.DAT files on that particular machine. HKEY_LOCAL_MACHINE is the SYSTEM component of the Registry. HKEY_CURRENT_CONFIG is the system as it is currently configured. As such, HKEY_CURRENT_CONFIG is a subset of what is in HKEY_LOCAL_MACHINE.

HKEY_CLASSES_ROOT is another subset of what is beneath HKEY_LOCAL_MACHINE—a mirror of HKEY_LOCAL_MACHINE\SOFTWARE\Classes. This exists for one purpose only—to appease any old or new applications that may be looking for information in REG.DAT—the old Registry from Windows 3.*x* days. Many 32-bit applications use this top-level hive for searches for file extension mapping to applications.

HKEY_DYN_DATA is the dynamic data—also known as Plug and Play. On Windows 9*x*, there will be values held here that are generated each time the operating system starts up. One setting may appear in more than one location in the Registry. If it is because one is a subset of another (such as appearing in HKEY_CURRENT_CONFIG and HKEY_LOCAL_MACHINE), you really only have one setting. Regardless of where you choose to make a change, you are doing so for all other places it may appear.

LAB 8.1 SELF-REVIEW QUESTIONS

1) In which of the following files is the user portion of the Windows 95 registry stored?
   a) ___User.txt
   b) ___User.ini
   c) ___User.dat
   d) ___User.exe

2) Which file runs after COMMAND.COM ?
   a) ___CONFIG.SYS
   b) ___AUTOEXEC.BAT
   c) ___IO.SYS
   d) ___MSDOS.SYS

3) What is the purpose of the file COMMAND.COM?
   a) ___Serves as the command line interpreter for the DOS shell
   b) ___Contains all the DOS commands
   c) ___Manages the Registry
   d) ___Runs the IO.SYS file

4) What is the registry?
   a) ___A configuration file used by DOS
   b) ___A file that contains user preferences
   c) ___A centralized database containing configuration information
   d) ___An editing tool used in Win 95/98

5) Which of the following is the tool used to edit the Registry?
   a) ___Edit.exe
   b) ___Edit.com
   c) ___Regedit.exe
   d) ___Regedit.com

LAB 8.1

6) What is the purpose of the HKEY_LOCAL_MACHINE registry key file?
   a) ___Contains local user preferences
   b) ___Contains settings for the hardware installed on the computer
   c) ___Contains systems initialization settings
   d) ___Contains plug and play settings

7) A command that is not internal to COMMAND.COM is:
   a) ___Copy
   b) ___Xcopy
   c) ___Erase
   d) ___Del

8) The driver that can control screen attributes is:
   a) ___CONFIG.SYS
   b) ___AUTOEXEC.BAT
   c) ___MSDOS.SYS
   d) ___ANSI.SYS

9) Where are the INI files typically stored in Win3.1?
   a) ___C:\ (the root directory)
   b) ___In the Registry
   c) ___In My Documents
   d) ___C:\WINDOWS

Quiz answers appear in Appendix A, Section 8.1.

L A B   8.2

WORKING WITH FILES AND DIRECTORIES

LAB OBJECTIVES

After this Lab, you will be able to:

✓ Create and Edit Files and Directories in Different Operating Systems

✓ Assign and Modify File and Directory Attributes

The ability to create files and directories in an operating system is of critical importance. The ability to assign properties/attributes to those items is of equal importance. Both of those topics are examined in this section. The utilities that were there in DOS have remained and are still available from the command line, while the graphical interfaces have added means by which the same functions can be accomplished without going to the command line.

NAMING CONVENTIONS

DOS and Windows 3.*x* allow you to create a file or directory with a name of up to 8 characters in length and an optional 3 character extension. Windows 95 allows you to create names of up to 255 characters in length with the extension being within that number. One "gotcha" to watch for is that although 255 characters can be used for a filename, the path to that file can only be a maximum of 260 characters in length, so you may not see a complete filename when it is preceded by a long pathname.

The use of extensions is highly recommended with all files; although legal, it is frowned upon for subdirectories. All numbers and letters of the alphabet can be used in the name, as well as the following characters: ^, $, ~, !, #, %, &, -, {, }, (,).

Control characters should **not** be used in names (the first 32 ASCII character set), and you should also avoid the following characters: , \ <>/*?+.

Periods have special meaning—separating the name from the extension—and cannot be used within the file or directory name in DOS or Windows 3.*x*. Additional periods can be used in the names of Windows 95 files, but for compatibility purposes it is not recommended. Windows 95 will, by default, make an *alias* for every long file name that is stored on it for compatibility with the older operating systems.

You will explore some additional command-line options in this Lab's Exercises.

THE GRAPHICAL OPTIONS

LAB
8.2

In the graphical interfaces, the core remains the same, but you have other options available to you. As one example of the graphical alternative to the command-line option, to create a subdirectory when saving a file, you can click on the folder to the right of the asterisk, as shown in Figure 8.2. To move to a different directory, you can use the dropdown menu to move anywhere (even another drive), or click on the folder with the arrow on it to move back one directory, as shown in Figure 8.3.

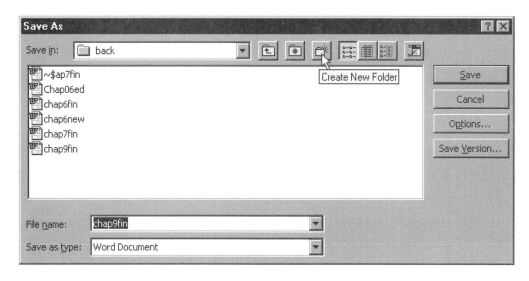

**Figure 8.2 ■ One Windows equivalent to creating a subdirectory at
the command line with the *mkdir* command is to click the Create New Folder button in the Save As dialog box when you are
saving a file.**

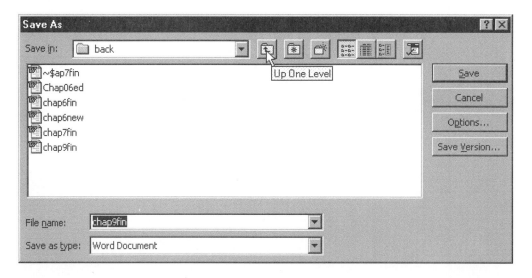

**Figure 8.3 ■ Here is another example of the ease of using a graphical
user interface as opposed to entering commands at the command line.**

LAB 8.2 EXERCISES

8.2.1 CREATE AND EDIT FILES AND DIRECTORIES IN DIFFERENT OPERATING SYSTEMS

Begin this Exercise by creating two directories on a floppy in Windows. Name one directory lab8_1 and the second lab8_2. Then create a new text file in a Windows word processor that reads:

> `This is a test of the Emergency Broadcasting System.`

Name this file ex_8_2_1.txt and save it to the floppy within the folder lab8_2.

In this Exercise, you will organize the files and directories that you've created in this chapter so far. You will also edit the text file that you just created.

1. Open a DOS window and change to the root directory on the C drive.

2. Enter the following command at the command line:

   `mkdir a_plus`

3. Return to Windows Explorer.

   a) Is there a folder on your C drive called a_plus?

   _____

   _____

4. Now enter the following command:

   `xcopy a: c:\a_plus /s`

If your floppy drive is not drive A, replace a: with the letter that corresponds to your floppy drive.

b) What happens?

_____

_____

c) Why do you suppose the subdirectory lab8_1 wasn't copied?

_____

_____

Create the subdirectory lab8_1 in the a_plus folder on your C drive.

d) How did you do this?

_____

_____

**LAB
8.2**

Move the file test2.txt from Exercise 8.1.1 into the lab8_1 subdirectory you just created.

e) What command did you use to move test2.txt?

_____

_____

Now enter the following command:

```
rd c:\aplustest
```

Return to Windows Explorer and open the directory aplustest.

f) What happens when you open the aplustest directory?

_____

_____

Next, you will edit the file ex_8_2_1.txt using DOS.

1. Enter the following command at the DOS command line:

   ```
   edit c:\a_plus\lab8_2\ex_8_2_1.txt
   ```

   g) What happens when you enter this command?

   _____

   _____

2. Without using your mouse, change the text in this file to read:

   ```
   This is a test of the Emergency Publishing System.
   ```

   h) How did you edit this text without using the mouse?

   _____

   _____

LAB 8.2

3. Press the Alt key on your keyboard, then press the Down Arrow key.

   i) What happens?

   _____

   _____

4. Use the Down Arrow key to select Save As from the File menu, then press the Enter key.
5. Save this file as ex_8_2_1a.txt
6. Press the Alt key again, then exit the Edit program.
7. Now, enter the following command:

   ```
   dir c:\a_plus /s/p
   ```

   j) What does DOS display for you?

   _____

   _____

k) What do you notice about the contents of the lab8_2 subdirectory?

_____

_____

8.2.2 ASSIGN AND MODIFY FILE AND DIRECTORY ATTRIBUTES

In this Exercise, you will explore the attributes, such as hidden or read-only, that can be assigned to a file or directory.

1. Enter the following command:

```
attrib +h c:\a_plus\lab8_2
```

**LAB
8.2**

2. Now list the directory contents of a_plus.

a) What happens?

_____

_____

3. Next, do a directory listing of a_plus\lab8_2.

b) Why do you think you can see the contents of lab8_2?

_____

_____

4. Enter the following command:

```
attrib c:\a_plus\lab8_2
```

c) What are the results of entering this command?

_____

_____

5. Finally, enter the following command, then try another directory listing of a_plus:

```
attrib -h c:\a_plus\lab8_2
```

d) What are the results?

_____

_____

LAB 8.2 EXERCISE ANSWERS

8.2.1 ANSWERS

a) Is there a folder on your C drive called a_plus?

Answer: There should be.

The mkdir command is used to create a directory or subdirectory. Another command that you can use is simply md (for make directory). Both commands accomplish the same thing.

You should note that you do not need to change to a specific directory in order to create a subdirectory within it. All you really need to do is enter the complete path name.

■ *FOR EXAMPLE:*

In this Exercise, regardless of which directory you were currently in (as specified on the command line prompt), you could have created a_plus on your C drive by entering the following command:

```
mkdir c:\a_plus
```

This works similarly with any DOS command, as long as you enter the complete path name. Try this:

```
cd c:\windows\system\color
```

This should change your prompt to read:

```
C:\WINDOWS\SYSTEM\COLOR>
```

Without cd'ing back to c:\a_plus, you can still do a directory listing of it by entering:

```
dir c:\a_plus
```

b) What happens?

Answer: You should see the following:

```
lab8_2\ex_8_2_1.txt
lab8_2\ex_8_2_1a.txt
 2 File (s) copied
```

Files can be copied from one location to another with the copy command, moved with the move command, and renamed with the ren command. To copy an entire directory and all of its contents, use xcopy.

Here we used the /S parameter when copying, which is used to copy as well as list files. The /E parameter will get subdirectories even if they are empty, which explains why the subdirectory lab8_1 wasn't copied in this case (it was empty)

If you need to copy an entire disk, the DISKCOPY command is the one to use, with the syntax being source, then target.

■ FOR EXAMPLE:

The following will make an exact copy of the disk in drive A: on drive B:

```
DISKCOPY A: B:
```

c) Why do you suppose the subdirectory lab8_1 wasn't copied?

Answer: As you just learned, the /E parameter would have copied this subdirectory even though it's empty.

The syntax to accomplish this would have been:

```
xcopy a: c:\a_plus /s/e
```

d) How did you do this?

Answer: *You should have used the following command to create this subdirectory:*

```
mkdir c:\a_plus\lab8_1
```

The following would have worked as well:

```
md c:\a_plus\lab8_1
```

e) What command did you use to move test2.txt?

Answer: *You should have used the following command:*

```
move c:\aplustest\test2.txt c:\a_plus\lab8_1
```

You could also have simply copied this file using the `copy` command instead of the `move` command.

f) What happens when you open the aplustest directory?

Answer: *You can't. The rd command is responsible for removing empty directories.*

To remove a file, you would use `del` or `erase` (they are both the same). The `rd` command is used to remove a directory that is empty, and DOS 6.2 brought into existence the `deltree` command that can recursively delete a directory and all the subdirectories beneath it.

Next, you entered the following command:

```
edit c:\a_plus\lab8_2\ex_8_2_1.txt
```

g) What happens when you enter this command?

Answer: *This command opens the file ex_8_2_1.txt in a DOS utility called Edit.*

Edit is a very generic DOS utility used to create and edit simple ASCII text documents. It has none of the snazzy features as most Windows word processing programs, such as Microsoft Word, but it serves its purpose in DOS. Go ahead and explore this utility if you wish to learn more about its capabilities.

h) How did you edit this text without using the mouse?

Answer: *You should have used your keyboard's Arrow keys to navigate through the text.*

You can use the CTRL key and the Arrow keys to jump over words in the file, just like you can in Windows programs. You can also use the Shift and Arrow keys to highlight characters.

You should note that you can also use your mouse to interact with the Edit utility, but the purpose of this Exercise is to show you that your keyboard is a primary input device in DOS.

i) What happens?

Answer: Pressing the Alt key on your keyboard activates the menu bar. You use the Arrow keys to navigate the menu and make choices. Pressing the Enter key activates your selection.

Your final step in this Exercise was to enter the following command:

```
dir c:\a_plus /s/p
```

j) What does DOS display for you?

Answer: You should see the entire contents of the a_plus directory, including the contents of all subdirectories.

The /S parameter is only one parameter that can be used with the `dir` command. As you can see, it's a handy one. Table 8.4 lists other parameters that you can use with the `dir` command.

Table 8.4 ■ Parameters for the `dir` Command

Parameter	Effect
/S	To view the contents of all subdirectories
/P	To pause the display after each screen
/A	To see files only of a particular attribute
/W	To show the file names in a wide format (columnar display)
/O	To order (sort) the display
/L	To convert all names to lowercase
/B	To give a bare output—names only

k) What do you notice about the contents of the lab8_2 subdirectory?

Answer: The filename for ex_8_2_1a.txt is truncated to ex_8_2~1.txt.

This is called *aliasing*, as you saw in the Lab text. As you know, DOS can only handle file names of eight characters or less in length, followed by the three-character extension. Windows 95 automatically creates an alias for names that are longer than eight characters.

For example, if you name a file "My_Refrigerator_Warranty.txt", the alias becomes the first six characters, a tilde, and an incremental number, followed by the first three characters following the last period. Thus this file name would be aliased as:

```
My_Ref~1.txt
```

If you also had a file called "My_Refrigerator_Magnets.txt", it would become:

```
My_Ref~2.txt
```

LAB 8.2

and so on. After nine incremental numbers, only five letters of the name are reserved so the number can grow further:

```
My_Re~10.txt
```

and so on.

Paths to file and directory locations can be absolute or relative. An absolute path specifies how to get there regardless of where you are. Thus C:\A_PLUS\My_Ref~2.Doc will always point to that location regardless of what directory you happen to be in at the time. A relative path points to the location relative to where you are now. For example, if you are currently in that directory, you can reference the file simply as:

```
My_Ref~2.Doc.
```

If you are in a subdirectory of A_PLUS, you can signify moving back one directory with two periods:

```
..\My_Ref~2.Doc
```

and so on.

8.2.2 ASSIGN AND MODIFY FILE AND DIRECTORY ATTRIBUTES

In this Exercise, you entered the following command and listed the contents of a_plus:

```
attrib +h c:\a_plus\lab8_2
```

a)   What happens?

Answer: Only the directory lab8_1 shows up within a_plus.

This is an example of assigning an attribute (in this case, the Hidden attribute) to a directory. The ATTRIB command, used without parameters, will show the attributes of files and/or directories, and it can be used with parameters to turn the attributes on and off for the entity.

The four attributes that DOS and the other operating systems in question understand are:

- R—Read-Only
- H—Hidden
- S—System
- A—Archive

Read-Only mode allows the file to be listed and displayed, but keeps it from being modified or deleted.

The Hidden attribute prevents the file from being listed or displayed in a normal directory search. This feature can be useful for protecting system or other important files from being inadvertently deleted, overwritten, or modified.

The System attribute is used to tell the operating system that this file is crucial to system operations and should not be deleted.

The Archive attribute is used to signify whether a file has changed or been modified since the last time it was backed up. When you first create a new file, it has the archive bit turned on. Assuming you do a full backup that night, the archive bit would then be turned off. It would only be turned back on if you modify the file. This prevents it from being included in any incremental or differential backups that you may do during the week to shorten your backup time.

The plus sign before the attribute's letter tells DOS to activate that attribute. You can assign as many attributes to a file or directory within one command that you wish. So the following command would assign the Hidden, Read-Only, and System attributes to lab8_2:

```
attrib +h +r +s c:\ a_plus\lab8_2
```

b) Why do you think you can see the contents of lab8_2?

Answer: In this example, you can see the contents of lab8_2 because you know it's there and went directly to it.

The directory still exists, but as explained previously, the Hidden attribute "hides" it to protect it from being inadvertently deleted, overwritten, or modified.

Next, you entered the following command:

```
attrib c:\a_plus\lab8_2
```

c) What are the results of entering this command?

Answer: You should see something like the following:

```
   H        LAB8_2              c:\a_plus\lab8_2
```

As stated previously, the `attrib` command, when used without parameters will show the attributes of files and/or directories. This proves that lab8_2 has been assigned the Hidden attribute.

Finally, you entered the following command and did another directory listing of a_plus:

```
attrib -h c:\a_plus\lab8_2
```

d) What are the results?

Answer: The directory is listed this time.

The minus sign before the attribute's letter instructs DOS to deactivate that attribute for the referenced file or directory.

You can view the attributes of files and directories in Windows 95 directly in Windows Explorer. Simply select the file or directory and right-click on it. From the pop-up menu, choose Properties. Figure 8.4 shows the pop-up menu for a .BAK file.

LAB 8.2

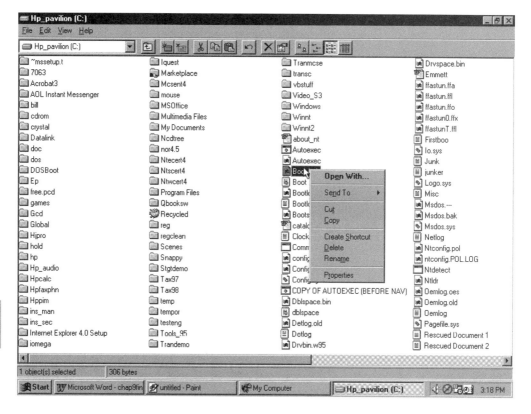

**LAB
8.2**

Figure 8.4 ■ Right-clicking on a file or directory brings up this menu.

Figure 8.5 shows the attributes at the bottom of the Properties page. A check in the checkbox indicates that the attribute currently exists on the file, and can be removed by removing the check. Conversely, an attribute can be assigned merely by placing a check in the box.

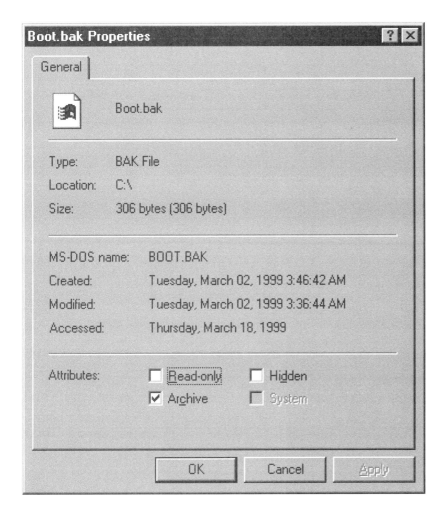

Figure 8.5 ■ **File and directory attributes are listed at the bottom of that item's Properties window.**

LAB 8.2 SELF-REVIEW QUESTIONS

In order to test your progress, you should be able to answer the following questions.

1) Which attribute is used to prevent a file from being erased?
   a) ___hidden
   b) ___system
   c) ___archive
   d) ___read-only

2) How many characters can a filename be—without the extension—in DOS:
   a) ___3
   b) ___8
   c) ___255
   d) ___260

3) How many characters can the filename be—with the extension—in Windows 95:
   a) ___3
   b) ___8
   c) ___255
   d) ___260

4) Which of the following is the command to copy a directory and all sub-directories—those with and without files beneath them ?
   a) ___XCOPY C:\ONE C:\TWO
   b) ___ XCOPY C:\ONE C:\TWO /E
   c) ___ XCOPY C:\ONE C:\TWO /S
   d) ___ XCOPY C:\ONE C:\TWO /S /E

5) Which of the following is the command to recursively delete a directory and all subdirectories?
   a) ___RD
   b) ___DEL
   c) ___DELTREE
   d) ___ERASE

Quiz answers appear in Appendix A, Section 8.2.

L A B   8.3

BASIC DISK MANAGEMENT

LAB OBJECTIVES

After this Lab, you will be able to:

✓ Run ScanDisk

✓ Identify Backup Statistics

✓ Run FDISK.EXE

✓ Understand Fragmentation and the Use of DEFRAG.EXE

The ability to manage the disk(s) on a machine is essential to properly interact with the system. As a general rule, the utilities that came with DOS and Windows 3.*x* have remained in Windows 95, with a few modifications and exceptions. The following is a breakout of the utilities and the operating systems they work with, in order of function.

FILE SYSTEMS

One of the first file systems ever created for the personal computer was the File Allocation Table (FAT). Over the years, several changes have been made to it, but it has remained essentially the same at its core that it always was. FAT is the only choice available in DOS and Windows 3.*x* and is limited to filenames of 8 characters in length, with 3-character extensions. Additionally, there is a maximum of 512 entries that can exist in the root partition.

When Windows 95 came out, it utilized a deviation of FAT called the Virtual File Allocation Table (VFAT). Essentially, it is the same as FAT, but uses multiple entries in the table for a single file that has a long character name. If you figure that FAT allows for 8 characters + 3 characters + 2 unused spaces, you can reason that the maximum number of characters in each entry is 13 characters. Under VFAT, when you save a file with a 40-character filename, it merely uses up four entries in the table 13+13+13+1.

When the user looks to see what files are there, he or she has no idea that multiple entries are being pieced together to make the long filenames visible. It is seamless to the user, and works quite well. The one area where problems can occur is that the root directory is still limited to 512 entries. If you have a user who is storing files on average of 200 characters in size in the root directory, then the 512 possibilities quickly dwindles to 32 (16 entries in the table are used for each file). This is a significant problem.

To correct this, Microsoft quickly released FAT32. FAT32 is a file system that does not have a root directory limitation and is only available in Windows 95 release B (and now in Windows 98). It cannot be used with the original release of Windows 95 or any other operating system. If you are running Win95B, when you choose to format a drive you are asked whether you want to enable large drive support or not. If you choose yes, the drive is formatted as FAT32. If you choose no, the drive is formatted as VFAT, also known as FAT16. Figure 8.6 shows the properties of a hard drive formatted with VFAT, while Figure 8.7 shows one formatted with FAT32.

Table 8.5 summarizes the differences between the FAT that exists with DOS and Windows 3.*x*, VFAT, and FAT32.

**LAB
8.3**

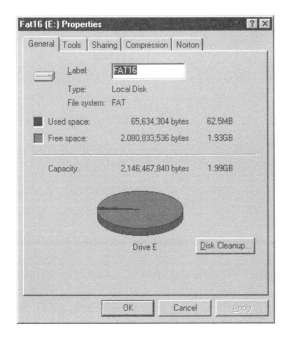

Figure 8.6 ■ **The properties of a hard drive formatted as VFAT.**

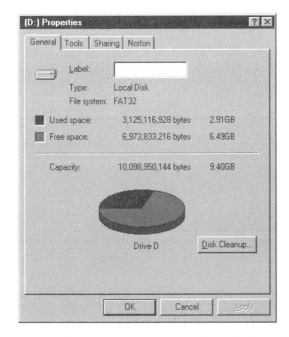

Figure 8.7 ■ **The properties of a hard drive formatted with FAT32.**

Table 8.5 ■ File System Feature Comparison

Feature	FAT	VFAT	FAT32
File name length	8.3	255	255
8.3 compatibility		Yes	Yes
Maximum files in root directory	512	512	No limit
Maximum files in nonroot directory	65,535	No limit	No limit
Partition size	2GB	4GB (but can only format 2GB)	4GB
Accessible from DOS	Yes	Yes	Yes
Accessible from OS/2	Yes	Yes	No
Case preserving	No	Yes	Yes

One feature of the FAT filesystem unique to hard drives is how sectors on the disk are grouped together into allocation units called "clusters." These clusters cannot be shared among multiple files, so any cluster space not used by a single file is essentially wasted. Over time, the number of non-filled clusters increases, leading to an accumulation of wasted disk space. FAT32 was released as the solution to the clustering and file allocation size problem.

LAB 8.3

BACKUP

The name of the backup utility in DOS 6.2 is MSBACKUP and in Windows 3.*x* it is MWBACKUP, while in Windows 95 it is just plain BACKUP. As an interesting aside, the name of the utility in DOS prior to 6.2 was BACKUP, but it was a very weak utility and should be shunned at all costs. MSBACKUP/MWBACKUP is based upon the best backup utility Symantec had at the time, and it is licensed from them. MSBACKUP and MWBACKUP files are compatible with each other and you can restore your Windows 3.*x* backup from the command line if the system has crashed.

The BACKUP utility in Windows 95 is not compatible with any of the others and cannot be used to restore a crashed system. One of the biggest reasons for this is incompatibility with long filenames.

Three locations for backups are supported:

- To floppy disks
- To a tape drive (preferred method)
- To a network location

COMPRESSION

All three operating systems give you the ability to compress the hard drive. When you do so, you are making a mirror, or virtual drive that you are really working on while all the data actually exists in one lone file. The compression in all the operating systems in question is at the drive level—you cannot take it down to the folder or file level as you can with Windows NT.

In DOS/Windows 3.*x*, the utility is called DoubleSpace, while in Windows 95 it is merely known as Disk Compression (though the executable is DriveSpace). Without the PLUS pack, the maximum size that can be compressed is 512MB, while with the PLUS pack (or Release B), the maximum size jumps to 2GB. Figure 8.8 shows the estimation before the utility is run. Notice that you can compress the drive or the free space.

LAB 8.3

DEFRAGMENT

It is a given that over time files become noncontiguous on a disk. This means that portions of them are stored on a disk in locations other than beside each other. The utility to defragment (place the files in contiguous order) in DOS/Windows 3.*x* is DEFRAG.EXE, while in Windows 95 it is merely called Disk Defragmenter. The purpose in all cases it to prevent file system performance degradation due to inefficient file storage.

FORMAT

The FORMAT executable exists in all the operating systems and can be used to format a disk—the first step in making it capable of storing data. In Windows 95, you can also choose to format from within the interface

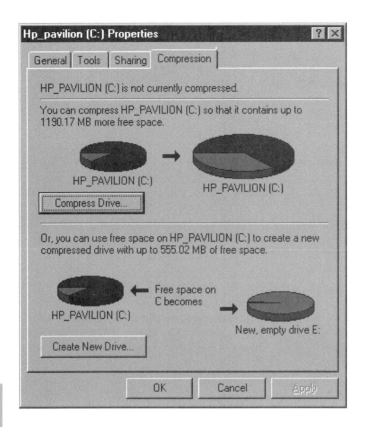

Figure 8.8 ■ Before you compress a drive, the Compression panel of the drive's Properties dialog box shows you approximately how much space you will gain.

by right-clicking on the drive and selecting Format from the pop-up menu, as shown in Figure 8.9.

If you are running Windows 95 release B, and the drive you are formatting is of large enough size, you will be presented with a question asking if you want to enable large drive support or not. If you choose yes, you are formatting with FAT32, and if you choose no, you are formatting with standard FAT. The file systems are discussed in more detail later in this Lab.

LAB
8.3

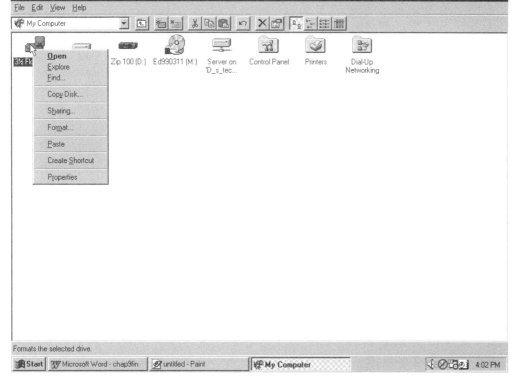

Figure 8.9 ■ Right-clicking on a drive in My Computer produces this pop-up menu.

PARTITIONING

In all cases of the operating systems discussed here, FDISK is the primary tool for partitioning the hard drive. Command-line in nature, it allows you to divide your hard drive into partitions—primary and extended, as well as logical. It allows you to specify which partition is active, and look at the current partition tables as well.

SCANDISK

In a category of its own, ScanDisk is the tool to use to look for errors on the hard drive. ScanDisk replaces the older ChkDsk utility and exists in all the operating systems you need to know for the exam. ScanDisk can look for errors by performing logical tests on the File Allocation Table as well as find invalid file names, dates, and time stamps.

In Windows 95, there are two versions of the utility—SCANDISK.EXE to run from the command line, and SCANDSKW.EXE to run from within Windows. When selected as a menu choice, the user never knows which is running, and it is automatically taken care of by the operating system. Figure 8.10 shows the standard ScanDisk configuration screen.

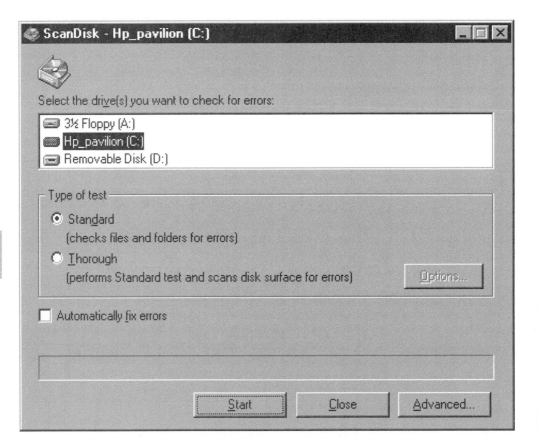

**LAB
8.3**

**Figure 8.10 ■ ScanDisk is used to detect and fix errors on the hard
    drive.**

LAB 8.3 EXERCISES

8.3.1 RUN SCANDISK

On Windows 95, run ScanDisk (choose Run from the Start menu and type in scandisk) on your primary drive in Standard test mode.

Run it once more in Thorough test mode.

> **a)** Can you identify the differences in items that were checked in the two modes?

_____

_____

8.3.2 EXAMINE BACKUP STATISTICS

On Windows 95, right-click on a drive on your system in either Windows Explorer or My Computer.

From the pop-up menu, select Properties.

In the Properties dialog, click the Tools tab.

Check to see when a backup program was last run on your system.

> **a)** When was the last time this drive was backed up?

_____

_____

LAB 8.3

8.3.3 RUN FDISK.EXE

Open a DOS session using the MS-DOS Prompt from the Programs group.

When the DOS prompt appears, typed "FDISK" and select option 4 (display partition information) from the menu that appears.

a) Identify how many partitions you have and what kinds of partitions they are.

_____

_____

8.3.4 UNDERSTAND FRAGMENTATION AND THE USE OF DEFRAG.EXE

On Windows 95, right-click on a drive on your system in either Windows Explorer or My Computer.

From the pop-up menu, select Properties.

In the Properties dialog, click the Tools tab.

a) When was the last time this drive was defragmented?

_____

_____

Click the Defrag Now button to have DEFRAG determine how fragmented your drive is.

b) What are the results?

_____

_____

c) Discuss why fragmentation is a problem.

_____

_____

LAB 8.3 EXERCISE ANSWERS

8.3.1 ANSWERS

For this Exercise, you ran ScanDisk twice on your primary drive, once in Standard test mode and once in Thorough test mode.

a) Can you identify the differences in items that were checked in the two modes?

Answer: Standard mode checks the file and directory structure only (the FAT table). Thorough mode actually performs checks on your hard drive to make certain there are no bad blocks, or that they have already been identified.

8.3.2 ANSWERS

For this Exercise, you checked to see when a backup program was last run on your system.

a) When was the last time this drive was backed up?

Answer: This will depend on your system.

You should see a dialog box similar to the one shown in Figure 8.11.

8.3.3 ANSWERS

For this Exercise, you ran FDISK.EXE on your system from a DOS window.

a) Identify the number and kinds of partitions you have.

Answer: The information that FDISK provides you should include the partition number, its status, size in megabytes, type, volume label, the FAT in use, and the percentage used.

Figure 8.11 ■ **The Properties dialog box for the selected drive. Tools tab is where you check the status of your system's properties.**

8.3.4 ANSWERS

This Exercise had you run DEFRAG.EXE on your system and observe how fragmented your drive is without actually starting the defragmentation process.

a) When was the last time this drive was defragmented?

Answer: This will depend on your system.

b) What are the results?

Answer: This, too, will depend on your system.

c) Discuss why fragmentation is a problem.

Answer: Fragmentation is a problem because, as files begin to be spread across non-contiguous space, file access and creation performance degrade because the disk's read-write heads must jump back and forth across the disk to "put together" pieces of the file that are divided across various chunks on the disk. The DEFRAG.EXE utility takes these disjointed files and portions of files and reallocates them across the disk, consolidating the fragments and files into contiguous space, so that the disk usage becomes more efficient again.

DEFRAG.EXE provides some options, like selecting the defragmentation level: standard or thorough. Depending on how much you use your system, you may want to run DEFRAG regularly, even as often as daily for high-use systems, because even a 2% gain in contiguous space may represent a significant system performance increase.

LAB 8.3 SELF-REVIEW QUESTIONS

In order to test your progress, you should be able to answer the following questions.

1) Which tool can you use to place files in contiguous order on a hard drive:
   a) ___ScanDisk
   b) ___Backup
   c) ___Defrag
   d) ___Format

2) Which file system is only available in Windows 95 release B:
   a) ___FAT16
   b) ___VFAT
   c) ___FAT32
   d) ___FAT64

3) Which file system(s) are case-preserving:
   a) ___FAT
   b) ___VFAT
   c) ___FAT32
   d) ___FAT64

LAB
8.3

4) Which utility would you use to divide a hard drive into partitions:

    a) ___FORMAT

    b) ___ FDISK

    c) ___ EDIT

    d) ___ SCANDISK

5) Which utility would you use to compress a hard drive in DOS:

    a) ___DoubleSpace

    b) ___DriveSpace

    c) ___Pack

    d) ___Compress

Quiz answers appear in Appendix A, Section 8.3.

**LAB
8.3**

C H A P T E R 8

TEST YOUR THINKING

In this chapter, you learned about how the DOS and Windows operating systems manage files. You saw that there are various tools for use in analyzing and optimizing filesystem performance.

Optimization of system performance is an art—one that is frequently crucial—but one that can be learned. Only experience in using the tools discussed here will prepare you for their use in the real world. As an experiment, you may want to try the following:

1) Examine the fragmentation of the system you are working on. Is it highly fragmented, or just minimally? Make a note of the percentage, along with statistics, about the size of the disk, what type of FAT scheme is used, etc.

2) Perform some file-related action, such as copying or moving a large file from one disk to another. Note how long it takes you currently to complete the task.

3) Run the defragmenting program and then redo your file transfer experiment in step #2. Note any differences in performance.

4) Now, repeat these steps on other computers, preferably ones that are similarly configured. Note your results. It may be helpful to create a spreadsheet of your results so you can take note of any trends or inconsistencies you may discover.

5) Finally, try the same experiments on systems using a variety of configurations, including systems using FAT32 instead of FAT16, or systems using larger partition sizes and disks as opposed to smaller ones. Again, compare your observations to previous ones noted. Do you find that things remain the same, or do they change?

You may want to keep a history of the types of results you encounter as you work with various systems. It is this type of experience that becomes the foundation for your success in recognizing subtle changes in system behavior and applying effective solutions.

C H A P T E R 9

MEMORY
MANAGEMENT

 . . . what was I going to say?

—Author

Understanding computer memory—the different types, the problems it can cause, and such—is essential not only for this exam, but for the real world (very much so). So many problems are caused by memory conflicts, and so many problems are solved by adding more memory that some could make a career from doing nothing but this. As a general rule of thumb, when there is a problem with performance, you will never go wrong throwing more RAM at it.

This chapter breaks the Memory Management category into two labs: Different Types of Memory and Memory Conflict Problems. This topic is worth 10% of the exam grade, but the questions can be especially tricky.

L A B 9.1

DIFFERENT TYPES OF MEMORY

LAB OBJECTIVES

After this Lab, you will be able to:

✓ Identify Memory Specifics on Your Machine

✓ Identify Additional System Information

Appendix B, which appears later in this book, will examine memory from the physical system's standpoint in preparation for the core exam. This chapter looks at the utilization of memory from the operating system's standpoint as it prepares you for the elective exam. For those purposes, memory here consists of any chips or modules (be they RAM, ROM, or other) that can hold data. There are four categories of memory, as follows:

- Conventional
- Extended and Upper
- High
- Expanded

Figure 9.1 shows how these four fall into a linear diagram.

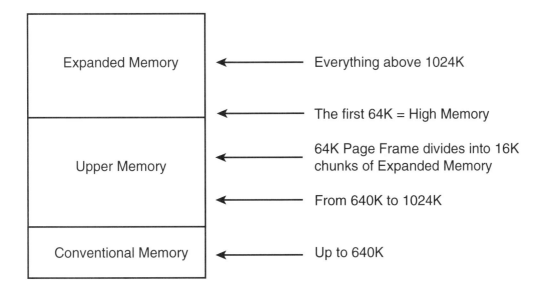

Figure 9.1 ■ **Memory can be divided into four main categories.**

CONVENTIONAL

Conventional memory—also known as base memory - is all memory in the lower 640K. Conventional memory is available on every PC and every operating system (DOS, Windows, Windows 95, and so forth).

On DOS machines, this is where the TSRs, device drivers, and such load. Old DOS-based machines (and thus programs written for those machines) could only access that amount of memory. In the days of DOS, when only that amount of memory was available, the application you were running had to share the memory with Terminate and Stay Resident (TSR) programs that were also running, assuring that they never had access to all the memory on the system.

EXTENDED AND UPPER

Upper memory (also known as Reserved Memory) follows Conventional and consists of the 384K between 640K and 1024K in the form of Upper Memory Blocks (UMBs). This was originally an area of memory set aside to store BIOS data and assign memory addresses—such as video. By so doing, it was possible to leave the lower 640K for the applications. Video ROM begins at 640K and extends to 768K. The area from 768K to 1024K is used by other BIOS programs. Placing TSRs (Terminate and Stay Resident programs) into upper memory frees additional conventional memory for application usage.

All memory above 1024K (1MB) is known as Extended memory. Extended memory is controlled by a device driver loaded by the operating system and was not a possibility before the 286 machines. Prior to Windows 95, SMARTDRV.EXE was used to manage disk caching. It was eliminated, with that function now built internally into the operating system.

HIGH MEMORY

The first 64K of Extended memory is known as High Memory. This area is set aside and often used by the operating system to store portions of itself there. Beginning with DOS 5.0, the operating system could be *loaded high*—or placed in this area.

EXPANDED

Expanded memory - also known as EMS memory - is a carry-over from the days of expanded memory boards and is memory accessed in pages (16K chunks) from upper memory page frames (a 64K chunk). As a general rule, programs that access expanded memory must be specifically written to do so. 386 machines and above can make their extended memory emulate expanded memory to make better use of it.

**LAB
9.1**

OTHER

A RAM drive can be created by setting aside a portion of RAM to emulate a drive. For example, on a machine that has a hard drive partitioned into drives C and D, a RAM drive of 2MB (2048K) can be created to be E with the command:

```
DEVICE=C:\DOS\RAMDRIVE.SYS 2048
```

in the CONFIG.SYS file. The RAM drive will always become the next available letter and can be of any size you specify up to the amount of RAM installed on the system. Because data stored on the RAM drive exists only in RAM, it is cleared on each reboot—not a good location for storing data files you are updating.

Another type of memory that we haven't yet discussed is *virtual memory*. Virtual memory is created by setting up paging in the CPU combined with the paging file. By so doing, you are able to offer to applications more memory (virtually) than the system has installed in it. Because the hard drive—generally the slowest component in the machine—must be accessed to read and write data, virtual memory is the slowest memory access model of any.

On older operating systems, there was often a permanent swap file, which had an extension of PAR. Today, most operating systems utilize temporary swap files with the extension of SWP.

LAB 9.1 EXERCISES

9.1.1 IDENTIFY MEMORY SPECIFICS ON YOUR MACHINE

From a clean machine boot, with nothing but your operating system running (i.e., no other applications), start the System applet in the Control Panel on a Windows 95 machine and choose the Performance tab.

a) Fill in the blanks in the following table to complete the specifications for your machine.

**LAB
9.1**

Item	Amount
Memory:	
System Resources:	
File System:	_____ -bit
Virtual Memory:	_____ -bit

Next, launch an application on your system. With that application still opened, start the System applet again and choose the Performance tab.

b) Fill in the blanks in the following table again. Compare your results from those found in Question a of this Exercise.

Item	Amount
Memory:	
System Resources:	
File System:	_____ -bit
Virtual Memory:	_____ -bit

9.1.2 IDENTIFY ADDITIONAL SYSTEM INFORMATION

Look for a file called MSINFO32.EXE on your system. This file ships with, and is installed on, most Microsoft systems.

a) Run the utility and fill in the blanks in the following table.

Item	Amount
Total physical memory	
Available physical memory	
USER memory available	
GDI memory available	
Swap file size	
Swap file usage	
Swap file setting	
Available space on drive ___:	

LAB 9.1 EXERCISE ANSWERS

9.1.1 ANSWERS

a) Fill in the blanks in the following table to complete the specifications for your machine.

Answer: Your answers will obviously vary, but Figure 9.2 shows an example of a Windows 95 system and the numbers returned at the Performance tab.

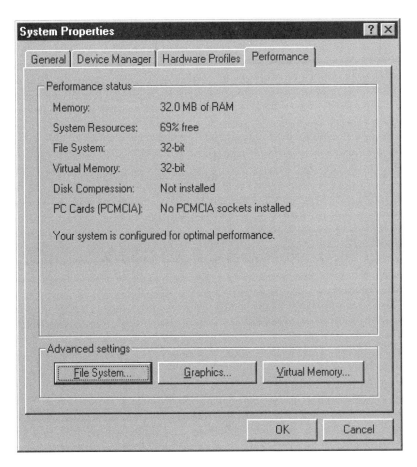

Figure 9.2 ■ **You can check your system resources by opening the System applet from the Control Panel and clicking the Performance tab.**

LAB 9.1

In terms of Performance Status, Memory refers to how much RAM you have installed on your system. The system shown in Figure 9.2 has 32MB of RAM installed. System Resources refers to the percentage of RAM that is currently available to your system. As you'll see in the next Question, the more applications that you have currently running, the lower the amount of RAM you'll have available.

The File System dialog allows you to configure and modify settings to optimize the type of access and behaviors of your hard disk and CD-ROM drives.

Virtual memory can be managed by the dialog accessed through the Virtual Memory button. You have the choice here to allow Windows to manage virtual memory for you (the most common option), or to specifically designate your own settings.

Next launch an application on your system. With that application still opened, start the System applet again and choose the Performance tab.

b) Fill in the blanks in the following table again. Compare your results from those found in Question a of this Exercise.

Answer: Chances are your System Resources are lower now that you have an application opened.

It should make sense that the more activity you have going on (e.g., the more applications you have opened), the more resources are utilized at any given time. You will see this again when you run the System Monitor in the next Lab's Exercises.

9.1.2 ANSWERS

a) Run the utility and fill in the blanks in the following table.

Answer: Again, your answers will vary. Figure 9.3 shows an example of a Windows 95 system and the information returned by the System portion of the MSINFO utility.

MSINFO32.EXE (Microsoft System Information) is a basic tool for gathering system configuration information. This tool is intended primarily to help technicians determine information that could indicate problems with the system.

Although there are many features available in this tool outlined in the Help file that comes with it, one of the most helpful is the ability to list all

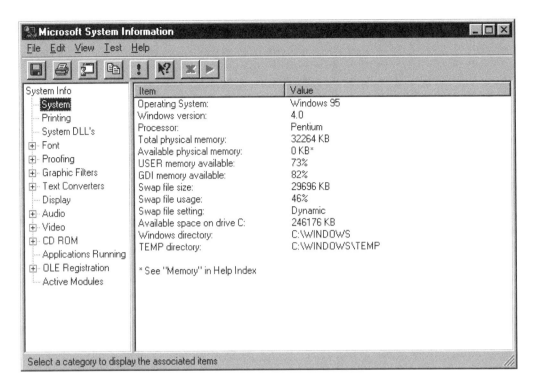

Figure 9.3 ■ The MSINFO utility gives you information about your system and its configuration.

Dynamic Linked Library files (DLLs) and all of their properties, including whether they are currently loaded. This tool will list all of the same information for the executables, including a special entry for 16-bit modules. A commonly used feature is review of the OLE registration entries in both the Registry and WIN.INI file.

LAB
9.1

LAB 9.1 SELF-REVIEW QUESTIONS

In order to test your progress, you should be able to answer the following questions.

1) What is all memory above 1024K called?
   a) ___Reserved
   b) ___Extended
   c) ___Conventional
   d) ___Expanded

2) What is another name for upper memory?
   a) ___Extended memory
   b) ___Expanded memory
   c) ___Reserved memory
   d) ___Conventional memory

3) A RAM drive can be created by adding the appropriate driver line to which of the following?
   a) ___CONFIG.SYS
   b) ___AUTOEXEC.BAT
   c) ___RAMDRIVE.SYS
   d) ___IO.SYS

4) Which of the following is the file extension on a temporary swap file?
   a) ___SWAP
   b) ___SWP
   c) ___PAR
   d) ___PER

5) The file extension on a permanent swap file is which of the following?
   a) ___SWAP
   b) ___SWP
   c) ___PAR
   d) ___PER

Quiz answers appear in Appendix A, Section 9.1.

**LAB
9.1**

L A B 9.2

OPTIMIZING MEMORY AND AVOIDING CONFLICTS

LAB OBJECTIVES

After this Lab, you will be able to:

✓ Use MEM and the System Applet Utility

✓ Configure a DOS Window

✓ View a Sample CONFIG.SYS

✓ Run System Monitor

LAB 9.2

To understand memory and its implementation, let's look at Windows 95 and the applications it can run. Windows 95 uses Virtual Memory consisting of RAM and a Swap file to meet the needs of all applications written up to the point of its release. This includes Windows 3.*x* applications (known as Win 16 for being 16-bit), Windows 95, Windows NT applications (known as Win 32 for being 32-bit), and old DOS applications.

The swap file can be noncontiguous on the hard drive (though it greatly deteriorates performance) and can even exist on a compressed drive. The three types of applications that run on Windows 95 differ in how they run as shown in Table 9.1.

Table 9.1 ■ Three Types of Applications That Run on Windows 95

DOS	Win 16	Win 32
Run in private Virtual DOS Machines (VDMs)	Run in common address space	Run in private address space
No message queue	Share single message queue	Each thread has its own message queue
Loaded in lower 1MB of virtual memory	Loaded in lower 2GB of virtual memory	Loaded in the 4MB to 2GB range of virtual memory

DOS applications were all written to run as the only application running on the machine, and in a small amount of memory; thus there was no need for messaging between them. Windows 95 attempts to run them in a virtual setting, which allows multiple DOS applications to run at the same time in their own window. Each window is given 1MB of RAM—far more than the application had access to natively. In short, DOS applications run better on Windows 95 than they ever ran in DOS. If, for some reason, a DOS application cannot run in a window (the virtual machine) due to conflicts, then there are two other modes that you can try:

- *In MS-DOS mode. Here, the graphical interface of Windows 95 shuts down and goes away and the DOS application runs. When the DOS application ends, the graphical interface of Windows 95 returns.
- *In MS-DOS mode outside of Windows 95 using parameters customized for the application. Here, Windows 95 never loads anything but the DOS application. This would be necessary if the application requires direct access to the hardware, has incompatible memory requirements, has video problems, or when its install program checks to see if Windows is running.

Windows 3.x (Win16) applications run in Windows 95 as if they were running on Windows 3.1. They run in a common address space because that is the way they were programmed. Additionally, they share a common, single message queue—again, because they were originally written to do so. This can cause problems with General Protection Faults (discussed later in this section). Each of them can be loaded in the lower 2GB of memory. If one 16-bit application crashes, it typically crashes all other

16-bit applications that are running as well. In short, Windows 16-bit applications do not gain any performance running on Windows 95 over what they would have had running on Windows 3.1.

Windows 32-bit applications, however, are a whole new breed. They each run in their own address space, with every thread (the lowest division of a process) having its own message queue. Additionally, they are loaded in the 4MB to 2GB memory range. If a 32-bit application goes awry and crashes, it crashes only itself and nothing else.

MEMORY MANAGEMENT

Memory Management is done by using a number of drivers:

- HIMEM.SYS: HIMEM.SYS is a driver loaded from the CONFIG.SYS file. It is the device driver for making memory above 640K available as extended memory.
- EMM386.EXE: EMM386.EXE emulates expanded memory and thus makes upper memory available for use.
- DOS=HIGH: When placed into the CONFIG.SYS file, it tells the operating system to load a portion of itself into high memory. This can be combined with DOS=UMB, which tells it to create an upper memory block.
- DEVICEHIGH: Device drivers can be used in the upper memory blocks once they have been loaded using this command.
- LOADHIGH: The LOADHIGH command is used a little differently than the drivers previously covered. Whereas DEVICEHIGH works in the CONFIG.SYS file, LOADHIGH can be used for a similar function in the AUTOEXEC.BAT file or at the command line. For example:

```
LOADHIGH C:\ABC.EXE
```

The LOADHIGH command can also be shortened to LH.

MEMMAKER

Beginning with DOS 6.0, a new utility, MEMMAKER was included to help simplify the task of placing TSRs into Upper Memory. It examines the amount of available space and the size of your TSRs and device drivers

LAB 9.2

and makes the best assumptions it can on what should be placed up there. Started from a DOS prompt, it walks you through the steps to make the appropriate entries in your CONFIG.SYS and AUTOEXEC.BAT (and SYSTEM.INI, if applicable) files.

The original versions of the configuration files are saved just in case there are any errors created by the changes MEMMAKER makes. Should this situation occur, you can use the following command to go back to the original configuration files:

`MEMMAKER /UNDO`

VIEWING MEMORY

Memory can be viewed with a number of utilities, based upon the operating system in question. The primary tools for checking are MEM (which exists in DOS after 5.0) and the System applet in Control Panel (in Windows 95 and after).

THE SYSTEM APPLET

With Windows 95, the MEM command is still available, but the System applet in Control Panel offers some quick information.

SYSTEM MONITOR

Windows 95 includes the System Monitor utility—a slimmed down version of Performance Monitor that is available in Windows NT. System Monitor allows you to look at your system and monitor certain events.

CONFLICTS

**LAB
9.2**

Memory conflicts can be caused by a number of things, such as two memory managers running at the same time (for example, the ones supplied with DOS and those from a third party). Using the MSD (Microsoft Diagnostics) utility, you can find those very easily.

A General Protection Fault is a carryover from the Windows 3.x world when Win 16 applications are run. It is typically caused by an application attempting to violate system integrity by any of the following:

- Making a request to read or write to a memory space owned by another application

- Attempting to access the system hardware directly
- Attempting to interact with a failing hardware driver

Other errors or conflicts can occur anytime there is more than one item (such as TSRs) accessing the same upper memory address. Before you can resolve them, you must identify where the conflicts are occurring using utilities such as the ones described in the preceding section. If you find the conflicting applications, you can then reassign them into memory—explicitly, if necessary—as described earlier in this chapter.

LAB 9.2 EXERCISES

9.2.1 USE *MEM* AND THE SYSTEM APPLET UTILITY

Open a DOS window, or go to a command prompt and run the MEM command. Use the various parameters that it allows and note the displays given for your machine.

a) Compare those numbers to what you saw in the Exercises from Lab 9.1.

_____

_____

b) Now, using the System Applet, examine the same settings and compare it to the information you got using MEM.

_____

_____

LAB 9.2

9.2.2 CONFIGURE A DOS WINDOW

Open a DOS window in Windows 95, then minimize it. Right-click on its icon in the task bar and choose Properties from the pop-up menu that appears. Choose the Memory tab.

a) Note the settings you can change there.

_____

_____

9.2.3 VIEW A SAMPLE *CONFIG.SYS*

Open your CONFIG.SYS file and examine the memory management utilities that you find there.

a) Do you find examples of the types of drivers described earlier in the text? Note the specific syntax of each.

_____

_____

9.2.4 RUN SYSTEM MONITOR

For this Exercise, you will configure and run System Monitor to examine various resources and usage.

1. To open the System Monitor utility, select Start -> Programs -> Accessories -> System Tools -> System Monitor.

    a) What items, if any, are being monitored on your machine currently?

_____

_____

2. Next, choose Add Item from the Edit menu.
3. Click on the various categories in the left panel of the Add Item dialog box and scan the Item panel on the right to see what items are stored in each category.

      b) In what category is the item *Page faults* stored?

_____

_____

4.   Next, open a category and select a number of items from it. You can do this by pressing the Ctrl or Shift key and choosing multiple items. Then click the OK button.

      c) How does your display change?

_____

_____

5.   Open the Add Item dialog box again and select the Dirty Data item from the File System category. Click on the Explain button at the bottom right of the window.

      d) What happens when you click on the Explain button?

_____

_____

Poke around the menu options and tool buttons in the System Monitor to get a feel for what options are available.

      e) What types of characteristics can you edit for any particular item?

_____

_____

LAB
9.2

With several items opened in the System Monitor, including *Allocated memory* from the Memory Manager category and *Bytes read/second* from the File System category, let the Monitor run and perform a few common tasks on your system, such as opening and closing applications. Note the effects of certain processes on your opened items.

LAB 9.2 EXERCISE ANSWERS

9.2.1 ANSWERS

Open a DOS window, or go to a command prompt and run the MEM command. Use the various parameters that it allows and note the displays given for your machine.

a) Compare those numbers to what you saw in the Exercises from Lab 9.1.

Answer: The MEM command shows you another look at the same information you saw in the earlier Exercise, but allows you to break it into finer granularity.

The MEM utility, used without parameters, presents a basic amount of information that will resemble the following display:

```
Memory Type        Total    Used     Free
---------------    --------  --------  --------
Conventional         640K      72K      569K
Upper                  0K       0K        0K
Reserved             384K     384K        0K
Extended (XMS)    31,744K     184K   31,560K
---------------   --------   --------  --------
Total memory      32,768K     640K   32,129K

Total under 1 MB    640K      72K      569K

Total Expanded (EMS)            32M (33,030,144 bytes)
Free Expanded (EMS)             16M (16,777,216 bytes)

Largest executable program size  568K (582,128 bytes)
Largest free upper memory block    0K (0 bytes)
MS-DOS is resident in the high memory area.
```

This indicates the total amount of memory on the system (32MB), how it is being divided between the main categories, and how much of each type is free. Using the /C parameter (MEM /C), it is possible to get additional information about specific programs and whether they are loaded into conventional or upper memory locations as shown in the following display:

```
Modules using memory below 1 MB:

Name           Total            Conventional        Upper Memory
--------  ----------------   ----------------   ----------------
MSDOS       39,184  (38K)       39,184  (38K)             0  (0K)
HIMEM        1,168   (1K)        1,168   (1K)             0  (0K)
ACER212H    14,464  (14K)       14,464  (14K)             0  (0K)
CS4232C         80   (0K)           80   (0K)             0  (0K)
IFSHLP       2,864   (3K)        2,864   (3K)             0  (0K)
SETVER         832   (1K)          832   (1K)             0  (0K)
WIN          3,600   (4K)        3,600   (4K)             0  (0K)
vmm32        3,424   (3K)        3,424   (3K)             0  (0K)
COMMAND      7,424   (7K)        7,424   (7K)             0  (0K)
Free       582,144 (569K)      582,144 (569K)             0  (0K)

Memory Summary:

Type of Memory     Total         Used          Free
----------------  -----------   -----------   -----------
Conventional          655,360        73,216       582,144
Upper                       0             0             0
Reserved              393,216       393,216             0
Extended (XMS)     32,505,856       188,416    32,317,440
----------------  -----------   -----------   -----------
Total memory       33,554,432       654,848    32,899,584

Total under 1 MB      655,360        73,216       582,144

Total Expanded (EMS)                33,030,144  (32M)
Free Expanded (EMS)                 16,777,216  (16M)
Largest executable program size        582,128 (568K)
Largest free upper memory block               0   (0K)
MS-DOS is resident in the high memory area.
```

You can now see exactly where the memory is being used. Table 9.2 shows you the parameters that can be used with MEM.

**LAB
9.2**

Table 9.2 ■ MEM Parameters

Parameter	Usage
/C	Use the /C parameter to receive additional information about specific programs and whether they are loaded into conventional or upper memory locations.
/F	Use the /F parameter to see the total amount of free memory available on the machine.
/D	Use the /D parameter to operate MEM in Debug mode.
/P	Use /P to pause the display for every screen.
/M	Use the /M parameter to see how much memory a particular module is using.

With regards to the /M parameter, for example, to see how the specific module WIN is using memory and in which locations, the command and result would be as follows:

```
C:\MEM /M WIN
WIN is using the following memory:

Segment  Region      Total              Type
-------  ------    ----------------    --------
00E49                       32 (0K)    Data
00E4B                      224 (0K)    Environment
00E59                    3,344 (3K)    Program
----------------
Total Size:              3,600 (4K)
```

b) Now, using the System Applet, examine the same settings and compare it to the information you got using MEM.

Answer: To view this information, select the System Icon from Control. Figure 9.4 illustrates the Performance tab, which identifies how much memory is installed and how much is free. Clicking on the Virtual Memory button takes you to the display shown in Figure 9.5. It is possible to limit the amount of virtual memory available on the machine. The default amount is equal to the current free space on the hard drive.

In order to provide more memory to applications than is physically present in the computer in the form of RAM, Windows uses hard disk space to simulate RAM. The amount of RAM in the computer plus the size

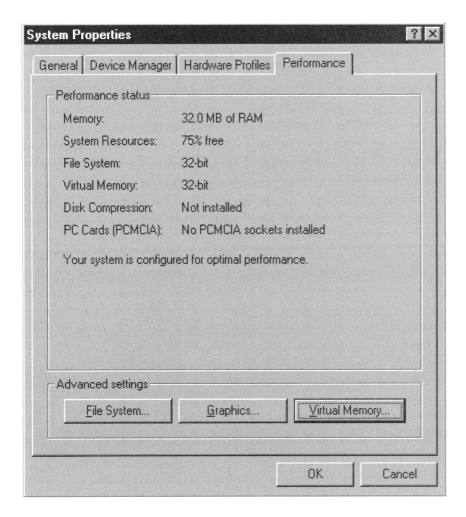

Figure 9.4 ■ Click on the System icon in the Control Panel to view System properties, such as Performance.

of the paging file (also known as the swap file) equals the total physical memory, or virtual memory, size. Windows uses a dynamic paging file that remains at a size of 0K until it is needed. The paging file can grow to use all the available space on the hard disk if it is necessary. This is the default setting for the paging file and you should use this setting if possible. If you do choose to manually adjust these settings, you will need to click on the Virtual Memory button on the System applet's Performance panel to change Virtual Memory settings.

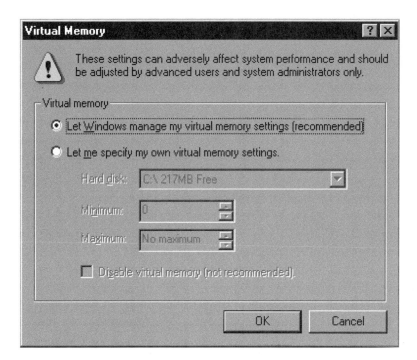

Figure 9.5 ■ The Virtual Memory dialog selected from the System Properties program within Control Panel.

9.2.2 ANSWERS

In this Exercise, you opened a DOS window in Windows 95, then minimized it. Right-clicking on its icon in the task bar and choosing Properties from the pop-up menu that appears allowed you to choose the Memory tab.

a) Note the settings you can change there.

Answer: While the default is for Auto to apply to every DOS window opened, you can set specific parameters for Conventional, Expanded, Extended, and Protected memory for that window, as shown in Figure 9.6.

Under most circumstances, the AUTO setting is ideal for DOS applications running on Windows 95. There are situations, however, where an application expects a certain environment, and that environment can be supplied by tweaking the parameters here.

LAB
9.2

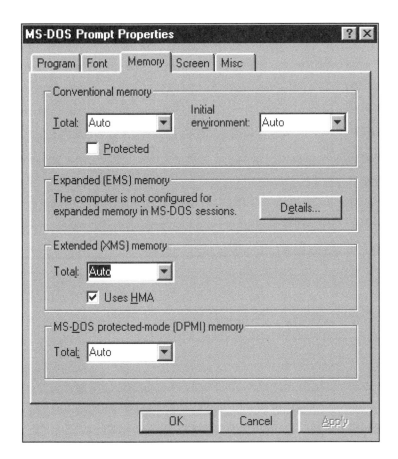

Figure 9.6 ■ **You open the MS-DOS prompt Properties dialog box by right-clicking its icon in the task bar.**

You can also create customized CONFIG.SYS and AUTOEXEC.BAT files that will be swapped with the standard versions of these files when you double-click the application's icon. For the settings in these customized files to take effect, Windows 95 must reboot the computer. If this is the case, one line that must always be present in the CONFIG.SYS file is DOS=SINGLE.

Figure 9.7 shows the configuration settings available for DOS programs in Windows 95.

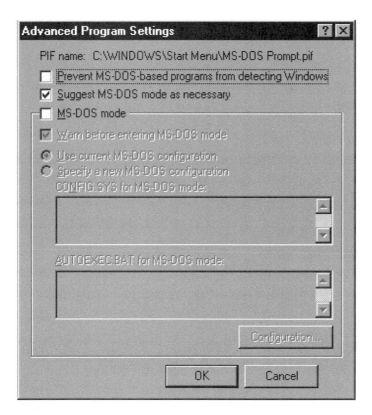

Figure 9.7 ■ Changing DOS program properties by selecting "Advanced..." from the Properties/Program tab.

LAB
9.2

9.2.3 ANSWERS

You opened your CONFIG.SYS file and examined the memory management utilities that you found there.

a) Did you find examples of the types of drivers described earlier in the text? What was the specific syntax of each?

Answer: Certainly your answers will vary depending on your environment, but a sample CONFIG.SYS file might look like the following:

```
DEVICE=C:\DOS\HIMEM.SYS
DEVICE=C:\DOS\EMM386.EXE NOEMS
```

```
DOS=HIGH, UMB
DEVICEHIGH=C:\DOS\MOUSE.SYS
```

The correct syntax for HIMEM.SYS is:

```
DEVICE=C:\DOS\HIMEM.SYS
```

This line should always be near the top of CONFIG.SYS as it must create the environment to be used by any subsequent lines interacting with memory management.

EMM386.EXE is loaded in CONFIG.SYS as well, and the correct syntax would be:

```
DEVICE=C:\DOS\EMM386.EXE NOEMS
```

The last part of the command line (NOEMS) tells the operating system not to convert extended memory to expanded memory.

DOS=HIGH and UMB can be used separately or together. Combined, the syntax becomes:

```
DOS=HIGH, UMB
```

The next line covers the driver DEVICEHIGH. To load the mouse driver high, as in our example, the CONFIG.SYS syntax would be:

```
DEVICEHIGH=C:\DOS\MOUSE.SYS
```

9.2.4 ANSWERS

For this Exercise, you configured and ran System Monitor to examine various resources and usage.

**LAB
9.2**

a) What items, if any, are being monitored on your machine currently?

Answer: Your answer will vary according to your system.

Each item that is currently active in the System Monitor is clearly labeled. If you have more than one item active, you may click on it in the main window and view the status bar at the bottom of the window to see details of that item, including its current value and its peak value.

b) In what category is the item *Page faults* stored?

Answer: The Page faults *item is stored in the Memory Manager category.*

Figure 9.8 shows the Add Item dialog box with the Memory Manager category selected; this brings up a number of items that can be chosen for monitoring.

c) How does your display change?

Answer: Your display will change to accommodate any new items that you've added to the System Monitor.

Depending on which View mode you have selected, your display may now look something like that shown in Figure 9.9.

This display is shown in the Line Charts View mode. Based on your preferences, you can change the View mode to either Line Charts, Bar Charts, or Numeric Charts. Do so by either clicking one of the corresponding toolbar buttons (the right three buttons affect the View mode), or selecting View from the menu bar and choosing the View that suits your needs.

**LAB
9.2**

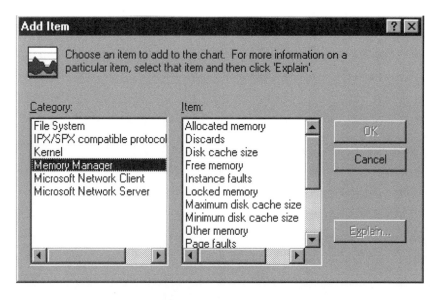

Figure 9.8 ■ The Add Item dialog box is where you can add a process to the System Monitor chart.

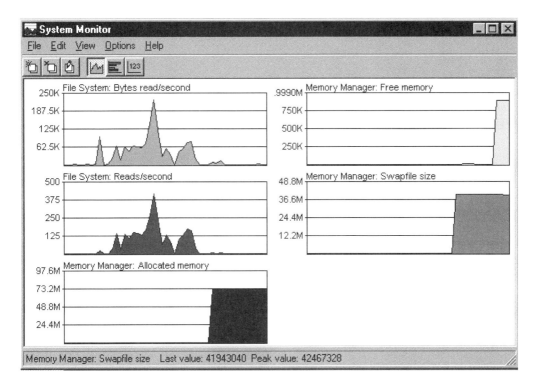

Figure 9.9 ■ The System Monitor utility presents you with a chart like this showing statistics for a number of system resources during a selected operation.

d) What happens when you click the Explain button?

Answer: You are given the definition of Dirty Data.

You can click the Explain button to gain more information about any item in the Item list. Simply click the item, and then click Explain. You will see a definition of the item you've selected.

e) What types of characteristics can you edit for any particular item?

Answer: You can only change the scale of the chart and the color representation for the item.

You should have noticed when you completed this Exercise that sizable operations, such as opening and closing applications, can have a dramatic

LAB 9.2

affect on your system resources. The System Monitor can be used to troubleshoot performance problems, or evaluate how effectively system resources are being used.

LAB 9.2 SELF-REVIEW QUESTIONS

In order to test your progress, you should be able to answer the following questions.

I) The command DEVICEHIGH goes into which configuration file?
    a) ___AUTOEXEC.BAT
    b) ___CONFIG.SYS
    c) ___SYSTEM.INI
    d) ___COMMAND.COM

2) The command LH goes into which configuration file?
    a) ___AUTOEXEC.BAT
    b) ___CONFIG.SYS
    c) ___SYSTEM.INI
    d) ___COMMAND.COM

3) Expanded memory is managed via which of the following?
    a) ___EMM386.EXE
    b) ___HIMEM.SYS
    c) ___SMARTDRV.EXE
    d) ___LOADHIGH.EXE

4) Which of the following is the program used to load TSRs into upper memory blocks?
    a) ___DEVICEHIGH
    b) ___LOADHIGH
    c) ___HIGHLOAD
    d) ___MEMMAKER

5) A General Protection Fault is most likely caused by which of the following?
    a) ___faulty cables
    b) ___hard drive
    c) ___application
    d) ___RAM

Quiz answers appear in Appendix A, Section 9.2.

LAB
9.2

C H A P T E R   9

TEST YOUR THINKING

Change the virtual memory settings on your system and observe how the performance changes by:

1) Creating a permanent swap file that is the same size as your physical RAM (i.e., if you have 32MB of physical RAM, create a 32MB permanent swap file).

2) Creating a permanent swap file that is half the size as your physical RAM.

3) Creating a permanent swap file that has a minimum and maximum size of twice your physical RAM (assuming you have that much free on your system).

CHAPTER 10

INSTALLATION, CONFIGURATION, AND UPGRADING

Your 'if' is the only peacemaker; much virtue in "if."

—William Shakespeare, *As You Like It*

This section constitutes 25 percent of the elective exam. It is imperative that you know as much as you can about the installation of Windows 95 and the boot sequence it uses.

L A B   10.1

INSTALLING AND UPGRADING OPERATING SYSTEMS

LAB OBJECTIVES

After this Lab, you will be able to:

✓ Install Windows 95

Before a hard drive can have an operating system placed on it, it must be partitioned and formatted. Partitioning a drive involves determining how much space will be available in a given block. Factors that play into this equation include the size of the drive itself, the file system structure you will be using, and the operating system you intend to use.

At one time, a 20MB hard drive was all that was available for the personal computer and it would cost you as much or more than you paid for the rest of the computer. In less than 12 years, that situation has changed dramatically. Now, it is not at all uncommon to find home machines with 10GB hard drives pre-installed. Should a home user decide to upgrade his or her existing drive, a large one can be found for only a few hundred dollars.

In Chapter 8, "Operating System Functions, Operation, and File Management," we saw that the file system chosen can make a significant impact on partition size as well. Running VFAT, the maximum partition size that

**LAB
10.1**

can be created is 2GB, and that can be seen by the operating system is 4GB. This means that you would have to divide your 8GB hard drive into at least two partitions/drive letters. If you are using Windows 95B, with FAT32, however, then you can use only one partition/drive letter for the whole hard drive.

As was also discussed in Chapter 8, FDISK is the all-purpose tool to use for creating partitions. It is run from the command line and has a limited menu of options with which you can interact to create or delete partitions.

Once partitioned, the next step in the process is to format the drive. The FORMAT command is used to accomplish this:

```
FORMAT /S
```

This command not only formats the drive but also places the operating system boot files on the drive (IO.SYS, MSDOS.SYS, and COM-MAND.COM). This makes it capable of being booted from as well as having the rest of the operating system installed on it.

If the drive is formatted, but does not have the boot files, you can place them there by using the SYS command. The syntax is:

```
SYS {where files are} {where you want them}
```

Thus the following command would place the system files on the hard drive by reading them from the floppy:

```
SYS A: C:
```

Specifying the source is optional.

For the exam, you should be familiar with the Windows 95 installation process. A walk-through of the installation steps is provided as an Exercise in this Lab.

LAB 10.1

UPGRADING VERSUS NEW INSTALL

When you install Windows 95 on a machine that has Windows 3.x on it, you have the choice of upgrading Windows 3.x to Windows 95, or doing a fresh installation. The key to it all is the location of the directory in which you place Windows 95. Under most circumstances, Windows 3.x is installed in the C:\WINDOWS directory. If you place Windows 95 in that same directory, it will automatically do an upgrade. If you install it in any other directory, it will not do an upgrade.

An upgrade implies that it will copy over all the information specific to your applications, preferences, and settings and use them in the new operating system. It also uses the settings in SYSTEM.INI, WIN.INI, and PROTOCOL.INI in building the Registry to get your desktop settings. If you do not upgrade, you will have to run the setup routine for all of your applications within the new operating system to configure them to run there.

When you upgrade from DOS to Windows 95, the two operating systems are different enough that none of the settings are maintained anyway: DOS is not a graphical environment, and that is all that Windows 95 is. If the DOS version you are coming from is 5.0 or higher, you will have a choice on the startup menu allowing you to boot into that previous version. If it is less than 5.0, that menu choice will not be present.

The minimum upgrade operating systems for Windows 95 are:

- MS-DOS 3.2 or higher (5.0 needed to enable the "Boot to previous version of DOS" option)
- Windows 3.x
- OS/2 2.x

LAB 10.1 EXERCISE

This Exercise is optional; if you have an old machine handy, you are welcome to step through it in "real time." Otherwise, performing this Exercise may result in your changing the installation settings and options on operational systems, which may not be practical for you. Follow along anyway, however, so that you understand the processes for the exam, which you will need to know. For this reason, these Exercises will be slightly different than those that you are used to in this book.

10.1.1 INSTALL WINDOWS 95

For this Exercise, you should find an old machine with an operating system other than Windows 95 on it and install the new operating system. Before you do so, however, make certain the machine on which you are installing can handle the new operating system.

a) What are the minimum hardware requirements for this operating system?

_____

_____

1. The first step in the installation process is the Startup and Information Gathering process. In this step, you interact with and accept the license agreement before continuing with the installation.
2. Next, you specify the directory in which you will install the operating system. The default is C:\WINDOWS, but you can select "Other directory" and the setup program will ask you to specify another directory name.
3. After you have entered the directory information, click the Next button and you are asked to specify the Setup options. For this Exercise, you choose "Typical."
4. The next screen asks you to supply a default user name and company information.

b) How many characters of text can each of these fields accept?

_____

_____

5. Next you're asked to enter your product information number, which ensures that you are performing a legal installation of the software, and not simply installing a pirated copy. This information is found on your warranty registration card or on the back cover of the CD case.

**LAB
10.1**

6. The next major step in the installation process is hardware detection. The Setup program attempts to identify all the hardware connected to your machine so that it knows which drivers it will need to install as part of the setup program. If you have devices such as network adapters, CD-ROM drives, or sound cards, you will want to check the appropriate boxes in the analysis dialog.

7. If a network card is installed on your computer, Setup will enter a network configuration stage in which you can customize the networking components for your system. This set of dialogs will ask you to identify the type of network you have, your computer name, description, and workgroup.

8. After you have completed the interactive dialogs for hardware detection, Setup presents you with a list of hardware that has been located and provides you with an opportunity to change any of these devices and the drivers that will be loaded.

9. As part of its process, Setup prompts you to make a start-up disk.

    c) Why do you suppose you are recommended to create a startup disk during the installation process?

    _____

    _____

10. The next significant step in the installation process is File Copy—during which files are copied to the system. The source files are all cabinet (CAB) files that are moved over and extracted.

11. The last step is that of final system configuration. During this step, you can set up the operating system for your monitor resolution preference, properly configure your time zone, and so forth. You will also be prompted to install and set up a default printer for your system using the Add Printer wizard.

**LAB
10.1**

At the end of this step, you will need to reboot your system.

The next procedure for this Exercise is to reformat the hard disk on which you just installed Windows 95 in order to erase the operating system completely.

Redo the installation. This time choose a "compact" installation. Note which files are different.

Do the installation a third time. Choose a custom installation and choose not to install any of the accessories. Once the system is installed, choose the Add/Remove Programs applet from the control panel and select the Windows Setup tab. Install all of the accessories and note which programs are installed.

> **d)** Do a couple of installations using various options to SETUP.EXE discussed in the Lab. Note how the behavior changes.

_____

_____

LAB 10.1 EXERCISE ANSWERS

10.1.1 ANSWERS

In this Exercise, you were asked to find an old machine with an operating system other than Windows 95 on it and install the new operating system (typical installation). Before you did so, you were to make certain the machine on which you were installing could handle the new operating system.

a) What are the minimum hardware requirements for this operating system?

Answer: The minimum hardware requirements for Windows 95 include a 386DX/20 processor (that is, not a B-step, or ID 0303 processor), 4MB of RAM (which jumps to 8MB with Exchange, MSN, or multiple 32-bit apps), VGA or better monitor, and at least 40MB of free disk space. The actual amount of memory space Windows 95 needs to run is 14MB, but it will use a swap file to make up the difference between this number and the amount of RAM you have installed.

 Note: You can copy the contents of the \WIN95 and root directories from the CD onto the hard disk to speed up the installation.

LAB 10.1

b) How many characters of text can each of these fields accept?

Answer: Each of these responses can be up to 15 characters in length, cannot include embedded spaces, and can contain any of these characters:

`!@#$%^&()-_`{}~.`

c) Why do you suppose you are recommended to create a start-up disk during the installation process?

Answer: The start-up disk is a precaution that you can use in the event the system will not boot after further steps are done.

The start-up disk contains a number of files, with important ones being:

- ATTRIB.EXE—Allows you to look at and change file attributes as needed.
- CHKDSK.EXE—Lets you check the drive for errors if Scandisk cannot run.
- COMMAND.COM—The command interpreter.
- DEBUG.EXE—The DOS interactive debugger program; not for the faint of heart.
- DRVSPACE.BIN—The older disk compression driver.
- EDIT.COM—A simple text editor.
- FDISK.EXE—A partition utility.
- FORMAT.COM—Lets you do any formatting that needs to be done.
- IO.SYS—Makes the disk bootable.
- MSDOS.SYS—Also makes the disk bootable.
- REGEDIT.EXE—Enables you to troubleshoot problems with the Registry.
- SCANDISK.EXE—Enables you to repair any problems with the disk.
- SYS.COM—Enables you to transfer the operating system from the disk to a drive.
- UNINSTAL.EXE—Uninstalls Windows 95 should it become apparent that the operating system will not run on the machine

d) Do a couple of installations using various options to SETUP.EXE. Note how the behavior changes.

Answer: After a drive has been formatted and made bootable, the next step is to run the appropriate set-up utility from your specific operating system disks to configure it to run the appropriate operating system. In all cases (DOS, Windows 3.x, Windows 95), the utility to use to install the operating system is SETUP.

In Windows 95, there are a number of switches that can be used with the utility to override routine operations it would normally do. Under most circumstances, you would never invoke anything other than SETUP without any switches, but if there is a problem, switches may be useful. Table 10.1 lists the available switches to the SETUP utility.

Table 10.1 ■ Setup Switches

Switch	Purpose
/?	Show all available options and appropriate syntax
/C	Do not load SmartDrive disk cache
/d	Do not use earlier version of Windows for setup phases
/id	Do not check for minimum disk space available
/ih	Run SCANDISK in the foreground
/iL	Load Logitech mouse driver
/im	Do not check for minimum conventional memory
/in	Do not run network setup module
/iq	Do not run SCANDISK from MS-DOS
/is	Do not run SCANDISK under any condition
/it	Skip the check TSR (Terminate and Stay Resident) programs that are known to cause problems with Windows 95
/iw	Bypass licensing agreement
/nostart	Load minimal drivers for Windows 3.x but do not install Windows 95
/t:temp	Allows you to specify a specific directory where temporary files will be placed
FILE.inf	Specify a settings file to use during installation

LAB 10.1

One of the more common uses of switches is to create a minimal installation of Windows using the /nostart option. If you have experienced problems with the hard disk and are reinstalling Windows, selecting /ih to run SCANDISK interactively may help you identify where on the drive problems are occurring prior to fully rebuilding the system.

LAB 10.1 SELF-REVIEW QUESTIONS

In order to test your progress, you should be able to answer the following questions.

1) Which of the following is the utility used to begin the installation of Windows 95?
   a) ___Install
   b) ___Start
   c) ___Setup
   d) ___Config

2) Which of the following is the parameter that loads the Logitech mouse?
   a) ___/iM
   b) ___/iL
   c) ___/ML
   d) ___/LM

3) Which of the following is the tool used to edit the Registry?
   a) ___Edit.exe
   b) ___Edit.com
   c) ___Regedit.exe
   d) ___Regedit.com

4) What is the minimum free hard drive space for Windows 95?
   a) ___4MB
   b) ___8MB
   c) ___16MB
   d) ___40MB

5) What is the minimum version of MS-DOS you can upgrade from and still be able to boot into?
   a) ___3.2
   b) ___3.3
   c) ___5.0
   d) ___6.2

   Quiz answers appear in Appendix A, Section 10.1.

L A B   10.2

BASIC BOOT SEQUENCES

LAB OBJECTIVES

After this Lab, you will be able to:

✓ Create an Emergency Boot Disk

✓ Interact with the Startup Menu While Booting

✓ Examine the WIN.INI File

The series of events that occur as part of the computer's start-up process is referred to as "booting." When the computer first starts up, the first process it runs is the POST (Power-On Self-Test), which is responsible for testing a number of devices. After the POST, the firmware inside the computer then looks to find the operating system installed on either a floppy or a hard drive. Once the DOS/Windows operating system is found, the boot loader program is run, which looks for the following files:

`IO.SYS`

`MSDOS.SYS`

At this point, the main DOS kernel is active, and it loads the command processor, COMMAND.COM, which, in turn, executes the two configuration files CONFIG.SYS and AUTOEXEC.BAT.

LAB 10.2

For an MS-DOS-based system, the boot sequence completes at this last file.

For Windows 3.*x* and Windows 95 systems, the next system file executed is:

```
WIN.COM
```

which was created at the Windows set-up time. WIN.COM loads another file, WIN.CNF, which contains the logo files for the start-up screen.

WIN.COM, when loading Windows in standard mode, runs DOSX.EXE and WIN386.EXE to create the environment and extended memory support. It also loads all the INI files that it needs to present your desktop to you, getting device drivers from SYSTEM.INI. Once all of these are up and running, USER.EXE controls the interaction between you and your windows, while the program GDI.EXE provides the graphics interface and KRNL386.EXE handles the memory management, task scheduling, and code execution.

With Windows 95, most of the 3.*x* INI files are no longer used, with the exception of SYSTEM.INI that is still looked at by WIN.COM and WIN.INI that is referenced later. Added to the mixture is VMM32.VXD that makes the virtual machine and loads all the virtual device drivers (VxDs). Next, it loads KERNEL32.DLL and KRNL386.EXE for the drivers and components. Following those are:

```
GDI.EXE and GDI32.EXE

USER.EXE and USER32.EXE

WIN.INI
```

And then the Registry files in the following order:

```
USER.DAT

SYSTEM.DAT
```

As a refresher, the USER.DAT portion of the Registry contains information about the user. At this point in the game, it is the default user's "profile" that is loaded as it does not know who the user is until the actual logon. The SYSTEM.DAT portion of the Registry contains the information about the machine itself—hardware attached to it, software installed on it, etc. For complete details about these files, the Registry, and how the system uses them, see Chapter 9.

If there are different profiles in use, the user will log on, and his or her USER.DAT file will be loaded, replacing the default user's in memory. As a very last step, if the system policies (CONFIG.POL) are utilized (their use is optional), this file will be read last and the settings will override everything else.

EMERGENCY BOOT DISK

The Windows 95 installation process allows you to make an Emergency Boot Disk to should your system become corrupted down the road. This is different from the start-up disk discussed earlier in this chapter. We will create an Emergency Boot Disk in an Exercise later in this chapter.

STARTUP MENU

The Windows 95 Startup Menu is accessible by pressing F8 when Windows 95 boots. The options presented on the menu are dependent upon the way in which Windows 95 was installed (upgrade versus new) and the settings in MSDOS.SYS.

LAB 10.2 EXERCISES

10.2.1 CREATE AN EMERGENCY BOOT DISK

Create an Emergency Boot Disk on a floppy disk. The most common method is from the Start menu.

1. Choose Start → Settings → Control Panel.
2. Click on Add/Remove Programs and select the Startup Disk tab.
3. When you have inserted a blank floppy disk and are ready, click on the Create Disk icon.

a) What happens when you select this option?

_____

_____

b) Do you know of an alternative way to create an Emergency Boot Disk?

_____

_____

10.2.2 INTERACT WITH THE STARTUP MENU WHILE BOOTING

Boot your system and press F8 as soon as you see the message "Starting Windows 95."

a) What does the system do?

_____

_____

b) What choices do you see?

_____

_____

Select "logged" and look at the file c:\bootlog.txt after the system boots into Windows.

c) What do you see?

_____

_____

Reboot your system again and press F8 when you see the "Starting Windows 95" message. This time, select "safe mode."

> **d)** How is the appearance and behavior different than a normal Windows boot?

_____

_____

Reboot your system again and press F8 when you see the "Starting Windows 95" message. This time, select "command prompt only."

> **e)** How is the appearance and behavior different than a normal Windows boot?

_____

_____

Reboot your system again and press F8 when you see the "Starting Windows 95" message. This time, select "safe mode command prompt only."

> **f)** How is the appearance and behavior different than a normal Windows boot?

_____

_____

10.2.3 EXAMINE THE WIN.INI FILE

In either DOS or Windows Explorer, locate your WIN.INI file and open it (it's usually located in the c:\windows directory)

> **a)** What programs are loaded with the line load= ?

_____

_____

LAB
10.2

b) What programs are started with the line run= ?

_____

_____

LAB 10.2 EXERCISE ANSWERS

10.2.1 ANSWERS

Create an Emergency Boot Disk on a floppy disk by using the Add/Remove Programs applet and choosing Create Disk from the Startup Disk tab.

a) What happens when you select this option?

Answer: Windows asks you to label the floppy disk in drive A: and warns you that any data on this disk will be deleted. Windows 95 will then format the disk in a bootable format, then it will copy the files you need to fix Windows 95 on the disk.

b) Do you know of an alternative way to create an Emergency Boot Disk?

Answer: Another way to create an Emergency Boot Disk is to use the ERU utility located in the Other\Misc directory of the installation CD—it is not copied to the machine by default. When run, it saves important Windows 95 files to a location you specify: a network drive, floppy disk, or other.

10.2.2 ANSWERS

For this Exercise, you pressed F8 during the boot process as soon as you saw the message "Starting Windows 95."

a) What does the system do?

Answer: The system stops booting and presents you with a text screen—the multiple boot manager—that contains a menu.

b) What choices do you see?

Answer: Generally, there are eight choices, as shown in the following discussion.

**LAB
10.2**

- **Normal mode**—This returns the system to the boot process, which results in what would be run by default if you had not pressed F8.
- **Logged mode**—All boot steps are written to bootlog.txt, an ASCII file you can examine in the event of hangs during boot. It shows all driver loads, VxD initializations, and so forth.
- **Safe mode**—When Windows 95 is started in safe mode, only the essential device drivers required by the operating system will be loaded. You will not be able to access printers, CD-ROM devices, or sound cards.
- **Safe mode with network support**—The same as safe mode, only now it also enables the NetBEUI and some of the Registry information needed to read networking parameters. You still have limited network access in this mode, enabling you to use services that may be necessary for troubleshooting, such as printing.
- **Step-by-step confirmation**—Walks through the start up process line by line asking you to answer yes or no to whether you want to perform each step. This step-by-step mode is often used to diagnose exactly where in the boot process a problem may exist. This is the same feature that existed in previous (DOS) operating systems when the F8 key was pressed at start up.
- **Command prompt only**—Use this option if you want to start the computer without starting Windows, and to skip your Autoexec.bat and Config.sys files and go directly to the command prompt.
- **Safe mode command prompt**—Similar to Command prompt only, it starts the computer without starting Windows. If you also want to skip your Autoexec.bat and Config.sys files and go to the command prompt without network support, choose this option.
- **Previous version of MS-DOS**—only available if you came from MS-DOS 5.0 or greater.

Next, you chose the "logged" mode from this menu.

c) What do you see?

Answer: This option produces a log output of the boot process, listing each driver and program started by the boot process and their outcomes.

Your own log will likely differ, but a portion from a sample bootlog.txt file looks like this:

```
[000C75E9] Loading Device = C:\WINDOWS\HIMEM.SYS
[000C75EC] LoadSuccess    = C:\WINDOWS\HIMEM.SYS
[000C75EC] Loading Device = C:\WINDOWS\IFSHLP.SYS
[000C75ED] LoadSuccess    = C:\WINDOWS\IFSHLP.SYS
[000C75ED] Loading Device = C:\WINDOWS\SETVER.EXE
[000C75EE] LoadFailed     = C:\WINDOWS\SETVER.EXE
[000C75F3] C:\PROGRA~1\NORTON~1\NAVDX.EXE[000C75F4] starting
[000C768E] c:\windows\COMMAND\DOSKEY.COM[000C768E] starting
[000C76D7] Loading Vxd = C:\WINDOWS\system\VMM32\VMM.VXD
[000C76DA] LoadSuccess = C:\WINDOWS\system\VMM32\VMM.VXD
[000C76DD] Loading Vxd = JAVASUP.VXD
[000C76DF] LoadSuccess = JAVASUP.VXD
[000C76DF] Loading Vxd = CONFIGMG
[000C76DF] LoadSuccess = CONFIGMG
[000C76E0] Loading Vxd = VSHARE
[000C76E0] LoadSuccess = VSHARE
[000C76E1] Loading Vxd = C:\WINDOWS\system\VMM32\VWIN32.VXD
[000C76E3] LoadSuccess = C:\WINDOWS\system\VMM32\VWIN32.VXD
[000C76E6] Loading Vxd = C:\WINDOWS\system\VMM32\VFBACKUP.VXD
[000C76E7] LoadSuccess = C:\WINDOWS\system\VMM32\VFBACKUP.VXD
[000C76E7] Loading Vxd = VCOMM
[000C76E7] LoadSuccess = VCOMM
[000C76E8] Loading Vxd = COMBUFF
[000C76E8] LoadSuccess = COMBUFF
[000C76EA] Loading Vxd = C:\WINDOWS\system\VMM32\IFSMGR.VXD
[000C76ED] LoadSuccess = C:\WINDOWS\system\VMM32\IFSMGR.VXD
[000C76EF] Loading Vxd = C:\WINDOWS\system\VMM32\IOS.VXD
[000C76F2] LoadSuccess = C:\WINDOWS\system\VMM32\IOS.VXD
[000C76F2] Loading Vxd = SPOOLER
[000C76F2] LoadSuccess = SPOOLER
```

```
[000C76F2]  Loading Vxd = VFAT

[000C76F2]  LoadSuccess = VFAT

[000C76F2]  Loading Vxd = VCACHE

[000C76F2]  LoadSuccess = VCACHE

[000C76F5]  Loading Vxd = C:\WINDOWS\system\VMM32\VCOND.VXD

[000C76F7]  LoadSuccess = C:\WINDOWS\system\VMM32\VCOND.VXD

[000C76F7]  Loading Vxd = VCDFSD

[000C76F7]  LoadSuccess = VCDFSD

[000C76F9]  Loading Vxd = C:\WINDOWS\system\VMM32\VXDLDR.VXD

[000C76FB]  LoadSuccess = C:\WINDOWS\system\VMM32\VXDLDR.VXD

[000C76FB]  Loading Vxd = VDEF

[000C76FB]  LoadSuccess = VDEF

[000C76FE]  Loading Vxd = C:\WINDOWS\system\VMM32\VPICD.VXD

[000C7700]  LoadSuccess = C:\WINDOWS\system\VMM32\VPICD.VXD

[000C7702]  Loading Vxd = C:\WINDOWS\system\VMM32\VTD.VXD

[000C7704]  LoadSuccess = C:\WINDOWS\system\VMM32\VTD.VXD

[000C7704]  Loading Vxd = REBOOT

[000C7704]  LoadSuccess = REBOOT
```

Next, you rebooted and selected the "Safe mode."

d) How is the appearance and behavior different than a normal Windows boot?

Answer: In Safe mode, most configuration and setting choices are ignored so that the operating system can load minimally, which reduces the risk of running into a problem. Safe mode loads only enough essential system's functionality to enable you to poke around and investigate where the true source of the problem might be.

When booting into Safe mode, these system files and resouces are completely ignored:

- CONFIG.SYS
- AUTOEXEC.BAT
- [Boot] section of SYSTEM.INI
- [386Enh] section of SYSTEM.INI
- Load= portion of WIN.INI
- Run= portion of WIN.INI

**LAB
10.2**

- All of the startup group
- The Registry
- All device drivers except keyboard, mouse, and standard VGA.

Next, you rebooted again and this time selected "Command prompt only."

e) How is the appearance and behavior different than a normal Windows boot?

Answer: In Command prompt only mode, only CONFIG.SYS, AUTOEXEC.BAT, COMMAND.COM, and the Registry are run—all graphical components are overlooked. The system boots into a mode that looks like the old, character-based DOS system, and you will need to issue commands directly to the system at the prompt.

Finally, you rebooted once again and chose "Safe mode command prompt."

f) How is the appearance and behavior different than a normal Windows boot?

Answer: Safe mode command prompt is the same as the previous choice, only now CONFIG.SYS and AUTOEXEC.BAT are not run.

10.2.3 ANSWERS

For this Exercise, you opened your WIN.INI file.

a) What programs are loaded with the line load= ?

Answer: This answer will depend on your system. You will see an example of the WIN.INI file after the next question. Load= automatically starts the program in a minimized fashion upon boot.

b) What programs are started with the line run= ?

Answer: As before, your actual WIN.INI file will contain different settings, but a sample file segment follows:

```
[windows]
load=
run=
NullPort=None
```

```
device=HP DeskJet 870 Series,HPRDJC08,LPT1:


[Desktop]
Wallpaper=C:\WINDOWS\LANEYE~2.BMP
TileWallpaper=0
WallpaperStyle=0


[intl]
iCountry=1
ICurrDigits=2
iCurrency=0
iDate=0
iDigits=2
iLZero=1
iMeasure=1
iNegCurr=0
iTime=0
iTLZero=0
s1159=AM
s2359=PM
sCountry=United States
```

Programs that are initialized by the "RUN" statement run normally (not minimized) upon execution of the WIN.INI file. Any programs you have in the Startup program group have a line in this file as well.

LAB
10.2

LAB 10.2 SELF-REVIEW QUESTIONS

In order to test your progress, you should be able to answer the following questions.

1) Which utility is used to make an emergency disk?
   a) ___EMR
   b) ___ERU
   c) ___EMG
   d) ___EDM

2) To bring up the boot menu in Windows 95, which key must you press during boot?
   a) ___F3
   b) ___F8
   c) ___F5
   d) ___F6

3) System Policy files have which of the following extensions?
   a) ___.CFG
   b) ___.SYS
   c) ___.VxD
   d) ___.POL

4) The first file processed during boot is which of the following?
   a) ___CONFIG.SYS
   b) ___ COMMAND.COM
   c) ___ MSDOS.SYS
   d) ___ IO.SYS

5) Booting in Logged mode creates which of the following files?
   a) ___Boot.txt
   b) ___Log.txt
   c) ___Bootlog.txt
   d) ___Logboot.txt

Quiz answers appear in Appendix A, Section 10.2.

LAB
10.2

L A B   10.3

PRINTING AND APPLICATION CONCEPTS

LAB OBJECTIVES

After this Lab, you will be able to:

✓ Turn on ECP Support
✓ Examine Printer Properties

The printing architecture in Windows 95 uses a unidriver/minidriver model. Microsoft supplies a universal driver with the operating system that speaks in a common language to most printers. The printer manufacturer writes only a mini driver that the universal driver then talks to in order to know specific features of that printer. There are actually two universal drivers—one for Postscript, and one for everything else. The non-Postscript driver can talk to many languages, including:

- Canon CaPSL
- EPSON ESC P/2
- HP PCL
- Lexmark PPDS
- Monochrome HP-GL/2
- Most dot-matrix printers

The printing process or model follows these steps:

1.   A user chooses to print a job within Windows.
2.   A local print spooler on the machine creates a temporary file on the hard disk (by default in C:\WINDOWS\SPOOL\PRINTERS).
3.   The Print Monitor begins sending the print job to the printer by writing the spooled data to a port or another print spooler on a network print server.
4.   The job is printed and Print Monitor can inform (if so told) the user the job is done.

In addition to the model, you should be familiar with a number of features available with Windows 95 for printing. These include:

- Point and Print setup. When a user points to a printer he or she wants to use for the very first time, regardless of where it is located, the drivers are downloaded to the client.
- Drag and Drop printing. A user can drag a file to a desktop icon of a printer and drop it there. The application associated with the file is automatically opened, the file is sent to the printer, and the application is automatically closed.
- Enhanced Metafile Spooling (EMF). Instead of sending raw data directly to the printer, the data can be processed and sent by the operating system—decreasing the printing time by about half.
- Plug and Play. The Windows 95 operating system is Plug and Play (PnP) throughout, with the printing component being no exception. Devices that comply with PnP standards are automatically recognized and configured by the operating system each time Windows 95 is started. If the device adheres to IEEE1284 standards, then bi-directional communication is also possible. With bi-directional communication, the printer can send unsolicited messages to the computer telling it that it is low on toner, out of paper, and so forth. However, PnP is not entirely foolproof, and can fail occasionally.
- Extended Capabilities Ports (ECP). This allows compression to be used by Windows 95 to send data to the printer quicker. This is not enabled by default, but can be turned on within the operating system if the printer you have is ECP-capable.

- Image Color Matching (ICM). This makes certain that the color you see on your screen is the same color that appears when you print. This is accomplished by using InterColor 3.0 specifications– a technology created by Kodak, Apple, Sun, and Silicon Graphics.

You should also know how to print from non-Windows applications. Here, the application sends the print job to the printer driver that translates everything into a language the printer will understand. Raw data is then sent to the print spooler and control is returned to the application.

RUNNING APPLICATIONS IN WINDOWS 95

Windows 3.*x* was built on the premise of cooperative multitasking between applications and processes. Windows 95 does that one better by going to preemptive multitasking, which keeps one process from tying up the system.

Windows 95 uses Virtual Memory consisting of RAM and a Swap file to meet the needs of all applications—Win 16, Win 32, and DOS. The swap file can be noncontiguous and even reside on a compressed drive. As a review from Chapter 9, remember that the three types of platforms differ in how they run applications, as shown in Table 10.2.

Table 10.2 ■ How the Three Types of Applications Run

DOS	Win 16	Win 32
Run in private Virtual DOS Machines (VDMs)	Run in common address space	Run in private address space
No message queue	Share single message queue	Each thread has its own message queue
Loaded in lower 1MB of virtual memory	Loaded in lower 2GB of virtual memory	Loaded in the 4MB to 2GB range of virtual memory

In order for Windows 95 to run Win 16-bit applications, the code must be converted to 32-bit, processed, then converted back to 16-bit. The process of converting from 16 to 32 is known as *thunking up*, while the process of converting from 32 to 16 is known as *thunking down*. In plain English, this means that Win 16 applications run worse on Windows 95 than they do on Windows 3.*x*. This is because an additional process must occur twice to carry out the operations. DOS applications, on the other hand, run far better on Windows 95 than they ever did anywhere else, and Win 32 applications run virtually flawlessly.

The Task Scheduler is responsible for seeing to it that every thread gets processed. There are 32 possible priority levels preassigned to a thread when it is submitted (ranging from 0 to 31). A primary scheduler also alters the priority of the thread to see to it that it eventually does get processed, and does not wait unprocessed for long:

- Threads waiting for user input get an automatic priority boost, thus making the system seem more responsive.
- All threads periodically receive a priority boost to prevent them from locking shared resources needed by higher priority threads.
- CPU-bound threads get a priority decrease so that I/O operations are not blocked.

When an application cannot be opened more than once, its code is said to be mutually exclusive. The way it identifies itself as being open is by setting a Mutex (for MUTually EXclusive) flag. If a user tries to open the application again, rather than a new instance of it beginning, the open instance comes to the front. This can cause problems with Win 16 applications that hang and crash. If the Mutex flag is still set to 1, the user cannot start the application again, even though there is not another instance of it open. While Windows 95 makes every attempt to solve this problem, if it does occur; the only solution is to shut down and restart.

LAB 10.3 EXERCISES

10.3.1 TURN ON ECP SUPPORT

For this Exercise, you will determine the IRQ or DMA settings for the ECP ports on your Windows 95 machine.

1. Open the System applet in the Control Panel and choose the Device Manager tab.
2. Expand Ports and double-click the Printer Port.

3. Choose the Resources tab in the Printer Port Properties dialog box and uncheck the Use Automatic Settings check box. Make note of the Interrupt Request value. You will need this later in this Exercise.

4. Click the down arrow to expand the Settings based on drop-down menu.

   a) What are your choices in the Settings based on drop-down menu?

   _____

   _____

5. Choose Basic Configuration 0002 from this menu.

   b) Does anything appear in the Conflicting device list at the bottom of this window?

   _____

   _____

6. Select the Interrupt Request , and click the Change Setting button. The Change Setting dialog will appear and allow you to enter a specific IRQ value.

7. Type in the IRQ from step 4 and click OK. Shut down and restart the computer. When it reboots, your printer has now been specifically assigned to operate on your designated interrupt.

10.3.2 EXAMINE PRINTER PROPERTIES

For this Exercise, you will check the properties of a printer you have installed to see if EMF is a feature of your printer.

1. From the Start menu, choose Settings, then Printers. Click on the icon for a printer whose properties you wish to examine.

2. Once the printer is selected, right-click to bring up the menu, then choose Properties. A multi-tab Properties dialog box for that printer will open.

3.   To determine whether you have EMF set for this printer, select the Details tab, then click the "Spool Settings..." button.

a) In the Spool Settings dialog box, what is listed in the Spool data format drop-down list?

_____

_____

You may now cancel out of these dialog boxes.

LAB 10.3 EXERCISE ANSWERS

10.3.1 ANSWERS

On a Windows 95 machine, you determined the IRQ or DMA settings for the ECP ports.

a)   What are your choices in the Settings based on drop-down menu?

Answer: As you can see in Figure 10.1, you should have three choices: Basic Configuration 0000, Basic Configuration 0001, and Basic Configuration 0002.

Next, you chose Basic Configuration 0002 from this menu.

b)   Does anything appear in the Conflicting device list at the bottom of this window?

Answer: This will depend on your system.

If there is a device listed, it may compete for system resources with your current device. You will need to reassign one or more devices until no more conflicts exist.

LAB
10.3

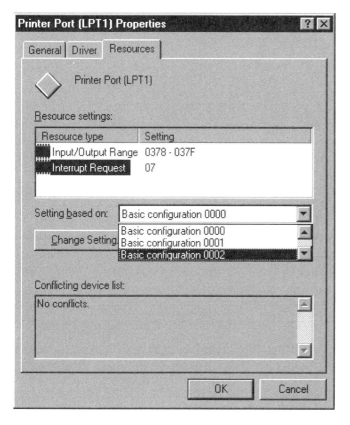

Figure 10.1 ■ You can change your printer configuration using the Resources panel of the Printer Port Properties dialog box.

10.3.2 ANSWERS

For this Exercise, you checked your printer's properties to see if EMF is a feature of your printer.

a) In the Spool Settings dialog box, what is listed in the Spool data format drop-down list?

Answer: This will depend on the printer you chose.

EMF is available only if both the printer and application support it. Usually, any program written specifically for Windows NT or Windows 95 will support EMF spooling. Otherwise, the default choice is RAW, which means that data is sent directly to the printer, without any intermediate spooling.

LAB 10.3 SELF-REVIEW QUESTIONS

In order to test your progress, you should be able to answer the following questions.

1) Converting 16-bit code to 32-bit code is known as which of the following?
   a) ___Porting
   b) ___Translating
   c) ___Thunking
   d) ___Mutex

2) Which types of applications run better on Windows 95 than in their own environment?
   a) ___DOS
   b) ___Win16
   c) ___Win32
   d) ___Win64

3) The default location for the internal print spool is which of the following?
   a) ___C:\Windows\Spool\Printers
   b) ___ C:\Windows\Spool
   c) ___ C:\Windows\Printers
   d) ___ C:\Spool\Printers

4) Win16 applications have how many message queues?
   a) ___0
   b) ___1
   c) ___8
   d) ___16

5) When you print from a non-Windows application, the application sends the print job to the printer driver that translates everything into a language the printer will understand. Raw data is then sent to the print spooler and control is returned to the application.
   a) _____True
   b) _____False

Quiz answers appear in Appendix A, Section 10.3.

C H A P T E R   10

TEST YOUR THINKING

1) Install a printer on one Windows 95 system and share it to the network. Observe what happens. Pay particular attention from where the files are loaded.

2) On a Windows 95 system that does not have the driver for that particular printer already installed, connect to the shared printer in the previous example across the network. Observe what happens. Pay particular attention from where the files are loaded.

CHAPTER 11

DIAGNOSING AND TROUBLESHOOTING: SOFTWARE

 The great weakness of Pragmatism is that it ends by being of no use to anybody.

—T.S. Eliot

CHAPTER OBJECTIVES

In this chapter, you will learn about:

- ✓ Recognizing Common Errors and Corrective   Page 426
  Steps

This section constitutes another 25 percent of the elective exam. Most of the problems truly are common ones that you will have encountered if you have spent any time servicing computers.

L A B   11.1

COMMON ERRORS AND CORRECTIVE STEPS

LAB OBJECTIVES

After this Lab, you will be able to:

✓ Troubleshoot When the Application Will Not Start or Load

✓ Fix a Problem with COMMAND.COM

✓ Identify the Source of Network Login Problems

✓ Repair a CONFIG.SYS Error

✓ Resolve Problems with the Print Spooler

✓ Improve System Performance by Optimizing Swap File Size

The problems you will encounter in the Exercises for this Lab are common ones that occur with operating systems, with the most likely cause and corrective step discussed for each of them. Before getting to the Exercises, however, you should apply several rules of logic to any situation (particularly for the exam):

- Never attempt to solve a problem without narrowing it down. If a user complains that he cannot print, you would never replace the printer as a first step. You would first try to narrow it down, such as testing if anyone else could print to it.
- Always try to refine the problem by starting broad and narrowing in as you go. A line of reasoning with a call from a user who cannot print would follow this train of logic:
  — Have you ever been able to print (it could be that the user has a new machine)?
  — Has it been to this printer (it could be that he has a new printer, or is trying to use a different one to get color copies that he never printed from before)?
  — When was the last time you did so (yesterday, or last month, or last year)?
  — What has changed since then (the answer will always be "nothing," but you still must ask)?

LAB 11.1

APPLICATION WILL NOT START OR LOAD

An application will not start or load if a portion of it is missing, or if it is unable to access the resources that it needs. The first step in troubleshooting should be to examine the means by which the application is called— by its actual EXE name, through a shortcut, a batch file, or other means.

BAD OR MISSING COMMAND.COM

There are three files necessary for any of the operating systems on this exam to boot: IO.SYS, MSDOS.SYS, and COMMAND.COM. The first two are hidden; COMMAND.COM is not, which leaves it susceptible to all kinds of problems. Many is the beginning user who several months after having gotten a new machine decides to clean it up a bit and deletes files not being used. This one sits right there in the root directory and screams to them, "Delete me! Delete me! Delete me!" When they do, they have no command interpreter—nothing to translate between them and the operating system, and thus they have no operating system.

BEEP CODES

During the POST operation, no operating system has been loaded, and the only way an error can be relayed is through the use of the internal speaker. A single beep tells you that the POST operation has completed successfully and the load process is continuing. No beep at all is indicative of a bad PC speaker, while more than one beep indicates a problem with memory.

BOOTING INTO SAFE MODE

If Windows 95 is improperly shut down—power turned off before first choosing Start—Shutdown and letting it go through its paces, Windows 95 will want to boot into Safe Mode. It does this because it does not know the extent—if any—of corruption that has occurred. As discussed in the previous chapter, in Safe Mode it bypasses most configuration settings and lets the operating system get loaded. From here, you can open the System applet from Control Panel and choose the Device Manager tab to look for any conflicts.

If there are no conflicts, you can reboot and come back in Normal mode. If there are conflicts, you can delete the items in disharmony and reboot. Since Windows 95 is a Plug and Play operating system, it will find the devices that have been altered during this step and reconfigure them upon boot, allowing you to continue on into Normal mode.

CANNOT LOG ONTO NETWORK

An inability to log onto the network can be caused by any number of factors—both hardware and software.

CMOS PROBLEMS

The CMOS stores the computer's date and time, hard drive configuration settings, and hardware password (with the default being that its use is disabled). If date/time and related information is lost when you boot, then the internal battery is no longer of sufficient charge to retain that information and must be replaced.

If a user loses his or her hardware password, the only solution is to disconnect and reconnect the internal battery. This defaults back to the setting of a hardware password not being used. Unfortunately, it also loses all the date/time, hardware, and other CMOS information, which must be reentered when the machine boots.

DEVICE REFERENCED IN SYSTEM.INI COULD NOT BE FOUND

The System.ini file is read when Windows 3.x or Windows 95 initializes and is used to load additional drivers, customized settings, and hardware configuration. When a device/driver cannot be found, the error is echoed back to the screen. Use this information to verify the device is still there.

LAB 11.1

If the device is not there, you can edit out the line referencing it with Edit.com, Sysedit, or any editor capable of working with ASCII files. If the file is still there, it has potentially become corrupted. Try replacing it with a back-up copy.

ERROR IN CONFIG.SYS

The CONFIG.SYS file runs before COMMAND.COM and is used to load drivers and create an environment for the command interpreter to run in.

GENERAL PROTECTION FAULT

One of the biggest complaints with Windows 3.x is the GPFs (General Protection Faults) that occur. From a user's standpoint, she is minding her own business and about ready to save files that she has been working with all day long when suddenly a blue screen comes up and reports that there has been a General Protection Fault, giving an error message understood only by the engineer who was hit by the bus right after Windows shipped.

Because all 16-bit applications share the same message queue, an error in one application can (and will) cause an error in all other applications. This means that the only way to correct the problem is to reboot—losing the data that the user had been modifying all day long. While there are a number of suggestions, there are no surefire answers. Among the more obvious, the user should save work more often, and upgrade to Windows 95. When upgraded, all 16-bit applications will still have the same problem because they still have the same code, but a GPF will affect only the 16-bit applications and not the operating system or any of the 32-bit applications.

After the upgrade to Windows 95, migrating applications to 32-bit applications will virtually eliminate GPFs altogether. This is because 32-bit applications run in their own space and queues and do not interact with one another—virtually eliminating the possibility of a protection fault.

HIMEM.SYS NOT LOADED OR CORRUPT

HIMEM.SYS is needed to load Windows 3.x in 386 enhanced mode and Windows 95, and in its absence you get the command line only. A very visible file that is loaded from CONFIG.SYS, it has the potential to become corrupt or deleted like any other file. Should this be the case, the best solution is to restore the file from your installation media.

ILLEGAL OPERATION

Illegal operations occur when an application attempts to do something it cannot do—such as divide by zero. This is an application-specific problem and you should carefully scrutinize the operation in question, the environment variables, and related factors to find the solution.

INCORRECT DOS VERSION

Many executables are written to a particular version of the operating system. When the version changes, they can fail to run—thinking features that they utilized no longer exist. In most cases, the operating system version changed because you upgraded from an older version to a newer one. In almost every case, the new operating system **does** have everything the older version had and more. It's now merely an issue of fooling the executable into thinking it is running on the older operating system. That is the purpose of the SETVER utility.

SETVER tricks the programs into thinking they are running on another version of the operating system by returning to them an entry from the system version table showing values you have placed there. If, for example, DS_TECH.EXE was written to run on MS-DOS version 5.0 and never updated, you could coerce it to work on DOS 6.2 by typing the command below:

```
SETVER DS_TECH.EXE 5.0
```

This would create an entry in the settings table telling the version number returned to be 5.0 should DS_TECH.EXE ever inquire.

INVALID WORKING DIRECTORY

An invalid working directory is most often one that does not exist, or is no longer accessible. If you are running an executable from the A: drive, and then remove the floppy from the drive, you no longer have a valid working directory. In Windows 95, a working directory is specified for every program.

The solution, simply enough, is to change the directory or its specification to a valid entry.

NO OPERATING SYSTEM FOUND

The three files necessary to make a bootable operating system for the purposes of the exam are IO.SYS, MSDOS.SYS, and COMMAND.COM. Should either of the first two become corrupted, deleted, or otherwise inaccessible, this error message will be returned. The solution is to boot from a bootable floppy and run the SYS command to restore them.

PRINT SPOOL IS STALLED

The biggest component (most likely to cause problems) with printing is spooling. Spool settings can make happy users or angry managers.

SWAP FILE PROBLEMS

The swap file is a large file on the hard drive used to hold data that is being processed that cannot be held in memory. In other words, it frees memory by writing some of the data to the hard drive. A swap file can be used for a temporary file, an application, or virtual memory. Temporary swap files have a .SWP extension, while permanent swap files have a .PAR extension.

The best example of a swap file in use is the Windows 95 operating system itself. If you read the box requirements, it states that it can run in 4MB of RAM. In reality, the Windows 95 operating system requires 14MB to run. Assuming absolutely no programs whatsoever, it takes the amount of RAM you have and uses it, then makes a swap file for the rest of its data.

If you have 4MB of RAM, the swap file is 10MB in size. If you have 8MB of RAM, the swap file is 6MB in size. For every major operation you do, Windows 95 must read from and write to the swap file to complete the operation. Since the hard drive is one of the slowest components in the entire PC, this adds considerably to the amount of processing time for every operation.

SYSTEM LOCKUP

A system lockup can be caused by any number of items and is incredibly difficult to diagnose. It usually occurs without regularity and only moments before you were going to do a full backup. The best trouble-shooting tool is to document the operations you are doing and see what combination of events led to the lockup. Lockups in DOS can and do occur when an application goes awry. Lockups in Windows 3.x are typically associated or preceded by General Protection Faults. Lockups in Windows 95 should be nonexistent, but do occasionally still occur.

UTILITIES

Most of the troubleshooting utilities available to you were discussed in the previous chapters of this book in relation to the components they pertain to. Make certain you know and understand why you would use:

- ATTRIB.EXE—to see and set file attributes
- DEFRAG.EXE—to place files in contiguous order on the drive
- Device Manager—to look for conflicts
- EDIT.COM—to edit any ASCII file
- EXTRACT.EXE—to uncompress files from the distribution media. Compressed files display the last character of the extension as an underscore; thus fdisk.ex_ would be the compressed version of fdisk.exe
- FDISK.EXE—to partition the drive
- MEM.EXE—to view memory statistics
- MSD.EXE—to gather information about your system
- SCANDISK—to look for drive errors and file allocation table errors
- SYSEDIT.EXE—to edit the system configuration files

Familiarity with this handful of utilities will greatly help you answer many of the questions on the elective exam.

VIRUSES

Viruses are malicious programs that run with the intent of doing harm to your system. They include instructions that run without the user summoning them and can be classified either as a program virus or a macro virus. A program virus attacks the operating system and the command interpreter, while a macro virus works within the program, such as Word or Excel.

A boot sector virus runs every time the PC boots and changes the boot sector to include its code. Viruses can be memory-resident (running as TSRs), stealth (hide their presence), and polymorphic (modifying themselves to escape detection). One of the key attributes of a virus is the inherent desire to multiple and spread to other machines through files, boot disks, downloads, etc.

Later versions of MS-DOS shipped with MSAV.exe, Microsoft's Anti-Virus software licensed from Central Point. Windows 3.x and Windows 95 do not include any anti-virus software and it is highly recommended that third-party utilities be purchased and utilized to save one's system from these programs. It is also recommended that newer third-party programs be purchased for DOS as well, to replace MSAV which has not been kept updated.

LAB 11.1 EXERCISES

For these Exercises, I present you with typical scenarios and ask you to troubleshoot them. Use your experience or your intuition to craft your answers and be as thorough as you possibly can.

11.1.1 TROUBLESHOOT WHEN THE APPLICATION WILL NOT START OR LOAD

For this Exercise, suppose you have an application—such as a spreadsheet or word processing program—that will not load.

a) What steps would you take to troubleshoot the problem?

_____

_____

11.1.2 FIX A PROBLEM WITH COMMAND.COM

While booting the computer, you receive a message "Bad or Missing Command.com."

a) How do you resolve this problem?

_____

_____

11.1.3 IDENTIFY THE SOURCE OF NETWORK LOGIN PROBLEMS

You discover you are unable to log into the network, although you were able to do so yesterday. You suspect a faulty NIC card.

a) What should you do to confirm your theory prior to replacing the NIC card?

_____

_____

11.1.4 REPAIR A CONFIG.SYS ERROR

You notice a problem with your CONFIG.SYS file.

a) How do you identify the source of the problem and repair it?

_____

_____

11.1.5 RESOLVE PROBLEMS WITH THE PRINT SPOOLER

A user calls to tell you that her printer is not printing a job she's sent. When you look at the system, you notice the print spooler is stalled.

a) What do you do next to resolve the problem?

_____

_____

11.1.6 IMPROVE SYSTEM PERFORMANCE BY OPTIMIZING SWAP FILE SIZE

A user's system performance has degraded substantially over a short period of time, and you've narrowed it down to a problem with the size of the swap file.

a) What would cause you to suspect this, and what do you do to resolve it?

_____

_____

LAB 11.1 EXERCISE ANSWERS

11.1.1 ANSWERS

In this scenario, you have an application—such as a spreadsheet or word processing program—that would not load.

a) What steps do you take to troubleshoot the problem?

Answer: If the application is launched by a batch file, try typing in the commands found in the batch file at a command prompt to see what messages are coming back. Most of the time, the problem will become obvious to you in this manner when an error message pops back.

All shortcuts are saved in Windows 95 with a .LNK extension. Examine the shortcut by right-clicking on it and choosing Properties. Figure 11.1 shows an example of the General tab of the Properties on a shortcut for a simple executable file, while Figure 11.2 shows the Shortcut tab. Notice that the Properties are all stored in a file aliased as DRAWIN~1.LNK and that it is pointing to a file DRAWTHR.EXE in the C:\VBSTUFF directory.

You should verify that the directory exists and has not been deleted, and that the executable is still there. If it has been moved, you can choose the Find Target button and redo the shortcut, or delete the shortcut altogether and re-create it.

If the executable does exist and is being called correctly—either directly, through a shortcut, or batch file—and the application still will not run, attempt to call the executable from a command line and look for error messages related to insufficient resources. If such an error message comes back, correct the resource situation and call the executable again. If no such error message occurs and there is no indication as to why the application will not run, it is possible the executable itself has become corrupted. Delete the executable portion of the application and reinstall from its native media.

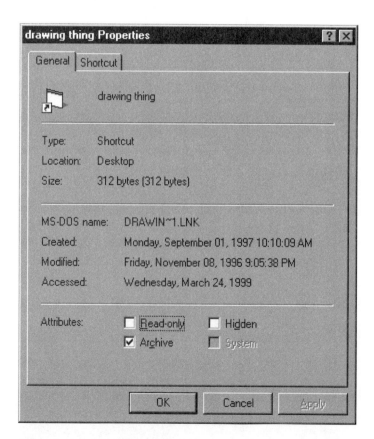

Figure 11.1 ■ General tab of a shortcut's Properties dialog box shows the general properties of the shortcut.

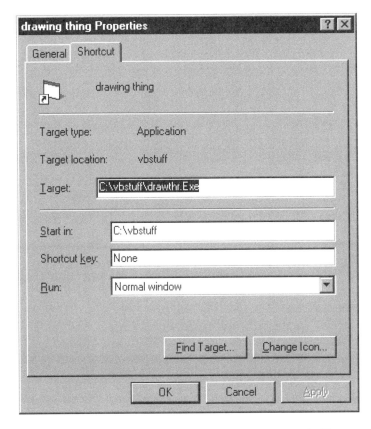

Figure 11.2 ■ Shortcut tab of a shortcut's Properties dialog box is where you can change the properties.

11.1.2 ANSWERS

While booting the computer, you receive a message "Bad or Missing Command.com."

a) How did you resolve this problem?

Answer: The solution is to boot from a bootable floppy and run the SYS command. The SYS command copies the operating system files (all three) over and makes the hard drive bootable once more.

11.1.3 ANSWERS

You discover you are unable to log into the network, although you were able to do so yesterday. You suspect a faulty NIC card.

a) What should you do to confirm your theory prior to replacing the card?

Answer: While a defective NIC is a possibility, there are a few items you should check first before replacing it:

- Can anyone else get on the network—is the network up?
- Has this client ever been on the network and when?
- Can the client get to another network?
- Are the protocols loaded and running on this client? If running TCP/IP, you can ping the loopback address (127.0.0.1) to see if the protocol is in working order.
- Can another client ping (if using TCP/IP) over to here?
- Are there lights on the NIC card and are they lit? Is there a conflict in Device Manager?
- Is the network cable properly and securely connected at both ends?
- Have you tried rebooting?

If you have moved through all the steps and not resolved the problem, then—and only then—should replacing the network interface card be considered a viable option.

11.1.4 ANSWERS

You notice a problem with your CONFIG.SYS file.

a) How do you identify the source of the problem and repair it?

Answer: Errors within this file are typically referenced by line number. You can find the line in question with any ASCII editor to make the changes that are needed.

For example, the following line points to an executable file:

```
DEVICE=C:\DOS\SETVER.EXE
```

In this case, you would make certain the file has not been deleted or moved.

In the following line, parameters are used:

```
SHELL=C:\COMMAND.COM /P /E
```

In this instance, make certain the correct syntax is used. In this example, the /E parameter requires specifying how much memory will be used with it, and the line really should be:

```
SHELL=C:\COMMAND.COM /P /E:2048
```

If the operating system in question is DOS, there is a utility included with it—MEMMAKER—that should be run. It optimizes the configuration files, mainly CONFIG.SYS, thereby optimizing performance.

11.1.5 ANSWERS

A user calls to tell you that her printer is not printing a job she's sent. When you look at the system, you notice the print spooler is stalled.

a) What do you do next to resolve the problem?

Answer: Windows 95 tries to print in the Enhanced Metafile (EMF) format to speed the printing process as much as possible. If you are having difficulties printing, particularly with older applications, change EMF to RAW. This will slow down the process somewhat, but there is not a printer made that does not understand the RAW language.

Change your print spooling characteristics by following these steps:

1. Select Start → Settings → Printers and then select your specific printer.
2. Right-click on the highlighted printer and select Properties from the pop-up menu.
3. Select the Details tab (see Figure 11.3) and then click on Spool Settings.
4. The "Spool data format" drop-down list box allows you to change your spooling characteristics (see Figure 11.4).

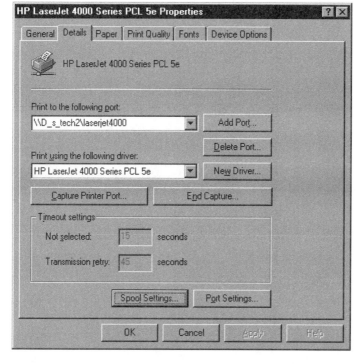

Figure 11.3 ■ **The printer's Properties dialog box. Details tab is where you access the Spool Settings dialog box.**

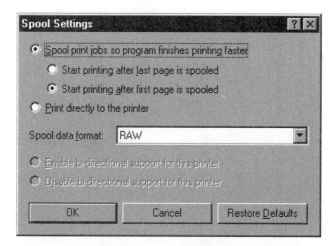

Figure 11.4 ■ **Click the down-arrow next to the Spool data format field to view the available options.**

In Windows 95, the Spool Settings dialog box in Figure 11.4 allows you to configure the spool specifications. Figure 11.3 points to something more troublesome—timeout factors. This is the number of seconds that the printer waits for data before it thinks the job is finished. If you are printing Microsoft Word documents, waiting 15 seconds after the print job comes to you before taking the next job is adequate. If you are printing TIF files, however (large, graphic files that must be rendered), then there could conceivably be a 30-second delay in portions of the data sent to the spool. Too short of timeout settings will have one user's print job clobbering another, while too long will merely require longer time periods between printed jobs. You must optimize both for your environment.

11.1.6 ANSWERS

A user's system performance has degraded substantially over a short period of time, and you've narrowed it down to a problem with the size of the swap file.

a) What would cause you to suspect this, and what do you do to resolve it?

Answer: In all cases of this sort, the best solution is to add more RAM to the system.

Again, assuming only Windows 95 and no applications, increasing the RAM in the machine from 4MB to 32MB allows the entire operating system to run in RAM and leaves 18MB left for other operations.

Problems can also occur when there is only a small amount of space remaining on the hard drive and/or that space is not contiguous. Since the swap file must be read, reading from noncontiguous sectors adds more time to an already slow process. The solution here is to free up disk space, add a larger hard drive, add a faster hard drive, or defragment the drive.

In Windows 95, you can go to the System applet in Control Panel and choose the Performance tab. From there, click the Virtual Memory button and you will see a dialog box like that shown in Figure 11.5. The default is for the swap file to be able to grow to the size of remaining free space on your hard drive. Under most circumstances, this is desirable and this setting should be kept, although you can modify it if you need to.

**LAB
11.1**

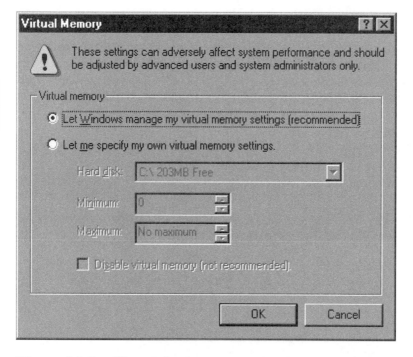

**Figure 11.5 ■ The default settings in the Virtual Memory dialog box
are usually the most desirable, though they can be changed.**

LAB 11.1 SELF-REVIEW QUESTIONS

In order to test your progress, you should be able to answer the following
questions.

1) The utility used to uncompress installation files is which of the follow-
    ing?
    a) ___Unpack
    b) ___Uncompress
    c) ___Compress
    d) ___Extract

2) HIMEM.SYS is loaded from which start-up file?
    a) ___System.ini
    b) ___Config.sys
    c) ___Autoexec.bat
    d) ___Win.com

3) The lack of any beep codes during start up indicates which of the following?

   a) ___Successful boot
   b) ___Memory error
   c) ___Bad PC speaker
   d) ___Bad power supply

4) Which of the following is the extension on a permanent swap file?

   a) ___SWP
   b) ___PAR
   c) ___PER
   d) ___PWS

5) The loopback address in TCP/IP is which of the following?

   a) ___255.255.255.0
   b) ___255.255.0.0
   c) ___255.0.0.0
   d) ___127.0.0.1

Quiz answers appear in Appendix A, Section 11.1.

C H A P T E R   11

TEST YOUR THINKING

1) Have a knowledgeable colleague deliberately disable a working PC (your colleague needs to carefully document what he did so that it can be undone; what is done should not precipitate permanent or unrecoverable damage). Some good ideas include changing or removing a display, network, or printer configuration, or removing an entry from CONFIG.SYS, WINDOWS.INI, or AUTOEXEC.BAT. Poor ideas include anything requiring the reinstallation of Windows or a software package.

Depending upon exactly what your friend does to the PC, a "complaint" may need to accompany the broken PC, such as "I cannot print" or "I cannot run this application."

 The point here is to create a realistic—but reversible—fault. However, if an "expendable" system is available, then the range of possibilities could include those requiring more time-consuming recovery.

Now, proceed with diagnosis of the system. Take thorough notes on the things you looked at, what you observed, and the steps you performed to further diagnose or resolve the situation. Answer the following questions:

a) What was the original set of symptoms?

b) What steps did you perform to diagnose and (hopefully) resolve the problem?

c) Is the system—once recovered—in its original condition, or is something different? (For example, if diagnosing a printer problem, you might have installed a newer version of a printer driver than what was originally on the system.)

d) How long did it take to resolve the problem?

e) Would you follow the same steps again? What—if anything—would you do differently?

Have your colleague describe exactly what he did to the system. Did your remediation effectively reverse his action?

 Run through this project several times and see if you can successfully diagnose the problem each time.

2) What online (and printed) resources can you find that will help to troubleshoot PC problems? Do those resources have specific troubleshooting steps, or are they in the form of general guidelines that add to one's knowledge and experience? What form of information is more useful to you?

NETWORKS

Isn't this what Chapter 6 was about?

—Average reader

CHAPTER OBJECTIVES

In this chapter, you will learn about:

✓ DOS and Windows Networking Capabilities   Page 448
✓ Internet Networking   Page 466

The Network section of the elective exam builds upon the Basic Networking section of the core exam. Whereas Chapter 6 explained concepts and components, this chapter focuses on the actual implementation. It is imperative that you read Chapter 6, "Basic Networking," before beginning this chapter.

L A B   12.1

DOS AND WINDOWS NETWORKING CAPABILITIES

LAB OBJECTIVES

After this Lab, you will be able to:

✓ Install TCP/IP Networking For Windows 95

✓ Configure Print and File Sharing Services

✓ Share Disk Drives and Directories

✓ Map a Drive

Windows 95 is one of the easiest operating systems ever created and we will examine it first to see how to properly configure network services for it. Essential to this discussion is a good understanding of the architecture, which we will look at first.

WINDOWS 95 NETWORKING ARCHITECTURE

Windows 95 has a modular, layered architecture. Each layer needs to communicate directly only with the layers immediately above and below it. Therefore, a component of the architecture, such as a network adapter driver, needs to be compatible only with the layer adjacent to it, which is the device driver interface in this case. Thus, only one version of the network adapter driver needs to be created as the driver will work with any of the Windows 95-compatible transport protocols.

The layers of the Windows 95 networking architecture, starting from the topmost layer, are:

1. Application Interface—The Application Interface layer contains two interfaces (the Win32 Print Applicator Programming Interface (API) and the Win32 WinNet Interface) that allow an application to access the Windows 95 networking services. The application interfaces contain a standardized set of commands and procedures that an application can use to communicate with the network provider.

2. Network Providers—The network providers allow access to shared files and printers and provide browsing services.

3. IFS (Installable File System) Manager—The IFS Manager handles the communication between the various IFSs (such as the CD File System, CDFS, VFAT), the Network Provider, and the network redirectors and services.

4. Redirectors and Services—Information passing between the application and transport protocol layers is processed and converted to the proper data format for the next layer. The redirectors and services residing at this layer each perform a specific function on the information.

5. Transport Programming Interface—This interface provides a standardized set of commands to allow the network redirector and services to send information to the underlying transport protocols. The Transport Programming Interface allows the services of the upper layers of the networking architecture to communicate with any of the Windows 95-compatible transport protocols, such as NetBEUI, TCP/IP, or IPX/SPX.

6. Transport Driver Protocols—There are responsible for putting the information in the correct format so that it can be understood by the network device to which the message is being sent. This could be TCP/IP, NetBEUI, IPX/SPX, and so forth.

7. Device Driver Interface—The Device Driver Interface handles communication between the transport protocol and the network card driver. This interface contains a standard-

ized set of commands and procedures that the protocol and network card driver can use to communicate with each other.

ADMINISTERING SECURITY ACCESS

Windows 95 enables you to leverage security access to users by utilizing either share-level or user-level security. Share-level security is used by default when File and Printer Sharing for Microsoft Networks is installed. With share-level security, passwords are assigned to each individual share to permit access to a directory or printer share. To access the share, a user must supply the correct password. This can become difficult to manage in even small workgroups. If no password is used, any user will have full or read-only access to the directory, depending on which option was specified when the shared directory was created. When creating a shared directory using share-level security, one of three types of access can be granted: Read, Full, or Depends on Password. Print queues also can be shared with other network users using share-level security. Printers are either shared or not shared in Windows 95.

Because share-level security relies on access passwords, this form of security has the following disadvantages:

- To access different shares, a network user has to know numerous passwords.
- Passwords can easily be forgotten. Windows 95 can cache passwords so that a user must enter them each time. However, if the creator of the share forgets the password, the password has to be changed to allow another user to access the share.
- Nothing prevents a user from disclosing the password to an unauthorized user.

With user-level security, specific user accounts or group accounts can be granted access to a shared directory or printer. Instead of relying on a password that could be used by anyone, the user account accessing a shared resource must be authenticated to ensure that the account has been granted access.

Windows 95 does not manage user accounts by itself. User-level security enables you to create a list of users who have access to a particular resource; you can store that list on a server (called the *central server*). Before a user can gain access to a resource, he or she must be on this list of users. When a user logs on to the server, he or she must use pass-through authentication to have a Windows NT or NetWare server authenticate the user who is trying to access the resource.

You can use user-level security to provide security for a variety of services beyond network access, such as Network management, Backup agents, and Dial-up networking.

To use user-level security, the Windows 95 computer must obtain a copy of the accounts list from one of the following sources:

- Windows NT Server or Workstation 3.5 (or later) computer.
- NetWare 3.x or 4.x.

**LAB
12.1**

With user-level security, when a directory is shared, the users or groups that have access to the share are assigned privileges allowing the appropriate levels of access to the resource. When sharing a printer, users or groups can be added to a list of users with access to that printer.

Although you can change from user-level to share-level security, or from share-level to user-level security, you probably should not. When you switch from one to the other, you lose all of the current security settings. You must re-create all security settings on each individual share.

Some of the same disadvantages found in share-level security also exist with user-level security, such as the user forgetting the password. However, with user-level security, this type of problem affects only the one user, and not the entire share. The steps you take to map a drive is covered in an Exercise later in this chapter.

UNDERSTANDING DRIVE MAPPING AND UNC PATHS

The *Universal Naming Convention* (UNC) is a standardized nomenclature for specifying a share name on a particular computer. The computer name is limited to 15 characters, and the share name is usually limited to 15 characters, depending on the network.

The UNC uniquely specifies the path to the share name on a network. The UNC path takes the form of *computername**sharename* [*optional path*]. If a dollar sign ($) is added to the end of the share name, it will prevent the share name from being visible to another computer through a browser, such as Network Neighborhood.

All Windows 95 functions support using a UNC name, including the Run option on the Start menu and the command prompt. NetWare servers, like Windows NT servers, can be accessed through a UNC name.

The UNC is used with some programs that require mapping of a local drive to a network folder. Mapping allows the assigning of a letter to a network drive or folder; all references to the drive can then use the letter "shortcut" instead of specifying the entire drive or folder path.

LAB 12.1 EXERCISES

12.1.1 INSTALL TCP/IP NETWORKING FOR WINDOWS 95

In addition to IPX/SPX and NetBEUI, the other protocol that is included with Windows 95 and can be installed is TCP/IP—the protocol of the Internet, Windows NT, Unix, and many other networked operating systems.

To install TCP/IP:

1. From the Start menu, choose Settings, then Control Panel.
2. Double-click on the Network icon to open the Network dialog box and select the Configuration tab.
3. Choose Add to open the Select Network Component Type dialog box, as shown in Figure 12.1.

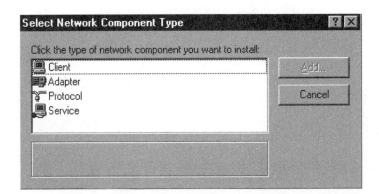

Figure 12.1 ■ Click on the type of network component you want to install in the Select Network Component Type dialog box.

4. Select Protocol and choose Add to open the Select Network Protocol dialog box.
5. Select Microsoft from the Manufacturers list and TCP/IP from the Network Protocols list.
6. Choose OK to return to the Network dialog box.

    a) Does Windows 95 tell you to reboot your machine?

_____

_____

LAB
12.1

The next step is to configure your TCP/IP properties, as follows:

1. From the Network dialog box Configuration tab, select TCP/IP and choose Properties. This opens the TCP/IP Properties dialog box shown in Figure 12.2.

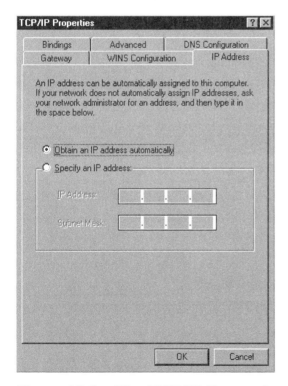

Figure 12.2 ■ The TCP/IP Properties dialog box. IP Address panel is where you specify an IP address.

2. From the TCP/IP Properties sheet, select the IP Address tab.

    b) Is there an IP address entered in the Specify an IP address portion of the panel?

    _____

    _____

3. Select Obtain an IP address automatically if there is a Dynamic Host Configuration Protocol (DHCP) server on the network configured to supply this machine with an IP address.

    Otherwise, type the IP address and subnet mask in the spaces provided. An incorrect IP address or subnet mask can cause communication problems with other TCP/IP nodes on the network. If an IP address is the same as another already on the network, it can cause either machine to hang.

4. Each of the other tabs in the TCP/IP Properties dialog box contains optional configuration information. For each of these tabs, enter the appropriate values as required. Choose OK when done to restart the computer and initialize TCP/IP.

    c) What other panels does your TCP/IP Properties dialog box contain?

    _____

    _____

12.1.2 CONFIGURE PRINT AND FILE SHARING SERVICES

Follow these steps to configure File and Print Sharing on Windows 95.

1. From the Start menu, choose Settings, then Control Panel.
2. Double-click on the Network icon and select the Configuration tab.
3. Choose Add to open the Select Network Component Type dialog box.

4. Select Service and choose Add, then File and Printer Sharing for Microsoft Networks.
5. Choose OK.
6. After rebooting, a new button appears on the same dialog box, as shown in Figure 12.3.

   a) Once your system reboots, what's different about the Configuration panel of the Network dialog box?

   _____

   _____

12.1.3 SHARE DISK DRIVES AND DIRECTORIES

Once print and file sharing services have been installed, you can share an entire drive, or only a folder. Windows 95 will not let you go down to the file level, but stops at the folder level.

For this Exercise, create the folder ACIW, for "A+ Certification Interactive Workbook," on your hard drive. We are going to enable sharing on this dummy folder.

To enable sharing, follow these steps:

1. Right-click on the item you want to share (in this case, the folder ACIW) and a pop-up menu appears as shown in Figure 12.3.
2. Choose Sharing from the pop-up menu, and select the Shared As radio button.

   a) What is the default share name of the item?

   _____

   _____

3. In the Comments field, type "Share Test—ACIW".
4. Choose an access level for the share—Read-Only, Full, or Depends on Password. If the latter is chosen, then two passwords must be specified—one for Read-Only and one for Full. Choosing either of

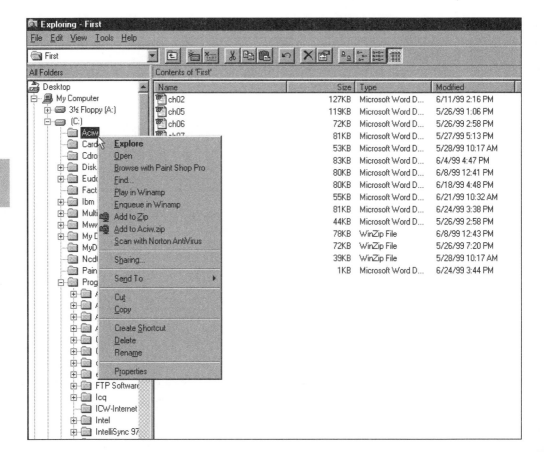

Figure 12.3 ■ To begin sharing an item, right-click on it and choose Sharing from the resulting pop-up menu.

the other two options does not require you to place a password on the share at all, though you can choose to do so.

5. Click on OK.

Now, return to Windows Explorer on your machine.

b) What do you notice about the item that you configured for sharing?

_____

_____

Move to another person's machine on the network and go to the Network Neighborhood.

> **c)** Is the ACIW folder available from that machine? What do you notice about its listing?

_____

_____

Again, the same sharing steps can be applied to any folder or the entire drive.

12.1.4 MAP A DRIVE

This Exercise requires you to have two machines running Windows 95, or a compatible operating system.

For purposes of illustration, we'll use a share called "market."

To map a drive, follow these steps:

1. Find the share on the remote computer through Network Neighborhood.
2. Right-click on the share from the remote computer and choose Map Network Drive from the pop-up menu, as shown in Figure 12.4.
3. Choose a drive letter to represent the share and the path, as shown in Figure 12.5.
4. Additionally, click the check box labeled Reconnect at logon to automatically recreate this assignment each time you logon, or leave the check box unchecked for this assignment to be in effect only for the duration of the current session.

> **a)** Do you know of another way to map a drive?

_____

_____

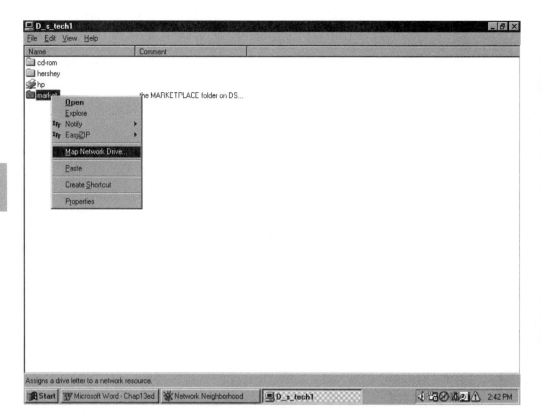

**LAB
12.1**

**Figure 12.4 ■ Choose Map Network Drive from this pop-up menu to
open the dialog box shown in Figure 12.5.**

After you have mapped a drive, now you will want to remove the
mapping. Use either this drive or another one that is presently
mapped.

b) How would you go about removing this mapping?

_____

_____

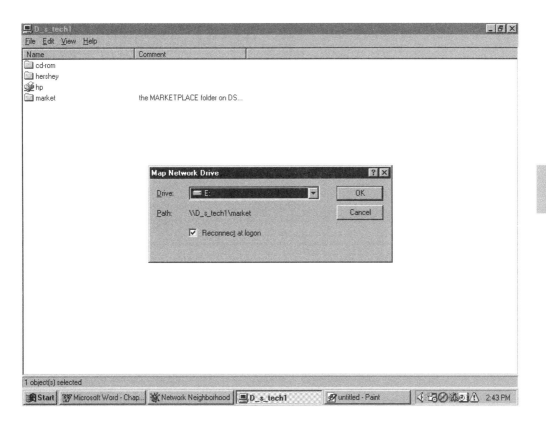

Figure 12.5 ■ **Note that the path here is a Universal Naming Convention (UNC) path.**

LAB 12.1 EXERCISE ANSWERS

12.1.1 ANSWERS

For this Exercise, you installed TCP/IP on your system.

a) Does Windows 95 tell you to reboot your machine?

Answer: You will be required to reboot the machine before the TCP/IP installation is complete.

The next step was to configure your TCP/IP properties.

b) Is there an IP address entered in the Specify an IP address portion of the panel?

Answer: There is an IP address in the Specify IP Address field only if the site lacks a DHCP server; this will require that each PC have a permanently assigned address. Otherwise, this field will be blank.

An IP address is a unique numeric identifier assigned to a computer connected to a local area network. This address is usually chosen from within a range of possible addresses administered by the network administrator.

A subnet mask is a numeric code used by a computer's network drivers to determine whether outbound packets should be sent directly to their destination or instead to the default router.

DHCP, or Dynamic Host Configuration Protocol, is used to dynamically assign IP addresses to computers on a network. Prior to DHCP, each device had a permanently assigned IP address.

c) What other panels does your TCP/IP Properties dialog box contain?

Answer: WINS Configuration (whether enabled and, if so, IP address(es) of WINS server(s)); Gateway (IP address(es) of network gateway(s)); DNS Configuration (whether enabled and, if so, the site domain name, host name, and IP address(es) of DNS server(s)); Bindings (which services are using TCP/IP); NetBIOS (whether NetBIOS applications are configured to use TCP/IP); and Advanced (additional configuration values for TCP/IP).

12.1.2 ANSWERS

In this Exercise, you configured File and Print Sharing on Windows 95:

a) Once your system reboots, what's different about the Configuration panel of the Network dialog box?

Answer: You should notice that there is a new button on the panel, called File and Print Sharing, as shown in Figure 12.6.

Now, if you choose the new File and Print Sharing button, it will bring you to the File and Print Sharing dialog box shown in Figure 12.7. This dialog only lets you set whether you want sharing to occur; it does not allow you to specify certain files or folders to share.

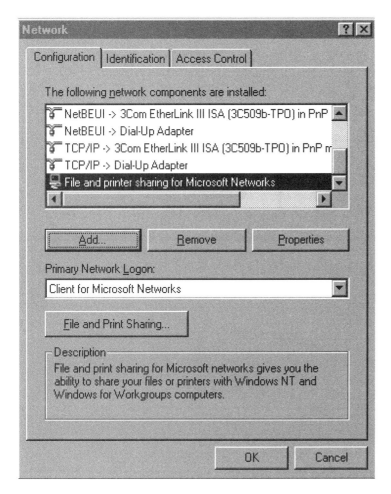

Figure 12.6 ■ Once you enable File and Print Sharing on Windows 95, the File and Print Sharing button becomes part of the Network dialog box's Configuration panel.

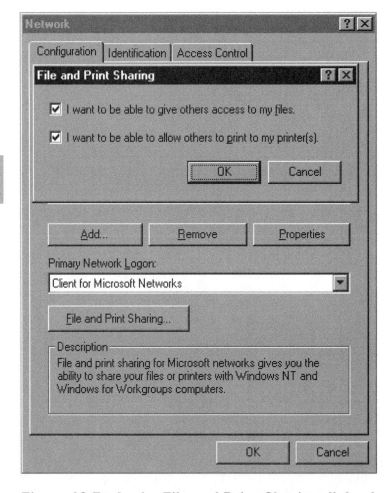

**LAB
12.1**

**Figure 12.7 ■ In the File and Print Sharing dialog box, you can choose
to share files, or the printer, or both.**

12.1.3 ANSWERS

In this Exercise, you performed the steps to enable sharing of a particular item.

a) What is the default Share Name of the item you chose?

*Answer: The default Share Name of the item you choose should be the original name
of the item.*

You can change the Shared Name of the item to any text value you want. For compatibility with older DOS machines, you should use a share name of eight characters or less.

b) What do you notice about the item that you configured for sharing?

Answer: The shared item will now appear on your system with a hand beneath the folder indicating that it is a shared folder.

Move to another person's machine on the network and go to the Network Neighborhood.

LAB
12.1

c) Is the ACIW folder available from that machine? What do you notice about its listing?

Answer: The shared file should be available from any machine on the network, if you did things correctly according to the Exercise. You should also note that the Comment you inserted in Step 3 of the Exercise, "Share Test—ACIW," appears in the Comments column when in Details view.

Again, the same sharing steps can be applied to any folder, or the entire drive. Comments are useful for sharing information about the shared item with others on your network. Note, however, that this Comments feature only supports 48 characters.

12.1.4 ANSWERS

For this Exercise, you were asked to select a shared network drive and map the drive path to a letter "shortcut."

a) Do you know of another way to map a drive?

Answer: Mappings can also be created at the command line through the use of the NET command, as illustrated by the following steps:

1. Share a folder on the first machine under the name IMAGES.
2. On the second machine, open a DOS window and type in the following command:

    NET USE X: \\{first machine name}\IMAGES.

3. Substitute the actual name of your machine in the appropriate spot in this command. On the second machine, you can now change to that "drive" and view the files within the folder.

b) How would you go about removing this mapping?

Answer: To unmap a drive, select the drive using Windows Explorer. When you've selected the drive, right-click and choose "Disconnect Network Drive."

You can also use the NET command for unmapping the drive. To remove the mapping to the drive, enter the following command on the second machine:

```
NET USE X: /DELETE
```

LAB 12.1 SELF-REVIEW QUESTIONS

In order to test your progress, you should be able to answer the following questions.

1) Windows 95 installs what two protocols by default when the first networking card is found in the machine?
   a) ___TCP/IP
   b) ___NetBIOS
   c) ___NetBEUI
   d) ___IPX/SPX-compatible

2) TCP/IP configuration information can be manually entered or automatically supplied by what type of server?
   a) ___WINS
   b) ___DNS
   c) ___PING
   d) ___DHCP

3) File and print sharing on Windows 95 is implemented as which of the following?
   a) ___a protocol
   b) ___an adapter
   c) ___a service
   d) ___a feature

4) The lowest item you can choose to share on a Windows 95 machine through file and print sharing is which of the following?
   a) ___a drive
   b) ___a folder
   c) ___a file
   d) ___a document

5) In the presence of a Windows 95-based network, and in the absence of a server, what is the highest level of security attainable?

    a) ___user-level

    b) ___share-level

    c) ___file-level

    d) ___folder-level

Quiz answers appear in Appendix A, Section 12.1.

LAB

12.1

L A B   12.2

INTERNET NETWORKING

LAB OBJECTIVES

After this Lab, you will be able to:

✓ Configuring TPC/IP

✓ Configuring Dial-Up Networking

TCP/IP is the protocol of the Internet. It must be loaded on the workstation for any and all communication to the Internet. When a network interface card is inserted into a Windows 95 computer and it is turned back on for the first time, the operating system will automatically install the IPX/SPX-compatible and NetBEUI protocols. It will not install TCP/IP. The means by which this protocol is installed is detailed in Exercise 12.2.1.

Existing within the TCP/IP protocol is support for a number of applications such as e-mail, file access, and a number of other protocols. These include:

- The HyperText Transfer Protocol (HTTP)—This is the protocol upon which the World Wide Web (WWW) content is transported. When you choose to access a site through an Internet Browser (such as Netscape's Navigator or Microsoft's Internet Explorer), you most often specify an address to go to such as:

```
http://www.ds-technical.com
```

This address is known as a Fully Qualified Domain Name (FQDN). It specifies the protocol to use (http), the type of site it is (World Wide Web), the type of organization (com for commercial) and the name (ds-technical). Domain names will be explored in more detail in a later section. Adding more syntax to this, such as identifying the page at the site to go to, creates a Universal Resource Locator (URL); for example:

```
http://www.ds-technical.com/mcse.html
```

Here, a specific page at the site has been added.

LAB
12.2

- The File Transfer Protocol (FTP)—This is the protocol used to transfer files from one location to another. FTP is the most commonly used protocol for this purpose and contains all the commands necessary to carry out these operations.
- Other applications/utilities include:
    — Simple Mail Transfer Protocol (SMTP): the protocol used to transport mail externally on the Internet and within many organizations.
    — Secure HTTP (HTTPS): an encrypted form of HTTP that provides secure transport of data.
    — Trivial File Transfer Protocol (TFTP): used to read or write files from/to a TFTP server. TFTP does not require a system or user to identify itself before allowing file transfers, so it's not good protocol for secure uses.
    — Network News Transfer Protocol (NNTP): the new method used to transmit UseNet content from site to site.

DOMAIN NAMES AND WEB SITES

Domain names are used to identify Web sites, ftp sites, mail servers, and other systems. The extension of the site identifies what type of organization is associated with the site. The possibilities include:

- COM—commercial site
- NET—Internet Service Provider (ISP)
- MIL—military

- ORG—organization; not a commercial venture
- EDU—educational institution
- GOV—government

Most Web sites are created using the HyperText Markup Language (HTML)—a scripting language that specifies how the Web page will look and allows for the inclusion of a number of different features. The extension on such files will be .HTM or .HTML to indicate what they are.

ACCESSING THE WEB WITH WINDOWS 95

To access the Web with Windows 95 clients, an account must first be established with an Internet Service Provider—a company whose purpose it is to provide Web access. Following that, you will need to configure your system to connect to the provider. Often, your provider will give you the dial-up and browser software you need for connecting to their site. Dial-Up Networking (DUN) over a modem is one way you might access the provider. Configuring DUN connection is presented as an Exercise.

LAB 12.2 EXERCISES

12.2.1 CONFIGURING TCP/IP

To configure TCP/IP on a Windows 95 machine to talk to the Internet through an Internet Service Provider (ISP), follow these steps:

1. Right-click on the Network Neighborhood icon and choose Properties (this is an alternative to choosing the Network applet from the Control Panel).
2. Double-click on TCP/IP on the Configuration tab.

   a) What is another way to open the TCP/IP Properties sheet?

   _____

   _____

3. From the TCP/IP Properties dialog, select the IP Address panel.

If you do not have an IP address provided by your ISP, check the checkbox next to "Obtain an IP address automatically." (The ISP will use DHCP to dynamically assign your PC an IP address when you log in. Your PC is a node on the ISP's network; the ISP dynamically assigns addresses in order to conserve IP address space, since at any given time most of an ISP's customers will not be logged in.)

If you do have an IP address provided by your ISP, check the "Specify an IP address" checkbox and insert the address in the space provided.

4. Click on the WINS Configuration tab to display Windows Internet Naming Service information.

   b) Which WINS options are configured on your system?

LAB 12.2

   _____

   _____

5. Click the Disable WINS Resolution option because you want to communicate outside your own network. Make sure none of the other options are selected on this panel.
6. Click on the DNS Configuration panel to display your Domain Name Server configuration.

   c) Under Enable DNS, what are your Host and Domain Name fields set to?

   _____

   _____

7. Click the OK button until you exit the configuration screens.

   d) What is the last thing that happens before these settings are activated?

   _____

   _____

12.2.2 CONFIGURING DIAL-UP NETWORKING

For this Exercise, you will create a new Dial-Up Network connection for use in accessing an ISP or other similar remote access site.

To get you started, follow these steps:

1. From the Start menu, select Programs, then Accessories, and finally Dial-Up Networking.
2. Double click on the item "Make New Connection." This opens the Make New Connection wizard.

a) Follow the remaining steps in this wizard and record each process.

_____

_____

LAB 12.2 EXERCISE ANSWERS

12.2.1 ANSWERS

a) What is another way to open the TCP/IP Properties sheet?

Answer: Double-clicking on the TCP/IP entry in the Network Configuration component list is a shortcut to selecting the entry and clicking the Properties button.

b) Which WINS options are configured on your system?

Answer: This will depend on your system.

WINS, the acronym for Windows Internet Naming Service, is a Windows NT Server method for associating a computer's host name with its IP address. It is also called INS, for Internet Naming Service. Not all systems use this method of addressing, so you may not have any WINS options in use on your particular system.

c) Under Enable DNS, what are your Host and Domain Name fields set to?

Answer: Under DNS configuration, your Host is usually your username, and your ISP is the Domain.

The IP configuration and other related data are sent by your ISP to your workstation during each session. You configure your host name to be your username and join their domain during each session.

d) What is the last thing that happens before these settings are activated?

Answer: You will need to reboot your system to activate these settings.

12.2.2 ANSWERS

a) Follow the remaining steps in this wizard and record each process.

Answer: Create a new DUN connection in the following way:

1. In the first wizard window, enter a new connection or computer name in the field labeled "Type a name for the computer you are dialing."
2. Next, select the modem you will want to use for this connection from the drop-down list box—most people only have one installed, so the connection will default to that one modem. Finally, click the Next button.
3. The next dialog box is where you enter the phone number you will be dialing. Windows 95 determines whether the phone number is a long-distance call during dialing and includes a "1" in front of the area code for you if it needs it, so there's no need to add it here.
4. Finally, click the Next button again to get to the final confirmation dialog box. Select Finish to complete the process and build the new connection.

LAB 12.2

LAB 12.2 SELF-REVIEW QUESTIONS

In order to test your progress, you should be able to answer the following questions.

1) The protocol that must be on the client and used for Internet access is which of the following?
    a) ___IPX/SPX
    b) ___FTP
    c) ___HTTP
    d) ___TCP/IP

2) The protocol/utility used for transferring files is which of the following?
    a) ___HTML
    b) ___TCP
    c) ___IP
    d) ___FTP

3) The language that Web pages are written in is which of the following?
   a) ___HTTP
   b) ___HTML
   c) ___Visual Basic
   d) ___Visual Studio

4) The address http://www.clockwork.org is known as which of the following?
   a) ___FQDN
   b) ___UNC
   c) ___HTTP
   d) ___Link

5) Acceptable extensions on HTML documents include which of the following (choose all that apply)?
   a) ___HT
   b) ___HTM
   c) ___HTML
   d) ___SHTML

Quiz answers appear in Appendix A, Section 12.2.

C H A P T E R   12

TEST YOUR THINKING

Earlier in this chapter, we presented the Windows 95 networking architecture. The astute reader may have picked up the similarities between the Win 95 architecture and that of the OSI model presented in Chapter 6. To test your thinking, map the Win 95 architecture layers against the OSI model.

APPENDIX A

ANSWERS TO SELF-REVIEW QUESTIONS

CHAPTER 1

Lab 1.1 ■ Self-Review Answers

Question	Answer	Comments
1)	b	You should not remove these screws when opening a case.
2)	a	This is easy to remember because it works just like a key.
3)	b	
4)	b	This describes the fan screws. Power supply screws do surround the fan and power cord connectors on the back of the PC, but they go through the back of the case.
5)	c	
6)	c	Sometimes newer modems will be connected via USB.
7)	e	
8)	b	SIMMs can have memory chips on both sides, but they can only be inserted one way. There is a notch in the SIMM card that should correspond to a plastic tab in the card slot.
9)	b	
10)	d	
11)	d	
12)	b	Make sure you understand the four stages of boot-up and what happens during each.
13)	e	

Lab 1.2 ■ Self-Review Answers

Question	Answer	Comments
1)	c	
2)	b	
3)	d	
4)	c	
5)	a	
6)	a	
7)	a	
8)	d	
9)	c	
10)	b	This is true of IRQs in some cases, but DMAs can never be shared.

Lab 1.3 ■ Self-Review Answers

Question	Answer	Comments
1)	c	
2)	a	
3)	b	
4)	b	The HDDB-15 connector is generally used for connecting a monitor to the PC, but this is a three-row connector, not a two-row connector.
5)	b	
6)	d	
7)	b	

Lab 1.4 ■ Self-Review Answers

Question	Answer	Comments
1)	b	It's the other way around—EIDE drives provide the best performance and can accommodate larger drives.
2)	a	
3)	d	
4)	b	
5)	b	
6)	a	This is accomplished using an inexpensive drive mounting kit.

Lab 1.5 ■ Self-Review Answers

Question	Answer	Comments
1)	b	SCSI drives are much better suited to support multitasking applications than IDEs. They are not as popular because they are much more expensive.
2)	b	
3)	a	
4)	a	Termination is related to where devices are located on the SCSI chain, and has nothing to do with the ID.
5)	d	Including the controller, Wide SCSI supports a total of 16 devices. Remember, the ID range for Wide SCSI is 0-15.

Lab 1.6 ■ Self-Review Answers

Question	Answer	Comments
1)	a	The System Monitor enables you to see what components are being exercised on your machine and assists in pinpointing what component or process could be causing the problem.
2)	a	When this total number drops below 4-8 MB on a personal PC, it's probably time to add RAM.
3)	c	
4)	a	You may want to defrag the suspect drive to see if performance improves before deciding to upgrade.
5)	d	Obviously you'd perform some analysis before doing anything else. Blindly making upgrades for people is the wrong thing to do.

CHAPTER 2

Lab 2.1 ■ Self-Review Answers

Question	Answer	Comments
1)	b	The four steps are to 1) Identify and understand the problem; 2) Hypothesize a solution; 3) Test the hypothesis; 4) If the test fails, go to step 1. Don't underestimate the importance of identifying the correct problem by hypothesizing a second solution to what you think is the problem. Analyze the situation carefully.
2)	c	
3)	a	If you have to test a voltage that is more than about 25 volts, either only hold on to one lead, or hold on to both leads with one hand. This prevents the power from taking a path across your heart, which could kill you.

Lab 2.1 ■ Self-Review Answers (Continued)

4)	d	
5)	a	All that's needed to test certain core components, such as the CPU, is the ability for POST to run before determining that there's no memory.

Lab 2.2 ■ Self-Review Answers

Question	Answer	Comments
1)	b	In this case, you'd replace the processor first because it is comparatively simple.
2)	c	
3)	b	
4)	b	The keyboard is the only peripheral input device natively detected on every PC.
5)	b	The PC cannot detect when there is a missing key, but can detect when there is a missing keyboard or a stuck key.
6)	a	
7)	a	
8)	a	Once again, the command first gets the modem's attention (AT). Then it tells it to start echoing characters back (E1). Then it tells the modem to not be quiet (Q0). Finally, it tells the modem to give back verbose responses (V1).
9)	b	
10)	c	
11)	b	While heat can affect, or even kill, the entire PC system, dirt is the most common cause of problems with a floppy drive.

CHAPTER 3

Lab 3.1 ■ Self-Review Answers

Question	Answer	Comments
1)	a	
2)	b	ZIF sockets lock a chip into place so it cannot "walk."
3)	b	There are many types of chips that still use standard sockets, such as SRAM chips. BIOS are just the most common.
4)	c	
5)	c	

Lab 3.2 ■ Self-Review Answers

Question	Answer	Comments
1)	a	AC stands for Alternating Current because the direction that the current is flowing changes.
2)	b	
3)	b	
4)	d	
5)	a	
6)	c	
7)	d	

Lab 3.3 ■ Self-Review Answers

Question	Answer	Comments
1)	a	The two primary high-voltage devices are the monitor and the power supply. A problem with the fan is usually indicative of a power-supply problem.
2)	b	NEVER try to repair a faulty monitor, not even with an ESD strap.
3)	b	Nothing can protect you from damaging your eyes by staring into a laser. Always look 30 degrees to any side of a light source.
4)	b	Remember that hazardous levels of power can be maintained in PC devices for a long time after the power is turned off. The PC chassis should always be grounded, and you should follow the precautions outlined in Exercise 3.3.1.

Lab 3.4 ■ Self-Review Answers

Question	Answer	Comments
1)	b	All batteries, even alkaline batteries, must be disposed of in accordance with regulations, some of which can very from state to state.
2)	b	Never assume that any solvent can be poured down a drain. You should always clearly know and understand the proper disposal procedures for any kinds of solvents that you use, whether or not you use it as part of computer maintenance.
3)	b	Mercury is extremely toxic to any living thing.
4)	a	
5)	c	

Lab 3.5 ■ Self-Review Answers

Question	Answer	Comments
1)	b	Anything under 30 percent is conducive to electrostatic discharge. 100 percent humidity is generally too uncomfortable for most. 65 percent is a good medium.
2)	b	Simply unplugging the machine will not safeguard against ESD. The machine must be grounded and other safety precautions should be employed, as outlined in this Lab.
3)	a	
4)	e	
5)	b	An AC/DC transformer won't help drain static electric charges. You need something that's directly plugged into the wall.

CHAPTER 4

Lab 4.1 ■ Self-Review Answers

Question	Answer	Comments
1)	a	
2)	d	
3)	d	
4)	b	You might have thought that only dot-matrix and daisy wheel printers could produce multi-part forms because they are the only two types of impact printers. However, laser printers, using special paper, are also capable of producing such forms.
5)	b	This is also known as the storage area.

Lab 4.2 ■ Self-Review Answers

Question	Answer	Comments
1)	b	
2)	d	
3)	b	
4)	c	
5)	a	The ozone filter should be replaced during all general maintenance laser printer calls.

Lab 4.3 ■ Self-Review Answers

Question	Answer	Comments
1)	a	
2)	b	
3)	d	
4)	a	
5)	d	

CHAPTER 5

Lab 5.1 ■ Self-Review Answers

Question	Answer	Comments
1)	c	Always investigate proper disposal requirements in your area for any computer component. Often, you will be able to return such components directly to the manufacturer, especially if you are ordering a replacement part.
2)	a	
3)	c	
4)	d	
5)	b	
6)	a	
7)	d	

Lab 5.2 ■ Self-Review Answers

Question	Answer	Comments
1)	a	
2)	d	
3)	b	PC cards are hot swappable and can be inserted and removed without powering down the system.
4)	c	

Lab 5.3 ■ Self-Review Answers

Question	Answer	Comments
1)	b	
2)	b	
3)	a	
4)	c	
5)	b	

Lab 5.4 ■ Self-Review Answers

Question	Answer	Comments
1)	c	
2)	Both a and b are correct	
3)	c	
4)	c	
5)	a	
6)	a	

CHAPTER 6

Lab 6.1 ■ Self-Review Answers

Question	Answer	Comments
1)	c	
2)	a	UTP is the cable that is most sensitive to EMI.
3)	d	
4)	Both a and b are correct.	
5)	c	

Lab 6.2 ■ Self-Review Answers

Question	Answer	Comments
1)	d	
2)	b	
3)	c	
4)	c	
5)	b	
6)	a	
7)	c	A network-monitoring or protocol-analysis tool often can determine the source of a broadcast storm.
8)	a	
9)	c	

CHAPTER 7

Lab 7.1 ■ Self-Review Answers

Question	Answer	Comments
1)	d	This is the most efficient solution. Most of the answers in this section should seem obvious to you. If two answers appear to be appropriate, pick the most appropriate one.
2)	b	
3)	c	
4)	d	
5)	a	
6)	d	
7)	b	
8)	a	
8)	c	All of the answers to this question are appropriate.
9)	d	

CHAPTER 8

Lab 8.1 ■ Self-Review Answers

Question	Answer	Comments
1)	c	
2)	b	AUTOEXEC.BAT sets variables and other parameters for the user.
3)	a	
4)	c	The Registry consists of two files—System.dat and User.dat—that hold all configuration information.
5)	c	
6)	b	
7)	b	
8)	d	
9)	d	

Lab 8.2 ■ Self-Review Answers

Question	Answer	Comments
1)	d	The hidden feature can be useful for protecting files from being inadvertently deleted, but read-only prevents it.
2)	b	
3)	c	
4)	d	
5)	c	

Lab 8.3 ■ Self-Review Answers

Question	Answer	Comments
1)	c	
2)	c	
3)	Both b and c are correct	
4)	b	
5)	a	

CHAPTER 9

Lab 9.1 ■ Self-Review Answers

Question	Answer	Comments
1)	b	
2)	c	
3)	a	The command for doing this is: DEVICE=C:\DOS\RAM-DRIVE.SYS 2048
4)	b	On older operating systems, there was often a permanent swap file, which had an extension of PAR.
5)	c	

Lab 9.2 ■ Self-Review Answers

Question	Answer	Comments
1)	b	
2)	a	
3)	a	
4)	d	
5)	c	

CHAPTER 10

Lab 10.1 ■ Self-Review Answers

Question	Answer	Comments
1)	c	
2)	b	
3)	c	
4)	d	
5)	c	

Lab 10.2 ■ Self-Review Answers

Question	Answer	Comments
1)	b	The most common method is to use the Add/Remove Programs applet from the Control Panel, but this utility, which is available on the installation CD, works as well.
2)	b	
3)	d	CONFIG.POL, an optional file, is the file that contains system policies.
4)	d	
5)	c	

Lab 10.3 ■ Self-Review Answers

Question	Answer	Comments
1)	c	
2)	a	
3)	a	
4)	b	
5)	a	

CHAPTER 11

Lab 11.1 ■ Self-Review Answers

Question	Answer	Comments
1)	d	
2)	b	
3)	c	
4)	b	
5)	d	

CHAPTER 12

Lab 12.1 ■ Self-Review Answers

Question	Answer	Comments
1)	Both c and d are correct.	TCP/IP is not installed by default when you install Windows 95.
2)	d	
3)	c	
4)	c	
5)	a	

Lab 12.2 ■ Self-Review Answers

Question	Answer	Comments
1)	d	
2)	d	
3)	b	
4)	a	You may have been confused by the absence of URL from the answer list, but remember that a URL adds more syntax, such as a specific page, to a Fully Qualified Domain Name.
5)	Both b and c are correct	

A P P E N D I X   B

MOTHERBOARDS, PROCESSORS, AND MEMORY

APPENDIX OBJECTIVES

This Appendix covers the following CompTIA Objectives:

This appendix reviews many of the concepts that we initially discussed in Chapter 1, attempting to dig into slightly more detail than we were able to do there. CompTIA has separated out these topics on the test and has specified that they will represent 10 percent of the core exam. In practice, it's difficult to decide which questions are questions from this domain, and which are from the initial (Installation, Configuration, and Upgrading) domain.

The material in this Appendix, together with the upgrading instruction in Chapter 1, "Installation, Configuration, and Upgrading," constitute the CompTIA requirements for Domain 4.0, Motherboards/Processors/Memory.

IDENTIFYING AND UPGRADING CPUS

Identifying a CPU is much like being a surgeon and identifying a heart. You know roughly where it's going to reside and roughly what it looks like but everyone is a little different. In this Lab, we'll learn how to positively identify different CPUs.

UNDERSTANDING CPU TECHNOLOGIES

Before we start to identify specific CPUs, it's important to understand Intel's processor families, as well as the families of clone CPU manufacturers.

The basic CPU lineage from Intel reads: 8086, 8088, 80186, 80286, 80386, 80486, Pentium, Pentium Pro, Pentium II, Pentium III. While that list may seem long, it only identifies the major categories in the family. There are also several variations of each processor chip, not including changes that are only changes in speed at which the chip runs.

THE WHOLE TRUTH

You may have noticed the inclusion of the 8086 and 80186 processors in the list of CPUs given here. They are parts of the Intel x86 line of processors, but they were never widely used in the PC market. The 8086 was ahead of it's time because it had a 16-bit external interface vs. the 8-bit external interface on the 8088 that IBM chose to start the PC line with. The 80186 never really caught on, however, but did find its way into specialized applications, such as embedded controllers in automobiles.

DIFFERENCES IN PERFORMANCE

Some of the variations, as we learned in Chapter 1, might be slight performance improvements within the CPU and are generally referred to as stepping levels, but there are other differences within the chips as well.

For instance, the 80386DX is a fully functional, 32-bit external memory interface while the 80386SX has a 24-bit external memory interface. The net effect of this is that the 386SX was cheaper to build and cheaper to outfit on a motherboard, but it could only address 16MB of RAM.

Similarly, the 80486DX included the 32-bit external interface and a math co-processor. The math co-processor allowed the motherboard to work with floating-point numbers at a much greater speed. The 80486SX didn't include the floating-point math co-processor. The 80486SX did, however, include a 32-bit external interface.

WHAT IS A FLOATING-POINT MATH CO-PROCESSOR?

CPUs operate on integer math very quickly. Integer math is numbers without anything behind the decimal point. For instance, -237, 0, 12, and 25 are all integer numbers. These numbers convert quite easily into binary, and thus performing addition, subtraction, and multiplication can be done relatively easily.

Numbers like 12.3456, -0.1242, 0.002345, and 87.34 are floating-point numbers. These are the numbers that we see more often in our daily lives. Because of their makeup, these numbers are not easily converted into binary numbers.

There is a standard for representing these floating-point numbers and processes by which they can be added, subtracted, multiplied, and divided; however, it's relatively complex to do this.

The Intel x86 line originally didn't include direct support for these types of numbers. Either you added a specialty floating-point math co-processor, or your software had to emulate a floating-point math co-processor.

Historically, even with the floating-point math co-processor, Intel's floating-point performance has been very poor relative to other processors. That is why some high-end graphics and CAD business is handled with Alpha processors, despite the prevalence of the x86 architecture.

DIFFERENCES IN VOLTAGE

Another change that is common particularly within the Pentium and newer lines, which wasn't quite so popular before, is the packaging and the voltage that the processor needs to function.

Changing the voltage that a processor needs to function can have great importance in both how well it stays cool and how well it is able to be installed in a notebook computer.

Heat generation is directly related to how much power a CPU consumes. The more power that is used by the processor, the more heat that is generated. Because the amperage used stays relatively the same when the operating voltage is lowered, the overall power used is reduced.

Lower voltages with notebooks are important for two reasons. First, the reduced heat is a great helper because heat in a notebook is a significant design concern. Because of the need to contain size, the power consumption fans are not normally used in notebooks. This means that the heat that is generated by the CPU isn't able to be dissipated as easily.

The second, obvious, reason to keep the power consumption low is that by reducing the power consumption, you can dramatically increase battery life. Because the primary problem with notebooks for some time has been battery life, it's no wonder that reducing the power consumption has been such a big push.

To give you an example of what the heat reduction means, the Pentium processor was originally released at 5 volts, (the 60MHz and 66MHz versions). These processors were notorious for overheating. Even with specially designed cooling systems and the introduction of CPU fans on a mass scale, there were still many stories of the processor overheating.

When Intel was able to develop a 3.3 volt version (90 MHz and 100 MHz) of the processor, it was much cooler and consequently the concerns about overheating were significantly reduced. Further progress on the Pentium processor has reduced the power consumption even further. This has resulted in a series of versions of the Pentium microprocessor that are well-suited for notebook use.

DIFFERENCES IN SIZE

The other variation that I mentioned was size, or packaging. This is how the chip is packaged for installation in a computer. The original Intel processors, like most processors of the time, were packaged in plastic casing in a dual inline pin (DIP) format. These processors fit into a rectangular socket. The pins on the processor itself were thin strips of flexible metal so that the chip could adapt to variations in the socket. You can still see chips using the DIP format today. Typically, you'll find BIOS in the DIP format.

This package worked well for the 8086 and 8088, but starting with the 80286, this package proved to be too cumbersome. The number of pins (or connection points) that the 80286 processor had made it necessary to move to a square package where pins were hard metal points coming straight down from the bottom of a ceramic package. This allowed for a much higher pin density.

This worked well for most desktop systems, but some systems and notebooks couldn't accommodate the size of the socket and the chip itself. To resolve this, Intel developed a surface mount or Quad-Flat package version of the processor, which could be installed directly on the motherboard without a socket. This mounting required special mounting hardware and locked the processor to the motherboard, meaning that quality had to be tightly controlled to prevent waste. However, by this time quality control was maintaining a very low dead on arrival (DOA) rate, so the efficiencies in manufacturing and the reduction in manufacturing cost (because of the removal of the socket) outweighed the scrap issue.

The Pentium II processor signaled the introduction of the single-edge connector. It's a slot, much like an AGP slot, which accepts a processor module. The processor module contains the processor and some support circuitry, most notably cache.

The SEC format looks like it's here to stay, despite the fact that Intel has not licensed it for use by any clone CPU manufacturer. They're stuck using the socket formats that Intel has abandoned. This is a slight technical disadvantage because of the inability to include cache on the processor module rather than on the chip itself. However, manufacturing processes have improved so that adding cache to a CPU chip isn't as difficult as it once was.

There are several socket formats that have been used for each of the different processors. The latest Intel-supported socket was Socket 8 and was used for its Pentium Pro family of processors. The predecessor was Socket 7 and was used for the Pentium family of processors. (Have you seen the pattern yet?) The clone manufacturers stuck with the Socket 7 design and have since designed their own socket for their chips, dubbed a Super 7 socket. This socket has the additional pins that the clone CPU manufacturers needed to make their CPUs work.

DIFFERENCES AMONG PROCESSORS

The differences between processors in the x86 family have been, for the most part, evolutionary. The 80286 processor was an evolutionary change from the 8086 processor. Although it offered a "protected mode," there was no way to get back to the previous "real" operating mode of the processor, so compatibility was a problem. The 80386 processor provided memory management and a way to get back out of protected mode. It was a great processor in terms of functionality, however there wasn't a huge performance increase. The 80486 was also evolutionary, with it's notable inclusion of a math co-processor in its DX versions.

All of these processors are fully CISC-based (Complex Instruction Set Computer) processors. This means that there is a large number of instructions that the CPU can execute directly. Complex instructions can do complex things. The alternative to CISC is RISC. RISC is a Reduced Instruction Set Computer. It maintains a small number of instructions that the CPU supports, but RISC can execute them faster. Since all of the CISC instructions can be performed by a set of RISC instructions it's not an issue of one processor being able to do something that the other can't. It's more of an issue of which one is faster.

On the surface, it may seem that CISC processors are better than their RISC counterparts because they have more and more complex instructions that they can execute. But all of this complexity comes at the cost of additional transistors, which in turn limits the rate of speed at which the processor can be run.

WHAT'S IN A CLOCK CYCLE?

When most people talk about CPUs they talk about their clock cycle, rated in megahertz. While this is a convenient way of measuring the relative performances of processors within a class, it's not very effective at measuring across processor families or even within different levels of the same family. There are two reasons for this.

First, CISC CPUs can execute a single instruction that it may take a RISC CPU several instructions to accomplish the same effect. This may result in the RISC CPU appearing to be faster. The question is: Which processor is actually faster, an Alpha 500 MHz (RISC based) or an Intel Pentium III 500 MHz (CISC based)? The answer is the Pentium III.

Second, CISC CPUs often take more than one clock cycle to complete an instruction. Just because the CPU understands the instruction doesn't mean that it can complete it within one unit of time. In practice, most instructions on a CISC computer take considerably longer than one clock cycle. RISC processors, however, almost always execute every instruction within one clock cycle. This means that some of the loss of executing multiple instructions to compete with the CISC CPU's complex instructions may be moot because the RISC processor can emulate the command faster than the CISC can execute it internally.

The moral of this story is that you should look at true performance rather than clock speeds to determine which CPU is best for you.

The argument for RISC processors has always been that the smaller number of transistors needed to implement the processor would mean that the CPU could be run at higher speeds and that this speed would offset the need to use several instructions to accomplish the same amount of work that could be done by a CISC processor.

Intel wasn't immune to this discussion, although it was already firmly committed to the CISC processor idea with its 8086 series of processors that already had a complex instruction set. With its Pentium computer, Intel maintained the CISC appearance to the programmer, and developed an internal structure that was both RISC and CISC.

The idea that the Intel processor designers had developed was to create a RISC core and place micro-code on the chip itself that would translate complex instructions into the necessary RISC instructions that the processor could execute.

The performance improvement that was gained with this structure cannot be understated. It was a huge jump from the performance of the 80486 processor. This success has encouraged Intel to develop its future processors with this same RISC-CISC mentality.

There've been other evolutionary improvements in processor design that have improved performance with each new processor released, but they've not made the kind of performance impact that the change from the 80486 processor to the Pentium processor did.

WHY ISN'T THE PENTIUM NAMED 80586?

At the time the Pentium processor was in development, Intel started having legal battles with the clone CPU manufacturers. These legal battles led to the name Pentium.

The dispute revolved around the use of the 80386 moniker that many of the clone CPU manufacturers had been using. Intel argued that they owned that moniker in the CPU market. However, a federal judge decided that numbers could not be trademarked. As a result, all future processors from Intel will likely have names, not numbers.

Despite the performance improvements made with the Pentium processor, there were still applications that couldn't run fast enough. Processing the sheer amount of data that these applications were trying to process just couldn't be done using the standard commands in the 8086 CPU language.

Primarily these applications were multimedia applications. Those applications that allowed animation or digital video continued to struggle on the Pentium computers. To respond to this need, Intel developed MMX extensions to the Pentium processor, which allowed it to work quicker on multimedia data.

The MMX instructions do this by performing the same process on multiple bytes of data at the same time. This can significantly improve performance because multimedia applications often process the same instructions on a plethora of data.

Although you won't be asked about it on the A+ exam, there's another multimedia instruction set developed by AMD called 3Dnow. 3Dnow includes all of the instructions provided by Intel's MMX specification, but adds additional instructions useful to applications trying to do 3D renderings.

BASIC CPU IDENTIFICATION

Identifying CPUs is based upon the size and shape, and final determination is made by the markings. The hardest part about final identification is that often CPUs have heat sinks or fans attached to them so the markings may be obscured.

Table B.1 shows all of the Intel microprocessors used in PCs. For these processors, it lists their packaging as well as their pin count. If for some reason you're not able to immediately identify a chip by its markings, this table can help you to identify it by its packaging.

Some definitions from Table B.1 you should know are:

- DIP—Dual-Inline Pin
- PGA—Pin Grid Array
- SPGA—Staggered Pin Grid Array
- QFP—Quad Flat Package
- SQFP—Small Quad Flat Package
- SEPP—Single Edge Peripheral Package
- BGA—Ball Grid Array

Although you can roughly identify a processor by its package, pinning down precisely what processor you have isn't possible by the package alone. If you look at Table B.1, you'll see that several processors use the 168 PGA package, for instance. So, to positively identify the CPU, you'll need to read the chip markings.

Figure B.1 shows an 8088 processor, which shows its markings directly on the top where they are clearly visible. Because these are the only commonly used 40-pin DIP CPUs, they are relatively easy to identify.

Figures B.2 and B.3 show the undersides of 286 CPUs. You'll notice that these chips are now in a pin grid array package or a surface mount contact package because the DIP proved to be too difficult to manufacture.

Figure B.4 shows a 80386 CPU PGA chip with the pin side down, so in this case you can see the markings on the top of the chip. The chip shown here has the double sigma mark, which indicates that it doesn't have the problems that the initial 386 chips had.

Figure B.5 shows a Celeron chip, designed to be a low cost chip, with it's adapter board, to allow it to plug into a SEPP slot. This chip initially shipped without a math co-processor, but subsequent versions of the chip did have the math co-processor, making them more suitable for mainstream computing. Note that the markings for the chip are present on the underside as well.

Processor	8086*	8088	80286	80386DX	80386SX	80486DX	80486SX	80486DX2	80486DX4	Pentium	Pentium MMX	Pentium Pro	Celeron	Pentium II	Pentium II Xeon	Pentium III	Pentium III Xeon
Package	DIP	DIP	DIP	PGA	QFP	PGA/PQFP/SQFP	PGA	PGA	PGA/SQFP	PGA/SPGA/TCP	PGA/TCP	DPGA	PGA/BGA/SEPP	SEPP/PGA	SEPP	SEPP	SEPP
Pin Count	40	40	68	132	100	168/196/208	168	168	168/208	296/296/320	296/320	387	370/615/242	242/615	242	330	330
Speed in Mhz	4.77, 8, 10	4.77, 8	6, 10, 12	16, 20, 25, 33	16, 20, 25, 33	25, 33, 50	16, 20, 25, 33	50, 66	75, 100	60, 66, 75, 90, 100, 120, 133, 150, 166, 200	166, 200, 233, 266, 300	150, 166, 180, 200	266, 300, 333, 366, 400, 433, 466	233, 266, 300, 333, 350, 400, 450	400/450	450/500/550	500/550
Num. of Transistors	29K	29K	134K	275K	275K	1.2M	1.185M/900K	1.2M	1.6M	3.1M/3.3M	4.5M	5.5M/15.5M/31M	19M	7.5M/27.4M	7.5M	9.5M	9.5M
Transistor Size in microns	3	3	1.5	1.5/1	1.5/1	1/0.8	1/0.8	0.8	0.6	0.8	0.25	0.35	0.25	0.18	0.18	0.25	0.25
Bus Speeds	4.77, 8, 10	4.77, 8	6, 10, 12	16, 20, 25, 33	16, 20, 25, 33	25, 33, 50	16, 20, 25, 33	25, 33	25, 33	60, 66	66	66	66	66, 100 (350+)	100	100	100
Ext. Bus Width in bits	16	8	16	32	16	32	32	32	32	64	64	64	64	64	64	64	64
x Times 8088	1x	1x	3-6x	8-20x	4x	50x	50x	80x	100x	300x	300-400x	500x	700x	1000x	1100x	1200x	1500x
Integrated FPU	No	No	No	No	No	Yes	No	Yes	Yes	Yes	Yes	Yes	No/Yes (Some Models)	Yes	Yes	Yes	Yes

* Performance numbers are rounded and may not represent the true difference between processing speeds, which are affected by the type of operation being performed.

Table B.1 Intel Microprocessor Specs

Figure B.1 ■ 8088 Processor

Figure B.2 ■ Underside of 286 CPU

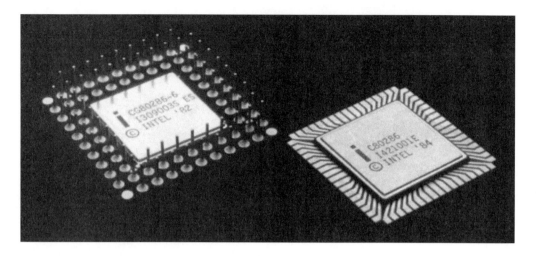

Figure B.3 ■ Underside of 286 CPU

Figure B.4 ■ 80386 CPU PGA Chip

Figure B.5 ▪ Celeron Chip

For this CompTIA objective, you are also required to understand what is involved with upgrading the CPU, which is covered in Chapter 1, "Installation, Configuration, and Upgrading."

IDENTIFYING AND UPGRADING ALL TYPES OF RAM

In this section, we'll learn how to identify the type of RAM in use in a PC and the different characteristics of RAM.

IDENTIFY RAM TECHNOLOGIES

RAM, or Random Access Memory, is as much responsible for the continuing improvements in PCs as the CPU. Without RAM, a CPU would be burdened with communicating with hopelessly slow devices such as a hard drive, or even a floppy drive.

When most people think of hard drives they don't think of slow. They think of a device capable of reading data at 5MB/sec or more. However, when you compare this with the speed of RAM, you begin to appreciate just how slow hard drives are.

The access time of a RAM chip, as we learned in Chapter 1, is measured in nanoseconds, or billionths of a second. Hard drive access times are measured in milliseconds, or thousandths of a second. The speed difference here is enormous.

As speedy as RAM is not all of it is able to keep up with today's CPUs. Only special kinds of RAM can meet the performance demands of a Pentium III Xeon. Where we could have memory that operated with a refresh cycle of 120ns-200ns back when the PC was new, it's typical to find RAM having a refresh cycle of 50ns or less today. That and the different operating frequencies of the RAM itself have made for a complex RAM landscape.

DRAM

The first RAM used in PCs was called DRAM or Dynamic Random Access Memory. You may also hear Fast Page Mode used to describe the DRAM we're talking about here. That is to differentiate it from some of the other memory types we'll be discussing in a minute. In fact it's still used today in conjunction with other types of RAM to improve performance. DRAM is characterized by it's need to be refreshed every so often so that it doesn't loose the information it's storing.

Because of the need to be refreshed, DRAM doesn't store anything permanent. It is the PC's working memory and doesn't remember anything after the power is removed. This is an important distinction. Most users can't differentiate between their hard disk size and the amount of RAM in their computers. Don't make this mistake. RAM is the PC's working space and the hard drive is for more permanent storage.

ROM

There is another type of memory that you will encounter in a PC that you need to make sure that you understand as well. That is ROM. ROM, or Read Only Memory, does keep its contents after the power has been turned off. ROM is what holds your BIOS (Basic Input/Output System) and why it's available when the PC boots.

ROM, however, is much slower than even DRAM, and thus most BIOSs allow you to copy the information in ROM into RAM at the same location as the ROM so that your PC can perform faster. This copy was accomplished by manipulating a memory management unit and remapping the RAM hidden behind the ROM into view of the CPU. This trick allowed many systems to improve performance with only a very slight change in the time it takes to boot up.

SRAM

As processors became faster, DRAM wasn't able to keep up with them. Soon it was necessary for CPUs to wait before writing or fetching information from memory. This resulted in what we called wait states. These were additional clock cycles where the CPU did literally nothing, waiting on the memory to catch up.

It was pretty obvious that this wasn't a desirable solution, but equipping a system with faster DRAMs, or an alternative Static Random Access Memory (SRAM), wasn't cost-effective. SRAM was much quicker and didn't need refreshing, so it was a great way to keep up with processors; however, it was also very expensive (and still is). This is where caches were born.

Motherboard manufacturers began placing memory management units on their motherboards that could allow a small amount of SRAM to be used to cache the slower DRAM that was the main memory. In caching the regular DRAM, the memory management unit tried to maintain a copy of the information the CPU would want next in SRAM. This meant that when the CPU asked for information, it was likely that the memory management unit could get it from SRAM rather than having to wait on the DRAM.

This could significantly improve performance because most of the time the CPU is always working on pretty much the same data. However, when the CPU started working on sets of data larger than the cache size on the motherboard, the performance benefits were eliminated.

Intel took this caching idea to heart and began integrating cache directly into the CPU. This allowed the CPU to quickly work on small amounts of data without waiting on the rest of the system. This is great, except that the caches on the CPU itself were very small and often needed to be backed up by larger caches on the motherboard.

ISN'T THIS GETTING OUT OF HAND?

Intel's newest Pentium II, Pentium II Xeon, Pentium III, and Pentium III Xeon have integrated cache on the CPU chip, additional cache on the CPU module, and are sometimes installed on motherboards with additional cache RAM.

If it seems like it's getting out of hand, you're right. Everyone's trying to squeeze that last little bit of performance out of their systems so that they can win the benchmarks, and hopefully sell a million PCs. Intel is now discouraging the use of additional cache on the motherboard to hopefully contain some of this insanity, but the jury is still out on whether they will be able to persuade the industry to stop putting cache on a motherboard.

EVOLUTION OF RAM

In Chapter 1 we talked about the different ways that RAM is packaged, everything from DRAM, SIPPs, SIMMs, and DIMMs. These different packages are just that—packages. Essentially all of the RAM is the same, despite the package.

There are some changes in the RAM, however, and the way that it works. Perhaps one of the most notable changes was the introduction of EDO (Enhanced Data Out) RAM. EDO RAM has a dual-pipeline architecture that allows it to leave data on its output lines for reading even after the computer has started requesting the next piece of data. This is an improvement because the next request can be processing while the current request is being read.

The most recent changes to memory in the PC have been the upgrade of the memory bus speed from 66MHz to 100MHz. This change has lead to RAM being designated with a "-100" to indicate that it's 100MHz compatible. This change was necessitated by the speed of the processor getting so fast that keeping the memory bus speed at 66MHz became a real bottleneck. Any Intel Processor from the Pentium II running at 350MHz or more requires 100MHz memory.

THE WHOLE TRUTH

Although it's probably not worth it today, the author purchased a dual 333MHz machine around the time that the 400MHz Pentium II machines were the hottest thing. The pricing was great. I was able to pay for the second processor by just the savings between the memory and the cost difference in processors. (The latest processors always have a fairly substantial markup on them.)

Though this won't be something I'd advise for you to do now, look for similar opportunities where you can get by with having *almost* the latest and greatest—not the latest and greatest. It can save you a lot of money.

In addition to the RAM on the motherboard, the video card generally has a large amount of RAM on it as well. This RAM is used to control the display the video card is outputting. It's typical for video cards to have in excess of 4MB of RAM on them, with high-end consumer video cards holding 16MB-32MB of RAM. Beyond this there are a variety of special purpose 3D accelerated video cards which have as much as 96MB of RAM (as of this writing) that is used for 3D geometry processing as well as controlling the display.

However, video memory has a different set of requirements than regular system RAM. In particular, the screen must be drawn several times a second. This means that the memory used to control the display must be read several times a second. This would be (and was) a performance problem when using conventional RAM, because conventional RAM can only be accessed by one device at a time. So the result is that the CPU would have to wait until the video card didn't need to read from a section of RAM to write to it.

That proved to be difficult as screen resolutions got larger and there was more RAM to be accessed by the CPU. The solution to this problem was to make special purpose Video RAM or VRAM, which was specifically designed to allow access on two different ports at the same time. This allows the CPU (or the video card's on-board processor) to write to the RAM even while it's being used to display the current image on the screen. VRAM was significantly faster than its DRAM cousin, but it came at a cost, so adding RAM to a video card used to be an expensive proposition.

The cost of VRAM led to a slight variation and performance improvement called WRAM. WRAM is similar to VRAM, but has features that allow it to perform better with accelerator cards.

In today's market there are also other specialized memory variations such as SGRAM, or Synchronous Graphics RAM, which can perform better with high-end graphics accelerators. However, these newer video RAM types are beyond the scope of the A+ exam. All you need to know for the A+ exam is DRAM, EDO DRAM, VRAM, and WRAM.

UPGRADING AND REPLACING RAM

One of the best upgrades that can be done to a PC is a RAM upgrade. It's cheap, easy, and most of the time it resolves performance issues. However, because of the RAM and motherboard options, it's hard to understand what you need.

Before attempting to upgrade or replace RAM, it's important to understand how the processor accesses memory, and how that changes from processor to processor. With the original 8088, things were simple. The CPU accessed memory one byte at a time. Today, most processors access memory 64 bits at a time, or 8 bytes at a time. This has important implications on how memory is installed on the motherboard.

The memory on the motherboard must be installed in the way in which the CPU accesses it. Thus, if the CPU accesses memory 32 bits at a time, the memory must be installed in at least 32-bit-wide chunks. It's this need to keep memory configured as the CPU needs it that lead to what we now call memory banking.

From a practical perspective memory banking just means that memory must be installed in pairs, or in sets of four. These pairs or banks allow the motherboard to arrange the memory as needed for the CPU to be able to access it. If you partially fill a bank, then the motherboard will mask out that RAM so the CPU doesn't get confused trying to access it.

From a technical perspective, the different types of RAM modules in use today, which we discussed fully in Chapter 1, are arranged to different widths on the modules themselves. For instance, a 30-pin SIMM has its memory arranged in 8 bit, or 1 byte, chunks. So when a 30-pin SIMM is used with a 486 computer (which accesses data 32 bits at a time), it takes four SIMMs to complete one bank. 72-pin SIMMs already have their data arranged 32 bits wide (4 bytes) so they don't need this memory banking to be able to work with processors that access memory 32 bits at a time. The Intel Pentium or better processors access memory 64 bits at a time, rather than 32, so even with 72-pin SIMMs you still have to bank two SIMMs together.

 For this CompTIA objective, you are also required to understand what is involved with installing a PC's RAM, which is covered in Chapter 1, "Installation, Configuration, and Upgrading."

IDENTIFYING MOTHERBOARD TYPES

Not all motherboards are created equal or the same. In fact, there are two different basic types of motherboards, as we discussed in Chapter 1. In this section, we'll more fully explore the differences between these two different types of motherboards.

UNDERSTANDING AT AND ATX MOTHERBOARDS

You may recall from our discussion in Chapter 1 that there are two basic styles of motherboards that are in use in PCs today. The first, older style is the AT motherboard. It's a true type, or class, because there are no rigid standards that control its size or the placement of mounting holes.

THE AT MOTHERBOARD

The AT motherboard style was the result of the industry trying to copy IBM's PC AT motherboard form factor. Apparently someone didn't copy very well because there soon became variations within the style that caused some motherboard and case combinations to work poorly together. There just weren't enough places where the motherboard and case lined up.

Selecting a motherboard, case, and power supply that all fit together well used to be a pain at times. Although today things have, for the most part, settled out where you can get motherboards and cases to work with one another, there were still those rare situations, which led in part to the creation of the ATX standard.

As we discussed in chapter 1, the AT style of motherboard has two connectors to the power supply. Each of these connectors is identical, except for the connections that they make. This leads to the problem that the connectors can be plugged into the wrong power supply cables, potentially burning out the motherboard. There's also a problem about getting the right kind of voltages to the motherboard itself.

THE WHOLE TRUTH

The specification says that the way the connectors are designed that you should rotate them in place by taking the tabs on the back of the wire-end connector and lock them into place under the bar on the motherboard-end connector, then slowly pivot them in place. In practice the pins on the motherboard are rarely strong enough to accept this kind of an installation. The best thing to do is to clip all of the tabs off the wire-end connector so that you can just push the connectors in place. I've never had a connector fall off in normal use, have been doing this for years. It certainly makes installing and removing motherboards much easier.

Earlier we discussed how Intel and Intel clone manufacturers were trying to reduce the voltage required by the processors so that they can be more efficient and run faster. This is great, except that you have to get power at that voltage to the CPU. The AT-style power supply was designed before this became an issue, so it only supplies 5 volt and 12 volt leads to the motherboard. Back when the AT-style power supply was new, you only needed these two because components either needed 12 volts for motors or high voltage circuits, or they needed 5 volt power for their standard logic circuits.

There are ways of stepping down, or transforming, 5 volt power into the lower voltages in use by processors today; however, they invariably generate heat and create more complexity for the motherboard manufacturers, creating added costs.

THE "BABY AT" MOTHERBOARD

Another consideration with AT-style systems is the so called "Baby-AT" motherboard, which was designed to fit in the smaller mini-tower cases. These Baby AT motherboards have the same positioning holes as a regular (full size) AT motherboard, except that they are smaller and are missing the mounting holes where they have no board (obviously).

Baby AT motherboards became possible because the support circuitry for the PC used to contain many different chips and required a great deal of motherboard space to mount. However, the introduction of VLSI (Very Large Scale Integration) motherboard chipsets dramatically reduced the footprint of the AT motherboard format. It's important to be careful when installing or upgrading a motherboard in older systems because full-size motherboards may not fit in a mid-size tower or mini-tower case designed for a Baby AT motherboard.

THE ATX MOTHERBOARD

The ATX style of motherboard, case, and power supply were created to solve all the mounting problems, as well as the power and installation issues. There were some significant changes made in how the power supply operates, and how things were mounted.

First it's important to point out that there are a series of sub-standards that we're lumping together as ATX. Each has a slightly different focus, and potentially a slightly different set of dimensions; however, all of the cases and power supplies that use the ATX standard, or one of the sub-standards such as NTX and WTX, adhere to the same rules.

The obvious change is the connectors. ATX motherboards and power supplies are connected to one another by a single-keyed connector that prevents misinstallation and potential damage. The connector is also physically easier to install and remove. Where the old AT power supply connectors required that you rotate them in and out around the back bar, the ATX power supply cable can be removed by depressing the release mechanism and pulling straight out. This eliminates collision problems associated with plugging and unplugging an AT motherboard.

One of the nonobvious changes is in the type of power being provided to the motherboard. In addition to the 5 volt and 12 volt leads provided by an AT power supply, there are also a set of 3.3 volt leads to allow for the newer processor voltages. Although some processors run at 2.8 volts or less, most desktop processors are still running at 3.3 volts, and in any case it's much easier to reduce 3.3 volts to 2.8 volts than it is to reduce 5 volts to 2.8 volts.

In addition to adding leads for the 3.3 volt power supply, it also added the leads necessary to manage power from the motherboard. Before ATX power supplies, the motherboard couldn't turn the power off by itself. You would get a message from Windows 9x on shutdown that it was safe to turn your computer off. However, with an ATX-based system you can tell Windows 9x to shutdown, and it will "fully" turn off your PC for you.

How this works is that there's always a small amount of current flowing to the processor. Whenever the processor detects that it's time to start up, it asks the power supply to turn on the rest of the power. This then allows the processor to spin backup hard drives and potentially to reinitialize any devices it put to sleep.

When the software tells the CPU to shut down it powers down anything it can and then asks the power supply to shut off power. It does, leaving the small trickle of power flowing through the system that the CPU needs to keep going. This soft power off, as it is called, has some potentially serious consequences in a PC environment.

The first consequence for a technician is that even when the PC is turned off it may not really be off. Most ATX computers have a master rocker switch which positively shuts down all power flow to the PC, but some don't. If you are taking a PC apart I suggest that you look at the motherboard/power supply connector(s) to determine if you need to unplug the power supply from the wall before proceeding with the upgrade or repair.

Another more global consequence is that spikes, surges, and other power problems that we discussed in Chapter 3 can still get through to your computer. While this isn't generally a big issue, it does increase your risk of PCs being damaged during a lightning storm.

Another change with the ATX style systems is that because it's a standard, mounting holes in the motherboard will match up with the holes and posts in the case. This is a welcome change for all of us who've struggled to get AT-style boards to work.

A more subtle change in the design of an ATX-style system is that the power supply pushes air through the computer rather than pulling it through. This actually improves cooling because the airflow is more directed, and holes don't have quite the disruptive tendency that they did with AT style power supplies.

 For this CompTIA objective, you are also required to understand what is involved with upgrading a PC's motherboard, which is covered in Chapter 1, "Installation, Configuration, and Upgrading."

APPENDIX C

A+ GLOSSARY

Word	Definition
Active matrix	Active matrix (also known as TFT or thin film transistor) is a technology used in the flat panel liquid crystal displays of notebook and laptop computers. Active matrix displays provide a more responsive image at a wider range of viewing angle than dual scan (passive matrix) displays.
Actuator arm	The physical device within the hard disk that moves the read/write heads over the platters.
Adapter	A physical device that allows one hardware or electronic interface to be adapted (accommodated without loss of function) to another hardware or electronic interface. An adapter is often built into a card that can be inserted into a slot on the computer's motherboard. The card adapts information that is exchanged between the computer's microprocessor and the devices that the card supports.
Address	An "address" can mean the unique location of either (1) an Internet server, (2) a specific file (for example, a Web page), or (3) an e-mail user. People use this word in several ways: to designate the address of their server, for their home page on the Web, or where to send e-mail.
Analog	Analog technology refers to electronic transmission accomplished by adding signals of varying frequency or amplitude to carrier waves of a given frequency of alternating electromagnetic current. Broadcast and phone transmission have conventionally used analog technology.

Word	Definition
ANSI	Acronym for American National Standards Institute and is the primary organization for fostering the development of technology standards in the United States. ANSI works with industry groups and is the U.S. member of the International Organization for Standardization (ISO). Long-established computer standards from ANSI include the American Standard Code for Information Interchange (ASCII) and the Small Computer System Interface (SCSI).
Application	1) In information technology, an application is the use of a technology, system, or product.
	2) The term *application* is a shorter form of *application program*. An application program is a program designed to perform a specific function directly for the user or for another application program. Examples of applications include word processors, database programs, Web browsers, development tools, drawing, paint, and image editing programs, and communication programs. Applications use the services of the computer's operating system and other supporting applications. The formal requests and means of communicating with other programs that an application program uses is called the application program interface (API).
Asynchronous	Asynchronous refers to processes that operate independently of each other until one process needs to "interrupt" the other process with a request. Using the client-server model, the server handles many asynchronous requests from its many clients. The client is often able to proceed with other work or must wait on the service requested from the server.
ASCII	Acronym for American Standard Code for Information Interchange. ASCII was developed by the American National Standards Institute (ANSI), and is the most common format for text files in computers and on the Internet. In an ASCII file, each alphabetic, numeric, or special character is represented with a 7-bit binary number (a string of seven 0s or 1s). 128 possible characters are defined.

Word	Definition
AT Command Set	Derived from the word ATttention, this is the set of commands used to communicate directly with a modem.
Attenuation	*Attenuation* is a general term that refers to any reduction in the strength of a signal. Attenuation occurs with any type of signal, whether digital or analog. Sometimes called *loss*, attenuation is a natural consequence of signal transmission over long distances. The extent of attenuation is usually expressed in units called decibels.
Backplane	A backplane is an electronic circuit board containing circuitry and sockets into which additional electronic devices on other circuit boards or cards can be plugged; in a computer, backplane is generally synonymous with or part of the motherboard.
Bad sector	An area on storage media (hard drive, floppy, etc) where data can no longer be written to or stored. Bad sectors can occur as a result of poor manufacturing or damage.
Bandwidth	The bandwidth of a transmitted communications signal is a measure of the range of frequencies the signal occupies. The term is also used in reference to the frequency-response characteristics of a communications receiving system. All transmitted signals, whether analog or digital, have a certain bandwidth. The same is true of receiving systems.
Baud rate	The rate at which information is transmitted. Baud is the unit of information carrying capacity or "signalling rate" of a communication channel. One baud is one symbol (state-transition or level-transition) per second. This coincides with bits per second only for two-level modulation with no framing or stop bits.
BIOS	BIOS (basic input/output system) is the program a personal computer's microprocessor uses to get the computer system started after you turn it on. It also manages data flow between the computer's operating system and attached devices such as the hard drive, video card, keyboard, mouse, and printers.

Word	Definition
Bit	A bit is the smallest unit of data in a computer. It has a single binary value, either 0 or 1.
Bitmap	A bitmap defines a display space and the color for each pixel or "bit" in the display space. A BMP or GIF file are examples of graphic image file types that contain bit-maps.
Blank	A piece of manufactured metal or plastic used to cover the space (slot) in the computer where a device can later be installed.
BNC Connector	A BNC (Bayonet Neil-Concelman) connector is a type of connector used to connect a computer to a coaxial cable in a 10BASE-2 Ethernet network. 10BASE-2 is a 10MHz network on a cable extending up to 185 meters—the 2 is a rounding up to 200 meters—without a repeater cable. The BNC connector in particular is generally easier to install and less expensive than other coaxial connectors.
Boot	To boot a computer is to load an operating system into the computer's main memory or RAM (random access memory). Once the operating system is loaded, it is ready for users to run programs. Sometimes you'll see an instruction to "reboot" the operating system. This simply means to reload the operating system (the most familiar way to do this on PCs is pressing the Ctrl, Alt, and Delete keys at the same time).
Bootable disk	A bootable floppy is a diskette containing a backup copy of your hard disk master boot record (MBR). In the event that the master boot record becomes corrupted or "infected" by a boot virus, having a bootable floppy will allow you to load it back onto your hard disk.
BPI	BPI (Bits Per Inch) is a measure of the recording density of a magnetic tape or disk.
BPS	Bits per second (abbreviated bps) is a common measure of data speed for computer modems and transmission carriers. As the term implies, the speed in bps is equal to the number of bits transmitted or received each second. Also known as the *baud rate*.

Word	Definition
Broadband	Broadband refers to telecommunication that provides multiple channels of data over a single communications medium using frequency division multiplexing.
Broadcasting	In general, to broadcast is to cast or throw forth something in all directions at the same time. A radio or television broadcast is a program that is transmitted over airwaves for public reception by anyone with a receiver tuned to the right signal channel. The term is sometimes used in e-mail or other message distribution for a message sent to all members, rather than specific members, of a group such as a department or enterprise.
Brownout	A low-voltage condition that is temporary, usually caused by utility system overload. Although seemingly not as severe as a blackout (where there is total loss of power), brownouts can nonetheless cause the computer to crash or damage to occur to components.
Browser	A browser is an application program that provides a way to look at and interact with the information on the World Wide Web.
Bug	In computer technology, a bug is a coding error in a computer program.
Bus	A bus is a transmission path on which signals are dropped off or picked up at every device attached to the line. Only devices addressed by the signals pay attention to them; the others discard the signals.
Byte	In most computer systems, a byte is a unit of information that is eight bits long. A byte is the unit most computers use to represent a character such as a letter, number, or typographic symbol (for example, "g," "5," or "?"). A byte can also hold a string of bits that need to be used in some larger unit for application purposes (for example, the stream of bits that constitute a visual image for a program that displays images).

Word	Definition
Cache	A cache is a place to store something more or less temporarily. Web pages you request are stored in your browser's cache directory on your hard disk. That way, when you return to a page you've recently looked at, the browser can get it from the cache rather than the original server, saving you time and the network the burden of some additional traffic. You can usually vary the size of your cache, depending on your particular browser.
Cache memory	Cache memory is random access memory (RAM) that a computer microprocessor can access more quickly than it can access regular RAM. As the microprocessor processes data, it looks first in the cache memory and if it finds the data there (from a previous reading of data), it does not have to do the more time-consuming reading of data from larger memory.
Caliper	The unit of measure that describes the thickness of an individual sheet of paper.
Capacitor	A capacitor is a passive electronic component that stores energy in the form of an electrostatic field. In its simplest form, a capacitor consists of two conducting plates separated by an insulating material called the dielectric. The capacitance is directly proportional to the surface areas of the plates, and is inversely proportional to the separation between the plates.
Card	A card (or *expansion card*, board, or adapter) is circuitry designed to provide expanded capability to a computer. It is provided on the surface of a standard-size rigid material (fiberboard or something similar) and then plugged into one of the computer's expansion slots in its motherboard (or backplane).
Carrier	A carrier (or *carrier signal*) is a transmitted electromagnetic pulse or wave at a steady base frequency of alternation on which information can be imposed by increasing signal strength, varying the base frequency, varying the wave phase, or other means. This variation is called *modulation*. With the advent of laser transmission over optical fiber media, a carrier can also be a laser-generated light beam on which information is imposed.

Word	Definition
CD-ROM	CD-ROM technology is a format and system for recording, storing, and retrieving electronic information on a compact disk that is read using an optical drive. A CD-ROM player or drive does not allow writing to the disk. A WORM (write once, read many) device is used to write information to a master disk from which CD-ROM disks are replicated.
CGA	A type of video display that stands for Color Graphics Adapter (CGA). This display system is capable of rendering four colors, and had a maximum resolution of 320 pixels horizontally by 200 pixels vertically.
Checksum	A checksum is a count of the number of bits in a transmission unit that is included with the unit so that the receiver can check to see whether the same number of bits arrived. If the counts match, it's assumed that the complete transmission was received. Both TCP and UDP communication layers provide a checksum count and verification as one of their services.
Circuit	1) In electronics, a circuit is a path between two or more points along which an electrical current can be carried. (A *circuit breaker* is a device that interrupts the path when necessary to protect other devices attached to the circuit, for example, in case of a power surge.) 2) In telecommunications, a circuit is a discrete (specific) path between two or more points along which signals can be carried. Unless otherwise qualified, a circuit is a physical path, consisting of one or more wires and possibly intermediate switching points.
Client	A client is the requesting program or user in a client-server relationship. For example, the user of a Web browser is effectively making client requests for pages from servers all over the Web. The browser itself is a client in its relationship with the computer that is getting and returning the requested HTML file. The computer handling the request and sending back the HTML file is a server.

Word	Definition
Clock speed	Clock speed refers to the number of pulses per second generated by an oscillator that sets the tempo for the processor. Clock speed is usually measured in MHz (megahertz, or millions of pulses per second). A typical computer clock runs at several hundred megahertz.
Clone	Computer system hardware that is a copy from an original, such as the multitude of "IBM PC-compatible" systems that were based on the original IBM-AT model. Generally, clones are cheaper than the original, but the quality of the clones has often been relative to their price.
Cluster	A cluster is the logical unit of file storage on a hard disk; it's managed by the computer's operating system. Any file stored on a hard disk takes up one or more clusters of storage. A file's clusters can be scattered among different locations on the hard disk. The clusters associated with a file are kept track of in the hard disk's file allocation table (FAT). When you read a file, the entire file is obtained for you and you aren't aware of the clusters it is stored in.
CMOS	CMOS is the semiconductor technology used in the transistors that are manufactured into most of today's computer microchips. Semiconductors are made of silicon and germanium, materials that "sort of" conduct electricity, but not enthusiastically.
Coaxial cable	Coaxial cable is the kind of cable used by cable TV companies between the community antenna and user homes and businesses. Coaxial cable is sometimes used by telephone companies from their central office to the telephone poles near users. It is also widely installed for use in business and corporation Ethernet and other types of local area networks.
Cold boot	The booting process that begins from a complete power-off state of the computer.
COM port	A connector for a communications interface, usually a serial port.

Word	Definition
Command processor	The part of the operating system that displays the command prompt, accepts, interprets, and executes the command sent to it (hence its alternate name—the *command interpreter*), and controls the operating environment.
Compatibility	Different systems (e.g., programs, file formats, protocols, even programming languages) that can work together or exchange data are said to be compatible.
Coprocessor	Any computer processor that assists the main processor (the CPU) by performing certain special functions, usually much faster than the main processor could perform them in software. The co-processor often decodes instructions in parallel with the main processor and executes only those instructions intended for it. The most common example is a floating point or math co-processor (or FPU); others are graphics and networking.
CPU	CPU (central processing unit) is an older term for processor and microprocessor, the central unit in a computer containing the logic circuitry that performs the instructions of a computer's programs.
Crash	A crash is the sudden failure of a software application or operating system, or of a hardware device such as a hard drive.
CRT	A cathode-ray tube (CRT) is a specialized vacuum tube in which images are produced when an electron beam strikes a phosphorescent surface. Most desktop computer displays make use of CRTs. The CRT in a computer display is similar to the picture tube in a television receiver.
Cylinder	The set of tracks on a multi-headed disk that may be accessed without head movement. That is, the collection of disk tracks that are the same distance from the spindle about which the disks rotate. Each such group forms the shape of a cylinder. Placing data that are likely to be accessed together in cylinders reduces the access significantly as head movement (seeking) is slow compared to disk rotation and switching between heads.

Word	Definition
DAT	DAT (Digital Audio Tape) is a standard medium and technology for the digital recording of audio signal on tape at a professional level of quality. A DAT drive is a digital tape recorder with rotating heads similar to those found in a video deck. Most DAT drives can record at sample rates of 44.1 KHz, the CD audio standard, and 48 KHz. DAT has become the standard archiving technology in professional and semi-professional recording environments for master recordings.
Data-Link Layer	The Data-Link Layer is the protocol layer in a program that handles the moving of data in and out across a physical link in a network. The Data-Link Layer is layer 2 in the Open Systems Interconnect (OSI) model for a set of telecommunication protocols.
Daughter board	A daughterboard (or *daughter board*, *daughter card*, or *daughtercard*) is a circuit board that plugs into and extends the circuitry of another circuit board. The other circuit board may be the computer's main board (its motherboard), or it may be another board or card that is already in the computer, often a sound card.
DB connector	A type of connector that is used with several types of serial or parallel cable. The connector type is usually followed by a number, which describes how many pins the connector has; e.g., DD-9 has 9 pins.
Defragmentation	Defragmentation is the process used to reposition file fragments into contiguous portions of the hard disk. When a file is too large to store in a single location on a hard disk, it is stored on the disk in discontiguous (not adjacent) parts or fragments. This fragmentation is invisible to the user, however. The locations of the fragments are kept track of by the system. Over time, disk access time can be slowed by fragmentation since each fragmented file is likely to require multiple drive head repositionings and accesses.

Word	Definition
Device	A device is a unit of hardware, outside or inside the case or housing, for the computer (processor, memory, and data paths) that is capable of providing input to the essential computer or of receiving output, or both. When the term is used generally (as in *computer devices*), it can include keyboards, mice, display monitors, hard disk drives, CD-ROM players, printers, audio speakers and microphones, and other hardware units. Some devices such as a hard disk drive or a CD-ROM drive, while physically inside the computer housing, are considered devices because they are separately installable and replaceable. With notebook and smaller computers, devices tend to be more physically integrated with the "non-device" part of the computer.
Device driver	A device driver is a program that controls a particular type of device that is attached to your computer. There are device drivers for printers, displays, CD-ROM readers, diskette drives, and so on. When you buy a new computer, many device drivers are built into the operating system. However, if you later buy a new type of device that the operating system didn't anticipate, you'll have to install the new device driver. A device driver essentially converts the more general input/output instructions of the operating system to messages that the device type can understand.
DIMM	A DIMM (dual in-line memory module) is a double SIMM (single in-line memory module). Like a SIMM, it's a module containing one or several random access (RAM) chips on a small circuit board with pins that connect it to the computer motherboard.
Disk cache	A disk cache is a mechanism for improving the time it takes to read from or write to a hard disk. Today, the disk cache is usually included as part of the hard disk. A disk cache can also be a specified portion of random access memory (RAM). The disk cache holds data that has recently been read and, in some cases, adjacent data areas that are likely to be accessed next. Write caching is also provided with some disk caches.

Word	Definition
Disk controller	The circuit that allows the CPU to communicate with a hard disk, floppy disk, or other kind of disk drive. The most common disk controllers in use are IDE and SCSI controllers. Most home PCs use IDE controllers. High-end PCs, workstations, and network file servers mostly have SCSI controllers.
Diskette	A diskette is a removable data storage medium that can be used with personal computers. The term usually refers to the magnetic medium housed in a rigid plastic cartridge measuring 3.5 inches square and about 2 millimeters thick. Also called a "3.5-inch diskette," it can store up to 1.44 megabytes (MB) of data. Although most personal computers today come with a 3.5-inch diskette drive pre-installed, some network computers now omit them. Some older computers provide drives for magnetic diskettes that are 5.25 inches square, about 1 millimeter thick, and capable of holding 1.2 megabytes of data. These are sometimes called "floppy disks" or "floppies" because their housings are flexible. In recent years, 5.25-inch diskettes have been largely replaced by 3.5-inch diskettes, which are physically more rugged. Many people also call the newer, hard-cased diskette a "floppy."
Distributed processing	An arrangement of linked computer systems that allows processing to occur among several systems, each handling a portion of the total workload. Client-server is one form of distributed processing.
DMA	DMA (Direct Memory Access) is a capability provided by some computer bus architectures that allows data to be sent directly from an attached device (such as a disk drive) to the memory on the computer's motherboard. The microprocessor is freed from involvement with the data transfer, thus speeding up overall computer operation.
DNS	The Domain Name System (DNS) is the way that Internet domain names are located and translated into IP addresses. A domain name is a meaningful and easy-to-remember "handle" for an Internet address.

Word	Definition
Docking Station	A docking station is a hardware frame and set of electrical connection interfaces that enable a notebook or laptop computer to effectively serve as a desktop computer. The interfaces typically allow the notebook to communicate with a local printer, larger storage or backup drives, and possibly other devices that are not usually taken along with a notebook computer. A docking station can also include a network interface card (NIC) that attaches the notebook to a local area network (LAN).
	Variations include the *port replicator*, an attachment on a notebook computer that expands the number of ports it can use, and the *expansion base*, which might hold a CD-ROM drive, a floppy disk drive, and additional storage.
Domain	In computing and telecommunication in general, a domain is a sphere of knowledge or operation identified by a name. Typically, the knowledge is a collection of facts about some program entities or a number of network points or addresses.
DOS	DOS (Disk Operating System) was the first widely-installed operating system in personal computers. (Earlier, the same name had been used for an IBM operating system for a line of business computers).
DOS prompt	The prompt controlled and displayed by the DOC command processor at which operating-system level commands are entered. Usually appears as "C:>".
EISA	Acronym for Extended Industry Standard Architecture. EISA is a standard bus(computer interconnection) architecture that extends the ISA standard to a 32-bit interface. It was developed in part as an open alternative to the proprietary Micro Channel Architecture (MCA) that IBM introduced in its PS/2 computers.
	EISA data transfer can reach a peak of 33 megabytes per second.

Word	Definition
EPROM	EPROM (Erasable Programmable Read-Only Memory) is programmable read-only memory (PROM) that can be erased and re-used. Erasure is caused by shining an intense ultraviolet light through a window that is designed into the memory chip. (Although ordinary room lighting does not contain enough ultraviolet light to cause erasure, bright sunlight can. For this reason, the window is usually covered with a label when not installed in the computer.)
Extension	A filename extension is an optional addition to the file name in a suffix of the form ".xxx" where "xxx" represents a limited number of alphanumeric characters depending on the operating system. (In Windows 3.1, for example, a filename extension or suffix can have no more than three characters, but in Windows 95, it can have more.) The filename extension allows a file's format to be described as part of its name so that users can quickly understand the type of file it is without having to "open" or try to use it. The filename extension also helps an application program recognize whether a file is a type that it can work with.
FAT	A file allocation table (FAT) is a table that an operating system maintains on a hard disk that provides a map of the clusters (the basic unit of logical storage on a hard disk) that a file has been stored in. When you write a new file to a hard disk, the file is stored in one or more clusters that are not necessarily next to each other; they may be rather widely scattered over the disk. A typical cluster size is 2,048 bytes, 4,096 bytes, or 8,192 bytes. The operating system creates a FAT entry for the new file, which records where each cluster is located and their sequential order. When you read a file, the operating system reassembles the file from clusters and places it as an entire file where you want to read it.
FDDI	FDDI (Fiber Distributed-Data Interface) is a standard for data transmission on fiber optic lines in a local area network (LAN) that can extend in range up to 200 km (124 miles). The FDDI protocol is based on the token ring protocol. In addition to being large geographically, an FDDI local area network can support thousands of users.

Word	Definition
Fiber optic	Fiber optic (or *optical fiber*) refers to the medium and the technology associated with the transmission of information as light impulses along a glass or plastic wire or fiber. Fiber optic wire carries much more information than conventional copper wire and is far less sensitive to electromagnetic interference. Most telephone company long-distance lines are now fiber optic.
File system	A file system is the way in which files are named and where they are placed logically for storage and retrieval. The DOS, Windows, OS/2, Macintosh, and UNIX-based operating systems all have file systems in which files are placed somewhere in a hierarchical (tree) structure. A file is placed in a directory (*folder* in Windows) or subdirectory at the desired place in the tree structure.
FTP	FTP (File Transfer Protocol) is a standard protocol that is the simplest way to exchange files between computers on the Internet. Like the Hypertext Transfer Protocol (HTTP), which transfers displayable Web pages and related files, and the Simple Mail Transfer Protocol (SMTP), which transfers e-mail, FTP is an application protocol that uses the Internet's TCP/IP protocols. FTP is commonly used to transfer Web page files from their creator to the computer that acts as their server for everyone on the Internet. It's also commonly used to download programs and other files to your computer from other servers.
Full duplex	Full-duplex data transmission means that data can be transmitted in both directions on a signal carrier at the same time. For example, on a local area network with a technology that has full-duplex transmission, one workstation can be sending data on the line while another workstation is receiving data. Full-duplex transmission necessarily implies a bidirectional line (one that can move data in both directions).

Word	Definition
Gateway	A gateway is a network point that acts as an entrance to another network. On the Internet, in terms of routing, the network consists of gateway nodes and host nodes. The computers of network users and the computers that serve content (such as Web pages) are host nodes. The computers that control traffic within your company's network or at your local Internet service provider (ISP) are gateway nodes.
GB	A gigabyte is a measure of computer data storage capacity and is "roughly" a billion bytes. A gigabyte is two to the 30th power, or 1,073,741,824 in decimal notation.
GPF	A general protection fault (or *general protection error*) is a phrase that users of personal computers see when an application program they are running (for example, Microsoft Word or the Netscape Web browser) tries to access storage that is not designated for their use. An operating system (such as Windows 95) manages the use of random access memory (RAM) for its own needs and for those of the application programs that it manages. The application programs are actually managed as tasks. When a task attempts to write to a place in RAM that is outside its assigned storage area, the operating system requires that the task or application be closed. Users usually get a message that tells them this is happening, but there isn't much they can do about it other than to restart the program and hope it will run successfully the next time.
GUI	A GUI is a graphical (rather than purely textual) user interface to a computer. The term came into existence because the first interactive user interfaces to computers were not graphical; they were text-and-keyboard oriented and usually consisted of commands you had to remember and computer responses that were brief. The command interface of the DOS operating system (which you can still get to from your Windows operating system) is an example of the typical user-computer interface before GUIs arrived. An intermediate step in user interfaces between the command line interface and the GUI was the non-graphical menu-based interface, which let you interact by using a mouse rather than by having to type in keyboard commands.

Word	Definition
Half duplex	Half-duplex data transmission means that data can be transmitted in both directions on a signal carrier, but not at the same time. For example, on a local area network using a technology that has half-duplex transmission, one workstation can send data on the line and then immediately receive data on the line from the same direction in which data was just transmitted. Like full-duplex transmission, half-duplex transmission implies a bi-directional line (one that can carry data in both directions.
Hardware	Hardware is the physical aspect of computers, telecommunications, and other information technology devices. The term arose as a way to distinguish the "box" and the electronic circuitry and components of a computer from the program you put in it to make it do things. The program came to be known as the software.
Handshaking	Handshaking is the exchange of information between two modems and the resulting agreement about which protocol to use that precedes each telephone connection. You can hear the handshaking in those crunching and other sounds when you make a dial-out call from your computer.
	Since the modems at each end of the line may have different capabilities, they need to inform each other and settle on the highest transmission speed they can both use. At higher speeds, the modems have to determine the length of line delays so that echo cancellers can be used properly.
Hot swap	A hot swap is the replacement of a hard drive, CD-ROM drive, power supply, or other device with a similar device while the computer system using it remains in operation. The replacement can be because of a device failure or, for storage devices, to substitute other data.
IC	An integrated circuit (IC), sometimes called a *chip* or *microchip*, is a semiconductor wafer on which thousands or millions of tiny resistors, capacitors, and transistors are fabricated. A particular IC is categorized as either linear (analog) or digital, depending on its intended application.

Word	Definition
Impedance	Impedance, denoted by *Z*, is an expression of the opposition that an electronic component, circuit, or system offers to AC (alternating current). Impedance is comprised of two independent scalar (one-dimensional) phenomena: resistance and reactance. Both of these quantities are expressed in ohms.
	Resistance, denoted by R, is a measure of the extent to which a substance opposes the movement of electrons among atoms. The more easily the atoms give up and/or accept electrons, the lower the resistance. It is always a positive real-number quantity. Resistance is observed with AC and also with DC (direct current). Examples of materials with low resistance, known as electrical *conductors*, include copper, silver, and gold. High-resistance substances are called *dielectrics*. They include materials such as polyethylene, mica, and glass. Materials with intermediate levels of resistance are classified as *semiconductors*.
Internet	The Internet, sometimes called simply "the Net," is a worldwide system of computer networks—a network of networks in which users at any one computer can, if they have permission, get information from any other computer (and sometimes talk directly to users at other computers). It was conceived by the Advanced Research Projects Agency (ARPA) of the U.S. government in 1969 and was first known as theARPANet. The original aim was to create a network that would allow users of a research computer at one university to be able to "talk to" research computers at other universities. A side benefit of ARPANet's design was that, because messages could be routed or rerouted in more than one direction, the network could continue to function even if parts of it were destroyed in the event of a military attack or other disaster.
	Today, the Internet is a public, cooperative, and self-sustaining facility accessible to hundreds of millions of people worldwide. Physically, the Internet uses a portion of the total resources of the currently existing public telecommunication networks.

Word	Definition
Interrupt	An interrupt is a signal from a device attached to a computer or from a program within the computer that causes the main program that operates the computer (the operating system) to stop and figure out what to do next. Almost all personal (or larger) computers today are interrupt-driven—that is, they start down the list of computer instructions in one program (perhaps an application such as a word processor) and keep running the instructions until either (a) they can't go any further or (b) an interrupt signal is sensed. After the interrupt signal is sensed, the computer either resumes running the program it was running or begins running another program.
IP Address	An IP address is a 32-bit number that identifies each sender or receiver of information that is sent in packets across the Internet.
IRQ	The IRQ (Interrupt ReQuest) value is an assigned location where the computer can expect a particular device to interrupt it when the device sends the computer signals about its operation. For example, when a printer has finished printing, it sends an interrupt signal to the computer. The signal momentarily interrupts the computer so that it can decide what processing to do next. Since multiple signals to the computer on the same interrupt line might not be understood by the computer, a unique value must be specified for each device and its path to the computer. Prior to Plug and Play (PnP) devices, users often had to set IRQ values manually (or be aware of them) when adding a new device to a computer.
Jumper	A jumper is a pair of prongs that are electrical contact points set into the computer motherboard or an adapter card. When you set a jumper, you place a plug on the prongs that completes a contact. Jumper settings tell the computer how it is configured and what operations can be performed. Computers come with jumpers preset. Instructions are sometimes provided so that the owner can reset the jumpers when new equipment is added. The latest trend, however, is Plug and Play equipment that does not require manual setting of jumpers. A group of jumpers is sometimes called a *jumper block*.

Word	Definition
LAN	A LAN is a network of interconnected workstations sharing the resources of a single processor or server within a relatively small geographic area. Typically, this might be within the area of a small office building. However, FDDI extends a local area network over a much wider area. Usually, the server has applications and data storage that are shared in common by multiple workstation users. A local area network may serve as few as four or five users or, in the case of FDDI, may serve several thousand.
Latency	In a network, latency, a synonym for *delay*, is an expression of how much time it takes for a packet of data to get from one designated point to another. In some applications (for example, AT&T), latency is measured by sending a packet that will be returned back to the sender and thus the round-trip time is considered the latency.
Master Boot Record	The Master Boot Record (MBR) is the information in the first sector of any hard disk or diskette that identifies how and where an operating system is located so that it can be booted (loaded) into the computer's main storage (RAM). The Master Boot Record is also sometimes called the "partition sector" or the "master partition table" because it includes a table that locates each partition that the hard disk has been formatted into. In addition to this table, the MBR also includes a program that reads the boot sector record of the partition containing the operating system to be booted into RAM. In turn, that record contains a program that loads the rest of the operating system into RAM.
Modem	A modem modulates outgoing digital signals from a computer or other digital device to analog signals for a conventional copper twisted pair telephone line and demodulates the incoming analog signal and converts it to a digital signal for the digital device.
Motherboard	A motherboard is the physical arrangement in a computer that contains the computer's basic circuitry and components. On the typical motherboard, the circuitry is imprinted or affixed to the surface of a firm planar surface and is usually manufactured in a single step.

Word	Definition
Mouse	A mouse is a small device that a computer user pushes across a desk surface in order to point to a place on a display screen to select one or more actions to take from that position. The mouse first became a widely used computer tool when Apple Computer made it a standard part of the Apple Macintosh. Today, the mouse is an integral part of the graphical user interface (GUI) of any personal computer. The mouse apparently got its name by being about the same size and color as a toy mouse.
MS-DOS	MS-DOS (Microsoft Disk Operating System) was the Microsoft-marketed version of the first widely installed operating system in personal computers. It was essentially the same operating system that Bill Gates's young company developed for IBM as PC-DOS (Personal Computer DOS). Most users of either DOS system simply referred to their system as DOS. Like PC-DOS, MS-DOS was (and still is) a non-graphical, line-oriented, command-driven operating system with a relatively simple interface but not an overly "friendly' user interface.
Network	A network is a series of points or nodes interconnected by communication paths. Networks can interconnect with other networks and contain subnetworks. The most common topologies or general configurations of networks include the bus, star, and ring topologies. Networks can also be characterized in terms of spatial distance as local area networks (LANs), metropolitan area networks (MANs), and wide area networks (WANs).
Network services	Refers to the collection of programs, protocols, and utilities needed to provide connectivity over a network. TCP is one type of a network service.
Node	In a network, a node is a connection point, either a redistribution point or an end point for data transmissions. In general, a node has programmed or engineered capability to recognize and process or forward transmissions to other nodes.

Word	Definition
OCR	OCR (Optical Character Recognition) is the recognition of printed or written text characters by a computer. This involves photoscanning of the text character-by-character, analysis of the scanned-in image, and then translation of the character image into character codes, such as ASCII, commonly used in data processing. In OCR processing, the scanned-in image or bitmap is analyzed for light and dark areas in order to identify each alphabetic letter or numeric digit. When a character is recognized, it is converted into an ASCII code. Special circuit boards and computer chips designed expressly for OCR are used to speed up the recognition process.
Operating System	An operating system (frequently abbreviated as "OS") is the program that, after being initially loaded into the computer by a boot program, manages all the other programs in a computer. The other programs are called *applications*. The applications make use of the operating system by making requests for services through a defined *application program interface* (API). In addition, users can interact directly with the operating system through an interface such as a command language.
Packet	A packet is the unit of data that is routed between an origin and a destination on the Internet or any packet-switched network. When any file (e-mail message, HTML file, GIF file, URL request, and so forth) is sent from one place to another on the Internet, the Transmission Control Protocol (TCP) layer of TCP/IP divides the file into "chunks" of an efficient size for routing. Each of these packets is separately numbered and includes the Internet address of the destination. The individual packets for a given file may travel different routes through the Internet. When they have all arrived, they are reassembled into the original file by the TCP layer at the receiving end.

Word	Definition
Packet-switched	Packet-switched describes the type of network in which relatively small units of data called *packets* are routed through a network based on the destination address contained within each packet. Breaking communication down into packets allows the same data path to be shared among many users in the network. This type of communication between sender and receiver is known as *connectionless* (rather than *dedicated*). Most traffic over the Internet uses packet switching and the Internet is basically a connectionless network.
Parity	Parity refers to a technique of checking whether data has been lost or written over when it's moved from one place in storage to another or when transmitted between computers.
Parity bit	An additional bit, the parity bit, is added to a group of bits that are moved together. This bit is used only for the purpose of identifying whether the bits being moved arrived successfully. Before the bits are sent, they are counted and if the total number of data bits is even, the parity bit is set to one so that the total number of bits transmitted will form an odd number. If the total number of data bits is already an odd number, the parity bit remains or is set to 0. At the receiving end, each group of incoming bits is checked to see if the group totals to an odd number. If the total is even, a transmission error has occurred and either the transmission is retried or the system halts and an error message is sent to the user.
Partition	A partition is a logical division of a hard disk created so that you can have different operating systems on the same hard disk or create the appearance of having separate hard drives for file management, multiple users, or other purposes. A partition is created when you format the hard disk. Typically, a one-partition hard disk is labelled the "C:" drive ("A:" and "B:" are typically reserved for diskette drives). A two-partition hard drive would typically contain "C:" and "D:" drives. CD-ROM drives typically are assigned the last letter in whatever sequence of letters have been used as a result of hard disk formatting, or typically with a two-partition, the "E:" drive.

Word	Definition
PCMCIA	The PCMCIA (Personal Computer Memory Card International Association) is an industry group organized in 1989 to promote standards for a credit card-size memory or I/O device that would fit into a personal computer, usually a notebook or laptop computer. The PCMCIA 2.1 Standard was published in 1993. As a result, PC users can be assured of standard attachments for any peripheral device that follows the standard. The initial standard and its subsequent releases describe a standard product, the PC Card.
Peripheral	A peripheral is any computer device that is not part of the essential computer (the processor, memory, and data paths) but is situated relatively close by. A near synonym is *input/output (I/O) device*. Some peripherals are mounted in the same case with the main part of the computer, as are the hard disk drive, CD-ROM drive, and network interface cards (NICs). Other peripherals are outside the computer case, such as the printer and image scanner, attached by a wired or wireless connection.
Plug and Play	Plug and Play (PnP) is a standard that gives computer users the ability to plug a device into a computer and have the computer recognize that the device is there. The user doesn't have to tell the computer.
Port	A port is generally a specific place for being physically connected to some other device, usually with a socket and plug of some kind. Typically, a personal computer is provided with one or more serial ports and usually one parallel port. The serial port supports sequential, one bit-at-a-time transmission to peripheral devices such as scanners, and the parallel port supports multiple-bit-at-a-time transmission to devices such as printers.
Protocol	A protocol is the special set of rules for communicating that the end points use in a telecommunication connection when they send signals back and forth. Protocols exist at several levels in a telecommunication connection. There are hardware telephone protocols. There are protocols between the end points in communicating programs within the same computer or at different locations. Both end points must recognize and observe the protocol. Protocols are often described in an industry or international standard.

Word	Definition
Queue	A list of items or programs waiting for a service, such as the list of jobs in a print queue waiting for the printer's availability.
RAM	RAM (random access memory) is the place in a computer where the operating system, application programs, and data in current use are kept so that they can be quickly reached by the computer's processor. RAM is much faster to read from and write to than the other kinds of storage in a computer, the hard disk, floppy disk, and CD-ROM. However, the data in RAM stays there only as long as your computer is running. When you turn the computer off, RAM loses its data. When you turn your computer on again, your operating system and other files are once again loaded into RAM, usually from your hard disk.
Resistance	Resistance is the opposition that a substance offers to the flow of electric current. It is represented by the uppercase letter R. The standard unit of resistance is the ohm, sometimes written out as a word, and sometimes symbolized by the uppercase Greek letter omega. When an electric current of one ampere passes through a component across which a potential difference (voltage) of one volt exists, then the resistance of that component is one ohm.
Root	In a computer file system that is organized as a hierarchy or tree, the root directory is the one that includes all other directories. (Unlike a real tree, a tree file system has only one root!)
SCSI	SCSI (the Small Computer System Interface) is a set of evolving ANSI-standard electronic interfaces that allow personal computers to communicate with peripheral hardware such as disk drives, tape drives, CD-ROM drives, printers, and scanners faster and more flexibly than previous interfaces. Developed at Apple Computer and still used in the Macintosh, the present set of SCSIs are parallel interfaces. SCSI ports are built into most personal computers today and supported by all major operating systems.

Word	Definition
Server	In general, a server is a computer program that provides services to other computer programs in the same or other computers.
	The computer that a server program runs in is also frequently referred to as a server (though it may contain a number of server and client programs).
SIMM	A SIMM is a module containing one or several Random Access Memory (RAM) chips on a small circuit board with pins that connect to the computer motherboard. Since the more RAM your computer has, the less frequently it will need to access your secondary storage (for example, hard disk or CD-ROM). PC owners sometimes expand RAM by installing additional SIMMs. SIMMs typically come with a 32-data-bit (36 bits counting parity bits) path to the computer that requires a 72-pin connector. SIMMs usually come in memory chip multiples of four megabytes.
Slot	In computers, a slot, or *expansion slot*, is an engineered technique for adding capability to a computer in the form of connection pinholes (typically in the range of 16 to 64 closely-spaced holes) and a place to fit an expansion card containing the circuitry that provides some specialized capability, such as video acceleration, sound, or disk drive control.
Software	Software is a general term for the various kinds of programs used to operate computers and related devices.
Subnet	A subnet (short for "subnetwork") is an identifiably separate part of an organization's network. Typically, a subnet may represent all the machines at one geographic location, in one building, or on the same local area network (LAN). Having an organization's network divided into subnets allows it to be connected to the Internet with a single, shared network address. Without subnets, an organization could get multiple connections to the Internet, one for each of its physically separate subnetworks, but this would require an unnecessary use of the limited number of network numbers the Internet has to assign. It would also require that Internet routing tables on gateways outside the organization would need to know about and have to manage routing that could and should be handled within an organization.

Word	Definition
Subnet mask	This is an extension of the IP addressing scheme that allows a site to use a single IP network address for multiple physical networks. Gateways and hosts inside a site using subnet addressing interpret the local portion of the address by dividing it into physical network portion and host portion.
Switch	A switch is a network device that selects a path or circuit for sending a unit of data to its next destination. A switch may also include the function of the router, a device or program that can determine the route and specifically what adjacent network point the data should be sent to. In general, a switch is a simpler and faster mechanism than a router, which requires knowledge about the network and how to determine the route.
Synchronous	Synchronous data communication requires that each end of an exchange of communication respond in turn without initiating a new communication. A typical activity that might use a synchronous protocol would be a transmission of files from one point to another. As each transmission is received, a response is returned indicating success or the need to resend. Each successive transmission of data requires a response to the previous transmission before a new one can be initiated.
TCP/IP	TCP/IP (Transmission Control Protocol/Internet Protocol) is the basic communication language or protocol of the Internet. It can also be used as a communications protocol in the private networks called intranets and extranets. When you are set up with direct access to the Internet, your computer is provided with a copy of the TCP/IP program, just as every other computer that you may send messages to or get information from.
TFTP	TFTP (Trivial File Transfer Protocol) is a network application that is simpler than the File Transfer Protocol (FTP) but less capable. It is used where user authentication and directory visibility are not required. TFTP uses the User Datagram Protocol (UDP) rather than the Transmission Control Protocol (TCP).

Word	Definition
Twisted pair	Twisted pair is the ordinary copper wire that connects home and many business computers to the telephone company. To reduce crosstalk or electromagnetic induction between pairs of wires, two insulated copper wires are twisted around each other. Each connection on twisted pair requires both wires.
	Since some telephone sets or desktop locations require multiple connections, twisted pair is sometimes installed in two or more pairs, all within a single cable. For some business locations, twisted pair is enclosed in a shield that functions as a ground. This is known as *shielded twisted pair (STP)*. Ordinary wire to the home is *unshielded twisted pair* (UTP).
UDP	UDP (User Datagram Protocol) is a communications protocol that offers a limited amount of service when messages are exchanged between computers in a network that uses the Internet Protocol (IP). UDP is an alternative to the Transmission Control Protocol (TCP) and, together with IP, is sometimes referred to as UDP/IP. Like the Transmission Control Protocol, UDP uses the Internet Protocol to actually get a data unit (called a datagram) from one computer to another. Unlike TCP, however, UDP does not provide the service of dividing a message into packets (datagrams) and reassembling it at the other end.
USB	USB (Universal Serial Bus) is a Plug and Play interface between a computer and add-on devices (such as audio players, joysticks, keyboards, telephones, scanners, and printers). With USB, a new device can be added to your computer without having to add an adapter card or even having to turn the computer off. The USB peripheral bus standard was developed by Compaq, IBM, DEC, Intel, Microsoft, NEC, and Northern Telecom and the technology is available without charge for all computer and device vendors.

Word	Definition
UPS	A UPS (uninterruptible power supply) is a device that allows your computer to keep running for at least a short time when the primary power source is lost. It also provides protection from power surges. A UPS contains a battery that "kicks in" when the device senses a loss of power from the primary source. If you are using the computer when the UPS notifies you of the power loss, you have time to save any data you are working on and exit gracefully before the secondary power source (the battery) runs out. When all power runs out, any data in your computer's random access memory (RAM) is erased. When power surges occur, a UPS intercepts the surge so that it doesn't damage your computer.
Virtual memory	Virtual (or logical) memory is a concept that, when implemented by a computer and its operating system, allows programmers to use a very large range of memory or storage addresses for stored data. The computing system maps the programmer's virtual addresses to real hardware storage addresses. Usually, the programmer is freed from having to be concerned about the availability of data storage.
Wideband	Wideband is a transmission medium or channel that has a wider bandwidth than one voice channel (with a carrier wave of a certain modulated frequency). This term is usually contrasted with narrowband.

INDEX

539